Calling All Cooks four

Telephone Pioneers of America
Alabama Chapter No. 34

DEDICATION

This book is dedicated to all the members of the Alabama Bell South Pioneer Volunteers: our past members who have established our respected reputation of community service; our current members who are working hard to meet the growing needs of our communities; our future members who will carry on this tradition with pride.

Our special thanks to everyone who supports our community service projects by purchasing our cookbooks.

Sandra Cleveland
Chapter President 1999–2000

Tom Mirus
Chapter President 2000–2001

Calling All Cooks four

This book or any part thereof may not be reproduced in any form whatsoever without prior written permission from Telephone Pioneers of America, Alabama Chapter #34, except in the form of short passages within reviews or articles.

This cookbook is a collection of favorite recipes which are not necessarily original recipes.

Published by:
Telephone Pioneers of America
Alabama Chapter #34
3196 Highway 280 South, Room 301N
Birmingham, Alabama 35243

Designed, Edited, and Manufactured by
Favorite Recipes® Press
an imprint of

FRP
P.O. Box 305142
Nashville, Tennessee 37230
1-800-358-0560

Manufactured in the United States of America
First Printing: 2000   40,000 copies

CROCK-POT® is a registered trademark of The Rival Company,
Kansas City, Missouri

IN APPRECIATION

The first, second, and third editions of *Calling All Cooks* still proves to be very successful and prompted us to collect recipes for *Calling All Cooks four*. This is our seventy-fifth anniversary of Pioneering in the state of Alabama.

These recipes were collected from active and retired employees and their family members. Every effort has been made to identify and eliminate duplicate recipes that may have appeared in *Calling All Cooks one, two,* and *three*.

A very special thanks to the Presidents of the Clubs and Councils for their cooperation in obtaining recipes from their members.

Special thanks to Sandra Deason, Mary Boehm, Sandra Cleveland, Georgia Glenn, Alice Walski, Pauline Slusher, Narice Sutton, Hazel Campbell, Betty Moon, Mary Alice Real, and Peggy West.

We hope you will enjoy Volume Four.
Thanks for helping us celebrate our seventy-fifth anniversary.

Sara Cooley   Helen Shirley
Cookbook Chairmen

Club Presidents	
Moon	Birmingham Life Member Club
n King	Birmingham South Life Member Club
athryn Pager	Bon Secour Life Member Club
Betty Darnell	Gadsden Life Member Club
Shirley Helms	Montgomery Life Member Club
Ed Martin	Opelika Life Member Club
Joe Small	Selma Life Member Club
Mary Ann Fulmer	Shoals Life Member Club

Council Presidents	
Jim Miller	Anniston Council
Linda McGhee	Birmingham Metro Council
Donna Bowman	Birmingham South Cahaba Council
Judy Burrow	Decatur Council
Le Nora Focnt	Huntsville Council
Barbara B	Jasper Club
Cathy Mic te	Mobile Council
Debbie Spe s	Montgomery Council
Deborah Scalisi	Rive se Council
Dick Johnson	T oosa Council

Mary Boehm	Chapter Liaison
Sara Cooley and Helen Shirley	Chapter Cookbook Chairmen

CONTENTS

Huntsville Council, 6

Appetizers and Beverages, 7

Tuscaloosa Council, 46

Soups, 47

Clowns, 72

Salads, 73

Habitat for Humanity, 122

Meats, 123

Birmingham South Cahaba Council, 178

Poultry and Seafood, 179

Riverchase Council, 234

Breads, 235

Birmingham Metro Council, 272

Vegetables, 273

CONTENTS

Mobile Council, 310

Side Dishes, 311

I Like Me Books, 338

Desserts, 339

Environment, 390

Cakes, 391

Alabama Reading Initiative, 462

Candy and Cookies, 463

Physically and Mentally Challenged, 512

Pies, 513

Basic Substitutions, 556

Refrigeration Chart, 557

Index, 558

Order Information, 576

HUNTSVILLE COUNCIL

Our Huntsville Council tested hearing for 11,567 students in 53 schools in 1999. This project won national recognition due to the large number of students and schools who benefited from the project. This is an annual project for the Huntsville Council.

Appetizers and Beverages

Cheese Ball

16 ounces cream cheese, softened
1 cup chopped pecans
2 tablespoons chopped green onions
1/4 cup chopped green bell pepper
1 (8-ounce) can crushed pineapple
2 tablespoons seasoned salt
1 cup chopped pecans
Cherries (optional)

Combine the cream cheese, 1 cup pecans, green onions, bell pepper, pineapple and seasoned salt in a bowl and mix well. Shape into a ball and roll in 1 cup pecans, coating evenly. Decorate with cherries if desired. Wrap in plastic wrap and chill until serving time. YIELD: 16 SERVINGS.

Carolyn G. Wheeler
Selma Life

Cheese Ball

8 ounces cream cheese, softened
1 tube jalapeño pepper cheese, softened
1/2 onion, grated
1 teaspoon Worcestershire sauce
1 package sliced almonds
Wheat crackers or butter crackers

Combine the cream cheese, jalapeño pepper cheese, onion and Worcestershire sauce in a bowl and mix well. Shape into a ball and roll in the almonds, coating evenly. Wrap in plastic wrap and chill for 8 hours or longer. Serve with wheat crackers or butter crackers. YIELD: 12 SERVINGS.

Ruth Townley
Birmingham South Life

APPETIZERS

Cheese Ball

8 ounces mild Cheddar cheese, shredded
8 ounces sharp Cheddar cheese, shredded
16 ounces cream cheese, softened
1 tablespoon chopped onion
1 tablespoon chopped green bell pepper
1 tablespoon chopped pimento
1 tablespoon lemon juice
1 tablespoon Worcestershire sauce
½ cup chopped pecans
Crackers

Combine the Cheddar cheeses, cream cheese, onion, bell pepper, pimento, lemon juice and Worcestershire sauce in a bowl and mix well. Shape into a ball and roll in the pecans, coating evenly. Wrap in plastic wrap and chill until serving time. Serve with crackers. YIELD: 24 SERVINGS.

Kim Osvath
Birmingham South Cahaba Council

Ground Pepper Cheese Ball

16 ounces cream cheese, softened
Milk
2 garlic cloves, minced
1 bunch green onions, chopped
Coarsely ground pepper
Crackers

Mix the cream cheese with a small amount of milk in a bowl until smooth. Add the garlic and green onions and mix well. Shape into a ball and roll in the pepper, coating evenly. Wrap in plastic wrap and chill for 8 hours or longer. Serve with crackers. YIELD: 16 SERVINGS.

Susan Poe
Riverchase Council

Pineapple Cheese Ball

8 ounces cream cheese, softened
1 (8-ounce) can crushed pineapple, drained
Chopped green onions to taste
Chopped green bell pepper to taste
Chopped pecans

Combine the cream cheese, pineapple, green onions and bell pepper in a bowl and mix well. Shape into a ball and roll in the pecans, coating evenly. Wrap in plastic wrap and chill for 24 hours. YIELD: 12 SERVINGS.

Faye Grizzell
Birmingham South Life

Snowball Cheese Balls

16 ounces cream cheese, softened
1/3 cup drained crushed pineapple
1/3 cup minced green bell pepper
1/3 cup finely chopped pecans or walnuts
1/2 cup mayonnaise
2 dashes of Worcestershire sauce
1/4 teaspoon garlic salt
1 (7-ounce) can flaked coconut or chopped pecans
Crackers

Combine the cream cheese, pineapple, bell pepper, pecans, mayonnaise, Worcestershire sauce and garlic salt in a bowl and mix well. Shape into 2 balls. Roll in the coconut, coating evenly. Wrap individually in plastic wrap and chill in the refrigerator. Serve with crackers. YIELD: 16 SERVINGS.

Edith Dixon
Birmingham Life

Chicken Cheese Ball

1 (6-ounce) can chicken breast
16 ounces cream cheese, softened
2 tablespoons (rounded) sour cream
1 envelope ranch salad dressing mix
Chopped pecans, walnuts or almonds
Crackers

Drain and shred the chicken; rinse in cold water and drain again. Combine the chicken with the cream cheese in a bowl and mix well. Add the sour cream and salad dressing mix and mix well. Shape into a ball and roll in the pecans, coating evenly. Wrap in plastic wrap and chill in the refrigerator for 8 hours or longer. Serve with crackers. **YIELD: 16 SERVINGS.**

Paula Smith
Birmingham Metro Council

Chicken Cheese Ball

16 ounces cream cheese, softened
2 cans chunky chicken spread
1/2 cup mayonnaise
1/2 cup chopped pecans
1 teaspoon garlic powder
1 teaspoon parsley flakes
1 1/4 cups chopped pecans
Crackers

Combine the cream cheese, chicken, mayonnaise, 1/2 cup pecans, garlic powder and parsley flakes in a bowl and mix well. Shape into a ball and roll in 1 1/4 cups pecans, coating evenly. Wrap in foil and chill until serving time. Serve with crackers. **YIELD: 16 SERVINGS.**

Phoebe Arthur
Gadsden Life

Salmon Ball

1 (15-ounce) can salmon
8 ounces cream cheese, softened
2 tablespoons horseradish
1 tablespoon each grated onion and lemon juice
¼ teaspoon liquid smoke
¼ teaspoon salt
1 cup chopped nuts
¼ cup chopped fresh parsley

Combine the salmon, cream cheese, horseradish, onion, lemon juice, liquid smoke and salt in a bowl and mix well. Chill, covered, for 1 hour. Mix the nuts and parsley on waxed paper. Shape the salmon mixture into a ball or log. Roll in the parsley mixture. Refrigerate and serve with crackers. YIELD: 12 TO 15 SERVINGS.

Phoebe Arthur
Gadsden Life

Tuna Ball

8 ounces cream cheese, softened
1 (6-ounce) can tuna, drained
½ cup minced onion
1 cup chopped pecans
4 or 5 dashes of Tabasco sauce
Salt to taste
Dried parsley flakes
Butter crackers

Combine the cream cheese, tuna, onion, pecans, Tabasco sauce and salt in a bowl and mix well. Shape into a ball and wrap with plastic wrap. Chill in the refrigerator. Roll in parsley flakes, coating evenly. Serve with butter crackers. YIELD: 12 SERVINGS.

Adeline Neal
Birmingham Life

Charleston Cheese

8 ounces cream cheese, softened
1 cup shredded sharp Cheddar cheese
½ cup mayonnaise
12 butter crackers, crushed
8 slices bacon, crisp-fried, crumbled, or real bacon bits
Crackers

Combine the cream cheese, Cheddar cheese and mayonnaise in a bowl and mix well. Spoon into a greased quiche dish. Top with the cracker crumbs. Bake at 350 degrees for 15 to 20 minutes or until heated through. Sprinkle with the bacon and serve warm with crackers. **YIELD: 15 TO 20 SERVINGS.**

Leigh Rice
Birmingham South Cahaba Council

Cheese Ring Spread

4 cups shredded sharp Cheddar cheese
1 bunch green onions, finely chopped
1 cup chopped pecans
1½ cups (or more) light mayonnaise
2 teaspoons Tabasco sauce (optional)
2 teaspoons seasoned salt
1 teaspoon seasoned pepper
Strawberry preserves
Wheat crackers

Combine the cheese, green onions, pecans, mayonnaise, Tabasco sauce, seasoned salt and seasoned pepper in a bowl and mix well. Press into an oiled ring mold and chill in the refrigerator. Invert onto a serving plate and fill the center with the strawberry preserves. Serve with the crackers. **YIELD: 24 SERVINGS.**

Virginia Greene
Birmingham South Life

Herbed Cheese Spread

16 ounces cream cheese, softened
1/2 cup (1 stick) butter, softened
2 garlic cloves, minced
1/4 teaspoon dried dillweed
1/4 teaspoon dried basil
1/4 teaspoon dried marjoram
1/4 teaspoon dried thyme
1/4 teaspoon dried oregano
1/4 teaspoon salt
1/4 teaspoon black pepper
Cayenne pepper to taste
Crackers

Combine the cream cheese, butter, garlic, dillweed, basil, marjoram, thyme, oregano, salt, black pepper and cayenne pepper in a mixing bowl or food processor container and mix until smooth. Spoon into a serving crock or bowl. Serve with crackers. Store in the refrigerator for up to 3 weeks or in the freezer for up to 1 month. YIELD: 10 TO 12 SERVINGS.

Frankie Vaughn
Selma Life

Pineapple Almond Cream Cheese Spread

8 ounces cream cheese, softened
4 cups shredded Cheddar cheese
1/2 cup mayonnaise
1 tablespoon soy sauce
1/4 cup chopped green onions
2 (8-ounce) cans crushed pineapple, drained
1/2 cup finely chopped green bell pepper
1 cup almonds, toasted, chopped

Beat the cream cheese in a large mixing bowl until smooth. Add the Cheddar cheese, mayonnaise and soy sauce and mix well. Stir in the green onions, pineapple, bell pepper and almonds. Chill, covered, in the refrigerator. Allow to return to room temperature to serve. YIELD: 16 SERVINGS.

Susan Robinson
Birmingham Metro Council

Olive Pimento Cheese Spread

2 cups shredded Cheddar cheese
1/2 cup mayonnaise
1 tablespoon mustard
1/2 cup chopped pimento-stuffed green olives
1 teaspoon sugar
Salt and pepper to taste

Combine the cheese, mayonnaise, mustard, olives, sugar, salt and pepper in a bowl and mix well. Serve on crackers or as a sandwich spread. YIELD: 12 SERVINGS.

Eunice Henry
Selma Life

Raine's Shrimp Butter

2 (4-ounce) cans shrimp
1/4 cup vinegar
2 teaspoons cooking sherry
1/2 cup (1 stick) margarine, softened
8 ounces cream cheese, softened
3 tablespoons mayonnaise
1 tablespoon lemon juice
3 tablespoons grated onion
1/4 cup chopped parsley
1 teaspoon Worcestershire sauce
2 teaspoons Tabasco sauce
1/2 teaspoon garlic powder
1/2 teaspoon red pepper
Melba rounds or wheat crackers

Drain the shrimp and combine with the vinegar and sherry in a bowl. Let stand for 15 minutes. Rinse under running water and drain. Blend the margarine and cream cheese in a bowl. Add the shrimp, mayonnaise, lemon juice, onion, parsley, Worcestershire sauce, Tabasco sauce, garlic powder and red pepper and mix well. Shape as desired and chill until serving time. Serve with Melba rounds or wheat crackers. You may omit the vinegar and wine if preferred and just rinse and drain the shrimp. YIELD: 12 SERVINGS.

Virginia Greene
Birmingham South Life

Oyster Spread

1 cup minced cooked oysters
1/4 cup (1/2 stick) butter, melted
1 teaspoon minced onion
Juice of 1 lemon
1 teaspoon Worcestershire sauce
1 teaspoon prepared mustard
1/2 teaspoon paprika
1/2 teaspoon salt

Combine the oysters, butter, onion, lemon juice, Worcestershire sauce, mustard, paprika and salt in a bowl and mix well. Spoon into a serving bowl. YIELD: 8 SERVINGS.

Betty Etheredge
Bon Secour Life

Nana Stetson's Chopped Liver

1 1/4 to 1 1/2 pounds chicken livers
Chopped onion to taste
2 hard-cooked eggs, chopped
Finely chopped celery to taste
Mayonnaise
Celery sticks and/or party crackers

Grind the chicken livers with the onion and eggs in a meat grinder. Sauté the liver mixture with the celery in a nonstick skillet until the liver is cooked through and the celery is tender. Let stand until cool. Combine with enough mayonnaise to make of spreading consistency in a bowl and mix well. Chill, covered, until serving time. Serve with celery sticks and/or party crackers.
YIELD: 8 TO 10 SERVINGS.

Margie Stetson
Riverchase Council

Caramel Apple Dip

6 ounces butterscotch chips
1 (14-ounce) can sweetened condensed milk
2 teaspoons vinegar
Apples, sliced
Pineapple juice

Combine the butterscotch chips with the sweetened condensed milk and vinegar in a saucepan and heat until the chips melt, stirring to blend well. Spoon into a serving bowl and serve with apple slices which have been sprinkled with pineapple juice. **YIELD: 8 SERVINGS.**

Patsy Frost
Decatur Council

Black Bean Hummus

1 (16-ounce) can black beans, drained
1 garlic clove
1/4 cup cilantro leaves
2 tablespoons tomato paste
Juice of 1/2 lime
2 tablespoons cumin
1 teaspoon salt
1/2 cup olive oil
Chopped green onions, chopped tomatoes or sour cream
Tortilla chips

Combine the beans, garlic, cilantro, tomato paste, lime juice, cumin and salt in a food processor container and process until smooth. Add the olive oil gradually, processing constantly until well mixed. Spoon into a serving bowl and garnish with green onions, tomatoes or sour cream. Serve with tortilla chips. **YIELD: 12 SERVINGS.**

Celia Bengel
Riverchase Council

Bean Dip

1 pound ground beef
1 (16-ounce) can refried beans
1 (16-ounce) can medium salsa
1 (15-ounce) can crushed tomatoes (optional)
Nacho chips

Brown the ground beef in a skillet, stirring until crumbly; drain. Mix with the beans, salsa and tomatoes in a CROCK-POT® Slow Cooker. Cook for several hours. Serve with nacho chips. YIELD: 12 SERVINGS.

Mary D. Palmer
Birmingham Metro Council

Mexican Bean Dip

1 pound dried pinto beans, or 3 to 4 cans pinto beans
3 or 4 garlic cloves, minced
1 (16-ounce) jar picante sauce
1 cup chopped green onions
½ to 1 cup chopped jalapeño peppers
16 ounces sour cream
½ to 1 cup chopped tomatoes
1 (2-ounce) can sliced black olives (optional)
Tortilla chips

Soak dried beans in water to cover in a bowl for 8 hours; drain. Combine with fresh water to cover and garlic in a saucepan and cook until tender, maintaining just enough water to cover. Mash the beans. Add the picante sauce, green onions and jalapeño peppers and mix well. Spoon into a serving bowl and spread the sour cream over the top. Sprinkle with the tomatoes and black olives. Serve warm with tortilla chips. YIELD: 20 SERVINGS.

Marjie Harden and Naomi Neaves
Birmingham Metro Council

Corn Dip

8 ounces cream cheese, softened
8 ounces sour cream
1 (8-ounce) can Mexicorn, drained
Chopped pimento to taste
¼ cup sugar
Chips

Combine the cream cheese and sour cream in a bowl and mix until smooth. Add the corn and pimento and mix well. Stir in the sugar. Serve with chips. You may also use this as stuffing for tacos or as a spread for French bread. **YIELD: 12 SERVINGS.**

Helen Smith
Birmingham Metro Council

Chunky Guacamole

2 avocados
Juice of ½ lemon
1 large tomato, chopped
1 tablespoon chopped garlic
Salt and pepper to taste
Chips

Mash the avocados in a bowl. Add the lemon juice, tomato, garlic, salt and pepper and mix well. Serve with chips. **YIELD: 8 SERVINGS.**

Elaine Hyatt, niece of Warren and Marion Thompson
Gadsden Life

▨ ▨ ▨ HELPFUL HINT ▨ ▨ ▨

If you heat the nail before driving it into the wall when hanging a picture, you will not crack or chip the plaster.

Peach Mango Guacamole

2 avocados
Juice of 1/2 lemon
1 large peach, chopped
1/2 mango, chopped
1/2 cup chopped pineapple
3/4 cup salsa
Chips

Mash the avocados in a bowl and add the lemon juice; mix well. Add the peach, mango and pineapple and mix well. Stir in the salsa. Serve with chips. YIELD: **8 TO 10 SERVINGS**.

Elaine Hyatt, niece of Warren and Marion Thompson
Gadsden Life

Veggie Guacamole

2 avocados
Juice of 1/2 lemon
Salt and pepper to taste
1 large tomato, chopped
3/4 cup drained canned black beans
Kernels of 1 roasted ear of corn
1 teaspoon chopped garlic
1 tablespoon chopped green onions
2 tablespoons chopped canned jalapeño peppers
Chips or tortillas

Mash the avocados in a bowl and add the lemon juice, salt and pepper; mix well. Stir in the tomato, beans, corn, garlic, green onions and jalapeño peppers. Serve with chips or tortillas. YIELD: **10 SERVINGS**.

Elaine Hyatt, niece of Warren and Marion Thompson
Gadsden Life

Outback-Style Dip

½ cup mayonnaise
2 teaspoons ketchup
2 teaspoons cream-style horseradish
¼ teaspoon paprika
⅛ teaspoon oregano
¼ teaspoon salt
Black pepper and cayenne pepper to taste

Combine the mayonnaise, ketchup, horseradish, paprika, oregano, salt, black pepper and cayenne pepper in a bowl and mix well. Store, tightly covered, in the refrigerator for up to 2 weeks. Serve as a dip or with Blooming Onions or fried turkey. **YIELD: 4 TO 6 SERVINGS.**

Mary Gillis
Mobile Council

Michelle's Black-Eyed Pea Dip

2 (16-ounce) cans black-eyed peas
1 green bell pepper, chopped
1 medium onion, chopped
1 (2-ounce) jar chopped pimentos, drained
1 (16-ounce) bottle of spicy Italian salad dressing
Scoop-size corn chips

Rinse and drain the peas. Combine the peas, bell pepper, onion and pimentos in a bowl. Add the salad dressing and mix well. Chill, covered, for 8 hours or longer. Serve with corn chips. **YIELD: 12 SERVINGS.**

Mary Ann Stanley
Mobile Council

Ro-Tel Dip

1 pound Velveeta cheese
1 (10-ounce) can Ro-Tel tomatoes with green chiles

Cut the cheese into chunks. Melt the cheese in a double boiler or microwave. Cook for 4 minutes and stir. Add the tomatoes with green chiles and mix well. Cook for 4 minutes. Serve with tortilla chips. YIELD: 20 SERVINGS.

Barbara S. Lagle
Birmingham Life

Pam's Homemade Salsa

1 gallon tomatoes
2 cups chopped onions
2 cups chopped green bell peppers
1/2 to 1 cup chopped jalapeño peppers
1/2 cup sugar
1 cup vinegar
2 tablespoons cumin
1 tablespoon garlic powder
1 1/2 tablespoons chili pepper
2 teaspoons black pepper

Combine the tomatoes, onions, bell peppers, jalapeño peppers, sugar, vinegar, cumin, garlic powder, chili pepper and black pepper in a saucepan and mix well. Cook for 30 minutes. Drain the mixture and spoon into sterilized 1-pint jars, leaving 1/2 inch headspace; seal with 2-piece lids. Process in a hot water bath for 10 minutes. You may chop the mixture in a food processor before spooning into the jars for a smoother salsa. YIELD: APPROXIMATELY 8 PINTS.

Pam Dyer
Riverchase Council

Spinach Dip

2 (2-pound) packages frozen chopped spinach
1 (16-ounce) can artichoke hearts, drained
1 to 2 cups (2 to 4 sticks) margarine
6 cups shredded Monterey Jack cheese
1/2 cup chopped onion
1 cup heavy cream
1 tablespoon garlic salt
2 teaspoons white pepper
1/2 cup shredded Monterey Jack cheese
Tortilla chips

Combine the spinach, artichoke hearts, margarine, 6 cups cheese, onion, cream, garlic salt and white pepper in a CROCK-POT® Slow Cooker. Cook until the cheese melts, stirring occasionally to mix well. Sprinkle with 1/2 cup cheese and serve hot with tortilla chips. You may reduce the recipe by half if desired. **YIELD: 30 SERVINGS.**

Anatalie Watson Fogg
Decatur Council

Taco Dip

1 pound ground beef
1 envelope taco seasoning mix
1 (4-ounce) can chopped black olives
8 ounces cream cheese, softened
8 ounces sour cream
2 cups shredded Cheddar cheese
Scoop-size corn chips

Brown the ground beef in a skillet, stirring until crumbly; drain. Stir in the taco seasoning mix. Spoon into a 9×9-inch baking dish and sprinkle with the olives. Blend the cream cheese and sour cream in a mixing bowl. Spread over the olives and sprinkle with the Cheddar cheese. Bake at 350 degrees until the cheese melts. Serve with corn chips. **YIELD: 12 SERVINGS.**

Donna Lee
Birmingham South Cahaba Council

Nine-Layer Taco Dip

1 (16-ounce) can refried
  beans
8 ounces avocado dip
8 ounces sour cream
1 envelope taco seasoning mix
1 (4-ounce) can chopped
  black olives
1 (4-ounce) can chopped
  green chiles
½ small head lettuce,
  chopped
1 medium tomato, chopped
2 small green onions with
  tops, chopped
Sliced jalapeño peppers
Scoop-size corn chips or
  taco chips

Spread the refried beans in a large serving dish and spread the avocado dip over the beans. Blend the sour cream and taco seasoning mix in a bowl. Spread over the avocado layer. Layer the olives, green chiles, lettuce, tomato, green onions and jalapeño peppers over the top. Serve with corn chips or taco chips. YIELD: 12 SERVINGS.

Marie P. Williams
Mobile Council

Hot Crab Dip

16 ounces cream cheese
½ cup shredded Cheddar
  cheese
1 cup sour cream
¼ cup mayonnaise
1 teaspoon lemon juice
1 teaspoon dry mustard
⅛ teaspoon garlic powder
1 pound backfin crab meat
½ cup shredded Cheddar
  cheese
Paprika to taste

Combine the first 7 ingredients in a double boiler. Cook until the cheeses melt, stirring to blend well. Fold in the crab meat. Spoon into an 8x8-inch baking dish. Top with ½ cup Cheddar cheese and sprinkle with paprika. Bake at 325 degrees for 45 minutes.
YIELD: 16 SERVINGS.

Chris Elsen
Gadsden Life

Shrimp Dip

8 ounces cream cheese, softened
½ cup mayonnaise-type salad dressing
1 (4-ounce) can tiny cocktail shrimp, rinsed, drained
⅓ cup finely chopped green onions
⅛ teaspoon garlic salt
Vegetable dippers
Crackers

Mix the cream cheese and salad dressing in a bowl until smooth. Stir in the shrimp, green onions and garlic salt. Serve with vegetable dippers and/or crackers. **YIELD: 8 SERVINGS.**

Eloise Bennett
Decatur Council

Bacon Appetizer Crescents

8 ounces cream cheese, softened
8 slices bacon, crisp-fried, crumbled
⅓ cup grated Parmesan cheese
2 tablespoons minced parsley
¼ cup finely chopped onion
1 tablespoon milk
2 (8-count) cans refrigerator crescent rolls
1 egg, beaten
1 teaspoon cold water
Poppy seeds (optional)

Beat the first 6 ingredients in a small bowl until smooth. Separate the crescent roll dough into 8 rectangles, pressing the diagonal perforations to seal. Spread the rectangles with the cream cheese mixture. Cut each rectangle into 4 triangles, cutting from corner to corner, then into halves crosswise to form 6 triangles. Roll up the triangles from the small end to enclose the filling. Place on a greased baking sheet. Beat the egg with the cold water in a small bowl. Brush on the rolls and sprinkle with the poppy seeds. Bake at 375 degrees for 12 to 15 minutes or until golden brown. **YIELD: 4 DOZEN.**

Susan Robinson
Birmingham Metro Council

Priatzo by Regina

3 pounds ground chuck
1 (16-ounce) can meat-flavor spaghetti sauce
2 cans refrigerator pizza crust dough
2 to 3 cups shredded mozzarella cheese

Brown the ground chuck in a skillet, stirring until crumbly; drain. Add the spaghetti sauce and simmer for 5 minutes. Roll the pizza dough on a floured surface and cut into 8 to 10 rectangles measuring 3x5 inches. Spoon the ground beef mixture onto 1/2 of each rectangle and sprinkle with the cheese. Fold the dough over to enclose the filling and press the edges with a fork to seal. Place on a greased baking sheet. Bake at 350 degrees for 15 to 25 minutes or until golden brown. YIELD: 8 TO 10 SERVINGS.

Helen Shirley
Birmingham Life

Cheddar Crisps

1¾ cups flour
½ cup yellow cornmeal
½ teaspoon baking soda
½ teaspoon sugar
½ teaspoon salt
½ cup (1 stick) butter or margarine
1½ cups shredded Cheddar cheese
½ cup cold water
2 tablespoons light vinegar
Pepper or poppy seeds

Mix the flour, cornmeal, baking soda, sugar and salt in a large bowl. Cut in the butter with a pastry blender or fork until crumbly. Add the Cheddar cheese, water and vinegar and mix with a fork to form a soft dough. Knead until smooth. Shape into a ball and wrap with plastic wrap. Chill for 1 hour or until easily handled. Divide the dough into 4 portions and roll 1 portion at a time into a large circle on a lightly floured surface; chill remaining dough until needed. Sprinkle the circle with pepper or poppy seeds. Cut with a pizza cutter or cookie cutter into desired shapes. Place on a greased baking sheet. Bake at 375 degrees for 8 to 10 minutes or until crisp and brown. Cool on a wire rack. Store in an airtight container.
YIELD: 5 DOZEN.

Susan Robinson
Birmingham Metro Council

Cheese Wafers

1 pound sharp Cheddar cheese, shredded
½ cup (1 stick) butter, softened
2 cups flour
1 teaspoon salt
½ teaspoon red pepper
1 cup finely chopped pecans

Combine the cheese and butter in a bowl and mix well. Add the flour, salt, red pepper and pecans and mix well. Shape into rolls 1 inch in diameter and wrap in waxed paper. Chill in the refrigerator. Cut into slices and place on a baking sheet. Bake at 400 degrees for 10 minutes. Cool on a wire rack. YIELD: **8 DOZEN**.

Dilla Samuel
Gadsden Life

Stuffed Mushrooms

1 pound medium mushrooms
8 ounces cream cheese, softened
1 cup chopped scallions
8 ounces bacon, crisp-fried, crumbled
Butter
1 cup burgundy (optional)

Remove the stems of the mushrooms and reserve for another use. Combine the cream cheese, scallions and bacon in a bowl and mix well. Spoon into the mushroom caps and dot each with butter. Place in a baking pan and pour the wine into the pan. Bake at 350 degrees for 15 minutes. YIELD: **16 SERVINGS**.

Faith Kirby Richardson
Gadsden Life

Sausage-Stuffed Mushrooms

12 to 15 large fresh mushrooms
2 tablespoons chopped onion
4½ teaspoons butter or margarine
1 tablespoon lemon juice
¼ teaspoon dried basil
Salt and pepper to taste
4 ounces bulk Italian sausage
1 tablespoon chopped fresh parsley
2 tablespoons dry bread crumbs
2 tablespoons grated Parmesan cheese
1½ teaspoons butter or margarine

Remove and chop the mushroom stems, reserving the caps. Press the chopped stems with paper towels to remove any moisture. Sauté the stems with the onion in 4½ teaspoons butter in a skillet until tender. Add the lemon juice, basil, salt and pepper. Cook until most of the liquid has evaporated. Cool to room temperature. Add the sausage and parsley. Spoon into the mushroom caps. Mix the bread crumbs and cheese in a bowl. Sprinkle over the mushroom stuffing and dot with 1½ teaspoons butter. Place in a greased baking pan. Bake at 400 degrees for 20 minutes, basting occasionally with accumulated pan juices. Serve hot. YIELD: 12 TO 15 SERVINGS.

Gail Hyatt
Anniston Council

HELPFUL HINT

When stung by a bee, apply an onion slice to the sting area and hold it there for a minute or two.

Olive Balls

1 (5-ounce) jar Old English cheese spread
1/2 cup (1 stick) margarine, softened
1 cup flour
1/2 teaspoon red pepper
36 small pimento-stuffed olives

Combine the cheese and margarine in a bowl and mix until smooth. Add the flour and red pepper and mix to form a dough. Pinch off small amounts of the dough and press flat in the hand. Place an olive in the center and shape the dough to enclose the olive completely. Place on a baking sheet and chill for 3 or 4 hours. Bake at 375 degrees for 15 minutes or until golden brown. You may freeze unbaked balls for up to 2 months. YIELD: **3 DOZEN**.

Nelda Goodwin
Birmingham Life

Cheesy Sausage Balls

1 pound mild bulk sausage
4 cups baking mix
1 pound extra-sharp Cheddar cheese,
finely shredded or melted

Crumble the sausage into a bowl and mix with the baking mix. Add the cheese and mix well. Shape into small balls and place on a baking sheet. Bake at 400 degrees for 15 to 20 minutes or until golden brown. YIELD: **8 DOZEN**.

Mary Ann Stanley
Mobile Council

Easy-as-Pie Sausage Balls

10 ounces sharp Cheddar cheese, shredded
1 pound hot or mild bulk sausage
3 cups baking mix

Melt the cheese in a saucepan over low heat. Add the sausage and baking mix and mix well. Shape into small balls and place on a baking sheet. Bake at 325 degrees for 25 minutes. **YIELD: 6 DOZEN.**

Betty M. Jones-Moon
Birmingham Life

Sausage Balls

4 cups baking mix
2 cups shredded mild or sharp Cheddar cheese
1 pound hot bulk sausage
1 pound mild bulk sausage

Combine the baking mix, cheese and sausage in a bowl and mix well. Shape into small balls and place on a baking sheet. Bake at 350 degrees for 20 minutes or until golden brown. **YIELD: 8 OR 9 DOZEN.**

Ann Moon
Decatur Council

HELPFUL HINT

Use corners cut from old envelopes as bookmarks.
They slip over the page you wish to mark.

Sausage Balls

1 pound bulk sausage
3 cups shredded cheese
1 cup baking mix

Crumble the sausage into a large bowl. Add the cheese and baking mix gradually, mixing well. Shape into 1-inch balls and place in a large shallow baking pan. Bake at 350 degrees for 30 minutes or until golden brown. YIELD: 5 DOZEN.

Jo Anne Norris Emery
Bon Secour Life

Cornelia's Party "Snausages"

1 pound smoked cocktail sausages
1 (1-pound) package dark brown sugar
1 cup whiskey

Combine the sausages, brown sugar and whiskey in a CROCK-POT® Slow Cooker. Cook on High for 5 to 6 hours, stirring occasionally. Serve hot. You may double the recipe if desired. YIELD: 10 SERVINGS.

Nita Furlong
Birmingham Metro Council

Cocktail Meatballs

2 pounds ground beef
1 egg
1 envelope onion soup mix
½ cup bread crumbs
¼ teaspoon salt
½ teaspoon black pepper
½ teaspoon red pepper
Sauce (below)

Combine the ground beef, egg, onion soup mix, bread crumbs, salt, black pepper and red pepper in a bowl and mix well. Shape into 1-inch balls. Add to the sauce in a saucepan. Cook over medium heat for 30 minutes. YIELD: **16 SERVINGS.**

Sauce

2 (14-ounce) bottles ketchup
1 (10-ounce) jar applesauce
½ cup packed brown sugar
1 teaspoon oregano
¼ teaspoon salt
½ teaspoon black pepper
½ teaspoon red pepper

Combine the ketchup, applesauce, brown sugar, oregano, salt, black pepper and red pepper in a saucepan and mix well. Bring to a simmer over medium heat. YIELD: **ABOUT 3 CUPS.**

Sue Bryars
Birmingham South Cahaba Council

McAllister Garlic Buffalo Wings

10 pounds chicken wings
Vegetable oil for deep-frying
Sauce (below)
1/4 large bottle Crystal Wing Sauce
Celery and Bleu Cheese (page 35)

Cut each chicken wing into 3 sections, discarding the wing tip sections. Deep-fry the wings in oil just until cooked through; drain. Arrange the chicken in a baking dish and pour the sauce over the top. Sprinkle with the Crystal Wing Sauce and stir to mix well. Bake at 325 degrees until chicken and sauce are heated through, stirring occasionally. Broil for several minutes for additional crispness if desired. Serve with Celery and Bleu Cheese. YIELD: 40 SERVINGS.

Sauce

1/2 cup (1 stick) butter
1 cup (about) olive oil
Crystal hot sauce to taste
3/4 large bottle Crystal Wing Sauce
1/2 onion, chopped
1 bulb garlic, separated into cloves
Salt to taste

Melt the butter with the olive oil in a medium saucepan over low heat. Add the Crystal hot sauce and Crystal Wing Sauce. Bring to a simmer. Press the juice from the onion into the saucepan and scrape the onion pulp from the press into the saucepan. Repeat the process with the garlic. Season with salt. Simmer until the flavors mix, adjusting the ingredients as desired. YIELD: 3 CUPS.

Celery and Bleu Cheese

1 package bleu cheese
Olive oil
16 ounces sour cream
Celery sticks

Crumble the bleu cheese and combine with a small amount of olive oil in a dish; mash slightly. Add the sour cream and mix gently. Chill for several hours before serving. Serve with celery sticks. **YIELD: VARIABLE.**

Bill McAllister
Birmingham South Cahaba Council

Hidden Valley Ranch Buffalo Wings

½ cup (1 stick) butter, melted
¼ cup hot sauce
2 tablespoons vinegar
24 chicken wing drumettes
1 envelope buttermilk-recipe ranch salad dressing mix
½ teaspoon paprika
Ranch salad dressing

Combine the butter, hot sauce and vinegar in a bowl and mix well. Dip the chicken drumettes into the butter mixture and arrange in a baking pan. Sprinkle with the salad dressing mix. Bake at 350 degrees for 25 to 30 minutes or until golden brown. Sprinkle with the paprika. Serve with ranch dressing for dipping. **YIELD: 12 SERVINGS.**

Narice Sutton
Birmingham Life

Appetillas

1 package large tortillas
16 ounces cream cheese, softened
1/3 cup mayonnaise
1/4 to 1/2 cup chopped green onions
1/4 cup chopped black olives
1/4 cup chopped green olives
1/4 cup grated Parmesan cheese
2 (2 1/2-ounce) packages thinly sliced cooked ham

Let the tortillas stand at room temperature for 15 minutes or longer. Combine the cream cheese, mayonnaise, green onions, black olives, green olives and Parmesan cheese in a bowl and mix well. Spread in a thin layer over the tortillas. Arrange the ham over the tortillas and roll up the tortillas tightly to enclose the filling. Wrap individually in plastic wrap and chill for 3 hours or longer. Slice 1/4 inch thick to serve. **Yield: 80 servings.**

Susan Robinson
Birmingham Metro Council

Pinwheel Chicken Roll-Ups

4 ounces light cream cheese, softened
2 tablespoons low-fat sour cream
1 tablespoon hot red pepper jelly
3 (9-inch) flour tortillas
1 cup chopped cooked chicken
½ cup chopped lettuce
½ cup shredded reduced-fat sharp Cheddar cheese
⅓ cup chopped green onions
⅓ cup chopped red bell pepper

Combine the cream cheese, sour cream and pepper jelly in a small bowl and mix well. Spread over the tortillas. Combine the chicken, lettuce, cheese, green onions and bell pepper in a medium bowl and mix well. Sprinkle over the tortillas. Roll up the tortillas to enclose the filling. Wrap individually in plastic wrap and chill for 2 hours or longer. Cut off and discard the ends of the rolls; cut each roll into 8 or 9 slices. **YIELD: 12 SERVINGS.**

Debbie Morris
Birmingham South Cahaba Council

HELPFUL HINT

If you can't sleep because a noisy cricket has come calling, try this. Place a wet dishcloth in your kitchen or bathroom sink at night. You will find your noisy "neighbor" hiding there in the morning.

Texas Tortillas

8 ounces cream cheese, softened
8 ounces sour cream
5 green onion tops, chopped
1 (4-ounce) can chopped green chiles
2 tablespoons chopped black olives
1/2 cup shredded Cheddar cheese
Large flour tortillas
Picante sauce

Combine the cream cheese, sour cream, green onion tops, green chiles, black olives and cheese in a bowl and mix well. Spread over the tortillas and roll up the tortillas tightly to enclose the filling. Wrap individually in damp paper towels. Chill for several hours. Cut into 1-inch slices and serve with picante sauce.
YIELD: 8 TO 10 SERVINGS.

Susan Robinson
Riverchase Council

Little Pizzas

1 pound hot bulk sausage
1 pound medium bulk sausage
8 ounces Velveeta cheese, chopped
1 loaf party rye bread
Pepperoni slices, cut into halves
Green or black olives

Brown the bulk sausage in a skillet, stirring until crumbly; drain. Add the cheese and cook until the cheese melts, stirring to mix well. Arrange the rye bread on a baking sheet. Spoon the sausage mixture onto the bread slices. Top with the pepperoni and olives. Bake at 350 degrees just until heated through. YIELD: 20 SERVINGS.

Lynn S. Herrer
Montgomery Council

Vegetable Pizza

2 cans refrigerator crescent rolls
16 ounces cream cheese, softened
1 envelope ranch salad dressing mix
3/4 cup mayonnaise
1 cup shredded lettuce
1 cup chopped tomato
1 cup chopped broccoli
1 cup chopped cauliflower
1 cup grated carrots
2 cups shredded Cheddar cheese

Unroll the crescent roll dough and place in an 11×18-inch baking pan for the crust, pressing the perforations and edges to seal. Bake at 350 degrees for 10 minutes. Cool to room temperature. Combine the cream cheese, ranch salad dressing mix and mayonnaise in a large bowl and mix well. Spread over the cooled crust. Layer the lettuce, tomato, broccoli, cauliflower, carrots and Cheddar cheese over the cream cheese layer. Cut into squares to serve. You may vary the vegetables to suit individual tastes. **YIELD: 20 SERVINGS.**

Mary Ann Sparks Fulmer
Shoals Life

HELPFUL HINT

Gently run a damp paper towel over your cat to reduce cat hair around your house. It collects both hair and dirt.

Marc's Pizza Dogs

1 package bun-size beef hot dogs
1 package hot dog buns
Sliced pepperoni
1 (14-ounce) jar pizza sauce
2 cups shredded mozzarella cheese

Cook the hot dogs in water to cover in a saucepan for 10 minutes; drain. Open the hot dog buns and arrange cut side up on a baking sheet. Place the hot dogs on the buns and arrange the pepperoni slices over the tops and sides of the hot dogs. Spoon 2 tablespoons of the pizza sauce over each hot dog and sprinkle with the cheese. Bake at 450 degrees for 10 minutes or until the cheese melts. Heat the remaining pizza sauce in a saucepan and serve with the pizza dogs for dipping. YIELD: 8 SERVINGS.

Renee McCreless
Birmingham Metro Council

Peanut Butter and Banana Sandwich

2 slices bread
Peanut butter
Mayonnaise
1 banana, sliced

Spread 1 slice of bread with peanut butter. Spread a small amount of mayonnaise over the peanut butter. Arrange the banana slices over the mayonnaise and top with the second slice of bread. YIELD: 1 SERVING.

Sherrie Poynor
Montgomery Council

APPETIZERS

Toasted Party Mix

2 cups each corn, rice and wheat or bran Chex
1 cup round oat cereal
1 cup pretzel sticks
1 cup nuts
1/2 cup vegetable oil
2 teaspoons Worcestershire sauce
1/2 teaspoon garlic salt
1/4 teaspoon salt

Combine the corn Chex, rice Chex, wheat Chex, oat cereal, pretzels and nuts in a 9×13-inch baking pan. Combine the oil, Worcestershire sauce, garlic salt and salt in a bowl and mix well. Drizzle over the cereal mixture, tossing to coat well. Bake at 275 degrees for 45 minutes, stirring occasionally. **YIELD: 20 SERVINGS.**

Eloise Bennett
Decatur Council

Glazed Pecans

1 1/2 cups sugar
1/2 cup milk
1 teaspoon corn syrup
1/4 teaspoon salt
Vanilla extract to taste
3 cups pecans

Combine the sugar, milk, corn syrup and salt in a saucepan. Cook to 235 degrees on a candy thermometer, soft-ball stage. Remove from the heat and stir. Add the vanilla and beat until thick and creamy. Add the pecans and mix well. Spread on waxed paper and separate with a fork. Let stand until cool. Store in an airtight container. **YIELD: 12 SERVINGS.**

Jeanette Norton
Shoals Life

Spiced Candied Pecans

1 cup sugar
½ cup cream
2 teaspoons water
½ teaspoon cinnamon
½ teaspoon vanilla extract
1½ cups pecans

Combine the sugar, cream, water and cinnamon in a saucepan. Cook to 236 degrees on a candy thermometer, soft-ball stage, stirring constantly. Remove from the heat and add the vanilla and pecans. Stir until the mixture becomes too thick to stir. Spread on waxed paper and separate with a fork. Let stand until cool. Store in an airtight container. YIELD: 6 SERVINGS.

Althea Dunn
Bon Secour Life

Fruity Smoothie

1 cup plain yogurt
Brown sugar or honey to taste
Strawberries and raspberries to taste
1 banana, sliced
Granola

Combine the yogurt and brown sugar with ice cubes in a blender container and process until smooth. Add the berries and banana and process until smooth. Serve in an ice cream sundae glass and top with granola. You may substitute kiwifruit, mango, passion fruit and/or watermelon for a Tropical Smoothie. YIELD: 1 SERVING.

Gussie Evans
Mobile Council

Tropical Berry Blast Smoothie

1 banana, cut into quarters
1 (8-ounce) can crushed pineapple, drained
1 cup skim milk
½ cup frozen strawberries, thawed

Combine the banana, pineapple, skim milk and strawberries in a food processor container and process until smooth. Serve immediately in tall glasses. **Yield: 2 servings.**

Gussie Evans
Mobile Council

Apple Punch

2 quarts apple cider, chilled
2 cups cranberry juice cocktail, chilled
2 teaspoons lemon juice
4 cups ginger ale, chilled
Mint leaves

Combine the apple cider, cranberry juice cocktail and lemon juice in a large pitcher and mix well. Add the ginger ale at serving time and mix gently. Serve over crushed ice in tall glasses. Garnish with mint leaves. **Yield: 14 servings.**

Barbara Odom Horton
Mobile Council

Punch

4 envelopes unsweetened fruit drink mix
4 (46-ounce) cans pineapple juice
2 (6-ounce) cans frozen lemonade concentrate, thawed
6 quarts plus 2 cups water
7 cups sugar
1/2 gallon pineapple sherbet
2 large bottles ginger ale, chilled

Combine the drink mix, pineapple juice, lemonade concentrate, water and sugar in a large container and mix well. Pour into 1/2-gallon containers and freeze until firm. Let stand at room temperature for several hours or until slushy. Place in a punch bowl and mash with a masher. Add the sherbet and ginger ale, mixing gently. YIELD: 100 SERVINGS.

Mary C. Martin
Birmingham Life

Simple Punch

1 (46-ounce) can pineapple juice
1 1/2 cups sugar
1 1/2 teaspoons coconut extract
1 1/2 teaspoons almond extract
1 drop of yellow food coloring
1 (12-ounce) can lemon-lime soda
Pineapple sherbet (optional)

Combine the pineapple juice, sugar, flavorings and food coloring in a 1-gallon container with a wide mouth and shake to mix well. Chill in the refrigerator for several hours. Freeze until slushy. Combine with the lemon-lime soda in a punch bowl and mix gently. Add the sherbet if desired. YIELD: 12 SERVINGS.

Felicia Cooper
Decatur Council

Sparkling Summer Tea

2 family-size tea bags
4 cups boiling water
1/2 cup sugar
1 (12-ounce) can frozen lemonade concentrate, thawed
4 cups cold water
1 (1-liter) bottle ginger ale
Lemon slices

Steep the tea bags in the boiling water in a pitcher for 15 minutes. Squeeze the tea bags into the tea and discard the tea bags. Add the sugar, lemonade concentrate and cold water. Chill in the refrigerator. Add the ginger ale and mix gently. Serve immediately over crushed ice. Garnish with lemon slices. **Yield: 14 servings.**

Jo Ann Thomas
Selma Life

Spiced Tea Mix

2 cups sweetened orange drink mix
1 cup instant tea granules
1 large package lemonade mix
1 1/4 cups sugar
1 teaspoon cinnamon
1/2 teaspoon ground cloves
1/2 teaspoon ground allspice

Combine the orange drink mix, instant tea granules, lemonade mix, sugar, cinnamon, cloves and allspice in a bowl and mix well. Store in an airtight container. Combine 1 to 3 teaspoons of the mix with 1 cup of boiling water for each serving. You may substitute sugar substitute for some of the sugar if desired. **Yield: 30 servings.**

Betty Foshee
Decatur Council

TUSCALOOSA COUNCIL

The Tuscaloosa Council has a continuing relationship with Sprayberry School, which serves special-needs students. Pioneer volunteers have wired the school for the Internet and the local education Intranet. They have raised money to buy and install adaptive playground equipment. The Pioneers present a special award to the student who makes the most progress each year.

Soups

Broccoli Mushroom Chowder

1 pound broccoli, cut into
  ½-inch pieces
½ cup water
1 cup (2 sticks) butter
1 cup flour
1 quart chicken broth
8 ounces mushrooms, sliced
1 quart half-and-half
1 teaspoon salt
¼ teaspoon pepper

Steam the broccoli in the water in a saucepan until tender. Set aside without draining. Melt the butter in a saucepan over medium heat. Add the flour gradually, stirring constantly. Cook for 2 to 4 minutes or until brown, stirring constantly. Add the chicken broth, whisking constantly. Bring to a boil; reduce the heat to low. Add the broccoli, mushrooms, half-and-half, salt and pepper and mix well. Cook until heated through; do not boil.
YIELD: 10 TO 12 SERVINGS.

Martha G. Shelton
Tuscaloosa Council

Tex-Mex Corn Chowder

1 (15-ounce) can corn
  kernels, drained
1 (14-ounce) can cream-style
  golden sweet corn
1 (14-ounce) can chopped
  tomatoes with garlic and
  onion
1 (15-ounce) can black or
  red kidney beans, rinsed,
  drained
½ cup chicken broth
½ cup water
Shredded Cheddar cheese or
  chopped fresh chiles

Combine the first 6 ingredients in a medium saucepan. Bring to a boil; reduce the heat. Simmer, covered, for 5 minutes. Ladle into bowls. Sprinkle each serving with cheese or chiles. Serve with Mexican corn bread or crackers. YIELD: 4 TO 6 SERVINGS.

Eloise Bennett
Decatur Council

Cheddar Chowder

3 slices bacon
1 cup chopped onion
2 cups chicken broth
3 cups cubed potatoes
1 cup chopped carrots
1 (15-ounce) can corn
1 (10-ounce) package frozen chopped spinach
4 cups milk
6 tablespoons flour
1/2 teaspoon salt
3 cups shredded Cheddar cheese
1/2 cup sliced green onions

Cook the bacon in a 5-quart saucepan until crisp; drain well, reserving 2 teaspoons drippings. Crumble the bacon and set aside. Sauté the onion in the reserved drippings in the saucepan until tender. Add the chicken broth, potatoes, carrots, corn and spinach. Bring to a boil; reduce the heat. Simmer, covered, for 15 minutes or until the vegetables are tender. Combine the milk, flour and salt in a bowl, whisking until blended. Add to the vegetable mixture in the saucepan. Simmer for 3 minutes or until slightly thickened, stirring constantly. Add the cheese, stirring until melted. Ladle into bowls. Top each serving with crumbled bacon and green onions. **Yield: 10 to 12 servings.**

Kelli Lee
Anniston Council

▪ ▪ ▪ HELPFUL HINT ▪ ▪ ▪

For an interesting garnish for soup, try peanuts, almonds, cashews or roasted soybeans.

Ham Chowder

4 medium potatoes, cut into cubes
1 cup sliced celery
1 cup sliced carrots
½ cup chopped onion
2 teaspoons salt
1 teaspoon pepper
3 cups water
½ cup (1 stick) butter
½ cup flour
4 cups milk
2 cups shredded cheese
2 cups cubed ham

Cook the potatoes, celery, carrots, onion, salt and pepper in the water in a large saucepan until tender; set aside and keep warm. Melt the butter in a saucepan over low heat. Add the flour, stirring until smooth. Cook for 1 minute, stirring constantly. Add the milk gradually. Cook over medium heat until thickened, stirring constantly. Add the cheese, stirring until melted. Add the cheese mixture to the vegetable mixture in the large saucepan. Add the ham and mix well. Cook until heated through; do not boil.
YIELD: 1 GALLON.

Melda H. Hicks
Anniston Council

HELPFUL HINT

To dress up a sparse dinner, serve an easy first-course soup: combine asparagus soup with a little sherry, shredded cheese and slivered almonds.

Very Quick-and-Easy Chicken Gumbo Soup

6 to 8 chicken thighs, skin removed
1 large onion, cut into quarters
Salt to taste
1 teaspoon thyme
1 teaspoon ground bay leaf
1 teaspoon gumbo filé
1 tablespoon Worcestershire sauce
1 cup uncooked rice
8 ounces (about) spaghetti, broken into pieces
Dash of Creole seasoning
1 package frozen gumbo vegetable mix
½ teaspoon salt

Combine the chicken, onion and salt to taste with water to cover in a saucepan. Cook until the chicken is tender. Remove the chicken from the saucepan. Remove and discard the chicken bones. Return the chicken to the saucepan. Add the thyme, bay leaf, gumbo filé, Worcestershire sauce, rice, spaghetti, Creole seasoning, vegetable mix and ½ teaspoon salt and mix well. Bring to a boil; reduce the heat. Simmer, covered, until all the vegetables are tender. **YIELD: 4 TO 6 SERVINGS.**

Billie Woodruff
Mobile Council

HELPFUL HINT

For a quick soup, add a rounded tablespoon of shredded crab meat per serving to hot chicken broth and season lightly with soy sauce or dry sherry and chopped green onions.

Seafood Gumbo

5 ribs celery, chopped
1 large bell pepper, chopped
1 large onion, chopped
Butter
5 to 6 slices bacon
4 to 5 tablespoons (heaping) flour
4 cups water
2 cans stewed tomatoes
1 pound shrimp, peeled
1 pint oysters (optional)
1 can crab meat, or 1 can boned chicken
1 tablespoon thyme
1 tablespoon ground bay leaf, or 3 bay leaves
1 teaspoon gumbo filé
1 teaspoon Creole seasoning
1 to 2 tablespoons Worcestershire sauce
1 to 2 teaspoons salt
1 package frozen okra

Sauté the celery, bell pepper and onion briefly in butter in a saucepan. Set aside. Cook the bacon in a large stockpot until crisp. Remove the bacon; crumble and set aside. Add the flour to the bacon drippings in the stockpot. Cook until golden brown and of a syrupy consistency, stirring constantly. Add the sautéed vegetables, water, tomatoes, shrimp, oysters and crab meat and mix well. Add the thyme, bay leaf, gumbo filé, Creole seasoning, Worcestershire sauce, salt and okra and mix well. Bring to a boil; reduce the heat to low. Simmer for 30 minutes or until the shrimp turn pink and the okra is tender. **YIELD: 4 TO 6 SERVINGS.**

Billie Woodruff
Mobile Council

Tabasco Seafood Gumbo

16 ounces fresh or frozen oysters
3/4 cup vegetable oil
1/4 cup flour
1 large onion, chopped
1 green bell pepper, chopped
2 ribs celery, chopped
3 garlic cloves, chopped
1 pound fresh-frozen okra, or 3 tablespoons filé powder
3 quarts water
1 tablespoon each salt and pepper
1 teaspoon Tabasco sauce
1 1/2 pounds fresh or frozen shrimp, peeled
8 ounces fresh or frozen crab meat
1/2 cup chopped green onions
1/2 cup chopped parsley
1 teaspoon Tabasco sauce
Hot cooked rice

Drain the oysters, reserving the liquor. Heat the vegetable oil in a large heavy stockpot or Dutch oven. Stir in the flour. Cook over medium heat until the flour is darker than peanut butter, stirring constantly. Add the onion, bell pepper, celery, garlic and okra. Cook over medium-high heat for 10 minutes, stirring frequently. Stir in the water gradually. Bring to a boil. Add the salt, pepper, 1 teaspoon Tabasco sauce and reserved oyster liquor. Reduce the heat. Simmer for 1 hour. Add the oysters, shrimp, crab meat, green onions, parsley and 1 teaspoon Tabasco sauce. Cook for 10 minutes longer. Remove from the heat. Adjust the seasonings. Serve over hot cooked rice. **Note:** If using filé powder instead of okra, stir in the filé powder at the end of the cooking time and let stand for 5 minutes before serving. Do not boil the gumbo after filé powder has been added or it will become stringy. **YIELD: 8 TO 10 SERVINGS.**

Candis Greenlee
Riverchase Council

Mexican Bean Soup

1½ pounds ground chuck
1 (28-ounce) can chopped tomatoes
1 (14-ounce) can chopped tomatoes
2 (10-ounce) cans tomatoes with green chiles
2 (11-ounce) cans Shoe Peg corn
1 (16-ounce) can black beans
1 (16-ounce) can pinto beans
1 (16-ounce) can red kidney beans
3 cups water
1 envelope taco seasoning mix
1 envelope ranch salad dressing mix
Sour cream
Shredded cheese (optional)

Brown the ground chuck in a skillet, stirring until crumbly; drain well. Combine the ground chuck and the next 10 ingredients in a large stockpot and mix well. Bring to a boil; reduce the heat. Simmer for 30 to 45 minutes. Ladle into bowls. Top each serving with a dollop of sour cream. Sprinkle with cheese. Serve with tortilla chips. YIELD: 8 TO 10 SERVINGS.

Marie Hartley
Birmingham South Life

Spicy Cabbage Beef Soup

1 pound lean ground beef
1 large onion, chopped
5 cups chopped cabbage
2 (16-ounce) cans Mexican-style beans or kidney beans
3 (8-ounce) cans tomato sauce
4 beef bouillon cubes
1½ teaspoons cumin
½ teaspoon salt

Brown the ground beef with the onion in a Dutch oven or large saucepan, stirring frequently until the ground beef is crumbly; drain well. Add the cabbage, beans, tomato sauce, bouillon cubes, cumin and salt and mix well. Bring to a boil; reduce the heat. Simmer, covered, for 5 to 6 hours. YIELD: 4 TO 6 SERVINGS.

Anne Hancock
Gadsden Life

Healthy Chicken Soup

1/4 cup olive oil
2 carrots, chopped
1 medium onion, chopped
1 rib celery, chopped
2 tablespoons basil
2 tablespoons garlic powder
10 cups water
1 large can mixed soup vegetables, drained, or
1 package frozen soup vegetables
4 chicken bouillon cubes
2 large boneless chicken breasts, finely chopped
1 (10-ounce) can cream of chicken soup
Salt and pepper to taste
1 small package spaghetti, broken into 2-inch pieces

Heat the olive oil in a large stockpot. Add the carrots, onion, celery, basil and garlic powder. Sauté until the onion is translucent. Add the water. Bring to a boil. Add the mixed vegetables and bouillon cubes. Boil for 5 minutes. Add the chicken and cream of chicken soup and mix well. Season with salt and pepper. Return the mixture to a boil. Add the spaghetti and reduce the heat. Simmer for 15 minutes. Cover and let stand for 20 minutes. YIELD: 4 TO 6 SERVINGS.

Pam Dyer
Riverchase Council

HELPFUL HINT

Congealed fat can be easily skimmed off the top of soup stock if you chill it before using. Each tablespoon of fat removed eliminates about 100 calories.

Forgotten Minestrone

1 pound ground chuck or ground round
6 cups water
1 (28-ounce) can tomatoes
1 medium onion, chopped
1 beef bouillon cube
2½ teaspoons salt
1½ teaspoons ground thyme
½ teaspoon pepper
1 medium zucchini, thinly sliced
2 cups chopped cabbage
1 cup uncooked elbow or shell macaroni
¼ cup grated Parmesan cheese

Combine the ground chuck, water, tomatoes, onion, bouillon cube, salt, thyme and pepper in a CROCK-POT® Slow Cooker. Cook, covered, on Low for 7 to 9 hours. Add the zucchini, cabbage and macaroni. Cook, covered, on High for 45 minutes. Ladle into bowls. Sprinkle each serving with cheese. YIELD: 4 TO 6 SERVINGS.

Debbie Morris
Birmingham South Cahaba Council

Barb's Minestrone Soup

1 medium onion, finely chopped
1 large garlic clove, chopped
2 teaspoons butter
12 ounces hot Italian sausage, sliced
4 cups chicken stock
1½ cups chopped celery or cabbage
1½ cups chopped carrots
1 large can kidney beans, drained
1 quart tomatoes, chopped
¾ cup macaroni, cooked, drained, rinsed
Grated Parmesan cheese (optional)

Sauté the onion and garlic in the butter in a saucepan. Add the sausage, chicken stock, celery, carrots, beans and tomatoes and mix well. Bring to a boil; reduce the heat. Simmer, covered, for 1 hour. Stir in the macaroni. Cook until heated through. Ladle into bowls. Sprinkle each serving with cheese. **YIELD: 4 TO 6 SERVINGS.**

Francis Tucker
Selma Life

French Onion Potato Soup

6 to 8 potatoes, chopped
½ small onion, chopped
2 (10-ounce) cans cream of chicken soup
2 soup cans milk
1 (8-ounce) container French onion dip
Shredded cheese
Bacon bits

Combine the potatoes and onion with water to cover in a saucepan. Cook until tender; drain well. Combine the potatoes, onion, cream of chicken soup, milk and onion dip in a saucepan and mix well. Cook over low heat until heated through. Ladle into bowls. Sprinkle with cheese and bacon bits. **YIELD: 6 SERVINGS.**

Linda D. Jackson
Montgomery Council

Hearty Potato Soup

6 medium potatoes,
 cut into cubes
6 ribs celery, chopped
2 carrots, chopped
2 quarts water
1 onion, chopped

6 tablespoons butter
6 tablespoons flour
1 teaspoon salt
½ teaspoon pepper
1½ cups milk

Combine the potatoes, celery, carrots and water in a large stockpot. Cook for 20 minutes or until tender; drain well, reserving the cooking liquid and vegetables separately. Sauté the onion in butter in the stockpot until tender. Stir in the flour, salt and pepper. Stir in the milk gradually. Cook until thickened, stirring constantly. Stir in the potato mixture gently. Stir in enough of the reserved cooking liquid gradually to make the soup the desired consistency. YIELD: 8 TO 10 SERVINGS.

Mauntez Mayer
Anniston Council

Low-Fat Potato Soup

1 (16-ounce) package frozen
 shredded hash brown
 potatoes
1 cup chopped onions
2 (14-ounce) cans fat-free
 chicken broth
1 cup skim milk

1 (10-ounce) can reduced-fat
 cream of celery soup
¼ teaspoon pepper, or to taste
2 ounces reduced-fat Velveeta
 cheese, chopped

Combine the potatoes, onions and chicken broth in a soup pot. Cook over medium heat until the potatoes and onions are tender. Add the skim milk, celery soup and pepper. Cook until heated through. Add the cheese and stir until melted. YIELD: 6 SERVINGS.

Dot Johnson
Gadsden Life

Potato Soup

*2 (20-ounce) packages shredded potatoes, or
8 cups shredded potatoes (see Note)
2 quarts water
Salt and pepper to taste
1 (10-ounce) can cream of celery soup
1 (10-ounce) can cream of onion soup
1 (5-ounce) can evaporated milk
8 ounces Velveeta cheese, cut into cubes*

Combine the potatoes, water, salt and pepper in a large stockpot. Bring to a boil; reduce the heat. Simmer, covered, for 30 minutes, stirring frequently. Stir in the cream of celery soup, cream of onion soup and evaporated milk. Add the cheese gradually, stirring constantly until melted. Simmer, covered, for 15 to 20 minutes or until of the desired consistency, stirring frequently. **Note:** Use shredded potatoes from the refrigerator section of the supermarket, not the frozen ones. YIELD: 10 TO 12 SERVINGS.

*Eunice Henry
Selma Life*

Potato Soup

1 (32-ounce) package frozen diced hash brown potatoes
2 bunches small green onions, chopped
1 (14-ounce) can chicken broth
3 cups water
2 cups milk
1 (10-ounce) can cream of celery soup
1 (10-ounce) can cream of chicken soup
Salt and pepper to taste

Combine the potatoes, green onions, chicken broth and water in a large stockpot. Simmer for 30 minutes. Stir in the milk, cream of celery soup, cream of chicken soup, salt and pepper. Cook until heated through. Serve with corn bread muffins.
YIELD: 4 TO 6 SERVINGS.

Sheila P. Brothers
Anniston Council

Potato Soup

1 large onion, chopped
2 (16-ounce) packages frozen hash brown potatoes
1 (10-ounce) can cream of chicken soup
4 cups milk
1/2 cup (1 stick) margarine
Salt and pepper to taste

Combine the onion, potatoes, cream of chicken soup, milk, margarine, salt and pepper in a saucepan. Cook until the onion and potatoes are tender. You may add chopped Velveeta cheese.
YIELD: 4 TO 6 SERVINGS.

Anatalie Watson Fogg
Decatur Council

Easy Potato Soup

1 (16-ounce) package frozen hash brown potatoes
1 cup chopped onion
1 (14-ounce) can chicken broth
3 cups water
1 (10-ounce) can cream of celery soup
1 (10-ounce) can cream of chicken soup
2 cups milk
Salt and pepper to taste

Combine the potatoes, onion, chicken broth and water in a Dutch oven. Bring to a boil; reduce the heat. Simmer for 30 minutes. Stir in the cream of celery soup, cream of chicken soup, milk, salt and pepper. Cook until heated through. You may add 1 chopped potato with the hash brown potatoes for a chunkier soup. YIELD: 6 SERVINGS.

Judy Evans
Decatur Council

Potato Soup

3 large potatoes, cut into cubes
1 carrot, grated
1/2 medium onion, chopped
1 tablespoon margarine
1 (10-ounce) can cream of celery soup
1 1/2 cups milk
Salt and pepper to taste

Combine the potatoes, carrot and onion with water to cover in a saucepan. Cook until the vegetables are tender. Add the margarine, cream of celery soup, milk, salt and pepper. Cook until the margarine is melted. YIELD: 4 TO 5 SERVINGS.

Hazel E. Campbell
Birmingham Life

Potato Soup

10 medium potatoes, cut into cubes
1 medium onion, chopped
½ cup (1 stick) margarine
1 (8-ounce) container French onion dip
2 (10-ounce) cans cream of chicken soup
2 soup cans milk

Boil the potatoes in water to cover in a saucepan until tender; drain well. Sauté the onion in the margarine in a Dutch oven until tender. Add the onion dip, cream of chicken soup and milk, stirring until smooth. Add the potatoes. Cook over medium heat until of the desired consistency. You may top each serving with crumbled bacon, shredded cheese or chopped onion. **YIELD: 6 TO 8 SERVINGS.**

Debbie Speaks
Montgomery Council

Potato Soup

6 medium potatoes, chopped
6 ribs celery, chopped
2 carrots, chopped
2 quarts water
1 medium onion, chopped
6 tablespoons butter
6 tablespoons flour
1 teaspoon each salt and pepper
1½ cups milk

Combine the potatoes, celery, carrots and water in a saucepan. Cook for 20 minutes or until the vegetables are tender; drain well, reserving the cooking liquid. Sauté the onion in butter in a large saucepan until translucent. Add the flour, salt and pepper. Stir in the milk gradually. Cook until thickened, stirring constantly. Add the potato mixture. Add enough of the reserved cooking liquid to make the soup the desired consistency. **YIELD: 4 TO 6 SERVINGS.**

Sue Walton
Birmingham Life

Santa Fe Soup

1 pound ground round
1 large onion, chopped
2 envelopes ranch salad dressing mix
2 envelopes taco seasoning mix
2 (11-ounce) cans Shoe Peg corn, drained
2 cups water
1 (16-ounce) can black beans
1 (16-ounce) can pinto beans
1 (16-ounce) can kidney beans
1 (14-ounce) can whole tomatoes
1 (10-ounce) can tomatoes with green chiles
Shredded fat-free cheese
Fat-free sour cream
Chopped green onions

Brown the ground round with the onion in a Dutch oven, stirring frequently until the ground round is crumbly; drain well. Add the salad dressing mix, taco seasoning mix, corn, water, black beans, pinto beans, kidney beans, whole tomatoes and tomatoes with green chiles; mix well. Bring to a boil; reduce the heat. Simmer, covered, for 2 hours. Ladle into bowls. Top each serving with cheese, sour cream and green onions. Serve with tortillas or corn bread. YIELD: 8 SERVINGS.

Bertha Capps
Birmingham Life

HELPFUL HINT

Don't throw away leftover vegetables. Store them in an airtight container in the freezer to use in a quick vegetable soup.

Santa Fe Soup

1½ pounds ground chuck
1 large onion, chopped
2 envelopes ranch salad dressing mix
1 envelope taco seasoning mix
2 (11-ounce) cans Shoe Peg corn
1 (16-ounce) can black beans
1 (16-ounce) can pinto beans
1 (16-ounce) can kidney beans
1 (14-ounce) can tomatoes
1 (10-ounce) can tomatoes with green chiles
2 cups water
Shredded cheese (optional)
Sour cream (optional)

Brown the ground chuck with the onion in a large saucepan, stirring frequently until the ground chuck is crumbly; drain well. Add the salad dressing mix, taco seasoning mix, corn, black beans, pinto beans, kidney beans, tomatoes, tomatoes with green chiles and water; mix well. Bring to a boil; reduce the heat. Simmer for 2 hours. Ladle into bowls. Top each serving with cheese and a dollop of sour cream. YIELD: 8 TO 10 SERVINGS.

Frances Cook
Birmingham South Life

HELPFUL HINT

Sauté vegetables in a small amount of oil before adding to soup. This keeps them firm and seals in their flavor.

Santa Fe Soup

2 pounds ground chuck
1 large onion, chopped
2 envelopes taco seasoning mix
2 envelopes ranch salad dressing mix
1 (14-ounce) can stewed tomatoes
1 (10-ounce) can tomatoes with green chiles
1 (16-ounce) can pinto beans
1 (16-ounce) can kidney beans
1 (16-ounce) can black beans
2 (15-ounce) cans whole kernel corn

Brown the ground chuck with the onion, taco seasoning mix and salad dressing mix in a skillet, stirring until the ground beef is crumbly; drain well. Combine the stewed tomatoes, tomatoes with green chiles, pinto beans, kidney beans, black beans and corn in a large stockpot and mix well. Add the ground chuck mixture. Simmer until heated through. Serve with rice, sour cream, green onions and chips. YIELD: **4** TO **6** SERVINGS.

Anatalie Watson Fogg
Decatur Council

Five-Can Soup

1½ to 2 pounds ground beef
1 large onion, chopped
1 (16-ounce) can Mexicorn
1 (15-ounce) can green beans, drained
2 (14-ounce) cans tomatoes, or 1 can tomatoes and 1 can Italian or Mexican-style tomatoes
1 (15-ounce) can hot chili

Brown the ground beef with the onion in a large stockpot, stirring frequently until the ground beef is crumbly; drain well. Add the Mexicorn, green beans, tomatoes and chili and mix well. Bring to a boil; reduce the heat. Simmer for 2 hours or longer, stirring frequently and adding water if needed to prevent scorching. This recipe makes a lot and can be frozen. You may add 1 small can tomato sauce for extra tomato flavor. **YIELD: 10 TO 12 SERVINGS.**

Elsie Fowler
Jasper Council

Seven-Can Soup

1 pound ground chuck
1 (14-ounce) can stewed tomatoes
1 (10-ounce) can tomatoes with green chiles
1 (10-ounce) can tomato soup
1 (15-ounce) can chili with beans
1 (10-ounce) can vegetable soup, or 1 can mixed soup vegetables and 1 bouillon cube
1 (15-ounce) can chili without beans
1 (15-ounce) can whole kernel corn or Mexicorn

Brown the ground chuck in a saucepan, stirring until crumbly; drain well. Add the stewed tomatoes, tomatoes with green chiles, tomato soup, chili with beans, vegetable soup, chili without beans and corn and mix well. Cook until thickened, stirring occasionally. **YIELD: 6 TO 8 SERVINGS.**

Anatalie Watson Fogg
Decatur Council

Squash Soup

5 or 6 squash, sliced
1 onion, sliced
Tomatoes, peeled, sliced
Salt and pepper to taste
½ cup (1 stick) butter or margarine, cut into pieces

Layer half the squash, half the onion and half the tomatoes in a microwave-safe bowl. Season with salt and pepper and dot with half the butter. Repeat the layers and seasonings. Cover with plastic wrap. Make several holes in the plastic wrap. Microwave on High just until the squash is tender. **YIELD: 4 TO 6 SERVINGS.**

Anatalie Watson Fogg
Decatur Council

Taco Soup

1 pound ground sirloin
1 large onion, chopped
1 envelope ranch salad dressing mix
1 envelope taco seasoning mix
1 (16-ounce) can ranch-style beans
1 (16-ounce) can pinto beans
1 (14-ounce) can stewed tomatoes
1 (10-ounce) can tomatoes with green chiles
1 (15-ounce) can whole kernel or cream-style corn

Brown the ground sirloin with the onion in a saucepan, stirring until the ground sirloin is crumbly; drain well. Add the salad dressing mix and taco seasoning mix; mix well. Add the ranch-style beans, pinto beans, stewed tomatoes, tomatoes with green chiles and corn and mix well. Bring to a boil; reduce the heat. Simmer for 1 hour. **YIELD: 4 TO 6 SERVINGS.**

Melda H. Hicks
Anniston Council

Taco Soup

2 pounds ground chuck or ground turkey
1 onion, chopped
2 envelopes taco seasoning mix
2 envelopes ranch salad dressing mix
2 (16-ounce) cans black beans
1 (16-ounce) can pinto beans
1 (10-ounce) can tomatoes with green chiles
1 (15-ounce) can tomato wedges
2 (11-ounce) cans white corn
2 cups water or broth
Sliced green onions (optional)
Sour cream (optional)
Shredded sharp Cheddar cheese (optional)

Brown the ground chuck with the onion in a saucepan, stirring until the ground chuck is crumbly; drain well and then rinse with hot water. Return the ground chuck mixture to the saucepan. Sprinkle the mixture with taco seasoning mix and salad dressing mix; stir to mix well. Add the black beans and pinto beans, tomatoes with green chiles, tomato wedges, corn and water and mix well. Bring to a boil; reduce the heat. Simmer for 2 hours, adding additional water if needed. Ladle into bowls. Top each serving with green onions, sour cream and cheese. YIELD: **4 QUARTS**.

Mrs. Virginia Greene
Birmingham South Life

HELPFUL HINT

As a quick substitute for white sauce or cream sauce, use canned cream soup.

SOUPS

Taco Soup

2 pounds chopped 90% fat-free sirloin or ground beef
1 medium onion, chopped
2 (10-ounce) cans tomatoes with green chiles
2 (15-ounce) cans hot chili beans
1 (10-ounce) package frozen Shoe Peg corn, or 2 (11-ounce) cans Shoe Peg corn
1 envelope ranch salad dressing mix
1 envelope taco seasoning mix
2 cups water

Brown the chopped sirloin with the onion in a saucepan, stirring until the sirloin is crumbly; drain well. Add the tomatoes with green chiles, beans, corn, salad dressing mix, taco seasoning mix and water and mix well. Bring to a boil; reduce the heat. Simmer for 2 hours. YIELD: 4 TO 6 SERVINGS.

Mary Loftin
Montgomery Council

Vegetable Soup with Beef

1 pound ground beef
1 (16-ounce) can mixed soup vegetables
1 (16-ounce) can cream-style or whole kernel corn
1 (16-ounce) can Spanish rice, partially drained
1 (14-ounce) can stewed tomatoes, partially drained
1 (10-ounce) can tomatoes with green chiles, partially drained
Salt to taste

Brown the ground beef in a skillet, stirring until crumbly; drain well. Combine the ground beef and the next 5 ingredients in a 3½- or 4-quart saucepan; mix well. Season with salt. Bring to a boil; reduce the heat. Simmer for 30 minutes. This soup is even better the second day. YIELD: 10 TO 12 SERVINGS.

Mary K. Forman
Birmingham South Life

Quick-and-Easy Ground Beef Vegetable Soup

1 pound lean ground beef
1 package frozen
  seasoning mix
1 (16-ounce) can
  cream-style corn
1 (10-ounce) can tomatoes
  with green chiles
1 (14-ounce) can stewed
  tomatoes
1 large can vegetable juice
  cocktail
2 (10-ounce) cans mixed soup
  vegetables, drained
1 (15-ounce) can Spanish rice

Brown the ground beef in a saucepan, stirring until crumbly; drain well. Add the seasoning mix, corn, tomatoes with green chiles, stewed tomatoes, vegetable juice cocktail, mixed vegetables and Spanish rice and mix well. Bring to a boil; reduce the heat. Simmer over low heat for 30 to 40 minutes. YIELD: 4 TO 6 SERVINGS.

Patricia V. Allen
Selma Life

Vegetable Soup

Kernels of 8 medium ears corn
5½ pounds tomatoes, chopped
3 medium onions, chopped
3 medium potatoes, chopped
2 medium green bell peppers,
  chopped
2 cups water
1 cup lima beans
1 cup sliced okra
1 whole hot chile (do not
  chop)
¼ cup sugar
¼ cup vinegar
2 teaspoons salt

Combine the corn, tomatoes, onions, potatoes, bell peppers, water, beans, okra, chile, sugar, vinegar and salt in a large Dutch oven and mix well. Cover and bring to a boil; reduce the heat. Simmer for 1 hour. To freeze the soup, cool completely, then ladle into 1-pint freezer containers. YIELD: 7½ PINTS.

Faith Kirby Richardson
Gadsden Life

Vegetable Chicken Soup

1 tablespoon olive oil
8 ounces boneless skinless chicken breast, cut into 1-inch pieces
1 medium yellow onion, chopped
2 large garlic cloves, minced
3/4 cup sliced carrots
1 cup chopped cauliflower
2 cups undrained canned chopped tomatoes
4 cups nonfat chicken broth
1 cup spinach leaves, torn into pieces
5 drops of hot chili sauce
Salt and pepper to taste

Heat the olive oil in a large saucepan. Add the chicken. Sauté until light brown. Remove the chicken to a bowl. Add the onion, garlic and carrots to the saucepan. Cook for 3 minutes or until the onion is tender-crisp, stirring constantly. Stir in the sautéed chicken, cauliflower, tomatoes and chicken broth. Bring to a boil; reduce the heat. Simmer, partially covered, for 20 to 25 minutes. Stir in the remaining ingredients. Simmer for 5 minutes. YIELD: 4 SERVINGS.

Helen Baker
Gadsden Life

Vegetable Soup for Canning

5 quarts tomatoes
2 quarts cabbage
2 quarts sliced okra
2 quarts green lima beans
2 quarts corn
2 quarts chopped potatoes
12 large onions, chopped
2 tablespoons sugar
Salt

Combine the first 8 ingredients in a large stockpot. Add enough water to cover and mix well. Cook for 5 minutes. Ladle into hot sterilized 1-quart jars, leaving 1/2 inch headspace. Add 1 teaspoon salt to each jar and seal with 2-piece lids. Process in a boiling water bath for 1 hour. YIELD: 10 TO 12 QUARTS.

Ann Moon
Decatur Council

CLOWNS

The Alabama Chapter has a clown corp with Pioneer Volunteers from all parts of the state. The clowns bring a smile to the faces of children and adults at Camp Smile-A-Mile (cancer camp), Camp ASCCA (camp for children with disabilities), and Camp Mash (children with arthritis). Our volunteers clown at nursing homes, hospitals, and schools. Clowns assist in fund-raising activities and fund-raising walks.

Salads

Tappy Apple Salad

2 (8-ounce) cans crushed pineapple
2 cups miniature marshmallows
1/2 cup sugar
1 tablespoon flour
1 egg, beaten
1 tablespoon vinegar
4 to 6 apples
1 1/2 cups unsalted roasted peanuts (optional)
8 to 12 ounces whipped topping

Drain the pineapple, reserving the juice. Mix the pineapple and marshmallows in a bowl. Chill, covered, for 8 to 10 hours. Mix the reserved juice, sugar, flour, egg and vinegar in a saucepan. Cook over medium heat until of pudding consistency, stirring frequently. Strain the mixture if the egg curdles. Spoon into a bowl. Chill, covered, for 8 to 10 hours. Cut the apples into cubes. Combine the pineapple mixture with the pudding mixture in a large serving bowl and mix well. Stir in the apples and peanuts. Fold in the whipped topping. Serve immediately. YIELD: 10 TO 12 SERVINGS.

Linda McAdams
Shoals Life

HELPFUL HINT

*Janice Foshee, daughter-in-law of James Foshee, Decatur Council, provides a **Recipe for Discovery**.*

Combine 1 talented teacher and 8 to 12 eager young minds. Add 1 to 2 cups of curiosity and 4 to 5 spoonfuls of fun. Blend in generous amounts of hands-on participation mixed with patience. Sprinkle with laughter and serve with enthusiasm.
YIELD: LEARNING AT ITS BEST.

Apple Salad

4 medium apples
2 ribs celery
1 cup purple grapes
1 cup chopped pecans
½ to 1 cup mayonnaise

Cut the apples and celery into small pieces. Cut the grapes into halves. Combine the apples, celery, grapes and pecans in a serving bowl and toss to mix. Add mayonnaise and mix well. Serve immediately or chill, covered, until serving time. YIELD: 8 SERVINGS.

Ruth Ann Edson
Gadsden Life

Apricot Salad

2 (3-ounce) packages apricot gelatin
1 cup sugar
1 (20-ounce) can crushed pineapple, drained
8 ounces cream cheese, softened
2 cups buttermilk
8 ounces whipped topping
¾ cup chopped pecans

Combine the apricot gelatin, sugar and pineapple in a saucepan and mix well. Bring to a boil. Boil for 1 minute, stirring constantly. Remove from the heat. Let stand until cool. Beat the cream cheese and buttermilk in a mixing bowl. Fold in the whipped topping and ½ cup of the pecans. Stir in the gelatin mixture. Spoon into a serving dish. Sprinkle with the remaining ¼ cup pecans. Chill, covered, for 8 to 10 hours. Serve with vegetables or meat. YIELD: 6 SERVINGS.

Lola Duffey
Shoals Life

Apricot Salad

1 (6-ounce) package apricot gelatin
1 (20-ounce) can crushed pineapple
2 cups buttermilk
16 ounces whipped topping
1 cup chopped nuts
1 cup chopped cooked dried apricots, cooled (optional)

Mix the gelatin and pineapple in a saucepan. Cook until the gelatin is dissolved, stirring frequently. Let stand until cool. Add the buttermilk and mix well. Chill, covered, until partially set. Fold in the whipped topping, nuts and dried apricots. Spoon into a serving dish. Chill, covered, until set. YIELD: 8 SERVINGS.

*Liddie Reding
Decatur Council*

Berry 'n' Banana Salad

1 pint fresh strawberries
1 pint fresh blueberries
4 medium bananas, sliced
1/2 to 1 1/2 cups freshly squeezed orange juice
1/3 cup toasted flaked coconut

Rinse the strawberries and blueberries. Drain on paper towels. Arrange the bananas in a large glass bowl. Layer with the strawberries and blueberries. Pour the orange juice over the fruit. Refrigerate, covered, until well chilled. Sprinkle with the coconut just before serving. YIELD: 6 SERVINGS.

*Mrs. Vauline Terry
Tuscaloosa Council*

Cherry Salad

1 (21-ounce) can cherry pie filling
1 (20-ounce) can crushed pineapple
1 (14-ounce) can sweetened condensed milk
2 cups miniature marshmallows
8 ounces whipped topping

Mix the cherry pie filling and pineapple in a bowl. Stir in the sweetened condensed milk. Fold in the marshmallows and whipped topping. Spoon into a 9×13-inch dish. Chill, covered, until set.
YIELD: 10 TO 12 SERVINGS.

Dorthy Kimbrough
Decatur Council

Cherry Salad

1 (6-ounce) package cherry gelatin
2 cups boiling water
1 (21-ounce) can cherry pie filling
1 (8-ounce) can crushed pineapple
8 ounces cream cheese, softened
1 cup sour cream
1/2 cup sugar
1/2 cup chopped pecans

Dissolve the gelatin in the boiling water in a large bowl. Stir in the cherry pie filling and undrained pineapple. Spoon into a serving dish. Chill, covered, until set. Beat the cream cheese, sour cream and sugar in a mixing bowl until smooth. Spread over the gelatin mixture. Sprinkle with the pecans. Serve immediately.
YIELD: 10 TO 12 SERVINGS.

Earline Weaver
Shoals Life

Cranberry Salad

8 ounces cranberries
1 orange, seeded
1 (6-ounce) package cherry gelatin
1 cup boiling water
2 cups sugar
1 cup drained crushed pineapple
1 cup ground celery
1 cup broken nuts
1 cup pineapple juice
2 teaspoons lemon juice
1 envelope unflavored gelatin

Grind the cranberries and unpeeled orange in a food grinder. Dissolve the cherry gelatin in the boiling water in a large bowl. Stir in the sugar, pineapple, cranberries, orange, celery, nuts, pineapple juice and lemon juice. Soften the unflavored gelatin in a small amount of cold water in a small bowl. Add a small amount of boiling water,stirring to dissolve the gelatin. Stir into the cherry gelatin mixture. Spoon into a serving dish. Chill, covered, until set.
YIELD: 10 TO 12 SERVINGS.

Linda McAdams
Shoals Life

HELPFUL HINT

Styrofoam cups can be used as molds for congealed salads. The salad will congeal faster and cleanup will be easier.

Cranberry Salad

2 cups cranberries
2 oranges, seeded
2 apples, chopped
1 cup chopped celery
1 cup chopped nuts

1 cup sugar
2 (3-ounce) packages cherry
   gelatin
2 cups boiling water

Grind the cranberries, 1 unpeeled orange and 1 peeled orange in a food grinder. Combine the cranberries, oranges, apples, celery, nuts and sugar in a large bowl and mix well. Dissolve the gelatin in the boiling water in a bowl. Chill until of the consistency of unbeaten egg white. Stir into the cranberry mixture. Spoon into a serving dish. Chill, covered, until set. YIELD: 10 TO 12 SERVINGS.

Margaret W. Wilborn
Gadsden Life

For Goodness Sakes Salad

1 (3-ounce) package lemon
   gelatin
1 (3-ounce) package lime
   gelatin
1 cup boiling water
1 (20-ounce) can crushed
   pineapple

1 cup evaporated skim milk
1 cup low-fat mayonnaise
8 ounces light cottage cheese
1 cup chopped nuts
1 tablespoon horseradish
   sauce

Dissolve the lemon gelatin and lime gelatin in the boiling water in a large bowl. Let stand until slightly cool. Stir in the undrained pineapple, evaporated milk, mayonnaise, cottage cheese, nuts and horseradish sauce. Spoon into a serving dish. Chill, covered, for 6 to 12 hours. YIELD: 12 TO 16 SERVINGS.

Hester P. Thompson
Birmingham Life

Fresh Fruit with Lemon Yogurt Dressing

2 oranges, sectioned
1 grapefruit, sectioned
2 bananas, sliced
1 cup sliced strawberries
3 kiwifruit, sliced
Lemon Yogurt Dressing (below)

Layer the oranges, grapefruit, bananas, strawberries and kiwifruit in a salad bowl. Pour the Lemon Yogurt Dressing over the fruit. Toss lightly to mix. YIELD: 4 SERVINGS.

Lemon Yogurt Dressing

1 cup plain yogurt
1 1/2 tablespoons sugar
1 teaspoon fresh lemon juice

Mix the yogurt, sugar and lemon juice in a small bowl. YIELD: 1 CUP.

Susan Robbins
Riverchase Council

Fruit Salad

1 (20-ounce) can pineapple chunks, drained
1 (10-ounce) jar maraschino cherries, drained
3 bananas, sliced
3 tablespoons lemon juice
1 (6-ounce) package vanilla instant pudding mix

Drain the pineapple and maraschino cherries, reserving the juices. Arrange the bananas in a small bowl. Drizzle with the lemon juice and set aside. Combine the pudding mix and reserved juices in a mixing bowl and beat well. Stir in the pineapple and cherries. Drain the bananas. Add to the pudding mixture and mix well. Spoon into a serving dish. Refrigerate, covered, until well chilled. YIELD: 8 SERVINGS.

Margaret W. Wilborn
Gadsden Life

Brandon's Fruit Salad

1 (15-ounce) can fruit cocktail, drained
1 (11-ounce) can mandarin oranges, drained
1 (21-ounce) can peach pie filling
1 red apple, chopped
1 yellow apple, chopped
2 bananas, sliced

Combine the fruit cocktail, mandarin oranges, peach pie filling, apples and bananas in a bowl and mix well. Chill, covered, for 8 to 10 hours. YIELD: 8 SERVINGS.

Henry Eli Daniel
Opelika Life

Old-Fashioned Fruit Salad

2 (11-ounce) cans pineapple tidbits
4 oranges, finely chopped
2 apples, finely chopped
1½ bunches red grapes, cut into halves
1½ bunches white grapes, cut into halves
6 bananas, sliced
1 cup (or more) sugar
Orange juice

Mix the pineapple, oranges, apples, grapes and bananas in a bowl. Stir in enough sugar to sweeten as desired. Add enough orange juice to cover the fruit. YIELD: 10 TO 12 SERVINGS.

Margaret W. Wilborn
Gadsden Life

7-Cup Salad

1 cup pineapple
1 cup fruit cocktail
1 cup chopped cherries
1 cup miniature marshmallows
1 cup shredded coconut
1 cup cottage cheese
1 cup sour cream

Drain the pineapple and fruit cocktail. Mix the pineapple, fruit cocktail, cherries, marshmallows, coconut, cottage cheese and sour cream in a large bowl. Refrigerate, covered, until chilled. May be served with plain cake. YIELD: 12 SERVINGS.

Hazel E. Campbell
Birmingham Life

Sunshine Salad

1 (3-ounce) package lemon or orange gelatin
1 cup boiling water
1 (8-ounce) can crushed pineapple
1 tablespoon cider vinegar
¼ teaspoon salt
2 large carrots, peeled, shredded
Mayonnaise and heavy cream

Dissolve the gelatin in the boiling water in a bowl. Drain the pineapple, reserving the juice in a 1-cup measure. Add enough water to the juice to make 1 cup. Combine the juice, vinegar and salt in a small bowl and mix well. Stir into the gelatin. Chill, covered, until slightly thickened. Fold in the carrots and pineapple. Spoon into a 5x9-inch loaf pan. Chill until set. Cut into squares. Serve on beds of shredded lettuce. Mix a small amount of mayonnaise with enough cream to make of a sauce consistency. Spoon over the squares. Garnish with chopped pecans or walnuts.
Yield: 6 servings.

Edith Dixon
Birmingham Life

Stained Glass Salad

1½ cups water
2 (3-ounce) packages sparkling white grape gelatin
2 cups chilled ginger ale
1 cup seedless red grapes
1 (11-ounce) can pineapple tidbits, drained
1 (11-ounce) can mandarin oranges, drained

Bring the water to a boil in a small saucepan. Add the gelatin. Cook for 2 minutes or until the gelatin dissolves, stirring constantly. Pour into a bowl. Chill, covered, for 15 minutes. Stir in the ginger ale. Chill, covered, for 1 hour or until the mixture is the consistency of unbeaten egg white. Stir for 15 seconds. Fold in the grapes, pineapple and mandarin oranges. Spoon into a lightly oiled 6-cup mold. Chill, covered, until set. Invert onto a lettuce-lined serving plate. Garnish with additional grapes. YIELD: 10 TO 12 SERVINGS.

Anatalie Watson Fogg
Decatur Council

Lime Jello Salad

1 cup water
1 (3-ounce) package lime gelatin
3 ounces cream cheese
1 cup cold water
1 (8-ounce) can crushed pineapple
1 cup whipping cream, whipped
½ cup chopped pecans

Bring 1 cup water to a boil in a saucepan. Add the gelatin, stirring to dissolve. Add the cream cheese. Cook until melted, stirring constantly. Let stand until cool. Stir in 1 cup cold water, pineapple, whipped cream and pecans. Spoon into a serving dish. Chill, covered, until set. YIELD: 8 SERVINGS.

Dorothy Yarber
Shoals Life

Molded Lime Salad

1 (3-ounce) package lime gelatin
1 cup hot water
1 cup crushed pineapple
1 cup cottage cheese
Pinch of salt
2 tablespoons mayonnaise-type salad dressing or mayonnaise

Dissolve the gelatin in the hot water in a large bowl. Stir in the pineapple, cottage cheese, salt and salad dressing. Spoon into a serving dish. Chill, covered, until set. YIELD: 4 TO 6 SERVINGS.

Virginia Sherrer
Selma Life

Orange Jello Salad

6 to 8 ounces mandarin oranges
12 ounces cottage cheese
1 (3-ounce) package orange gelatin
1 (8-ounce) can crushed pineapple, drained
8 ounces whipped topping

Drain the mandarin oranges and cut into pieces. Combine the cottage cheese and gelatin in a large bowl and mix well. Fold in the mandarin oranges, pineapple and whipped topping. Spoon into a serving dish. Chill, covered, until set. Garnish with additional mandarin orange sections. You may use low-fat cottage cheese, sugar-free gelatin and light whipped topping. YIELD: 6 TO 8 SERVINGS.

Marie Beaty
Anniston Council

Orange Jello Salad

1 (6-ounce) package orange gelatin
1 1/2 cups boiling water
2 cups reduced-fat sour cream
2 (11-ounce) cans mandarin oranges, drained
1 (8-ounce) can crushed pineapple
12 ounces light whipped topping
Chopped pecans

Dissolve the gelatin in the boiling water in a large bowl. Let stand for 10 minutes. Add the sour cream, mandarin oranges, pineapple and whipped topping 1 at a time, mixing well after each addition. Spoon into a greased 3-quart dish. Sprinkle with pecans. Chill, covered, until set. YIELD: 16 SERVINGS.

Jean Wharton
Birmingham Life

Romaine and Orange Salad

8 cups torn romaine
1 (11-ounce) can mandarin oranges, drained
2 green onions, sliced
1/4 cup sliced almonds, toasted
Oil and Vinegar Salad Dressing (below)

Combine the romaine, mandarin oranges, green onions and almonds in a salad bowl. Pour the Oil and Vinegar Salad Dressing over the top. Toss lightly to mix. YIELD: 8 SERVINGS.

Oil and Vinegar Salad Dressing

1/4 cup sugar
1/4 cup vegetable oil
1/4 cup white vinegar

Shake the sugar, oil and vinegar together in a covered jar. YIELD: 1/2 CUP.

Mrs. Vauline Terry
Tuscaloosa Council

Peach Salad

1 (6-ounce) package peach gelatin
2 cups boiling water
1 (21-ounce) can peach pie filling
1 (8-ounce) can crushed pineapple
Creamy Topping (below)

Dissolve the gelatin in the boiling water in a large bowl. Stir in the pie filling and undrained pineapple. Spoon into a serving dish. Chill, covered, until set. Spread with the Creamy Topping.
YIELD: 8 TO 10 SERVINGS.

Creamy Topping

8 ounces cream cheese, softened
1 cup sour cream
1/2 cup sugar
1/2 cup chopped pecans
1/2 teaspoon vanilla extract

Mix the cream cheese, sour cream and sugar in a bowl until smooth and creamy. Stir in the pecans and vanilla. **YIELD: 2 1/2 CUPS.**

Chris Elsen
Gadsden Life

HELPFUL HINT

*Susan Robbins, Riverchase Council, says it is **"For the Birds."***

Combine 1 part peanut butter, 2 parts bird seed, 5 parts cornmeal and 1 part beef suet in a large bowl. Press the mixture into paper-lined muffin cups. Chill in the refrigerator. Store in an airtight container in a cool place. Feed the Birds! They will thank you with a song.

Raspberry Congealed Salad

1 (6-ounce) package raspberry gelatin
1 cup boiling water
2 cups cold water
½ teaspoon lemon juice
1 (16-ounce) can whole cranberry sauce, crushed
1 (16-ounce) can pear halves, drained, chopped
½ cup chopped pecans

Dissolve the gelatin in 1 cup boiling water in a bowl. Stir in 2 cups cold water, lemon juice and cranberry sauce. Chill, covered, until slightly thickened. Fold in the pears and pecans. Spoon into a serving dish. Chill, covered, until set. YIELD: 8 TO 10 SERVINGS.

Carolyn G. Wheeler
Selma Life

Strawberry Almond Salad

1 large head curly green or red leaf lettuce
6 ounces baby spinach
½ cup toasted slivered almonds or walnuts
2 teaspoons butter, melted
1 pint strawberries, sliced
½ medium onion, chopped
Sweet/Sour Dressing (page 117)

Tear the lettuce and spinach into bite-size pieces. Arrange in a salad bowl. Sauté the almonds in the butter in a skillet until light brown. Add the almonds, strawberries and onion to the lettuce mixture. Pour the desired amount of Sweet/Sour Dressing over the top. Toss to mix. You may use red onions to add some color and substitute kiwifruit for the strawberries. YIELD: 6 SERVINGS.

Mrs. Virginia Greene
Birmingham South Life

Congealed Asparagus Salad

2 envelopes unflavored gelatin
½ cup cold water
1 cup sugar
1 cup water
½ cup white vinegar
2 (10-ounce) cans asparagus tips, drained
½ onion, finely chopped
½ cup chopped celery
1 (2-ounce) jar pimento, drained
Juice of ½ lemon
½ teaspoon salt
¾ cup chopped pecans
Sour Cream Dressing (below)

Soften the gelatin in ½ cup cold water in a bowl. Combine the sugar, 1 cup water and vinegar in a saucepan. Bring to a boil. Boil for 1 to 2 minutes; remove from the heat. Stir in the gelatin mixture. Add the asparagus, onion, celery, pimento, lemon juice, salt and pecans. Spoon into a 7×11-inch dish. Chill, covered, until set. Cut into squares. Top with Sour Cream Dressing. Garnish with olive slices. YIELD: 6 TO 8 SERVINGS.

Sour Cream Dressing

¼ cup sour cream
¼ cup mayonnaise

Combine the sour cream and mayonnaise in a small bowl and mix well. YIELD: ½ CUP.

Faith Kirby Richardson
Gadsden Life

Asparagus Mold

1 (10-ounce) can cream of asparagus soup
1 (3-ounce) package lemon gelatin
8 ounces cream cheese
½ cup cold water
½ cup mayonnaise
½ cup minced bell pepper
⅓ cup chopped pecans
1 tablespoon grated onion

Bring the soup to a boil in a saucepan. Remove from the heat. Add the gelatin, stirring to dissolve. Stir in the cream cheese until melted. Add the water and mayonnaise and mix well. Fold in the pecans and onion. Spoon into a serving dish. Chill, covered, until set. YIELD: 8 TO 10 SERVINGS.

Barbara Seegmiller
Decatur Council

Tuscan White Bean Salad

2 teaspoons sage
4 teaspoons extra-virgin olive oil
1 tablespoon dry white wine
1 tablespoon white wine vinegar
2 garlic cloves, minced
Black pepper to taste
1 (16-ounce) can cannellini beans, rinsed, drained
½ small red onion, chopped

Whisk the sage, olive oil, wine, vinegar, garlic and pepper in a large bowl. Add the beans and onion, tossing to coat. Let stand, covered, for 2 hours or until the flavors are blended. YIELD: 4 SERVINGS.

Rita Wilson
Birmingham Life

Broccoli Salad

2 crowns broccoli
1 medium red onion, finely chopped
16 ounces Cheddar cheese, finely shredded
1 pound bacon, crisp-cooked, crumbled
1 cup raisins
Mayonnaise Dressing (below)

Chop the broccoli into small pieces. Combine the broccoli, onion, cheese, bacon and raisins in a salad bowl. Pour the Mayonnaise Dressing over the top. Toss lightly to mix. Serve immediately. YIELD: 8 TO 10 SERVINGS.

Mayonnaise Dressing

1 cup mayonnaise
½ cup sugar
¼ cup white vinegar

Whisk the mayonnaise, sugar and vinegar in a bowl until well blended. YIELD: 1½ CUPS.

Adeline Neal
Birmingham Life

HELPFUL HINT

For quick salads, buy chopped vegetables at the supermarket produce section or salad bar and add your own greens.

Broccoli Salad

1 bunch broccoli
1 head cauliflower
1 small onion
1 cucumber
2 ribs celery
2 carrots
Buttermilk Dressing (below)

Chop the broccoli, cauliflower, onion, cucumber, celery and carrots. Combine the vegetables in a salad bowl and mix well. Pour the Buttermilk Dressing over the top. Toss to mix. Refrigerate, covered, until well chilled. YIELD: 8 TO 10 SERVINGS.

Buttermilk Dressing

1 cup buttermilk
1 cup mayonnaise
1/4 teaspoon onion salt
1/4 teaspoon garlic salt
1/4 teaspoon celery salt
1/8 teaspoon pepper

Combine the buttermilk, mayonnaise, onion salt, garlic salt, celery salt and pepper in a covered jar and shake well. YIELD: 2 CUPS.

Sara Cooley
Birmingham Life

Dot Salad and Dressing

1 (3-ounce) package ramen noodles, crumbled
1 cup chopped walnuts
1 bunch romaine, rinsed, torn
1 crown broccoli, chopped
4 green onions, chopped
Wine Vinegar Dressing (below)

Discard the ramen noodles seasoning packet. Toast the ramen noodles and walnuts on a baking sheet until light brown. Combine the ramen noodles, walnuts, romaine, broccoli and green onions in a salad bowl. Pour 1 cup of the Wine Vinegar Dressing over the top and toss lightly. Serve immediately. YIELD: 4 TO 6 SERVINGS.

Wine Vinegar Dressing

½ cup red wine vinegar
1 cup sugar
1 cup canola oil
2 tablespoons soy sauce

Combine the wine vinegar and sugar in a saucepan. Cook over medium heat until the sugar is dissolved. Add the canola oil and soy sauce and mix well. YIELD 1½ CUPS.

Kathryn Morgan
Gadsden Life

Garden Broccoli Cauliflower Salad

3/4 cup broccoli florets
3/4 cup cauliflower florets
1 small red bell pepper, chopped
Oil and Vinegar Dressing (below)
Lettuce leaves (optional)

Combine the broccoli and cauliflower in a 1½-quart casserole. Microwave, covered with plastic wrap, on High for 4 to 6 minutes or until tender-crisp. Drain well. Add the bell pepper, tossing gently. Pour Oil and Vinegar Dressing over the top. Toss gently to mix. Chill, covered, for 30 minutes or longer. Serve on a bed of lettuce leaves. **Yield: 4 servings.**

Oil and Vinegar Dressing

1 tablespoon vegetable oil
3 tablespoons white wine vinegar
1/4 cup water
1/4 teaspoon salt
1/4 teaspoon freshly ground pepper
1/8 teaspoon garlic powder

Mix the oil, wine vinegar, water, salt, pepper and garlic powder in a jar with a lid. Cover and shake vigorously to mix. **Yield: 1/2 cup.**

Gussie Evans
Mobile Council

Corn Salad

2 (11-ounce) cans Shoe Peg corn, drained
3 or 4 green onions with tops, chopped
1 bell pepper, chopped
Mayonnaise to taste

Mix the corn, green onions and bell pepper in a bowl. Stir in enough mayonnaise just to moisten. Chill, covered, for 1 hour or longer. YIELD: 6 TO 8 SERVINGS.

Dorthy Kimbrough
Decatur Council

Corn Salad

1 (16-ounce) can whole kernel corn, drained
1 small onion, chopped
½ green bell pepper, chopped
1 rib celery, chopped
1 small carrot, chopped
2 tablespoons mayonnaise

Combine the corn, onion, bell pepper, celery and carrot in a large bowl and mix well. Stir in the mayonnaise just until the vegetables are moistened. YIELD: 4 TO 6 SERVINGS.

Debbie Speaks
Montgomery Council

The Hog Pit Corn Salad with Hominy

1 (16-ounce) package frozen corn kernels, thawed, drained
1 tablespoon vegetable oil
Salt and pepper to taste
2 (15-ounce) cans golden hominy, rinsed, drained
1 each red and green bell pepper, chopped
3/4 cup finely chopped red onion
1/4 cup chopped fresh cilantro
2 tablespoons lemon juice
2 tablespoons red wine vinegar
1 tablespoon sugar
1 tablespoon chili powder

Mix the corn, oil, salt and pepper in a large bowl. Sauté the corn mixture in a hot skillet over high heat for 2 minutes or just until brown. Let cool. Remove the corn mixture to a large bowl. Add the hominy, bell peppers, onion, cilantro, lemon juice, wine vinegar, sugar and chili powder and mix well. Season with salt and pepper. Chill, covered, for 2 to 8 hours. YIELD: **6 SERVINGS**.

Frankie Vaughn
Selma Life

Corn Bread Salad

1 (8-ounce) package corn muffin mix
1 egg
⅓ cup milk
4 medium tomatoes, peeled, chopped
1 green bell pepper, chopped
1 medium onion, chopped
½ cup chopped sweet pickles
9 slices bacon, crisp-cooked, crumbled
1 cup mayonnaise
½ cup sweet pickle juice

Combine the corn muffin mix, egg and milk in a small bowl and mix well. Spoon into a greased 8-inch square baking ban. Bake at 400 degrees for 15 to 20 minutes or until light brown. Let stand until cool. Crumble into a large bowl. Combine the tomatoes, bell pepper, onion, pickles and bacon in a separate bowl and mix well. Combine the mayonnaise and pickle juice in a small bowl and mix well. Layer the corn bread mixture, tomato mixture and mayonnaise mixture ½ at a time in a large glass bowl. Chill, covered, for 2 hours. **YIELD: 8 SERVINGS.**

Mary C. Martin
Birmingham Life

HELPFUL HINT

For a creamy salad dressing base with a lower fat content, combine mayonnaise and yogurt. Add herbs, spices, garlic, lemon juice or fresh sprouts to complement the salad.

Corn Bread Salad

1 (8-ounce) package corn muffin mix
1 (8-ounce) can whole kernel corn, drained
1 (8-ounce) can green peas, drained
1 tomato, chopped
1 bunch green onions, chopped
1 (8-ounce) bottle ranch salad dressing
1 cup shredded cheese
8 ounces bacon, crisp-cooked, crumbled

Bake the corn muffins using the package directions. Let stand until cool. Crumble into a bowl. Add the corn, green peas, tomato and green onions and mix well. Stir in the salad dressing. Spoon into a 9×12-inch dish. Top with the cheese and bacon. Refrigerate, covered, until well chilled. YIELD: 8 TO 10 SERVINGS.

Cathy Midgette
Mobile Council

Corn Bread Salad

3 cups mayonnaise
1 cup sweet pickle juice
1 recipe corn bread, crumbled
2 (15-ounce) cans pinto beans, drained
1 cup chopped bell pepper
1 cup chopped onion
2 cups chopped tomatoes
2 pounds bacon, crisp-cooked, crumbled

Mix the mayonnaise and pickle juice in a small bowl. Layer the corn bread, pinto beans, bell pepper, onion, tomatoes, mayonnaise mixture and bacon 1/2 at a time in a large salad bowl. Let stand for 15 minutes. Serve immediately. You may store, covered, in the refrigerator. Microwave leftovers just until room temperature. YIELD: 10 TO 12 SERVINGS.

Mary M. Storey
Anniston Council

Cucumber Salad

1/2 cucumber, peeled
Salt and pepper to taste
Vinegar Salad Dressing (below)
Onions to taste
Tomatoes to taste

Cut the cucumber into thin slices. Arrange in a bowl. Sprinkle with salt and pepper. Let stand for 15 minutes; drain. Add the Vinegar Salad Dressing and mix well. Stir in the onions and tomatoes. Let stand for 1 hour before serving. YIELD: **2** TO **4** SERVINGS.

Vinegar Salad Dressing

3 tablespoons white vinegar
3 tablespoons water
3 tablespoons sugar
Salt and pepper to taste

Combine the vinegar, water sugar, salt and pepper in a bowl and whisk to blend well. YIELD: **1/3** CUP.

Francis Tucker
Selma Life

HELPFUL HINT

For delicious marinades for vegetables, use bottled salad dressings.

Cukes and Cream

1 cup reduced-fat sour cream
1/4 cup chopped green onions
1 tablespoon lemon juice
1 tablespoon sugar
1/4 teaspoon salt
6 cups sliced peeled cucumbers

Mix the sour cream, green onions, lemon juice, sugar and salt in a small bowl. Chill, covered, for 30 minutes. Combine the cucumbers and sour cream mixture in a large bowl and mix well. Chill until serving time. YIELD: 12 SERVINGS.

Debbie Morris
Birmingham South Cahaba Council

Frito Salad

1 (11-ounce) can Mexicorn, drained
1 (16-ounce) can kidney beans, drained
1 small green bell pepper, chopped
1 small red bell pepper, chopped
2 tomatoes, chopped
1 onion, chopped
4 ounces Cheddar cheese, finely shredded
1 package Frito corn chips
1 (8-ounce) bottle ranch salad dressing

Mix the Mexicorn, kidney beans, green pepper, red pepper, tomatoes, onion and cheese in a large bowl. Stir in the corn chips and dressing just before serving. YIELD: 8 TO 10 SERVINGS.

Mary Howle
Anniston Council

Green Bean Salad

1 (16-ounce) can French-style green beans, drained
1 (11-ounce) can Shoe Peg corn, drained
1 medium onion, chopped
1 bell pepper, chopped
1 carrot, grated
1 (16-ounce) can green peas, drained
Oil and Vinegar Dressing (below)

Mix the green beans, corn, onion, bell pepper, carrot and green peas in a salad bowl. Pour the Oil and Vinegar Dressing over the top. Chill, covered, for 8 to 10 hours. YIELD: **6 TO 8 SERVINGS**.

Oil and Vinegar Dressing

½ cup vegetable oil
¾ cup cider vinegar
1 cup sugar
1 tablespoon water

Combine the oil, vinegar, sugar and water in a bowl and mix until the sugar is dissolved. YIELD: **1½ CUPS**.

Mary Ann Sparks Fulmer
Shoals Life

HELPFUL HINT

Use three parts of vinegar or lemon juice to 1 part of vegetable oil for a lighter vinaigrette. Use lots of herbs and garlic and you will never miss the vegetable oil.

Kraut Salad

1 (29-ounce) can sauerkraut
1 large carrot, shredded
1 green bell pepper, chopped
1 onion, finely chopped
½ cup (or less) vegetable oil
½ cup cider vinegar
1½ cups (or less) sugar
½ teaspoon celery seeds

Mix the sauerkraut, carrot, bell pepper, onion, oil, vinegar, sugar and celery seeds in a large bowl. Chill, covered, for 8 to 10 hours. You may drain before serving if desired. You may store, covered, in the refrigerator for up to 1 week. **YIELD: 8 TO 10 SERVINGS.**

Linda McAdams
Shoals Life

Macaroni Salad

8 ounces shell pasta, cooked, cooled
¼ cup French salad dressing
1 tablespoon chopped onion
1 cup chopped celery
¼ cup chopped bell pepper
¼ cup sweet pickle relish
¾ cup finely shredded cheese
1 (2-ounce) jar pimentos
¾ cup mayonnaise

Combine the pasta and salad dressing in a large bowl and mix well. Chill, covered, for 8 to 10 hours. Add the onion, celery, bell pepper, pickle relish, cheese, pimentos and mayonnaise and mix well. Refrigerate, covered, until well chilled. **YIELD: 8 SERVINGS.**

Hazel E. Campbell
Birmingham Life

Polly's Oriental Salad

1½ cups sliced almonds
2 (3-ounce) packages oriental-flavor ramen noodles
1 bunch green onions, chopped
1 (15-ounce) package coleslaw
1½ packages lightly salted sunflower seed kernels
Oriental Salad Dressing (below)

Arrange the almonds on a baking sheet. Toast at 400 degrees for 2 to 3 minutes or until light brown. Break the ramen noodles into small pieces, reserving the seasoning packets for the Oriental Salad Dressing. Combine the almonds, ramen noodles, green onions, coleslaw and sunflower seed kernels in a large bowl and mix well. Add the Oriental Salad Dressing just before serving and toss lightly to mix. YIELD: 8 TO 10 SERVINGS.

Oriental Salad Dressing

2 seasoning packets from ramen noodles
½ cup canola oil
½ cup rice wine vinegar
⅓ cup sugar
1 teaspoon lemon juice

Combine the ramen noodles seasoning, canola oil, wine vinegar, sugar and lemon juice in a small bowl and mix well. YIELD: 1 CUP.

Linda McAdams
Shoals Life

English Pea Salad

2 (17-ounce) cans green peas, drained
2 eggs, hard-cooked, chopped
1 small red onion, finely chopped
½ cup chopped pecans
½ cup mayonnaise
Salt and pepper to taste

Combine the green peas, eggs, onion, pecans, mayonnaise, salt and pepper in a bowl and mix well. Refrigerate, covered, until well chilled. YIELD: 6 TO 8 SERVINGS.

Eunice Henry
Selma Life

Marinated Potato Salad

8 or 9 medium potatoes, boiled, peeled
1 small cucumber, sliced
⅔ cup vegetable oil
¼ cup cider vinegar
1 tablespoon sugar
2 teaspoons salt
½ teaspoon cracked pepper
1 tablespoon chopped fresh or frozen chives

Cut the potatoes into thin slices. Combine the potatoes and cucumber in a large bowl. Mix the oil, vinegar, sugar, salt, pepper and chives in a small bowl. Pour over the potato mixture, stirring to coat. Chill, covered, for 2 hours. YIELD: 8 SERVINGS.

Marie Beaty
Anniston Council

Perfect Potato Salad

5 to 8 pounds red potatoes, boiled, peeled
Salt to taste
12 eggs, hard-cooked
1 small onion
1 quart Hellmann's mayonnaise
2 tablespoons McCormick's black pepper

Chop the potatoes coarsely and place in a large bowl; sprinkle with salt. Combine the eggs, onion, mayonnaise and pepper in a blender or food processor container. Process until smooth. Add to the potatoes and mix well. Yield: 10 to 12 servings.

Susan Neuhoff
Montgomery Council

Blanch's Delicious Slaw

1 small package shredded cabbage
Chopped onion to taste
2 tablespoons pickle relish
2 tablespoons sugar
Seasoned rice vinegar to taste

Combine the cabbage, onion, pickle relish and sugar in a bowl. Add rice vinegar and mix just until moistened. Serve immediately. Yield: 4 to 6 servings.

Margaret Copelin
Montgomery Life

Broccoli Slaw

2 (3-ounce) packages ramen noodles
¾ cup slivered almonds
1 package angel hair shredded cabbage
1 (16-ounce) package broccoli slaw
8 green onions, thinly sliced
Olive Oil and Vinegar Dressing (below)

Crush the ramen noodles; discard the seasoning packets. Toast the almonds on a baking sheet at 325 degrees for 10 minutes. Combine the ramen noodles, almonds, cabbage, broccoli slaw and green onions in a large bowl. Pour the Olive Oil and Vinegar Dressing over the top. Toss lightly to mix. Serve immediately. YIELD: 12 SERVINGS.

Olive Oil and Vinegar Dressing

1 cup olive oil
6 tablespoons rice wine vinegar
¼ cup sugar
2 teaspoons salt
1 teaspoon pepper

Mix the olive oil, wine vinegar, sugar, salt and pepper in a jar with a lid. Cover and shake to mix. YIELD: 1½ CUPS.

Virginia Greene
Birmingham South Life

Cabbage Salad

1 large head cabbage, shredded
1 cup thinly sliced purple onion
1 cup sugar
1 cup vinegar

¾ cup vegetable oil
1 tablespoon sugar
1 teaspoon salt
1 teaspoon dry mustard
1 teaspoon celery seeds

Mix the cabbage and onion in a large bowl. Stir in the sugar and set aside. Combine the vinegar, oil, sugar, salt, dry mustard and celery seeds in a saucepan and mix well. Bring to a boil. Pour over the cabbage mixture. Refrigerate, covered, until well chilled. YIELD: 12 SERVINGS.

Faye King
Huntsville Council

Coleslaw

1 medium cabbage, shredded
2 medium onions, thinly sliced
1 cup sugar
1 cup vinegar
1 cup vegetable oil

2 teaspoons sugar
1 teaspoon dry mustard
1 teaspoon celery seeds
1 teaspoon salt

Layer the cabbage and onions in a large bowl. Sprinkle 1 cup sugar over the top. Combine the vinegar, oil, 2 teaspoons sugar, dry mustard, celery seeds and salt in a saucepan and mix well. Bring to a boil. Pour over the cabbage. Chill, covered, for 8 to 10 hours. Stir just before serving. YIELD: 8 TO 10 SERVINGS.

Fred H. Hicks
Tuscaloosa Council

Coleslaw

1 medium head cabbage, shredded
1 medium onion, thinly sliced
2/3 cup sugar
1 cup vinegar
3/4 cup vegetable oil
2 teaspoons dry mustard
1 teaspoon celery seeds

Layer the cabbage and onion slices in a large bowl. Sprinkle 2/3 cup sugar over the top. Combine the vinegar, oil, dry mustard and celery seeds in a saucepan and mix well. Bring to a boil. Pour over the cabbage. Chill, covered, for 4 to 6 hours. Stir just before serving. You may store, covered, in the refrigerator for up to 4 weeks.
YIELD: 8 TO 10 SERVINGS.

Jo Anne Norris
Bon Secour Life

Crunchy Slaw

6 tablespoons apple cider vinegar
1/4 cup sugar
1 cup vegetable oil
1 (3-ounce) package chicken flavor ramen noodles
1 large head cabbage, coarsely chopped
5 green onions with tops, chopped
1 cup sliced almonds
1/2 cup sunflower seed kernels

Heat the cider vinegar in a saucepan. Add the sugar, stirring to dissolve. Stir in the oil and the ramen noodles seasoning packet. Combine the cabbage, green onions, almonds and sunflower seed kernels in a large bowl and mix well. Pour the vinegar mixture over the cabbage mixture. Chill, covered, for 8 to 10 hours. Crumble the ramen noodles and add to the cabbage mixture just before serving, tossing to mix. **YIELD: 10 TO 12 SERVINGS.**

Willie Mae Jordan
Gadsden Life

Crunchy Coleslaw

1 cup vegetable oil
1/4 cup sugar
6 tablespoons rice vinegar
4 1/2 tablespoons red wine vinegar
1 teaspoon each pepper and salt
1 package shredded cabbage
6 to 8 green onions, sliced
1/2 cup slivered almonds, toasted
1/4 cup sesame seeds, toasted
2 (3-ounce) packages ramen noodles

Mix the oil, sugar, rice vinegar, red wine vinegar, pepper and salt in a covered jar and shake to mix. Refrigerate, covered, until well chilled. Combine the cabbage, green onions, almonds and sesame seeds in a large bowl. Discard the ramen noodles seasoning packet. Break the ramen noodles into small pieces. Add to the cabbage mixture. Stir in the chilled dressing just before serving. You may easily half the recipe. **YIELD: 8 TO 10 SERVINGS.**

Adeline Neal
Birmingham Life

Dreamland's Marinated Coleslaw

3 cups white wine vinegar
3 cups sugar
1 cup canola oil
2 teaspoons dry mustard
5 pounds cabbage, shredded
1 medium carrot, shredded
1 teaspoon each salt, pepper and seasoning salt
½ teaspoon celery salt

Combine the wine vinegar, sugar, canola oil and dry mustard in a saucepan and mix well. Bring to a boil. Mix the cabbage and carrot in a large bowl. Pour the vinegar mixture over the cabbage mixture. Add the salt, pepper, seasoning salt and celery salt and mix well. Let stand, covered, for 20 minutes. Chill, covered, for 4 hours or longer. Serve with a slotted spoon. YIELD: 16 SERVINGS.

Alice Walski
Birmingham Life

Marinated Slaw

1 head cabbage, chopped
1 onion, chopped
½ cup vegetable oil
½ cup white vinegar
¾ cup sugar
1 teaspoon prepared mustard

Combine the cabbage and onion in a large bowl and mix well. Combine the remaining ingredients in a small saucepan. Bring to a boil over low heat. Pour over the cabbage mixture, tossing to mix. Chill, covered, for 8 to 10 hours. Drain just before serving. YIELD: 10 SERVINGS.

Tammy Donner
Birmingham South Cahaba Council

Race Track Slaw

1 (5-ounce) package sliced almonds
¼ cup sesame seeds
2 (3-ounce) packages ramen noodles
1 (16-ounce) package slaw mix
1 bunch green onions, chopped
1 cup vegetable oil
6 tablespoons rice wine vinegar
¼ cup sugar
1 teaspoon salt
1 teaspoon pepper
1 teaspoon MSG

Toast the almonds and sesame seeds on a baking sheet in a 350-degree oven for 5 minutes or just until brown. Discard the ramen noodles seasoning packet. Combine the slaw mix, green onions, ramen noodles, almonds and sesame seeds in a large bowl and mix well. Combine the oil, wine vinegar, sugar, salt, pepper and MSG in a small bowl and mix well. Pour over the slaw mixture just before serving, tossing to mix. YIELD: 8 TO 10 SERVINGS.

Doris B. Thrasher
Gadsden Life

HELPFUL HINT

For the greatest concentration of minerals and vitamins, choose cabbage and salad greens with darker green leaves.

Spicy Coleslaw

2 cups finely shredded red cabbage
2 cups finely shredded green cabbage
1 cup finely chopped red onion
¾ cup mayonnaise
1 tablespoon cider vinegar
1 tablespoon fresh lemon juice
1 tablespoon Dijon mustard
¼ teaspoon sugar
¼ teaspoon Worcestershire sauce
⅛ teaspoon white pepper
⅛ teaspoon hot pepper sauce

Mix the red cabbage, green cabbage and red onion in a large bowl. Whisk the mayonnaise, cider vinegar, lemon juice, Dijon mustard, sugar, Worcestershire sauce, white pepper and hot pepper sauce in a small bowl. Pour over the cabbage mixture, tossing to coat. Chill, covered, for 1 hour or longer. YIELD: 8 SERVINGS.

Jane B. Weatherly
Mobile Council

HELPFUL HINT

Add toasted sesame seeds to salads for a rich and nutty flavor.

Pitty Pat's Sweet Potato Salad

8 large sweet potatoes, peeled
1 (8-ounce) 1/4-inch-thick ham slice
1 cup chopped green onions
1 cup chopped green bell pepper
1 cup spicy brown mustard
1/2 cup vegetable oil
1 tablespoon salt
1 tablespoon white pepper
1 tablespoon chopped fresh dill

Cut the sweet potatoes into 2-inch strips. Steam for 10 to 12 minutes or just until tender. Let stand until cool. Cut the ham into 1/2-inch pieces. Combine the sweet potatoes, ham, green onions and bell pepper in a large bowl. Mix the brown mustard, oil, salt, white pepper and dill in a small bowl. Add to the sweet potato mixture and mix well. Chill, covered, for 2 hours or longer. Serve with pork chops or chicken. YIELD: **6 SERVINGS.**

Alice Walski
Birmingham Life

Layered Taco Salad

½ large head iceberg lettuce
2 tomatoes, seeded, chopped
½ cup sliced olives
½ cup thinly sliced red onion
1 cup shredded sharp cheese
2 cups cooked black beans, drained
Mexican Dressing (below)
Tortilla chips, broken

Tear the lettuce into bite-size pieces. Arrange ⅔ of the lettuce in a salad bowl. Layer with the tomatoes, olives, remaining lettuce, red onion, cheese and black beans and press down. Spread the Mexican Dressing over the top. Chill, covered with plastic wrap, for 24 hours. Sprinkle with tortilla chips just before serving.
YIELD: 6 GENEROUS SERVINGS.

Mexican Dressing

1 cup frozen guacamole, thawed
½ cup sour cream
1 (4-ounce) can chopped green chiles
1½ teaspoons lemon or lime juice
1½ teaspoons heavy cream
1 teaspoon chili powder, or to taste

Combine the guacamole, sour cream, green chiles, lemon juice, heavy cream and chili powder in a bowl and mix well. YIELD: 2 CUPS.

Alice Walski
Birmingham Life

Marinated Vegetable Salad

1 cup sugar
¾ cup vinegar
½ cup vegetable oil
1 (16-ounce) can French-style green beans, drained
1 (11-ounce) can Shoe Peg corn, drained
1 (16-ounce) can tiny peas, drained
1 cup finely chopped celery
½ green bell pepper, chopped
2 medium onions, chopped
1 (2-ounce) jar pimentos

Combine the sugar, vinegar and oil in a small bowl, stirring to dissolve the sugar. Combine the French-style green beans, Shoe Peg corn, tiny peas, celery, bell pepper, onions and pimentos in a large bowl and mix well. Stir in the sugar mixture. Chill, covered, for 24 hours. You may store, covered, in the refrigerator for up to 2 weeks.
Yield: 8 to 10 servings.

Faith Kirby Richardson
Gadsden Life

Vegetable Salad

1 (16-ounce) can whole kernel corn, drained
1 (16-ounce) can French-style green beans, drained
1 (11-ounce) can Shoe Peg corn, drained
1 (16-ounce) can green peas, drained
1 bell pepper, chopped
1 red onion, chopped
1 cup sugar
3/4 cup white vinegar
1/2 cup vegetable oil
1 teaspoon salt
1 teaspoon pepper

Combine the corn, French-style green beans, Shoe Peg corn, green peas, bell pepper and onion in a large bowl and mix well. Combine the sugar, vinegar, oil, salt and pepper in a saucepan. Bring to a boil. Let stand until cool. Pour over the vegetable mixture. Chill, covered, for 24 hours. You may store, covered, in the refrigerator for up to 2 weeks. YIELD: 8 TO 10 SERVINGS.

Mary Howle
Anniston Council

HELPFUL HINT

Place an inverted saucer on the bottom of your vegetable salad bowl. Moisture will collect under the saucer and keep the salad crisp.

Sweet/Sour Dressing

1 cup olive oil
½ cup vinegar
½ cup sugar
1 teaspoon salt
1 teaspoon celery salt
1 teaspoon dry mustard
1 teaspoon paprika
1 teaspoon grated onion

Combine the olive oil, vinegar, sugar, salt, celery salt, dry mustard, paprika and grated onion in a jar with a lid. Cover and shake to mix. Chill for several hours. Shake just before pouring over salad. You may substitute 12 packets artificial sweetener for the sugar.
YIELD: 1½ CUPS.

Mrs. Virginia Greene
Birmingham South Life

Slaw Dressing

½ cup safflower oil
¼ cup apple cider vinegar
⅓ cup lemon juice
4 teaspoons sugar
1 tablespoon mayonnaise

Combine the safflower oil, cider vinegar, lemon juice and sugar in a jar with a lid. Cover and shake to mix. Refrigerate, covered, until chilled. Pour into a bowl. Stir in mayonnaise just before adding to slaw. YIELD: 1 CUP.

Doris B. Thrasher
Gadsden Life

Salad Lover's Delight

1 large package salad mix
1 head lettuce, optional
1 large package spinach mix
1 large package Caesar salad mix
1 large package slaw mix
1 large package shredded Cheddar cheese
1 large package shredded Swiss cheese
2 large tomatoes, coarsely chopped
2 large cucumbers, coarsely chopped
8 to 16 ounces ham, turkey and corned beef, chopped or shredded
Ranch or Italian salad dressing to taste

Mix the salad mix, lettuce, spinach mix, Caesar salad mix, slaw mix, Cheddar cheese, Swiss cheese, tomatoes, cucumbers, ham, turkey and corned beef in a large salad bowl. Toss with salad dressing. YIELD: 20 SERVINGS.

D. Christine Kinkley
Birmingham Life

Chicken Salad

5 chicken breasts
4 eggs, hard-cooked, grated
1 1/2 cups sliced grapes
1/2 cup chopped celery
1 cup mayonnaise
1 cup sour cream
2/3 cup slivered almonds

Boil the chicken breasts in enough water to cover in a saucepan until cooked through. Cool and cut into bite-size pieces. Combine the chicken, eggs, grapes and celery in a large bowl and mix well. Stir in a mixture of the mayonnaise and sour cream. Chill, covered, until serving time. Stir in the almonds just before serving. Serve on croissants or sliced bread. YIELD: 8 TO 10 SERVINGS.

Marsha Harbarger
Riverchase Council

Chicken Salad

3 chickens, cut into halves
Salt to taste
9 green onions
½ stalk celery
3 (8-ounce) cans sliced water chestnuts,
drained, chopped
Pepper to taste
Mayonnaise
Curly endive

Boil the chickens in salted water in a stockpot until cooked through. Remove the skin and bones. Process in a food processor until coarsely chopped. Combine the chicken, green onions, celery, water chestnuts and pepper in a large bowl and mix well. Stir in enough mayonnaise just to moisten. Line a salad bowl with curly endive. Spoon the chicken salad into the prepared bowl. Garnish with mandarin oranges and green grapes. Serve with unsalted butter crackers, strawberries dipped in white chocolate, cantaloupe wedges, purple grapes, cheese straws, tea cakes and iced or hot tea.
YIELD: 12 TO 16 SERVINGS.

Barbara O. Horton
Mobile Council

HELPFUL HINT

Salt salads just before serving because salt tends to wilt and toughen salad greens.

Creole Chicken Salad

1 cup mayonnaise
3/4 teaspoon Creole seasoning
1/4 teaspoon dillweed
1/4 teaspoon paprika
4 cups chopped cooked chicken
1 tablespoon finely chopped bell pepper
1/4 cup finely chopped celery
1/4 cup finely chopped onion
1/4 cup sweet pickle relish

Mix the mayonnaise, Creole seasoning, dillweed and paprika in a small bowl. Combine the chicken, bell pepper, celery, onion and pickle relish in a large bowl, tossing to mix. Stir in the mayonnaise mixture. YIELD: 6 SERVINGS.

Dot Johnson
Gadsden Life

Chicken Salad Supreme

4 pounds cooked chicken
5 or 6 Granny Smith apples, peeled
1 quart pecans
16 ounces pickle relish
Salt and pepper to taste
4 cups sour cream

Grind or shred the chicken, apples and pecans. Combine the chicken, apples and pecans in a large bowl and mix well. Add the pickle relish, salt and pepper and mix well. Stir in the sour cream. YIELD: 30 SERVINGS.

Helion C. Motes
Montgomery Life

Hot Chicken Salad

2 or 3 cups chopped cooked chicken
2 cups chopped celery
1 cup sliced water chestnuts
1/2 cup chopped toasted almonds
2 teaspoons grated onion
1 cup mayonnaise
2 tablespoons lemon juice
2 1/2 teaspoons tarragon wine vinegar
1/2 teaspoon MSG
1/2 teaspoon salt
1/2 cup finely shredded Cheddar cheese
1 cup crushed potato chips

Mix the chicken, celery, water chestnuts, almonds and onion in a large bowl. Combine the mayonnaise, lemon juice, wine vinegar, MSG and salt in a small bowl and mix well. Stir into the chicken mixture. Spoon into a well greased baking dish. Sprinkle with the Cheddar cheese and potato chips. Bake at 450 degrees for 10 minutes. YIELD: 6 TO 8 SERVINGS.

Mary Alice Neal
Birmingham Life

Exotic Turkey Salad

2 quarts chopped cooked turkey
1 (20-ounce) can sliced water chestnuts
2 pounds seedless grapes
2 cups chopped celery
2 cups slivered almonds
1 (20-ounce) can pineapple chunks, drained
3 cups mayonnaise
2 tablespoons soy sauce
1 tablespoon curry powder

Mix the turkey, water chestnuts, grapes, celery, almonds and pineapple in a large bowl. Combine the mayonnaise, soy sauce and curry powder in a bowl and mix well. Stir into the turkey mixture. Serve on lettuce leaves. YIELD: 18 TO 20 SERVINGS.

Virginia Sherrer
Selma Life

HABITAT FOR HUMANITY

In 1999, the Alabama Chapter of BellSouth Pioneer Volunteers built the first Ability House in the nation. This is a Habitat for Humanity house built with special adaptation for a physically impaired client. The house was totally built by disabled volunteers from all over the country. Pioneers assisted the "special" volunteers, donated the money to construct the house, and solicited donations from various community organizations to furnish the house.

Meats

Best-Ever Pot Roast

1 (3-pound) chuck roast
4 garlic cloves
Salt and pepper to taste
Flour for coating
2 tablespoons olive oil
1½ cups cooking wine
¾ cup brewed coffee
2 envelopes onion and mushroom soup mix
5 carrots, cut into 1-inch pieces
4 ribs celery, cut into 1-inch pieces
1 large onion, coarsely chopped
4 or 5 potatoes, cut into halves

Cut 4 slits in the sides of the roast and insert the garlic cloves. Sprinkle with salt and pepper. Coat lightly with the flour. Brown the roast in hot olive oil in a Dutch oven. Combine the wine, coffee and soup mix in a bowl and mix well. Pour over the roast. Bake at 350 degrees for 1 hour. Add the carrots, celery and onion. Bake for 1 hour. Add the potatoes. Bake for an additional hour. Place the vegetables in a serving bowl. Place the roast on a serving plate and cut into slices. Pour the gravy into a bowl. **Yield: 8 to 10 servings.**

Margie Stetson
Riverchase Council

HELPFUL HINT

Sprinkle salt in the pan before browning meat to keep it from sticking.

New England Boiled Dinner

1 (2½- to 3-pound) beef brisket
Salt and pepper to taste
1 medium head of cabbage, quartered
1½ leeks, cut into 1½-inch pieces
7 carrots, cut into halves
4 ears of corn, cut into halves
1 large onion, cut into quarters
3 turnips, cut into halves
5 potatoes, cut into halves

Place the brisket in a large soup pot. Add enough hot water to fill. Add the salt and pepper. Cook over medium to medium-high heat for 1 hour. Add the cabbage, leeks, carrots, corn and onion. Cook for 1 hour. Add the turnips and potatoes. Cook for 1 to 1½ hours or until the vegetables are tender. Serve with warm buttered bread.
YIELD: 8 TO 10 SERVINGS.

Margie Stetson
Riverchase Council

Roast Beef

1 (3- to 4-pound) chuck roast
Worcestershire sauce
1 envelope onion soup mix
1 (10-ounce) can cream of celery soup

Place the roast on a large sheet of foil in a roasting pan. Sprinkle with the Worcestershire sauce. Sprinkle the soup mix over the roast. Pour the celery soup over the top. Fold the foil over the roast and seal. Bake at 300 degrees until the roast registers 140 degrees on a meat thermometer for rare, or 160 degrees for medium.
YIELD: 10 TO 12 SERVINGS.

Barbara S. Lagle
Birmingham Life

Eye-of-Round Roast

1 tablespoon flour
1 (5-pound) eye-of-round roast
Seasoned salt
Garlic powder
Garlic pepper
Onion powder
1 envelope onion soup mix
1 large can 98% fat-free cream of mushroom soup
2 cups water
1 tablespoon beef bouillon granules

Place the flour in a plastic baking bag and shake to coat the inside of the bag. Sprinkle the roast generously with the seasoned salt, garlic powder, garlic pepper and onion powder. Place in the prepared baking bag and place in a roasting pan. Sprinkle the onion soup mix over the roast. Combine the mushroom soup, water and bouillon in a bowl and mix well. Pour over the roast. Tie the bag closed. Cut slits in the top of the bag. Bake at 325 degrees for 4 hours. Let stand for 10 minutes. Place the roast on a serving platter and cut into slices. Pour the liquid into a gravy bowl and serve with the roast. YIELD: 10 SERVINGS.

Mrs. Virginia Greene
Birmingham South Life

HELPFUL HINT

When broiling meat, place 1 or 2 slices of bread in the bottom of the broiler pan to absorb drippings and reduce spattering and cleanup.

Margaret's Special Roast Beef

1 (3- to 4-pound) sirloin tip roast
Vegetable oil
Steak sauce
Garlic salt
1 (10-ounce) can cream of mushroom soup
5 ounces water
1 tablespoon steak sauce
1 tablespoon Worcestershire sauce
Lemon pepper

Brown the roast on both sides in a small amount of oil in a heavy skillet. Soak all sides with steak sauce. Sprinkle all sides with garlic salt. Marinate, covered, in the refrigerator for 8 to 12 hours, turning occasionally; drain. Bake at 300 degrees for 2½ hours. Let stand until completely cool. Cut into slices. You may freeze the beef slices at this point. Arrange the beef slices in a baking dish. Combine the soup, water, 1 tablespoon steak sauce, Worcestershire sauce, garlic salt to taste and lemon pepper to taste in a bowl and mix well. Pour over the beef slices. Bake, tightly covered, at 300 degrees for 1 to 3 hours or until of the desired degree of doneness. You may make a gravy with the pan drippings. YIELD: 10 SERVINGS.

Margaret Jones
Birmingham Life

HELPFUL HINT

Cooking frozen beef without pre-thawing not only saves time but the beef also retains more flavor, more juices and more nutritive value.

Easy Roast Beef

1 (3-pound) eye-of-round beef roast
3 (10-ounce) cans brown gravy with onions
1 medium onion, chopped
Water (optional)

Trim the fat from the roast. Place in a small roasting pan. Pour 2 cans of gravy around the roast and 1 can over the roast. Sprinkle the onion over the top. Bake, covered, at 350 degrees for 1½ hours or until tender. Let stand until completely cool. Cut into thin slices. Whisk enough water into the gravy to make of the desired consistency. Layer the gravy and beef roast slices alternately in a baking dish, beginning and ending with the gravy. Bake at 350 degrees until heated through. You may freeze this. YIELD: 8 TO 10 SERVINGS.

Libby Harris
Birmingham South Life

Slow and Easy Roast

1 (4-pound) sirloin tip or chuck roast, trimmed
½ cup soy sauce
1 beef bouillon cube
1 bay leaf
4 or 5 peppercorns
1 teaspoon dried rosemary
1 teaspoon dried thyme
1 teaspoon garlic powder

Place the roast in a 5-quart CROCK-POT® Slow Cooker. Combine the soy sauce, bouillon cube, bay leaf, peppercorns, rosemary, thyme and garlic powder in a bowl and mix well. Pour over the roast. Add enough water to almost cover the roast. Cook on Low for 7 hours or until very tender. Place the roast on a serving platter. Remove and discard the bay leaf. Serve the sauce with the roast. YIELD: 10 TO 12 SERVINGS.

Shirley M. Helms
Montgomery Life

Rump Roast

Rump roast
2 tablespoons vegetable oil
3 onions, chopped
4 garlic cloves, chopped

1 cup ketchup
2 cups water
Salt and pepper to taste

Brown the roast on all sides in hot oil in a Dutch oven. Add the onions and garlic. Sauté until tender. Combine the ketchup, water, salt and pepper in a bowl and mix well. Pour over the roast. Simmer, covered, for 4 hours. You may make 1 day ahead for enhanced flavor, refrigerating the roast and stock separately.
YIELD: VARIABLE.

Margaret W. Wilborn
Gadsden Life

Italian Roast Beef Sandwich

Greek Italian spices
1 beef roast
2 envelopes brown gravy mix
2 cups water

Butter
Soft Hoagie rolls
Garlic salt
Greek peppers to taste

Sprinkle the Greek Italian spices generously over the roast. Place in a large pan. Add enough water to cover. Bring to a boil. Boil, covered, until tender; drain. Pull the roast apart into small pieces. Combine the gravy mix and 2 cups water in a saucepan and mix well. Cook over low heat until very thick. Spread the butter over the cut sides of the rolls. Sprinkle with garlic salt. Place the desired amount of meat into each roll. Place the peppers on the meat. Wrap each sandwich in foil. YIELD: VARIABLE.

Kathryn Morgan
Gadsden Life

Hungarian Goulash

2 pounds round steak, cut into 1/2-inch pieces
1 cup chopped onions
1 garlic clove, minced
2 tablespoons flour
1 teaspoon each paprika and salt
1/2 teaspoon pepper
1/4 teaspoon dried thyme, crushed
1 bay leaf
1 (28-ounce) can tomatoes
1 cup sour cream
Hot cooked noodles

Place the steak cubes, onions and garlic in a CROCK-POT® Slow Cooker. Add the flour, stirring to coat the steak. Add the paprika, salt, pepper, thyme, bay leaf and tomatoes and mix well. Cook on Low for 7 to 10 hours or on High for 5 to 6 hours, stirring occasionally. Add the sour cream 30 minutes before serving and mix well. Remove the bay leaf. Serve over the noodles. **YIELD: 8 SERVINGS.**

Francis Tucker
Selma Life

Swiss Steak

1½ pounds (1-inch thick) beef round or chuck steak
2 tablespoons flour
1½ teaspoons salt
¼ teaspoon pepper
3 tablespoons shortening
1 medium onion, sliced
1 (15-ounce) can tomato sauce
1 cup water
1 cup frozen English peas (optional)

Cut the steak into 4 equal pieces. Combine the flour, salt and pepper in a shallow dish. Coat the steaks lightly in the flour mixture. Pound until thin. Heat the shortening in a heavy skillet until melted. Separate the onions into rings. Sauté in the hot shortening until golden brown. Move to the side of the skillet. Reduce the heat. Add the steaks. Cook until brown on both sides. Arrange the onions over the steaks. Pour the tomato sauce and the water over the onions, stirring to blend. Bring to a boil. Simmer, tightly covered, for 2 hours. Add the peas. Cook for 10 minutes.
YIELD: 4 TO 6 SERVINGS.

Ila Skidmore
Shoals Life

HELPFUL HINT

Place a slice of bacon in the bottom of the baking pan to prevent meat loaf from sticking.

Easy Baked Beef Stew

2 pounds cubed beef for stew
Salt and pepper to taste
Paprika to taste
2 tablespoons onion soup mix
6 medium potatoes, cut into quarters
6 small white boiling onions
3 carrots, cut into quarters
1 (10-ounce) can cream of celery soup
1 cup water

Sprinkle the beef with the salt, pepper, paprika and soup mix. Place in a Dutch oven. Add the potatoes, onions and carrots. Combine the soup and water in a bowl and mix well. Pour over the top. Bake, covered, at 250 to 300 degrees for 5 hours. YIELD: **6 TO 8 SERVINGS**.

Betty Foshee
Decatur Council

One-Two-Three Stew

1 (2- to 3-pound) round steak, cut into cubes
1 envelope onion soup mix
1 (10-ounce) can cream of mushroom soup

Place the steak cubes in a baking dish. Combine the soup mix and soup in a bowl and mix well. Pour over the steak cubes. Bake, covered, at 300 degrees for 3 hours. Serve over rice. YIELD: **6 SERVINGS**.

Sue Small
Selma Life

Corned Beef and Cabbage Casserole

3 large white potatoes
1 large onion
1/4 cup (1/2 stick) margarine
Salt and pepper to taste
1/2 head (about) green cabbage, chopped
1 (12-ounce) can corned beef
1 (10-ounce) can cream of mushroom soup
1 to 1 1/2 cups shredded mild or medium Cheddar cheese

Peel and slice the potatoes. Arrange in a layer over the bottom of a 9×13-inch baking pan sprayed with nonstick cooking spray. Peel and slice the onion. Arrange in a layer over the potatoes. Dot with the margarine. Sprinkle with salt and pepper. Arrange the cabbage over the layers. Spread the corned beef over the cabbage. Spread the soup over the corned beef. Sprinkle the cheese over the top. Cover with foil sprayed with nonstick cooking spray. Bake at 375 degrees for 1 hour. **YIELD: 4 TO 6 SERVINGS.**

Bertha Capps
Birmingham Life

Asian Beef and Noodles

1¼ pounds ground chuck
2 (3-ounce) packages oriental ramen noodles, crumbled
2 cups water
2 cups frozen mixed vegetables
¼ teaspoon ginger
2 tablespoons thinly sliced green onions

Brown the ground chuck in a large nonstick skillet over medium heat for 10 to 12 minutes, stirring until crumbly; drain. Remove the cooked beef to a bowl. Add 1 seasoning package from the noodles and mix well. Add the water, vegetables, noodles, remaining seasoning package and ginger to the skillet and stir to combine. Bring to a boil. Reduce the heat. Simmer, covered, for 3 minutes or until noodles are tender, stirring occasionally; do not overcook. Add the beef to the noodle mixture. Stir in the green onions. **YIELD: 4 SERVINGS.**

Mabel Smartt
Decatur Council

Chloe Scott's Baked Beans

1 pound ground chuck
3 (16-ounce) cans or 2 (28-ounce) cans pork and beans
½ (16-ounce) package brown sugar
1 onion, chopped
Ketchup to taste
Mustard to taste
Chopped bell pepper to taste
2 packages Polish or smoked sausages, chopped

Brown the ground chuck in a skillet, stirring until crumbly; drain. Combine the pork and beans, brown sugar, onion, ketchup, mustard and bell pepper in a bowl and mix well. Stir in the ground chuck and sausages. Spoon into a baking dish. Bake at 350 degrees for 30 to 35 minutes or until bubbly. **YIELD: 10 TO 12 SERVINGS.**

Imogene Davis
Birmingham Life

Chili

2 pounds lean ground beef
½ cup chopped onion
5 slices bacon, crisp-cooked, crumbled
1 (16-ounce) can diced tomatoes
1 (16-ounce) can special tomato sauce
1 (16-ounce) can Italian tomato sauce
¼ cup chopped jalapeño pepper slices
2 tablespoons chili powder
2 tablespoons cayenne pepper
2 tablespoons oregano
2 tablespoons basil
1 tablespoon cinnamon
1 teaspoon black pepper
1 teaspoon white pepper
1 teaspoon cumin
½ teaspoon garlic salt
Dash of Tabasco sauce
1 (15-ounce) can red kidney beans, drained (optional)
1 cup shredded Cheddar cheese

Brown the ground beef with the onion in a skillet, stirring until the ground beef is crumbly; drain. Spoon into a large saucepan or Dutch oven. Add the bacon, tomatoes, tomato sauces, jalapeño peppers, chili powder, cayenne pepper, oregano, basil, cinnamon, black pepper, white pepper, cumin, garlic salt, Tabasco sauce and kidney beans and mix well. Bring to a boil. Reduce the heat. Simmer for 45 minutes, stirring occasionally. Ladle into bowls. Sprinkle with the cheese. YIELD: 8 TO 10 SERVINGS.

Renee McCreless
Birmingham Metro Council

Chauvinist Chili

6 to 8 slices bacon
1 pound lean ground beef
1 pound hot Italian sausage, casing removed
1 or 2 large Spanish onions, chopped
2 garlic cloves, smashed or chopped
1 cup dark red wine
1/2 cup Worcestershire sauce
1 teaspoon hot dry mustard
1 teaspoon celery seeds
1 1/2 teaspoons chili powder
1/2 teaspoon salt
1 1/2 teaspoons freshly ground black pepper
2 (28-ounce) cans Italian pear shaped tomatoes, or 2 large cans diced Italian tomatoes
1 small can jalapeño relish
1 (15-ounce) can pinto beans
1 (15-ounce) can kidney beans
1 (15-ounce) can garbanzo beans

Cook the bacon in a Dutch oven until crisp. Drain, reserving a small amount of the drippings in the Dutch oven. Remove the bacon and crumble into a large strainer. Brown the ground beef in the Dutch oven, stirring until crumbly. Drain, reserving a small amount of the drippings in the Dutch oven. Remove the cooked ground beef, placing in the strainer. Brown the sausage in the Dutch oven, stirring until crumbly. Drain, reserving a small amount of the drippings in the Dutch oven. Remove the cooked sausage, placing in the strainer. Cook the onions and garlic in the hot drippings over low heat for 2 to 3 minutes. Stir in the wine and Worcestershire sauce. Simmer for 10 minutes. Stir in the mustard, celery seeds, chili powder, salt and pepper. Simmer for 10 minutes. Stir in the tomatoes and relish. Stir in the cooked sausage, ground beef and bacon. Bring to a boil. Reduce the heat. Simmer, covered, for 30 minutes, stirring occasionally. Add the pinto beans, kidney beans and garbanzo beans. Bring to a boil. Reduce the heat. Simmer, covered, for 1 hour. You may refrigerate, covered, for 1 day for enhanced flavor and reheat before serving. YIELD: 10 TO 12 SERVINGS.

Sarah Spratt
Anniston Council

Beef and Bean Supper Dish

1 pound ground beef
1 onion, sliced
½ teaspoon salt
½ teaspoon pepper
1 (15-ounce) can pork and beans
½ cup ketchup
½ tablespoon Worcestershire sauce
2 tablespoons brown sugar
1 tablespoon vinegar

Brown the ground beef with the onion in a skillet, stirring until the ground beef is crumbly; drain. Add the salt, pepper, pork and beans, ketchup, Worcestershire sauce, brown sugar and vinegar and mix well. Simmer, covered, for 20 to 30 minutes. YIELD: 6 TO 8 SERVINGS.

Sue Small
Selma Life

Green Enchiladas

2 (10-ounce) cans cream of chicken soup
1 pound Velveeta cheese, chopped
2 (4-ounce) cans chopped green chilies
1 jar pimentos
1 small can sweetened condensed milk
1 pound ground beef
Vegetable oil
12 corn tortillas
1 medium onion, chopped
Shredded Cheddar cheese

Combine the first 5 ingredients in a saucepan. Cook until the cheese melts, stirring constantly. Brown the ground beef in a skillet, stirring until crumbly; drain. Heat the oil in a separate skillet. Dip the tortillas one at a time in the hot oil until pliable. Spoon an equal amount of the cooked beef, onion and shredded cheese down the middle of each tortilla. Roll to enclose the filling. Arrange seam side down in a glass baking dish. Pour the cheese sauce over the tortillas. Bake at 350 degrees for 35 minutes. YIELD: 6 SERVINGS.

Frances Hyatt
Gadsden Life

Enchilada Pie

2 pounds ground chuck
1 medium onion, chopped
½ teaspoon salt
1 (10-ounce) can tomato soup
2 (10-ounce) cans mild enchilada sauce
1 cup water
12 or more (8-inch) tortilla shells
2 cups shredded cheese

Brown the ground chuck with the onion and salt in a Dutch oven or large saucepan, stirring until the ground chuck is crumbly; drain. Add the soup, enchilada sauce and water and mix well. Simmer for 5 minutes. Spoon ¾ of the ground chuck mixture into a bowl. Arrange 2 or 3 tortillas over the remaining ground chuck mixture in the Dutch oven. Sprinkle with ¼ of the cheese. Repeat the ground chuck mixture, tortilla and cheese layers 3 more times. Simmer, covered, for 10 minutes or until the cheese melts and the tortillas soften. YIELD: ABOUT 10 SERVINGS.

Gloria "Carol" Lindley
Birmingham South Cahaba Council

Stuffed Green Peppers

6 large green bell peppers
1 pound ground beef
1 large onion, minced
1 garlic clove, minced
3 tablespoons margarine, melted
3 tomatoes, peeled, chopped
1 tablespoon Worcestershire sauce
1/2 teaspoon salt
1/4 teaspoon pepper
1 cup cooked rice
1/2 cup bread crumbs

Cut the tops off the bell peppers. Bring enough water to cover the bell peppers to a boil in a large saucepan. Add the bell peppers. Cook for 5 minutes; drain. Brown the ground beef with the onion and garlic in the margarine in a large skillet, stirring until the ground beef is crumbly; drain. Stir in the tomatoes. Simmer for 10 minutes. Add the Worcestershire sauce, salt, pepper and rice and mix well. Spoon into the bell peppers. Place the bell peppers upright in a shallow baking dish. Sprinkle the bread crumbs over the top. Bake at 350 degrees for 25 minutes. **Yield: 6 servings.**

Joann Ford
Gadsden Life

HELPFUL HINT

Invert a metal colander over the skillet when browning ground beef. This allows steam to escape and reduces spattering.

Ground Beef Casserole

1 pound ground chuck
1 garlic clove, minced
Salt and pepper to taste
1 teaspoon sugar
1 (15-ounce) can tomato sauce
1 cup sour cream
6 ounces cream cheese, softened
1 bunch green onions, chopped
1½ cups shredded Cheddar cheese
1 (5-ounce) package egg noodles
½ cup shredded Cheddar cheese

Brown the ground chuck in a skillet, stirring until crumbly. Stir in the garlic, salt, pepper, sugar and tomato sauce. Simmer for 15 minutes. Combine the sour cream, cream cheese, green onions and 1½ cups Cheddar cheese and mix well. Cook the noodles using the package directions; drain. Alternate layers of the noodles, ground chuck mixture and cheese mixture in a baking dish until all ingredients are used, ending with the cheese mixture. Sprinkle ½ cup Cheddar cheese over the top. Bake at 350 degrees for 30 minutes.
YIELD: 4 TO 6 SERVINGS.

Narice Sutton
Birmingham Life

HELPFUL HINT
Cinnamon and cloves are delicious additions to pork dishes.

Goulash

1 pound ground chuck
1/2 medium onion, chopped
1/2 medium bell pepper, chopped
1 (15-ounce) can tomatoes
1 cup macaroni, cooked
Salt and pepper to taste

Brown the ground chuck with the onion and bell pepper in a skillet, stirring until the ground chuck is crumbly; drain. Stir in the tomatoes and macaroni. Simmer for 30 minutes, adding additional liquid as needed. Season with salt and pepper. **YIELD: 4 SERVINGS.**

Hazel Campbell
Birmingham Life

Hamburger Pepper Casserole

1 pound ground beef
2 medium potatoes, peeled, chopped
2 medium green bell peppers, chopped
1 rib celery, chopped
1 (4-ounce) can mushrooms, drained
1 cup shredded Cheddar or Colby cheese
1 tablespoon butter or margarine

Brown the ground beef in a skillet, stirring until crumbly; drain. Layer the cooked ground beef, potatoes, bell peppers, celery and mushrooms in a greased baking dish. Bake, covered, at 375 degrees for 15 to 20 minutes. Sprinkle the cheese over the layers. Dot with butter. Bake until the cheese melts. **YIELD: 6 SERVINGS.**

Hannah M. Segrest
Montgomery Life

Hash

8 to 16 ounces ground beef
½ cup (1 stick) butter
2 medium onions, sliced
1 teaspoon garlic powder
2 teaspoons Tabasco sauce
Dash dry mustard
2 teaspoons Worcestershire sauce
Salt and pepper to taste
4 or 5 potatoes, sliced
1 to 2 cups beef bouillon

Brown the ground beef in the butter in a skillet, stirring until crumbly. Add the onions, garlic powder, Tabasco sauce, dry mustard, Worcestershire sauce, salt, pepper, potatoes and bouillon and mix well. Cook until potatoes are tender. Skim off the fat. YIELD: 4 TO 6 SERVINGS.

Margaret W. Wilborn
Gadsden Life

Macaroni and Cheese Casserole

1 package macaroni and cheese
1 pound ground beef
2 (15-ounce) cans tomatoes with onions, celery and peppers
½ to 1 cup shredded cheese

Prepare the macaroni and cheese using the package directions. Brown the ground beef in a skillet, stirring until crumbly; drain. Combine the prepared macaroni and cheese, ground beef and tomatoes in a bowl and mix well. Spoon into a baking dish. Sprinkle the cheese over the top. Bake at 350 degrees until heated through and bubbly. YIELD: 6 SERVINGS.

Rubie McInnis
Birmingham Life

CROCK-POT® Lasagna

1½ pounds ground chuck
½ large onion, chopped
2 garlic cloves, chopped
2 (15-ounce) cans tomato sauce
1 cup water
1 (6-ounce) can tomato paste
1 teaspoon salt
1 teaspoon oregano
4 cups shredded mozzarella cheese
1½ cups cottage cheese
½ cup grated Parmesan cheese
1 (16-ounce) package whole wheat lasagna noodles

Brown the ground chuck with the onion and garlic in a skillet over medium heat, stirring until the ground chuck is crumbly. Drain and rinse with hot water. Combine the cooked ground chuck mixture with the tomato sauce, water, tomato paste, salt and oregano in a bowl and mix well. Combine the mozzarella cheese, cottage cheese and Parmesan cheese in a separate bowl and mix well. Spread ¼ of the ground chuck mixture over the bottom of a 5-quart CROCK-POT® Slow Cooker. Layer the noodles, cheese mixture and remaining ground chuck mixture ⅓ at a time in the CROCK-POT® Slow Cooker. Cook on High for 5 hours or until noodles are tender. YIELD: **6** TO **8** SERVINGS.

Mrs. Virginia Greene
Birmingham South Life

HELPFUL HINT

Enhance the flavor of pork dishes by serving with fresh lime.
Limes can also be used in marinades for grilled pork.

Meal-in-One Casserole

1 pound ground beef
1 medium onion, chopped
1 medium green bell pepper, chopped
1 (15-ounce) can whole kernel corn
1 (4-ounce) can mushrooms, drained
1 teaspoon salt
1/4 teaspoon pepper
1 (11-ounce) jar salsa
5 cups medium egg noodles
1 (28-ounce) can diced tomatoes
1 cup water
1 cup shredded cheese

Brown the ground beef with the onion in a skillet over medium heat, stirring until the ground beef is crumbly; drain. Layer the ground beef mixture, bell pepper, corn, mushrooms, salt, pepper, salsa and noodles in a CROCK-POT® Slow Cooker. Pour the tomatoes and water over the layers. Sprinkle the cheese over the top. Cook on Low for 4 hours or until the noodles are tender.

YIELD: 4 TO 6 SERVINGS.

Mary Crittenden
Decatur Council

HELPFUL HINT

Use dried mushrooms, mushroom flakes or canned mushrooms in main dish recipes when you do not have fresh mushrooms.

Meal-in-One Casserole

5 or 6 medium potatoes
1 1/2 pounds ground beef
1 small onion, chopped (optional)
1 bell pepper, chopped (optional)
Sliced mushrooms (optional)
1 (16-ounce) can green beans
1 (10-ounce) can tomato soup
Shredded cheese (optional)

Combine the potatoes with enough water to cover in a saucepan. Bring to a boil. Boil until tender; drain. Beat in a mixing bowl until smooth. Brown the ground beef with the onion, bell pepper and mushrooms in a skillet, stirring until the ground beef is crumbly; drain. Stir in the green beans and soup. Simmer for 10 minutes, stirring occasionally. Spoon into a baking dish. Spread the potatoes over the ground beef mixture. Sprinkle the cheese over the top. Bake at 400 degrees for 20 to 25 minutes or until bubbly.

Yield: 6 to 8 servings.

Louise Morrison
Tuscaloosa Council

Barbecued Meatballs

1 1/2 cups bread crumbs
1/2 cup water
1 pound ground beef
8 ounces ground pork
1 cup dry milk
1 egg, lightly beaten
1 teaspoon salt
1/4 teaspoon pepper
1/4 cup (1/2 stick) butter
1 small onion, chopped
1 slice lemon
1/2 teaspoon chili powder
2 teaspoons celery seeds
2 tablespoons vinegar
1 teaspoon Worcestershire sauce
2/3 cup ketchup
1 cup water
Dash of Tabasco sauce

Combine the bread crumbs and water in a bowl and mix well. Combine the ground beef, ground pork, dry milk, egg, salt, pepper and bread crumb mixture in a large bowl and mix well. Shape into 12 meatballs. Arrange the meatballs in a baking dish. Heat the butter in a saucepan until melted. Sauté the onion in the hot butter. Add the lemon, chili powder, celery seeds, vinegar, Worcestershire sauce, ketchup, water and Tabasco sauce and mix well. Bring to a boil. Pour over the meatballs. Bake at 350 degrees for 40 minutes, turning occasionally. YIELD: 4 TO 6 SERVINGS.

Ila Skidmore
Shoals Life

Meatballs

2 pounds ground steak
½ teaspoon sage
2 teaspoons salt
½ teaspoon pepper
¼ cup vegetable oil or ¼ cup (½ stick) margarine
4 medium onions, sliced
3 tablespoons flour
1 pint tomatoes, chopped
1 cup bread crumbs

Shape the ground steak into meatballs. Sprinkle each meatball with the sage, salt and pepper. Arrange in a baking dish. Heat the oil in a skillet. Stir-fry the onions in the hot oil. Remove the onions, reserving the oil. Arrange the onions over the meatballs. Stir the flour into the hot oil. Stir in the tomatoes. Pour over the onions. Sprinkle the bread crumbs over the top. Bake, covered, at 350 degrees for 1 hour. Remove the cover. Bake an additional 30 minutes. You may partially cook the meatballs before placing in the baking dish to decrease the baking time. **YIELD: 6 TO 8 SERVINGS.**

Mary Ann Sparks Fulmer
Shoals Life

▪ ▪ ▪ HELPFUL HINT ▪ ▪ ▪

Just add a small amount of baking soda to gravy if it is greasy.
Begin with ¼ teaspoon and add a little more if necessary.

Meat Loaf

2/3 cup dry bread crumbs
1 cup milk
1 1/2 cups ground beef
2 eggs, beaten
1/4 cup grated onion

1 teaspoon salt
1/2 teaspoon sage
6 tablespoons brown sugar
1 cup ketchup
1/2 teaspoon dry mustard

Soak the bread crumbs in the milk in a large bowl. Add the ground beef, eggs, onion, salt and sage and mix well. Pat into a loaf pan. Combine the brown sugar, ketchup and dry mustard in a bowl and mix well. Spread over the top. Bake at 350 degrees for 1 hour.
Yield: 4 to 6 servings.

Ann Moon
Decatur Council

Meat Loaf

1/2 cup milk
2 eggs
4 slices bread, cubed
1 1/2 pounds ground round
1 1/2 cups chopped onions
1 1/2 teaspoons salt

1/8 teaspoon pepper
3 tablespoons ketchup
1 tablespoon Worcestershire sauce
1 envelope onion soup mix

Combine the milk and eggs in a large bowl and mix well. Soak the bread in the milk mixture. Add the ground round, onions, salt, pepper, ketchup, Worcestershire sauce and soup mix and mix well. Pack into a loaf pan. Bake at 350 degrees for 1 hour.
Yield: 5 to 6 servings.

Margaret W. Wilborn
Gadsden Life

MEATS 149

Cottage Meat Loaf

1/2 cup ketchup
1/3 cup tomato juice
1/2 teaspoon salt
1/2 teaspoon black pepper
1/8 teaspoon red pepper
2 eggs, beaten
3/4 cup fresh bread crumbs
1/4 cup finely chopped onions
2 teaspoons mustard
1 1/2 pounds lean ground beef
1/4 cup ketchup
1/2 teaspoon mustard
2 teaspoons brown sugar

Line a 5x9-inch loaf pan with foil. Combine 1/2 cup ketchup, tomato juice, salt, black pepper, red pepper, eggs, bread crumbs, onions and 2 teaspoons mustard in a bowl and mix well. Add the ground beef and mix well. Pack into the prepared pan. Combine 1/4 cup ketchup, 1/2 teaspoon mustard and brown sugar in a small bowl and mix well. Spread over the top of the meat loaf. Bake at 400 degrees for 35 to 45 minutes or until cooked through. Skim off the fat. Let stand for 5 minutes. YIELD: 5 TO 6 SERVINGS.

Mary Alice Neal
Birmingham Life

HELPFUL HINT

To add flavor to meat pies, add curry powder or chili powder to the pastry.

Mexican Meat Loaf

2 pounds ground beef
1 onion, chopped
½ bell pepper, chopped
1 (6-ounce) can tomato paste
1 (10-ounce) can chicken with rice soup
1 (10-ounce) can cream of mushroom soup
1 (4-ounce) can green chilies
Salt, pepper and garlic to taste
1 (10-ounce) can mild enchilada sauce
1 (9-ounce) package nacho cheese tortilla chips
1 pound cheese, shredded

Brown the ground beef in a skillet, stirring until crumbly; drain. Stir in the onion, bell pepper, tomato paste, chicken with rice soup, cream of mushroom soup, green chilies, salt, pepper, garlic and enchilada sauce. Simmer for 20 minutes. Line a baking dish with the chips. Layer the cheese and ground beef mixture ½ at a time over the chips. Bake at 350 degrees for 20 minutes. **YIELD: 6 TO 8 SERVINGS.**

Patricia V. Allen
Selma Life

Micro Meat Loaf

1½ pounds ground beef
1 envelope onion soup mix
1½ cups water
¾ cup herb-seasoned stuffing mix
½ cup ketchup
¼ cup packed brown sugar
2 teaspoons Dijon mustard

Mix the ground beef, soup mix, water and stuffing mix in a bowl. Press into an 4x8-inch microwave-safe loaf pan. Cover with waxed paper. Microwave on High for 10 minutes, rotating the pan once; drain. Mix the remaining ingredients in a bowl. Spoon over the meat loaf. Microwave, uncovered, on High for 3 to 4 minutes or until cooked through. Let stand for 10 minutes. YIELD: **5 TO 6 SERVINGS**.

Elba Skinner
Selma Life

Rotel Spicy Meat Loaf

1½ pounds ground chuck
3 slices bread, torn into small pieces
1 egg
1 (16-ounce) can Rotel diced tomatoes with green chilies
1 small onion, chopped
2 teaspoons chili powder
¼ teaspoon pepper
⅓ cup chili sauce

Combine the ground chuck, bread, egg, tomatoes, onion, chili powder and pepper in a bowl and mix well. Press into an 4x8-inch loaf pan. Bake at 375 degrees for 1 hour; drain. Spoon the chili sauce over the top. Bake for 15 minutes longer. YIELD: **8 SERVINGS**.

Anatalie Watson Fogg
Decatur Council

Stuffed Meat Loaf

8 ounces fresh mushrooms, sliced
1 medium onion, chopped
2 tablespoons butter or margarine
2 cups soft bread crumbs
2 tablespoons chopped fresh parsley
½ teaspoon dried thyme
½ teaspoon salt
⅛ teaspoon pepper
2 eggs
2 tablespoons milk
¼ cup ketchup
1½ teaspoons salt
⅛ teaspoon pepper
1 teaspoon brown sugar
1½ pounds lean ground beef

Sauté the mushrooms and onion in the butter in a skillet for 3 minutes or until tender. Add the bread crumbs, parsley, thyme, ½ teaspoon salt and ⅛ teaspoon pepper and mix well. Sauté until bread crumbs are light brown. Beat the eggs, milk, ketchup, 1½ teaspoons salt, ⅛ teaspoon pepper and brown sugar together in a large bowl. Add the ground beef and mix well. Press ½ of the ground beef mixture over the bottom of a greased 5x9-inch loaf pan. Spoon the bread crumb mixture over the ground beef layer. Press the remaining ground beef mixture over the bread crumb mixture gently. Bake at 350 degrees for 1 hour or until cooked through; drain. YIELD: **6 SERVINGS**.

Hester P. Thompson
Birmingham Life

Mexican Casserole

1 (12-count) package corn tortillas
Vegetable oil for frying
1½ pounds ground beef
1 small onion, chopped
1 (4-ounce) can diced green chilies
1 (10-ounce) can cream of chicken soup
1 (10-ounce) can cream of mushroom soup
Shredded American or Cheddar cheese

Fry the tortillas briefly in hot oil in a skillet. Drain on paper towels. Brown the ground beef with the onion in a skillet, stirring until the ground beef is crumbly; drain. Add the green chilies, cream of chicken soup and cream of mushroom soup and mix well. Arrange a layer of overlapping tortillas 3-deep over the bottom of a baking dish. Layer the ground beef mixture, cheese and remaining tortillas ½ at a time over the bottom layer of tortillas. Bake at 350 degrees until bubbly. **YIELD: 4 TO 6 SERVINGS.**

Mary C. Martin
Birmingham Life

Quick Mushroom Supper

1 pound ground beef
1 (10-ounce) can cream of mushroom soup
Hot cooked rice

Brown the ground beef in a skillet, stirring until crumbly; drain. Stir in the soup. Serve over hot cooked rice. **YIELD: 4 SERVINGS.**

Barbara S. Lagle
Birmingham Life

Oriental Casserole

1½ pounds ground beef
1 onion, chopped
1 green bell pepper, chopped
1 or 2 ribs celery, chopped
1 cup water
1 tablespoon water
2 teaspoons ground ginger
2 tablespoons cornstarch
½ cup soy sauce
1 (16-ounce) can chop suey vegetables
Chow mein noodles, cooked

Brown the ground beef in a skillet, stirring until crumbly; drain. Add the onion, bell pepper, celery and 1 cup water and mix well. Bring to a boil. Combine 1 tablespoon water, ginger, cornstarch and soy sauce in a small bowl and mix well. Pour into the ground beef mixture. Cook until bubbly. Stir in the vegetables. Spoon into a 2-quart baking dish. Bake at 350 degrees for 45 minutes. Serve over the chow mein noodles. YIELD: **6** TO **8** SERVINGS.

Jo Anne Norris
Bon Secour Life

HELPFUL HINT

Allow a roast to "rest" for 15 to 20 minutes after removing it from the oven before carving.

Ho-Bo Potatoes

2 pounds ground beef
2½ pounds potatoes, sliced
Carrots, chopped
2 large onions, chopped
2 bell peppers, chopped
4 hot peppers, chopped
16 ounces sharp cheddar cheese, shredded
1 tablespoon garlic powder
1 (10-ounce) can cream of mushroom soup

Brown the ground beef in a skillet, stirring until crumbly; drain. Layer the ground beef, potato slices, carrots, onions, bell peppers, hot peppers, cheese and garlic powder in a baking dish. Spoon the soup over the top. Bake at 350 degrees for 2 hours.
YIELD: 8 TO 10 SERVINGS.

Margaret W. Wilborn
Gadsden Life

Spaghetti Sauce

2 pounds ground beef
1 medium onion, chopped
1 (15-ounce) can stewed tomatoes
1 (12-ounce) can tomato paste
1¾ cups water
1 (8-ounce) can tomato sauce
1 tablespoon oregano
1 tablespoon garlic powder
1 tablespoon sugar
1 or 2 carrots, chopped
Red wine to taste

Brown the ground beef with the onion in a Dutch oven, stirring until the ground beef is crumbly; drain. Add the tomatoes, tomato paste, water, tomato sauce, oregano, garlic powder, sugar, carrots and wine and mix well. Simmer for 3 to 4 hours adding additional water or wine as needed, stirring occasionally. YIELD: 10 TO 12 SERVINGS.

Frances Hyatt
Gadsden Life

Beef Stroganoff

½ onion, minced
¼ cup (½ stick) butter
1 garlic clove, minced
2 tablespoons flour
1 pound ground sirloin
2 teaspoons salt
¼ teaspoon pepper
1 can sliced mushrooms
¼ teaspoon MSG
¼ teaspoon paprika
1 (8-ounce) can sliced water chestnuts
1 (10-ounce) can cream of chicken soup
1 cup sour cream

Sauté the onion in the butter in a skillet. Add the garlic. Cook for 2 to 3 minutes. Stir in the flour. Add the ground sirloin. Cook until brown, stirring until crumbly; drain. Stir in the salt, pepper, mushrooms, MSG, paprika, water chestnuts and soup. Simmer for 45 minutes. Stir in the sour cream. Serve over rice. **YIELD: 4 TO 6 SERVINGS.**

Faith Kirby Richardson
Gadsden Life

HELPFUL HINT

When roasting meat, place a cup of water in the bottom of the broiler pan before placing it in the oven. This will help to absorb smoke and grease.

Spoonburgers

1 pound ground beef
2 tablespoons drippings
2/3 cup chopped onion
1 tablespoon ketchup
1/2 teaspoon salt

1/8 teaspoon pepper
1/4 cup water
1 (10-ounce) can chicken gumbo soup
Hamburger buns

Brown the ground beef in the drippings in a skillet, stirring until crumbly. Add the onion. Cook until golden brown. Stir in the ketchup, salt, pepper, water and soup. Simmer over low heat for 30 minutes. Spoon into the buns. YIELD: 8 SERVINGS.

Francis Tucker
Selma Life

Tater Tot Casserole

2 pounds ground beef
1 small onion, chopped
Salt and pepper to taste
2 (10-ounce) cans cream of mushroom soup
1 cup milk
1 envelope brown gravy mix

2 (16-ounce) cans mixed vegetables
2 cups shredded Cheddar cheese
1 (2-pound) package Tater Tots

Brown the ground beef with the onion, salt and pepper in a skillet, stirring until the ground beef is crumbly; drain. Add the soup, milk, gravy mix, vegetables and cheese and mix well. Spoon into a baking dish. Arrange the Tater Tots over the top. Bake at 375 degrees for 30 minutes. YIELD: 8 TO 10 SERVINGS.

Mauntez Mayer
Anniston Council

Elloise's Teenagers Delight

1 medium onion, chopped
2 tablespoons vegetable oil
1 pound ground beef
1 teaspoon salt
1/2 teaspoon pepper
1 1/2 cups chopped celery
1 teaspoon chili powder
1 teaspoon each Worcestershire sauce and mustard
1 (10-ounce) can cream of tomato soup
1 teaspoon Italian seasoning
1 tablespoon ketchup

Cook the onion in hot oil in a skillet until golden brown. Add the ground beef, salt and pepper. Cook until ground beef is brown and crumbly, stirring constantly; drain. Add the celery, chili powder, Worcestershire sauce, mustard, soup, Italian seasoning and ketchup and mix well. Simmer, covered, for 30 minutes. Serve over rice or toasted buns. YIELD: 4 SERVINGS.

Margaret Copelin
Montgomery Life

MEATS

Farmhouse Muffins

1 (8-count) package refrigerated buttermilk biscuits
1 pound ground beef or chuck
1/2 cup ketchup
3 tablespoons brown sugar
1/2 teaspoon chili powder
1 cup shredded sharp Cheddar cheese

Separate the biscuits and flatten into circles. Press each biscuit over the bottom and up the side of a greased muffin cup. Brown the ground beef in a skillet, stirring until crumbly; drain. Combine the ketchup, brown sugar and chili powder in a bowl and mix well. Stir in the cooked ground beef. Spoon 1/4 cup of the ground beef mixture into each biscuit-lined muffin cup. Sprinkle with the cheese. Bake at 375 degrees for 18 to 20 minutes. YIELD: 8 SERVINGS.

Debbie Morris
Birmingham South Cahaba Council

Bourbon-Glazed Ham

1 (10- to 12-pound) cooked ham
1 cup bourbon
1 cup packed light brown sugar
1 teaspoon grated orange zest
1/4 teaspoon ground cloves
Whole cloves

Place the ham in a roasting pan. Bake at 325 degrees for 2 hours. Combine the bourbon, brown sugar, orange zest and ground cloves in a bowl and mix well. Let stand for 30 minutes, stirring occasionally. Remove the skin from the ham. Score the fat into 1-inch diamonds. Insert a clove in each diamond point. Brush with 1/2 of the bourbon mixture. Bake for 1 hour longer, basting frequently with the remaining bourbon mixture. YIELD: 24 SERVINGS.

Mrs. Barclay Dempster
Mobile Council

My Mother's Great Ham

1 cooked ham butt
1/2 cup water
1 (12-ounce) can Coca-Cola
Brown sugar

Line a roasting pan with foil, allowing enough foil to hang over the edge to cover the ham. Place the ham on the foil in the pan. Pour the water around the ham. Pour the Coca-Cola over the ham. Pat the brown sugar over the ham. Seal the foil around the ham. Bake at 325 degrees for 15 minutes per pound. YIELD: VARIABLE.

Jack D. Phillips
Birmingham South Life

Grilled Ham Steak

1/4 cup apricot or plum preserves
1 tablespoon prepared mustard
1 teaspoon lemon juice
1/8 teaspoon cinnamon
1 (2-pound 1-inch thick) ham steak

Combine the preserves, mustard, lemon juice and cinnamon in a saucepan. Cook over medium heat for 2 to 3 minutes, stirring constantly. Score the fat edge of the ham. Grill over medium-hot coals for 8 to 10 minutes per side, brushing with the preserve mixture during the last 5 minutes. YIELD: 6 SERVINGS.

Alice Walski
Birmingham Life

Weekend Breakfast Casserole

4 or 5 slices wheat or pumpernickel bread, toasted, cubed
Lean ham to taste, cooked, cubed
Maple-flavored bacon to taste, crisp-cooked, crumbled
Chopped green bell pepper to taste
Chopped onion to taste
1 can sliced mushrooms, drained
1 medium tomato, sliced
Shredded Cheddar cheese
6 eggs, beaten
Salt and pepper to taste
1½ tablespoons milk

Combine the bread, ham, bacon, bell pepper, onion and mushrooms in a bowl and mix well. Spoon into a greased baking dish. Arrange the tomato slices over the ham mixture. Sprinkle the cheese over the tomatoes. Combine the eggs, salt, pepper and milk in a bowl and mix well. Pour over the layers. Bake at 350 degrees for 30 to 40 minutes or until set. Cut into squares. You may substitute cooked, crumbled sausage or corned beef hash for the ham.
YIELD: 6 SERVINGS.

Gussie Evans
Mobile Council

HELPFUL HINT

To reduce cleanup and enhance flavor, use celery tops as a basting brush.

Ham and Egg Pizza

1 (8-count) package crescent rolls
2 cups finely chopped cooked ham
1 cup frozen shredded hash brown potatoes
1 cup shredded Cheddar cheese
3 eggs, beaten
2 tablespoons milk
1/8 teaspoon pepper
1/2 cup grated Parmesan cheese

Unroll the crescent roll dough. Place over the bottom and up the side of a 12-inch pizza pan, pressing the perforations to seal. Bake at 350 degrees for 5 minutes. Sprinkle the ham, potatoes and Cheddar cheese over the crust. Combine the eggs, milk and pepper in a bowl and mix well. Pour over the layers. Sprinkle the Parmesan cheese over the top. Bake for 25 to 30 minutes or until eggs are set. YIELD: 6 SERVINGS.

Vauline Terry
Tuscaloosa Council

Ham and Cheese Quiche

1 (1-crust) pie pastry
½ cup milk
½ cup mayonnaise
2 eggs, lightly beaten
1 tablespoon cornstarch
1½ cups diced ham
1½ cups cubed Swiss cheese
⅓ cup chopped green bell pepper
½ cup sliced green onions
Dash of pepper

Line a 9-inch deep-dish quiche or pie pan with the pastry, trimming the excess pastry around the edge. Place a piece of buttered foil buttered side down over the pastry. Place dried beans in the foil-lined shell. Bake at 400 degrees for 10 minutes. Remove the beans and foil. Prick the shell several times with a fork. Bake for 3 to 5 minutes or until light brown. Let stand until cool. Combine the milk, mayonnaise, eggs and cornstarch in a bowl and mix until smooth. Stir in the ham, cheese, bell pepper, green onions and pepper. Spoon into the pie shell. Bake at 350 degrees for 40 to 50 minutes or until set. YIELD: 4 SERVINGS.

Neida Taylor
Bon Secour Life

HELPFUL HINT

Use ground or chopped leftover meats as sandwich spreads.

Rio Grande Pork Roast

½ teaspoon salt
½ teaspoon garlic salt
½ teaspoon chili powder
1 (4- to 5-pound) boneless rolled pork loin roast
1 cup apple jelly
1 cup ketchup
2 tablespoons vinegar
1 teaspoon chili powder
1 cup crushed corn chips

Combine the salt, garlic salt and ½ teaspoon chili powder in a bowl and mix well. Rub over the roast. Place the pork fat side up on a rack in a shallow roasting pan. Roast at 325 degrees for 2 to 2½ hours or until the pork registers 165 degrees on a meat thermometer. Combine the jelly, ketchup, vinegar and 1 teaspoon chili powder in a small saucepan and mix well. Bring to a boil. Reduce the heat. Simmer for 2 minutes. Reserve ½ of the glaze. Brush the remaining glaze over the roast. Sprinkle with the corn chips. Bake for an additional 10 to 15 minutes or until the pork registers 170 degrees on a meat thermometer. Let stand for 10 minutes. Serve with the reserved glaze. YIELD: 12 TO 15 SERVINGS.

Judy Brantley
Gadsden Life

HELPFUL HINT

Cut several slits in the fat on the edge of steak to keep it from curling.

CROCK-POT® Pork Chops

8 to 10 pork chops
Salt and pepper to taste
2 cups flour
1/4 cup water
2 (10-ounce) cans cream of celery soup
1 (10-ounce) can Cheddar cheese soup
1 onion, chopped
1/2 cup chopped celery
1/4 cup chopped bell pepper
1 cup shredded Cheddar cheese

Season the pork chops with the salt and pepper. Coat with the flour. Brown on both sides in a skillet. Arrange 1/2 of the pork chops over the bottom of the CROCK-POT® Slow Cooker. Pour the water over the pork chops. Layer 1/2 of the celery soup, 1/2 of the cheese soup, 1/2 of the onion, 1/2 of the celery and 1/2 of the bell pepper over the pork chops. Arrange the remaining pork chops over the layers. Layer the remaining celery soup, remaining cheese soup, remaining onion, remaining celery and remaining bell pepper over the pork chops. Sprinkle the cheese over the top. Cook on High for 5 to 6 hours or on Low for 8 to 12 hours. Serve over rice.
YIELD: 8 TO 10 SERVINGS.

Barbara Seegmiller
Decatur Council

HELPFUL HINT

Use rib, blade, arm and loin and pork chops instead of center cuts. They are just as delicious and nutritious and cost less.

Pork Chop Bake

4 pork chops
Flour for coating
Vegetable oil
1 cup rice
1 cup water
1 (10-ounce) can cream of
 mushroom soup
1 envelope onion soup mix
Chopped onion (optional)

Coat the pork chops with the flour. Brown the pork chops on both sides in hot oil in a skillet. Combine the rice, water, soup, soup mix and onion in a bowl and mix well. Spoon into a baking dish. Arrange the pork chops over the rice mixture. Bake, covered, at 350 degrees for 1 to 1 1/4 hours or until rice is tender and pork chops are cooked through. **YIELD: 4 SERVINGS.**

Fay Clark
Riverchase Council

Cuban Pork Chops

1 (15-ounce) can black beans,
 drained, rinsed
4 bone-in pork chops
1 (15-ounce) can sweet
 potatoes in syrup, drained
1/3 cup frozen orange juice
 concentrate, thawed
1 1/2 teaspoons cumin
1 teaspoon garlic salt
1 teaspoon hot sauce

Cut four 12×18-inch pieces of heavy duty foil. Place 1/4 of the beans in the center of each piece. Place a pork chop on top of the beans. Arrange 1/4 of the sweet potatoes around each pork chop. Combine the orange juice concentrate, cumin, garlic salt and hot sauce in a bowl and mix well. Spoon evenly over the tops of the pork chops. Seal the sides of the foil loosely over the pork chops. Place the foil packets on a baking sheet. Bake at 450 degrees for 25 to 30 minutes or until pork chops are cooked through. **YIELD: 4 SERVINGS.**

Billie Harrison
Shoals Life

Mandarin Pork Chops

4 (4-ounce) center-cut pork chops
1 tablespoon vegetable oil
½ cup orange juice
¼ cup water
3 tablespoons brown sugar
2 tablespoons lemon juice
1 tablespoon cornstarch
2 teaspoons chicken bouillon granules
1 (11-ounce) can mandarin oranges, drained
1 medium green bell pepper, sliced

Brown the pork chops on both sides in the oil in a skillet. Remove from the skillet and set aside. Add the orange juice, water, brown sugar, lemon juice, cornstarch and bouillon to the skillet. Cook until thickened, stirring constantly. Add the pork chops. Simmer, covered, for 20 minutes or until pork chops are tender and cooked through. Add the oranges and bell pepper. Cook until heated through. YIELD: 4 SERVINGS.

Hazel E. Campbell
Birmingham Life

Sweet and Sour Pork Chops

6 (4- to 5-ounce) center-cut pork chops
Vegetable oil
1 (20-ounce) can pineapple chunks in heavy syrup
1/2 cup lemon juice
3 tablespoons cornstarch
1/2 cup packed brown sugar
1/4 cup chopped onion
1 tablespoon soy sauce
1 teaspoon chicken bouillon granules, or
1 chicken bouillon cube
1 cup thinly sliced carrots
Green bell pepper rings

Brown the pork chops on both sides in hot oil in a large ovenproof skillet; drain. Remove from the skillet. Drain the pineapple, reserving the syrup. Combine the lemon juice and cornstarch in the skillet and mix well. Add the brown sugar, onion, soy sauce, bouillon and reserved pineapple syrup. Cook until thickened and bouillon is dissolved, stirring constantly. Add the pork chops and carrots. Bake, covered, at 350 degrees for 1 hour or until pork chops are tender and cooked through. Add the pineapple. Bake, covered, for an additional 10 minutes. Garnish with the bell pepper rings. Serve with rice. YIELD: 6 SERVINGS.

Hazel E. Campbell
Birmingham Life

Stuffed Pork Chops

3 tablespoons butter
2 tablespoons chopped onion
1 cup chopped celery
1/2 teaspoon poultry seasoning

2 cups bread crumbs
4 pork chops with pockets
Paprika

Heat the butter in a skillet until melted. Add the onion, celery and poultry seasoning. Cook until onion and celery are tender, stirring frequently. Add the bread crumbs and mix well. Spoon the bread crumb mixture into the pork chop pockets. Place the stuffed pork chops in a baking pan. Sprinkle with the paprika. Bake at 350 degrees for 45 minutes or until cooked through. YIELD: 4 SERVINGS.

Ila Skidmore
Shoals Life

Pork Chops and Vegetables

4 pork chops
Salt and pepper to taste
2 tablespoons vegetable oil
1/2 cup water

4 potatoes, cut into pieces
3 carrots, cut into pieces
2 cabbage wedges

Season the pork chops with salt and pepper. Heat the oil in a large pot. Add the pork chops. Brown on both sides. Pour the water over the pork chops. Add the potatoes and carrots. Add the cabbage. Sprinkle with salt and pepper. Cook, covered, over low heat for 1 hour or until vegetables are tender and pork chops are cooked through. YIELD: 4 SERVINGS.

Margaret W. Wilborn
Gadsden Life

Brunch Puff

8 slices bacon
2 onions, sliced
12 slices white bread, cut into quarters
8 ounces Swiss cheese, shredded
8 eggs
4 cups milk
1 1/2 teaspoons salt
1/4 teaspoon pepper

Cook the bacon in a skillet until crisp. Remove the bacon and crumble. Cook the onions in the bacon drippings until tender. Layer the bread, bacon, onions and cheese 1/2 at a time in a greased 9x13-inch baking pan. Combine the eggs, milk, salt and pepper in a bowl and mix well. Pour over the layers. You may refrigerate, covered, at this point. Bake at 350 degrees for 45 to 50 minutes or until set and puffed. YIELD: 8 SERVINGS.

Hazel E. Campbell
Birmingham Life

Brunch Casserole

1 1/2 pounds mild sausage
9 eggs
2 1/2 cups milk
1 teaspoon salt
1 teaspoon dry mustard
6 slices bread, cubed
1 1/2 cups shredded cheese

Brown the sausage in a skillet, stirring until crumbly; drain. Beat the eggs in a mixing bowl. Beat in the milk, salt and dry mustard. Arrange the bread cubes evenly over the bottom of a large baking pan. Sprinkle the sausage and cheese over the bread. Pour the egg mixture over the top. Refrigerate, covered, for 8 to 12 hours. Bake at 350 degrees for 45 minutes. YIELD: 12 SERVINGS.

Mary Haynes
Birmingham South Cahaba Council

Grits and Sausage Casserole

1 cup quick-cooking grits
4 cups water
1 teaspoon salt
½ cup (1 stick) margarine
1 pound pork sausage
4 eggs, beaten
½ cup milk
1½ cups shredded Cheddar cheese

Place the grits in a saucepan. Add the water, stirring constantly. Stir in the salt. Cook for 5 minutes. Remove from the heat. Add the margarine to the hot mixture, stirring until melted. Brown the sausage in a skillet, stirring until crumbly; drain. Whisk the eggs and milk together in a bowl. Add the sausage and egg mixture to the grits and mix well. Stir in 1 cup of the cheese. Spoon into a 9×13-inch baking dish. Sprinkle the remaining ½ cup cheese over the top. Bake at 350 degrees for 40 minutes or until set and bubbly.
Yield: 8 to 10 servings.

Emogene Husby
Mobile Council

Andrea's Hash Brown Casserole

2 pounds hot or mild sausage
2 cups shredded Cheddar cheese
1 (10-ounce) can cream of chicken soup
1 cup sour cream
1 (8-ounce) container French onion dip
1 cup chopped onion
1/4 cup chopped green bell pepper
1/4 cup chopped red bell pepper
Salt and pepper to taste
1 (30-ounce) package frozen hash brown shredded potatoes, thawed

Brown the sausage in a skillet, stirring until crumbly; drain. Combine the cheese, soup, sour cream, dip, onion, bell peppers, salt and pepper in a bowl. Fold in the potatoes. Layer the potato mixture and sausage 1/2 at a time in a greased 9x13-inch baking pan. Bake at 350 degrees for 1 hour or until golden brown.
YIELD: 8 TO 10 SERVINGS.

Andrea Dutton
Anniston Council

Make Ahead Breakfast Bake

1 pound sausage, cooked, crumbled
3 slices bread, cubed
1 cup shredded Cheddar cheese
4 eggs, lightly beaten
1 cup milk
1/2 teaspoon salt

Combine the sausage, bread, cheese, eggs, milk and salt in a bowl and mix well. Spoon into a greased 9x13-inch baking pan. Chill, covered, for 12 hours. You may freeze at this point and thaw in the refrigerator before baking. Bake at 350 degrees for 35 minutes. Cut into squares and serve hot. YIELD: 6 SERVINGS.

Patricia Allen
Selma Life

Sausage Casserole

1 pound sausage
1 (10-ounce) can cream of chicken soup
2 eggs
1/4 cup milk
1 cup crisp rice cereal
3/4 cup rice
1 cup shredded cheese
1 cup crisp rice cereal

Brown the sausage in a skillet, stirring until crumbly; drain. Combine the soup, eggs and milk in a bowl and mix well. Layer 1 cup rice cereal, sausage, rice, cheese, egg mixture and 1 cup rice cereal in a greased 9×13-inch baking dish. Bake at 350 degrees for 30 minutes. **YIELD: 8 TO 10 SERVINGS.**

Willie Mae Jordan
Gadsden Life

Sausage, Egg and Cheese Quiche

1 pound sausage
1 large yellow onion, chopped
1 green bell pepper, chopped
6 eggs
2 cups shredded extra-sharp Cheddar cheese
2 all-ready pie pastries

Brown the sausage with the onion and bell pepper in a skillet, stirring until sausage is crumbly; drain. Add the eggs and cheese and mix well. Fit one of the pastries into a pie plate. Spoon the sausage mixture into the pastry-lined pie plate. Top with the remaining pastry, sealing the edge and cutting vents. Bake at 350 degrees for 45 to 55 minutes or until set. **YIELD: 6 SERVINGS.**

Mary Ann Stanley
Mobile Council

Karmen's Breakfast Pizza

1 pound bulk pork sausage
1 (8-count) package
  crescent rolls
3 eggs
1/4 cup milk
1/2 teaspoon salt
1/8 teaspoon pepper
1 cup frozen hash brown
  potatoes, thawed
1 cup shredded sharp Cheddar
  cheese
2 tablespoons grated
  Parmesan cheese

Brown the sausage in a skillet, stirring until crumbly; drain. Separate the crescent roll dough into triangles. Arrange dough over the bottom of a 12-inch pizza pan, pressing up the side of the pan and pressing the perforations to seal. Combine the eggs, milk, salt and pepper in a bowl and mix well. Layer the sausage, potatoes, Cheddar cheese and egg mixture over the dough. Sprinkle the Parmesan cheese over the top. Bake at 375 degrees for 25 to 30 minutes or until set. YIELD: 6 SERVINGS.

Karmen Patterson-Sutton
Birmingham Life

Sausage Roll

2 cups baking mix
Water
1 pound mild bulk sausage,
  room temperature

Combine the baking mix with enough water in a bowl to make crumbly. Roll into a thin rectangle. Spread the sausage over the dough. Roll to enclose the filling. Chill, covered, for 4 to 5 hours. Cut into 1/4- to 1/2-inch-thick slices. Arrange the slices on a baking sheet. Bake at 400 degrees until brown. You may use hot sausage and add shredded cheese to the dough.
YIELD: 13 TO 15 SERVINGS.

Tammy Donner
Birmingham South Cahaba Council

German Cabbage and Sausage

1 or 2 onions, thinly sliced
1 medium package smoked beef sausage or polish link sausage
2 cups water
2 or 3 carrots, sliced
2 or 3 potatoes, sliced
¼ teaspoon salt
¼ teaspoon pepper
1 head of cabbage, cut into quarters
2 teaspoons sugar
1 (12-ounce) can beer

Combine the onions, sausage and water in a large pot. Bring to a boil. Boil for 5 minutes.; drain Layer the carrots, potatoes, salt and pepper ½ at a time in a large pot. Add the sausage mixture and cabbage. Sprinkle with sugar. Pour the beer over the layers. Cook, covered, over medium heat for 30 to 40 minutes or until vegetables are tender. **Yield: 4 to 6 servings.**

Neida Taylor
Bon Secour Life

Easy Red Beans and Rice

1 pound dried red kidney beans
1 large onion, chopped
1 teaspoon garlic salt, or to taste
1½ tablespoons chili powder
1 tablespoon parsley
Salt to taste
1 pound smoked sausage, cut into bite-size pieces

Rinse and sort the beans. Combine the beans, onion, garlic salt, chili powder, parsley and salt in a large saucepan. Cook using the package directions on the beans until the beans are almost tender. Stir in the sausage. Cook until the beans are tender. Remove ½ cup of the beans and place in a bowl; mash. Stir into the bean mixture. Simmer until mixture thickens. Serve over hot cooked rice.
Yield: 4 to 6 servings.

Rubie McInnis
Birmingham Life

Tramp Eggs

6 teaspoons bacon drippings
6 tablespoons milk
6 eggs
Salt and pepper to taste
Shredded cheese

Place 1 teaspoon bacon drippings into each of 6 buttered muffin cups. Add 1 tablespoon milk to each muffin cup. Break 1 egg into each cup. Sprinkle with salt and pepper. Sprinkle shredded cheese over each egg. Bake at 300 degrees until cheese is bubbly and eggs are cooked through. YIELD: 6 SERVINGS.

Adeline Neal
Birmingham Life

Venison Roast

Venison roast
1/2 cup steak sauce
1 onion, chopped
1 bell pepper, chopped
1 tablespoon dried celery
1 (12-ounce) can cola
Barbeque sauce

Rinse the venison roast. Place in a CROCK-POT® Slow Cooker. Pour the steak sauce over the roast. Sprinkle the onion, bell pepper and celery over the roast. Pour the cola over the top. Cook on Low until the roast is cooked through. Remove the roast and chop. Combine the chopped roast and barbecue sauce in a large bowl and mix well. YIELD: 10 SERVINGS.

Jim Miller
Anniston Council

Barbecue Rabbit in Barbecue Sauce

Rabbit
Salt to taste
Barbecue Sauce (below)

Sprinkle the rabbit with salt. Coat with Barbecue Sauce. Place in a greased non-recycled paper bag. Bake at 350 degrees for 1½ hours. Reduce the oven temperature to 250 degrees. Bake for 15 minutes longer. YIELD: VARIABLE.

Barbecue Sauce

For a small amount:
- 3 tablespoons ketchup
- 2 tablespoons vinegar
- 1 tablespoon lemon juice
- 2 tablespoons Worcestershire sauce
- ¼ cup water
- 2 tablespoons butter or margarine
- 3 tablespoons brown sugar
- 1 teaspoon salt
- 1 teaspoon dry mustard
- 1 teaspoon chili powder
- 1 teaspoon paprika
- ½ teaspoon red pepper

For a large amount:
- 1 cup ketchup
- ⅔ cup vinegar
- ⅓ cup lemon juice
- ⅔ cup Worcestershire sauce
- 1½ cups water
- ½ cup (1 stick) butter or margarine
- 1 cup packed brown sugar
- 2 tablespoons salt
- 2 tablespoons dry mustard
- 2 tablespoons chili powder
- 2 tablespoons paprika
- 1 tablespoon red pepper

Combine the ketchup, vinegar, lemon juice, Worcestershire sauce, water, butter, brown sugar, salt, dry mustard, chili powder, paprika and red pepper in a saucepan. Cook over low heat until butter melts, stirring frequently.

Eloise Bennett
Decatur Counci

BIRMINGHAM SOUTH CAHABA COUNCIL

Pioneer Volunteers in the Birmingham South Cahaba Council provide Christmas gifts for more than 440 Angel Tree "Angels" each Christmas. The organization and delivery of more than 3,000 gifts involved 500 members. These members and employees make donations of time and money to create a joyous Christmas for children identified by local agencies and schools.

Poultry and Seafood

Capital Chicken Casserole

1/4 cup (1/2 stick) butter
1 tablespoon vegetable oil
1 (3-pound) chicken, cut up
8 ounces fresh mushrooms, sliced
1 tablespoon flour
1 (10-ounce) can cream of chicken soup
1 cup dry white wine
1 cup water
1/2 cup cream
1 teaspoon salt
1/4 teaspoon tarragon
1/4 teaspoon pepper
1 (15-ounce) can artichoke hearts, drained
6 green onions with tops, chopped
2 tablespoons chopped fresh parsley

Heat the butter and oil in a large skillet over medium heat until the butter melts. Add the chicken. Cook for 10 minutes or until the chicken is brown on all sides, turning occasionally. Remove the chicken to a baking dish using a slotted spoon, reserving the pan drippings. Sauté the mushrooms in the reserved pan drippings for 5 minutes or until tender. Stir in the flour. Add the soup, wine and water and mix well. Simmer for 10 minutes or until thickened, stirring frequently. Stir in the cream, salt, tarragon and pepper. Pour over the chicken. Bake at 350 degrees for 1 hour. Stir in the artichokes, green onions and parsley. Bake for 5 minutes longer or until the chicken is cooked through. You may substitute boneless skinless chicken breasts for the whole chicken. YIELD: 4 SERVINGS.

Ann S. Pierce
Birmingham South Cahaba Council

Joyce's Barbecued Chicken

1 (3-pound) chicken, cut up
6 tablespoons mayonnaise
2 tablespoons sugar
1 tablespoon salt
1 tablespoon pepper
3 tablespoons lemon juice
3 tablespoons white vinegar

Arrange the chicken in a single layer in a baking dish. Combine the mayonnaise, sugar, salt and pepper in a bowl and mix well. Stir in the lemon juice and vinegar. Reserve 2 tablespoons of the mayonnaise mixture. Spoon the remaining mayonnaise mixture over the chicken. Bake at 350 degrees for 2 hours or until cooked through, basting with the reserved mayonnaise mixture occasionally. YIELD: 4 SERVINGS.

Lillian Simpson
Decatur Council

Drunk Chicken

1 (3-pound) chicken
Cajun seasoning or your favorite seasoning to taste
1 (12-ounce) can beer

Sprinkle the outside surface of the chicken with Cajun seasoning. Sit the chicken upright on the open can of beer. Cook in a smoker for 3½ hours. Be careful when removing the chicken from the smoker. Use a spatula under the can of beer to help remove the chicken. YIELD: 4 SERVINGS.

Sara Cooley
Birmingham Life

Copycat Kentucky Fried Chicken

3 pounds chicken parts
1/4 cup lemon juice
1 1/2 cups baking mix
2 envelopes Italian salad dressing mix
3 tablespoons flour
2 teaspoons salt
1 teaspoon paprika
1/2 teaspoon sage
1/4 teaspoon pepper
1 cup milk
2 tablespoons butter, melted
Vegetable oil for frying

Combine the chicken and lemon juice in a bowl and toss to coat. Marinate, covered, in the refrigerator for 30 to 60 minutes; drain. Combine the baking mix, salad dressing mix, flour, salt, paprika, sage and pepper in a shallow dish and mix well. Whisk the milk and butter in a bowl until blended. Dip the chicken in the milk mixture and coat with the flour mixture. Fry the chicken in hot oil in a skillet until brown on both sides; drain. Arrange on a baking sheet. Bake at 350 degrees until cooked through and crispy. YIELD: 5 SERVINGS.

Barbara Seegmiller
Decatur Council

HELPFUL HINT

Chop leftover chicken and freeze in measured amounts for use in chicken salads.

Terri's Chicken String Bean Casserole

1 (7-ounce) package chicken-flavor Rice-A-Roni
1 (3-pound) chicken, cooked
2 (15-ounce) cans French-cut string beans, drained
2 (10-ounce) cans cream of chicken soup
½ cup mayonnaise
1 (2-ounce) jar chopped pimento, drained
Salt and pepper to taste
½ cup (1 stick) margarine, melted
1 sleeve butter crackers, crushed

Cook the Rice-A-Roni using package directions. Chop the chicken into bite-size pieces, discarding the skin and bones. Combine the rice, chicken, beans, soup, mayonnaise, pimento, salt and pepper in a bowl and mix well. Spoon into two 9×13-inch baking dishes. Combine the margarine and crackers in a bowl and mix well. Sprinkle over the chicken mixture. Bake at 350 degrees for 45 minutes. You may substitute 4 boneless skinless chicken breasts for the whole chicken. YIELD: 12 TO 18 SERVINGS.

Jo Ann Thomas
Selma Life

Alma's Baked Chicken

3 tablespoons flour
1/2 teaspoon seasoned salt
1/2 teaspoon garlic salt
1/2 teaspoon paprika
1/3 cup margarine, melted
6 chicken breasts, skinned

Combine the flour, seasoned salt, garlic salt and paprika in a bowl and mix well. Stir in the margarine. Coat the chicken the flour mixture. Arrange the chicken in a single layer in a baking pan lined with foil. Bake at 450 degrees for 20 minutes. Reduce the oven temperature to 350 degrees. Bake for 1 hour longer or until cooked through. YIELD: 6 SERVINGS.

Marie Hartley
Birmingham South Life

Baked Chicken

4 boneless skinless chicken breasts
1 tablespoon prepared mustard
Salt and pepper to taste
1/2 (6-ounce) can French-fried onions, crushed

Arrange the chicken in a single layer in a baking pan. Spread the prepared mustard over the chicken. Sprinkle with salt, pepper and onions. Bake at 350 degrees for 30 minutes or until the chicken is cooked through. YIELD: 4 SERVINGS.

Gloria "Carol" Lindley
Birmingham South Cahaba Council

Baked Chicken Breasts

Juice of 3 lemons
1/4 cup olive oil
2 teaspoons oregano
3 garlic cloves, finely chopped
Salt and pepper to taste
6 chicken breasts
Greek seasoning

Whisk the first 6 ingredients in a bowl. Coat the chicken with the lemon juice mixture. Sprinkle with the Greek seasoning. Arrange the chicken in a single layer in a baking dish; do not allow the chicken to touch. Bake at 450 degrees for 10 minutes; cover with foil. Reduce the oven temperature to 350 degrees. Bake for 1 1/2 to 2 hours longer or until the chicken is cooked through. **YIELD: 6 SERVINGS.**

Virginia Greene
Birmingham South Life

Creamy Chicken Bake

4 boneless skinless chicken breasts, split, flattened
4 (4x8-inch) slices Swiss cheese
1 (10-ounce) can cream of broccoli soup
1 cup milk
1 cup herb stuffing mix, crushed
1/4 cup (1/2 stick) butter or margarine, melted

Arrange the chicken in a single layer in a greased 9x13-inch baking pan. Top with the cheese. Combine the soup and milk in a bowl and mix well. Spread over the cheese. Toss the stuffing mix and butter in a small bowl until mixed. Sprinkle over the cheese. Bake at 350 degrees for 30 minutes or until the chicken is cooked through. **YIELD: 4 SERVINGS.**

Donna Jean Bowman
Birmingham South Cahaba Council

Deborah's Chicken Delight

1/2 cup seasoned bread crumbs
1/2 cup finely shredded Cheddar cheese
1/4 cup finely grated Parmesan cheese
1/2 teaspoon salt, or to taste
1/8 teaspoon pepper, or to taste
4 chicken breasts
1/2 cup (1 stick) margarine, melted

Combine the bread crumbs, Cheddar cheese, Parmesan cheese, salt and pepper in a shallow dish and mix well. Dip the chicken in the margarine and coat with the bread crumb mixture. Arrange the chicken in a single layer in a baking pan. Drizzle with any leftover butter and sprinkle with any leftover bread crumb mixture. Bake at 350 degrees for 30 to 40 minutes or until cooked through. YIELD: 4 SERVINGS.

Virginia Bowen
Shoals Life

Lipton Chicken

2 cups water
1/2 cup (1 stick) butter, melted
1 envelope Lipton's onion soup mix
1 cup uncooked rice
6 chicken breasts

Combine the water, butter and soup mix in a bowl and mix well. Stir in the rice. Spread in a baking dish. Arrange the chicken skin side down over the rice mixture. Bake, covered, at 350 degrees for 1 hour or until the chicken is cooked through and the rice is tender. YIELD: 4 SERVINGS.

Sheila P. Brothers
Anniston Council

Pan-Fried Chicken

4 boneless skinless chicken breasts
1 cup dry bread crumbs

1/2 teaspoon garlic powder
1/8 teaspoon light salt
1 tablespoon vegetable oil

Pound the chicken lightly between sheets of waxed paper. Mix the bread crumbs, garlic powder and salt in a shallow dish. Coat the chicken with the crumb mixture. Let stand for several minutes to allow the coating to adhere. Spray a skillet with nonstick cooking spray. Heat over medium heat until hot. Add 1 1/2 teaspoons of the oil, tilting the skillet to coat the bottom. Add the chicken. Panfry until brown on 1 side. Add the remaining 1 1/2 teaspoons oil. Turn the chicken. Panfry until cooked through. YIELD: 4 SERVINGS.

Gloria "Carol" Lindley
Birmingham South Cahaba Council

Angel Chicken Pasta

6 chicken breasts
Garlic powder to taste
Pepper to taste
1/4 cup (1/2 stick) butter or margarine
1 (10-ounce) can golden mushroom soup

1/2 cup white wine
4 ounces cream cheese, softened
1 envelope Italian salad dressing mix
12 ounces angel hair pasta, cooked, drained

Sprinkle the chicken with the garlic powder and pepper. Arrange in a single layer in a baking pan. Heat the butter in a saucepan until melted. Stir in the soup, wine, cream cheese and salad dressing mix. Cook until blended, stirring constantly. Spoon over the chicken. Bake at 325 degrees for 1 hour or until the chicken is cooked through. Spoon over the pasta on dinner plates. YIELD: 6 SERVINGS.

Sara Hyatt
Gadsden Life

Shirley's Chicken and Rice

4 chicken tenderloins
2½ cups water
2 cups instant rice
Salt and pepper to taste

Combine the chicken and water in a large saucepan. Cook until the chicken is cooked through. Stir in the rice. Bring to a boil. Boil until the rice is tender and the liquid has been absorbed. Season with salt and pepper. YIELD: 4 SERVINGS.

Margaret Copelin
Montgomery Life

Chicken Casserole

1 (6-ounce) can French-fried onions
1½ cups instant rice
¼ cup shredded cheese
4 chicken breasts, or 4 to 6 chicken parts
1 (10-ounce) can cream of mushroom soup
½ soup can water
Paprika to taste

Grease the bottom and sides of a baking dish. Layer the onions, rice and cheese in the order listed in the prepared baking dish. Arrange the chicken skin side up over the prepared layers. Combine the soup and water in a bowl and mix well. Spread over the chicken. Sprinkle with paprika. Bake, covered, at 300 degrees for 1½ hours or until the chicken is cooked through, removing the cover 10 minutes before the end of baking. YIELD: 4 SERVINGS.

Mary Alice Neal
Birmingham Life

Chicken-Rice Casserole

1 (10-ounce) can cream of mushroom soup
1 (10-ounce) can cream of chicken soup
1 cup rice
1 cup shredded cheese
3 boneless skinless chicken breasts

Combine the soups in a bowl and mix well. Rinse the soup cans, adding enough water to the soup mixture to measure ½ cup. Stir in the rice and cheese. Spoon the rice mixture into a baking dish. Arrange the chicken over the rice mixture. Bake at 350 degrees for 1 hour or until the chicken is cooked through. YIELD: 3 SERVINGS.

Elise C. Riddle
Opelika Life

Light and Sticky Chicken

⅓ cup honey
¼ cup prepared mustard
2 tablespoons butter
1 teaspoon curry powder
¼ teaspoon salt
4 (8-ounce) chicken breasts, skinned

Combine the first 5 ingredients in a saucepan. Cook over low heat until blended, stirring frequently. Place the chicken in a sealable plastic bag. Pour the honey mixture over the chicken and seal tightly. Turn to coat. Marinate in the refrigerator for 2 to 10 hours, turning occasionally. Arrange the undrained chicken in a single layer in a 9x13-inch baking pan sprayed with nonstick cooking spray. Bake at 400 degrees for 30 to 40 minutes or until the chicken is cooked through, basting with the pan juices 3 times. YIELD: 4 SERVINGS.

Mary C. Martin
Birmingham Life

Carrot and Zucchini-Stuffed Chicken Breasts

4 boneless chicken breasts
1 cup shredded carrots
1 cup shredded zucchini
1 teaspoon salt
1/4 teaspoon poultry seasoning
1/4 cup water
1 chicken bouillon cube, crushed

Cut a lengthwise slit in the side of each chicken breast to form a pocket. Combine the carrots, zucchini, salt and poultry seasoning in a bowl and mix well. Spoon equal amounts of the carrot mixture into each pocket. Secure with wooden picks. Pour the water into a skillet. Add the chicken. Sprinkle with the crushed bouillon. Bring to a boil over medium-high heat. Reduce the heat. Simmer, covered, for 35 to 40 minutes or until the chicken is cooked through. Discard the wooden picks. Serve over steamed rice. **Yield: 4 servings.**

Gussie Evans
Mobile Council

Sticky Chicken

1 cup packed brown sugar
3/4 cup soy sauce
1/2 cup teriyaki sauce
1/2 cup (1 stick) butter or margarine, melted
1 tablespoon Creole seasoning
1 teaspoon dry mustard
2 pounds chicken wings

Combine the brown sugar, soy sauce, teriyaki sauce, butter, Creole seasoning and dry mustard in a bowl and mix well. Pour over the chicken in a sealable plastic bag and seal tightly. Turn to coat. Marinate in the refrigerator for 1 to 10 hours, turning occasionally; drain. Arrange the chicken in a baking pan. Bake at 375 degrees for 1 hour. **Yield: 20 servings.**

Frankie Vaughn
Selma Life

Cashew Chicken

1½ cups milk
¾ cup soy sauce
6 eggs, beaten
1½ teaspoons garlic salt
1 teaspoon curry powder
6 boneless skinless chicken breasts, cut into 1-inch pieces
4 cups self-rising flour
Vegetable oil for frying
1 quart chicken broth
½ cup soy sauce
1 teaspoon garlic salt
Cornstarch
1½ cups rice, cooked
Chopped green onions
Cashews to taste

Whisk the milk, ¾ cup soy sauce, eggs, garlic salt and curry powder in a bowl until blended. Add the chicken and turn to coat. Marinate, covered, in the refrigerator for 8 to 10 hours, or as long as possible. Drain, reserving the marinade. Coat the chicken with the flour and dip in the reserved marinade twice. Fry the chicken in hot oil in a skillet until golden brown and cooked through; drain. Remove the chicken to a platter. Cover to keep warm. Combine the broth, ½ cup soy sauce and 1 teaspoon garlic salt in a saucepan and mix well. Add a mixture of cornstarch and a small amount of water to the broth mixture. Cook until thickened and of a gravy consistency, stirring constantly. Serve the chicken with rice. Drizzle with the gravy. Top with green onions and cashews. **Yield: 6 servings.**

Virginia Sims
Montgomery Life

Chicken Cannelloni

1 (3-pound) chicken
1 green bell pepper
1 tomato
2 large carrots
1 medium onion
2 ribs celery
1 (6-ounce) can tomato paste
1 package cannelloni or large shell macaroni
2 cups sour cream
2 cups shredded cheese

Combine the chicken, bell pepper, tomato, carrots, onion and celery with enough water to cover in a stockpot. Bring to a boil over high heat; reduce the heat. Simmer until the chicken is cooked through. Remove the chicken to a platter, reserving the vegetables and liquid. Press the vegetables through a sieve and return the mixture to the reserved liquid. Bring to a boil. Stir in the tomato paste. Boil for 20 minutes longer or until of a sauce consistency, stirring occasionally. Chop the chicken, discarding the bones and skin. Dip the chicken in the sauce. Cook the pasta using package directions until al dente; drain. Stuff the cannelloni with the chicken. Layer the stuffed cannelloni, sauce, sour cream and cheese in the order listed in a baking dish sprayed with nonstick cooking spray. Bake at 350 degrees for 30 to 45 minutes or until bubbly.
YIELD: 8 SERVINGS.

Bill Cole
Tuscaloosa Council

Chicken Casserole

1 (6-ounce) package long grain and wild rice
1 (3½- to 4-pound) chicken, cooked, drained
1 (16-ounce) can French-style green beans, drained
1 (10-ounce) can cream of celery soup
1 soup can water
1 (8-ounce) can sliced water chestnuts, drained
1 cup mayonnaise
1 medium onion, chopped
1 (2-ounce) jar chopped pimento, drained

Cook the rice using package directions. Chop the chicken, discarding the skin and bones. Combine the rice, chicken, green beans, soup, water, water chestnuts, mayonnaise, onion and pimento in a bowl and mix well. Spoon into a baking dish sprayed with nonstick cooking spray. Bake at 350 degrees for 30 to 35 minutes or until brown and bubbly. YIELD: 10 TO 14 SERVINGS.

Blanche T. Hooper
Anniston Council

Chicken Casserole

4 to 6 chicken breasts, cooked, drained
2 cups cream of chicken soup
1 cup sour cream
1 sleeve butter crackers, crushed
½ cup (1 stick) butter, melted

Chop the chicken, discarding the skin and bones. Arrange the chopped chicken in a baking dish. Combine the soup and sour cream in a bowl and mix well. Spread over the chicken. Sprinkle with the crackers and drizzle with the butter. Bake at 350 degrees for 30 to 40 minutes or until bubbly. YIELD: 4 TO 6 SERVINGS.

Fay Clark
Riverchase Council

Chicken Cordon Bleu Casserole

4 cups chopped cooked chicken
3 cups cubed cooked ham
1 cup shredded Cheddar cheese
1 cup chopped onion
1/4 cup (1/2 stick) butter or margarine
1/3 cup flour
2 cups light cream
1 teaspoon dillweed
1/8 teaspoon dry mustard
1/8 teaspoon nutmeg
1 cup dry bread crumbs
2 tablespoons butter or margarine, melted
1/4 teaspoon dillweed
1/4 cup shredded Cheddar cheese
1/4 cup chopped walnuts

Toss the chicken, ham and 1 cup cheese in a bowl. Sauté the onion in 1/4 cup butter in a skillet until tender. Add the flour, stirring until a paste forms. Add the cream gradually, stirring constantly. Bring to a boil. Boil for 1 minute or until thickened, stirring constantly. Stir in 1 teaspoon dillweed, dry mustard and nutmeg. Remove from the heat. Add to the chicken mixture and mix well. Spoon into a greased 9×13-inch baking dish. Toss the bread crumbs, 2 tablespoons butter and 1/4 teaspoon dillweed in a bowl. Stir in 1/4 cup cheese and walnuts. Sprinkle over the top. Bake at 350 degrees for 30 minutes or until bubbly. Yield: **8 to 10** servings.

Hester P. Thompson
Birmingham Life

Chicken Crunc[h]

2½ cups chopped cooked chicken
1 (8-ounce) can sliced water chestnuts, drained
1 (3-ounce) can mushrooms, drained
1½ cups chopped celery
½ cup ch[opped onion]
1 tablesp[oon lemon juice]
Salt and [pepper to taste]
1 cup mayonnaise
1 (10-ounce) can cream of chicken soup

Combine the chicken, water chestnuts, mushrooms, celery, onion, lemon juice, salt and pepper in a bowl and mix well. Combine the mayonnaise and soup in a bowl and mix well. Add to the chicken mixture, stirring until coated. Spoon the chicken mixture into a lightly buttered 9×13-inch baking pan. Bake at 350 degrees for 20 minutes or until brown and bubbly. You may top with crushed potato chips, shredded cheese or almond slivers before baking.
YIELD: 6 TO 8 SERVINGS.

Virginia Murphy
Montgomery Life

Great Chicken

8 cups chopped cooked chicken
2 (10-ounce) cans cream of chicken soup
1 cup sour cream
25 crackers, crushed
2 tablespoons butter, melted
1 teaspoon celery seeds

Combine the chicken, soup and sour cream in a bowl and mix well. Spread in a 9×13-inch baking dish sprayed with nonstick cooking spray. Toss the cracker crumbs, butter and celery seeds in a bowl. Sprinkle over the prepared layer. Bake at 350 degrees for 30 to 35 minutes or until brown and bubbly. **YIELD: 10 TO 12 SERVINGS.**

Virginia Sherrer
Selma Life

Oriental Chicken Casserole

2 cups chopped cooked chicken
1 (3- to 5-ounce) can chow mein noodles
1 (3-ounce) can chopped mushrooms, drained
1 cup chopped celery
1/2 cup chopped onion
1 (2-ounce) can chopped pimentos, drained
1 (10-ounce) can cream of chicken soup
3/4 cup mayonnaise

Combine the chicken, noodles, mushrooms, celery, onion and pimentos in a bowl and mix well. Stir in a mixture of the soup and mayonnaise. Spoon into a buttered 9x13-inch baking dish. Bake at 350 degrees for 30 minutes. You may reserve 1/3 of the chow mein noodles and sprinkle over the top just before serving. YIELD: 8 SERVINGS.

Dilla Samuel
Gadsden Life

Poppy Seed Chicken Casserole

1 (3-pound) chicken, cooked, drained
1 (10-ounce) can cream of chicken soup
1 (10-ounce) can cream of mushroom soup
1 cup sour cream
1/4 cup poppy seeds
2 envelopes ranch salad dressing mix
65 butter crackers, crushed
1/2 cup (1 stick) butter, melted

Chop the chicken, discarding the skin and bones. Combine the chicken, soups, sour cream, poppy seeds and dressing mix in a large bowl and mix well. Spoon into a baking dish sprayed with nonstick cooking spray. Combine the cracker crumbs and butter in a bowl and mix well. Sprinkle over the chicken mixture. Bake at 375 degrees for 35 minutes. YIELD: 8 SERVINGS.

Lynn Sherrer
Montgomery Council

Chicken and Shrimp Casserole

2 cups chopped cooked chicken
2 cups deveined peeled steamed shrimp
1 cup chopped onion
1 cup chopped celery
1 cup sliced water chestnuts
1 cup rice, cooked
1 (10-ounce) can cream of celery soup
1 cup mayonnaise
1 cup chicken broth
1/4 cup sherry
1 1/2 teaspoons Worcestershire sauce
3 to 4 dashes of Tabasco sauce
Salt and pepper to taste
Grated Parmesan cheese
Butter crackers, crushed
Butter to taste

Combine the chicken, shrimp, onion, celery, water chestnuts and rice in a bowl and mix well. Combine the soup, mayonnaise, broth, sherry, Worcestershire sauce, Tabasco sauce, salt and pepper in a bowl and mix well. Add to the chicken mixture, stirring until coated and adding additional broth if needed for a soupy consistency. Spoon the chicken mixture into a 9x13-inch baking dish sprayed with nonstick cooking spray. Sprinkle with cheese and cracker crumbs. Dot with butter. Bake at 350 degrees for 1 hour.
YIELD: 12 SERVINGS.

Frankie Vaughn
Selma Life

HELPFUL HINT

Defrost frozen chicken faster by immersing in a bowl of cold water.

CROCK-POT® Chicken Dressing

1 (3-pound) chicken, cut up
8 slices white bread, torn
1 (8-inch) skillet corn bread, crumbled
2 (10-ounce) cans cream of chicken soup
1 medium onion, chopped
½ cup chopped celery
4 eggs, beaten
2 teaspoons sage
Salt and pepper to taste
2 tablespoons butter or margarine

Combine the chicken with enough water to cover in a stockpot. Bring to a boil; reduce the heat. Simmer, covered, for 45 minutes or until cooked through. Remove the chicken to a platter with a slotted spoon, reserving the broth. Cool the chicken. Chop the chicken, discarding the skin and bones. Combine the torn white bread and corn bread in a bowl and mix well. Stir in the soup, onion, celery, eggs, sage, salt and pepper. Add enough reserved broth to measure 2 soup cans. Stir in the chicken. Spoon into a CROCK-POT® Slow Cooker. Dot with the butter. Cook, covered, on Low for 4 to 5 hours or until of the desired consistency.
YIELD: 12 TO 14 SERVINGS.

Mauntez Mayer
Anniston Council

HELPFUL HINT

For a delicious apple stuffing, combine equal parts of chopped apples and bread cubes. Season the stuffing with onion, celery, sage and salt.

Chicken Dressing

1 small hen, cut up
1 (9-inch) skillet corn bread, crumbled
(about 4 to 6 cups)
1 (13-ounce) package cornflakes
4 or 5 slices white bread, torn
1 medium onion, chopped
1/2 cup chopped celery
1 tablespoon sage
2 teaspoons poultry seasoning
Salt and pepper to taste
2 eggs, beaten

Combine the chicken with enough water to cover in a stockpot. Bring to a boil; reduce the heat. Simmer until the chicken is cooked through. Drain, reserving 6 to 7 cups of the broth. Let cool. Chop the chicken, discarding the skin and bones. Combine the chicken, 6 cups of the reserved broth, corn bread, cornflakes, white bread, onion, celery, sage, poultry seasoning, salt and pepper in a large bowl and mix well, adding the remaining broth if needed for the desired consistency. Adjust the seasonings. Stir in the eggs. Spoon into a large baking pan. Bake at 400 degrees for 30 to 35 minutes or until light brown. **YIELD: 8 TO 10 SERVINGS.**

Betty Foshee
Decatur Council

HELPFUL HINT

Buy chicken breast fillets or bone chicken breasts ahead of time and refrigerate or freeze them. They will cook in about half the usual time.

Liz's Chicken and Dressing

4 chicken leg quarters, cooked
1 (9-inch) skillet corn bread, crumbled
1 large onion, chopped
1 large green bell pepper, chopped
1 cup chopped celery
1½ cups chicken broth
Sage to taste
Salt and pepper to taste

Chop the chicken, discarding the skin and bones. Combine the chicken and corn bread in a bowl and mix well. Sauté the onion, bell pepper and celery in 1 cup of the broth in a skillet. Add to the chicken mixture and mix well. Stir in the remaining ½ cup broth, sage, salt and pepper gradually, stirring until of the desired consistency. Spoon into a baking pan. Bake at 365 degrees for 45 minutes or until brown and bubbly. Yield: 4 to 6 servings.

Elizabeth S. Hatcher
Riverchase Council

Mother's Chicken Dressing

1 small hen
⅓ cup chopped onion
1½ teaspoons minced celery (optional)
⅓ cup margarine
2 cups crumbled corn bread
2 cups crumbled biscuits
3 hard-cooked eggs, chopped
½ teaspoon salt
¼ teaspoon pepper

Combine the hen with enough water to cover in a stockpot. Bring to a boil; reduce the heat. Simmer until the chicken is cooked through. Drain, reserving 3 cups of the broth. Chop the chicken, discarding the skin and bones. Sauté the onion and celery in the margarine in a skillet until tender. Combine 3 cups reserved broth, 1½ cups of the chopped chicken (reserve the remaining for another recipe), onion mixture, corn bread, biscuits, eggs, salt and pepper in a bowl and mix well. Spoon into a baking pan sprayed with nonstick cooking spray. Bake at 400 degrees until brown.

YIELD: **6 TO 8** SERVINGS.

Joyce LaTaste
Anniston Council

HELPFUL HINT

For few calories, bake or roast chicken instead of stewing. Remove the skin to further reduce the calories.

Easy Chicken and Dumplings

4 to 6 boneless skinless chicken breasts
1 (8-count) package flour tortillas
Salt and pepper to taste
1/2 cup (1 stick) butter or margarine
1/2 cup milk
2 tablespoons flour

Combine the chicken with enough water to cover in a large saucepan. Bring to a boil; reduce the heat. Simmer until the chicken is tender. Remove the chicken to a platter with a slotted spoon, reserving the broth. Let cool. Chop the chicken. Cut the tortillas into strips or bite-size pieces. Bring the reserved broth to a boil. Add the tortilla strips gradually to the boiling broth. Stir in the salt, pepper and butter. Cook until the tortillas are tender. Add the chicken and mix gently. Stir in a mixture of the milk and flour. Cook until thickened, stirring constantly. YIELD: 6 SERVINGS.

Donna Jean Bowman
Birmingham South Cahaba Council

Chicken and Dumplings

1 (3-pound) chicken, cut up
1 (10-ounce) can cream of mushroom soup
Salt and pepper to taste
1/2 package flour tortillas, cut into 1-inch strips

Combine the chicken with enough water to cover in a stockpot. Bring to a boil; reduce the heat. Simmer until the chicken is tender. Remove the chicken to a platter with a slotted spoon, reserving the broth. Skim the broth. Stir the soup, salt and pepper into the broth. Chop the chicken. Return the chicken to the stockpot. Bring to a boil. Drop the tortilla strips into the boiling broth mixture; reduce the heat. Simmer, covered, for 15 minutes. YIELD: 6 SERVINGS.

Linda McKee
Decatur Council

Chicken and Dumpling Casserole

½ cup chopped onion
½ cup chopped celery
2 garlic cloves, minced
¼ cup (½ stick) butter or margarine
½ cup flour
2 teaspoons sugar
1 teaspoon salt
1 teaspoon basil
½ teaspoon pepper
4 cups chicken broth
1 (10-ounce) package frozen green peas
4 cups chopped cooked chicken
2 cups baking mix
2 teaspoons basil
⅔ cup milk

Sauté the onion, celery and garlic in the butter in a saucepan until the vegetables are tender. Stir in the flour, sugar, salt, 1 teaspoon basil and pepper. Add the broth, stirring until mixed. Bring to a boil. Boil for 1 minute, stirring constantly; reduce the heat. Stir in the peas. Cook for 5 minutes, stirring constantly. Add the chicken and mix well. Spoon into a greased 9×13-inch baking dish. Combine the baking mix and 2 teaspoons basil in a bowl and mix well. Add the milk gradually, stirring constantly until moistened. Drop the dough by tablespoonfuls over the chicken mixture (about 12 dumplings). Bake at 350 degrees for 30 minutes; cover. Bake for 10 minutes longer or until the dumplings are done. YIELD: **6 TO 8 SERVINGS**.

Hester P. Thompson
Birmingham Life

Chicken Enchiladas

1/4 cup chopped pecans
1/4 cup chopped onion
2 tablespoons butter
3 ounces cream cheese, softened
2 tablespoons milk
1 teaspoon cumin
1/2 teaspoon salt
2 cups chopped cooked chicken
6 (8-inch) flour tortillas
2 (10-ounce) cans cream of chicken soup
1 cup sour cream
1 cup milk
1/4 cup chopped sliced jalapeño chiles
1 cup shredded Monterey Jack cheese or mozzarella cheese
2 tablespoons chopped pecans, toasted (optional)

Sauté 1/4 cup pecans and onion in the butter in a skillet until light brown. Remove from the heat. Combine the cream cheese, milk, cumin and salt in a bowl and mix well. Stir in the pecan mixture. Spoon about 1/3 cup of the chicken mixture onto each tortilla and roll to enclose the filling. Arrange the tortillas seam side down in a greased 7×12-inch baking dish. Combine the soup, sour cream, milk and chiles in a bowl and mix well. Spoon over the tortillas. Bake, covered with foil, at 350 degrees for 35 minutes or until heated through; remove the foil. Sprinkle with the cheese and 2 tablespoons pecans. Bake for 5 minutes longer or until bubbly.
YIELD: 6 SERVINGS.

Renee McCreless
Birmingham Metro Council

Chicken Enchiladas

2 cups sour cream
1 (10-ounce) can cream of chicken soup
2 large chicken breasts, chopped or cut into strips
1 onion, julienned
Butter
1 large package tortillas
2 cups shredded mozzarella cheese

Combine the sour cream and soup in a bowl and mix well. Sauté the chicken and onion in the butter in a skillet until the chicken is cooked through. Add half the sour cream mixture and mix well. Simmer for 10 minutes, stirring frequently. Spoon the chicken mixture onto the tortillas and roll to enclose the filling. Arrange the tortillas seam side down in a greased baking dish. Spread with the remaining sour cream mixture. Bake at 350 degrees for 15 minutes. Sprinkle with the cheese. Bake just until the cheese melts.
YIELD: 8 TO 10 SERVINGS.

Sally McCrorie
Riverchase Council

Chicken Fantastic

1 (3-pound) chicken
1 (6-ounce) package chicken-flavor rice
1 (16-ounce) can French-style green beans, drained
1 (10-ounce) can cream of celery soup
1 cup mayonnaise
1 (8-ounce) can sliced water chestnuts, drained
2 tablespoons chopped pimentos (optional)
Salt and pepper to taste

Combine the chicken with enough water to cover in a stockpot. Bring to a boil; reduce the heat. Simmer until the chicken is cooked through; drain. Let cool. Chop the chicken, discarding the skin and bones. Cook the rice using package directions. Combine the chicken, rice, green beans, soup, mayonnaise, water chestnuts, pimentos, salt and pepper in a bowl and mix well. Spoon into a baking dish. Bake at 350 degrees for 30 minutes. You may substitute any type of rice for the chicken-flavor rice. If using white rice, cook the rice in 1 cup chicken broth with 1 chopped onion. YIELD: 6 SERVINGS.

Susan Neuhoff
Montgomery Council

HELPFUL HINT

For a quick source of chopped cooked chicken, use canned chunk chicken.

Chicken Jun Jun

1 (3-pound) chicken
2 tablespoons vegetable oil
3/4 cup water
1/4 cup soy sauce

1 1/2 tablespoons sugar
3 bunches green onions with tops, cut into 2-inch pieces

Chop the chicken, discarding the skin and bones. Heat the oil in a wok or large skillet until hot. Add the chicken. Stir-fry just until the chicken turns white. Stir in the water, soy sauce and sugar; reduce the heat. Simmer for 30 minutes, stirring occasionally and adding additional water as needed. Add the chopped green onion bulbs. Cook for 1 to 2 minutes. Add the green onion tops. Cook for 5 minutes longer, stirring frequently. Serve over hot cooked rice. YIELD: **6 SERVINGS**.

Margaret W. Wilborn
Gadsden Life

Chicken Pie

3 cups chopped cooked chicken
4 hard-cooked eggs, chopped
1 1/2 cups chicken broth
1 (10-ounce) can cream of celery soup

1 (10-ounce) can cream of chicken soup
1 cup self-rising flour
1/2 cup milk
1/2 cup mayonnaise

Combine the chicken, eggs, broth and soups in a bowl and mix gently. Spoon into a baking dish. Combine the self-rising flour, milk and mayonnaise in a bowl, stirring until blended. Spread over the chicken mixture. Bake at 350 degrees for 1 hour or until light brown and bubbly. Add chopped carrots, green peas and chopped potatoes to the chicken mixture for variety. YIELD: **6 SERVINGS**.

Ella Skinner
Selma Life

Chicken Potpie

4 chicken breasts
1 (15-ounce) can Veg-All, drained
1 (2-ounce) jar chopped pimentos, drained
2 (10-ounce) cans cream of chicken soup
2 cups chicken broth
1 cup self-rising flour
1 cup buttermilk
½ cup (1 stick) butter or margarine, melted

Combine the chicken with enough water to cover in a saucepan. Bring to a boil; reduce the heat. Simmer until the chicken is cooked through; drain. Let cool. Chop the chicken, discarding the skin and bones. Line the bottom of a 9×13-inch baking dish sprayed with nonstick cooking spray with the chicken. Layer with the Veg-All and pimentos. Combine the soup and broth in a saucepan and mix well. Bring to a boil, stirring occasionally. Pour over the chicken and vegetables. Combine the self-rising flour, buttermilk and margarine in a bowl, stirring until blended. Pour over the top. Bake at 350 degrees for 30 minutes. Increase the oven temperature to 450 degrees. Bake for 20 minutes longer. You may freeze, covered, for future use. **YIELD: 6 TO 8 SERVINGS.**

Eulene Miller
Birmingham South Cahaba Council

HELPFUL HINT

For a delicious gravy, stir orange juice and a small amount of peanut butter into the skimmed juices from roast chicken.

Chicken Potpie

4 boneless skinless chicken breasts, cooked, chopped
2 (16-ounce) cans mixed vegetables, drained
1 cup chicken broth
1 (10-ounce) can cream of celery soup
1 (10-ounce) can cream of potato soup
1 cup self-rising flour
1 cup milk
1/4 cup (1/2 stick) margarine, melted

Line the bottom of a baking dish sprayed with nonstick cooking spray with the chicken. Spread the vegetables over the chicken. Combine the broth and soups in a bowl and mix well. Pour over the chicken and vegetables. Combine the remaining ingredients in a bowl and stir until blended. Spoon over the top. Bake at 350 degrees for 45 to 55 minutes or until brown. YIELD: 6 TO 8 SERVINGS.

Kathryn Morgan
Gadsden Life

Chicken Potpie

1 (3-pound) chicken, cooked, drained
1 (16-ounce) can peas and carrots, drained
2 (10-ounce) cans cream of chicken soup
1 medium onion, chopped
1 (10-ounce) can cream of celery soup
1 cup flour
1 cup milk
3/4 cup mayonnaise

Chop the chicken, discarding the skin and bones. Combine the chicken, peas and carrots, chicken soup, onion and celery soup in a bowl and mix gently. Spoon into a 9x12-inch baking pan sprayed with nonstick cooking spray. Combine the flour, milk and mayonnaise in a bowl, stirring until blended. Pour over the chicken mixture. Bake at 350 degrees for 1 hour. YIELD: 6 TO 8 SERVINGS.

Margaret W. Wilborn
Gadsden Life

Easy Chicken Potpie

*4 boneless skinless chicken breasts,
cooked, drained
2 refrigerator pie pastries
2 (16-ounce) cans Veg-All, drained
1 (10-ounce) can cream of mushroom soup
1 (10-ounce) can cream of chicken soup
1 (10-ounce) can cream of celery soup
4 hard-cooked eggs, chopped
1 onion, chopped, or onion flakes to taste
Salt and pepper to taste*

Tear the chicken into bite-size pieces. Line the bottom of a baking dish with 1 of the pie pastries. Combine the chicken, Veg-All, soups, eggs, onion, salt and pepper in a bowl and mix gently. Spoon into the prepared dish. Top with the remaining pastry and cut several vents. Bake at 350 degrees for 30 to 40 minutes or until brown. You may freeze the unbaked potpie for future use. Thaw in the refrigerator and bake just before serving. YIELD: **6 TO 8 SERVINGS**.

*Linda Wong
Birmingham South Cahaba Council*

HELPFUL HINT

To make quick chicken and dumplings, tear flour tortillas into strips and drop into simmering chicken stock and cook until tender. Add canned chunk chicken.

Provençal Chicken

12 ounces boneless skinless chicken, cut into strips
2 teaspoons olive oil
6 scallions, sliced
2 garlic cloves, minced
8 plum tomatoes, chopped
2 tablespoons chopped fresh parsley
1 tablespoon capers
1 teaspoon red wine vinegar
1/4 teaspoon rosemary, crushed
3 cups hot cooked wide noodles

Sauté the chicken in the olive oil in a skillet for 4 minutes. Add the scallions and garlic. Cook for 3 to 4 minutes or until the chicken is cooked through, stirring frequently. Stir in the tomatoes, parsley, capers, wine vinegar and rosemary. Reduce the heat. Simmer for 10 minutes or until the liquid evaporates, stirring occasionally. Spoon over the hot noodles on a serving platter. **YIELD: 4 SERVINGS.**

Rita Wilson
Birmingham Life

POULTRY

Chicken with a Spanish Flair

3 chicken breasts, cooked, drained
1 (10-ounce) can cream of chicken soup
1 (10-ounce) can cream of mushroom soup
2 cups chopped green chiles
1 onion, finely chopped
1/2 cup chicken broth
1/3 cup milk
1 package tortilla chips or corn chips, broken
2 cups shredded cheese

Chop the chicken, discarding the skin and bones. Mix with the next 6 ingredients in a bowl. Layer the chips, chicken mixture and cheese 1/2 at a time in a 9×13-inch baking pan. Bake at 300 degrees for 35 to 45 minutes or until brown and bubbly. **YIELD: 8 SERVINGS.**

Mary Gillis
Mobile Council

Chicken Supreme

1/2 cup finely chopped onion
1/2 cup finely chopped celery
2 tablespoons butter
1 (15-ounce) can chicken broth or stock
1 (10-ounce) can cream of mushroom soup
2 tablespoons lemon juice
1 tablespoon soy sauce
2 tablespoons cornstarch
2 cups chopped cooked chicken
Salt and pepper to taste
Chow mein noodles

Sauté the onion and celery in the butter in a skillet until tender. Stir in the broth and soup. Combine the lemon juice and soy sauce in a bowl and mix well. Add the cornstarch, stirring until blended. Stir the cornstarch mixture into the soup mixture. Cook until thickened, stirring constantly. Add the chicken, salt and pepper and mix well. Cook just until heated through, stirring constantly. Spoon over the noodles on a serving platter. **YIELD: 4 TO 6 SERVINGS.**

Sue Bryars
Birmingham South Cahaba Council

Zippy Chicken Stir-Fry

½ cup mayonnaise-type salad dressing
1 tablespoon soy sauce
½ teaspoon ginger
¼ teaspoon red pepper flakes (optional)
2 tablespoons vegetable oil
3 boneless skinless chicken breasts, cut into thin strips
1 cup broccoli florets
1 cup julienned red bell pepper
1 cup carrot sticks
¼ cup sliced green onions
1 garlic clove, minced
4 cups hot cooked rice

Combine the salad dressing, soy sauce, ginger and red pepper flakes in a bowl and mix well. Heat the oil in a wok or large skillet over medium-high heat until hot. Add the chicken. Stir-fry for 4 minutes. Add the broccoli, bell pepper, carrot, green onions and garlic. Stir-fry for 3 to 4 minutes or until the vegetables are tender-crisp. Stir in the salad dressing mixture. Simmer for 30 seconds, stirring constantly. Spoon over the rice on a serving platter.
YIELD: 3 TO 4 SERVINGS.

Mary Alice Neal
Birmingham Life

HELPFUL HINT

Store meal-size portions of chopped chicken in plastic bags in the freezer to have ready for a busy-day meal.

Chicken Salad Tacos

1 (10-ounce) can chunk white chicken, drained, flaked
1/3 cup salsa
1/4 cup sour cream
1 rib celery, chopped
1 teaspoon cumin
8 taco shells
1 cup shredded iceberg lettuce
1 small tomato, chopped
1/2 cup shredded Cheddar cheese

Combine the chicken, salsa, sour cream, celery and cumin in a bowl and mix well. Spoon the chicken mixture into the taco shells. Top each taco with lettuce, tomato and cheese. Serve immediately. YIELD: **8 SERVINGS**.

Mary C. Martin
Birmingham Life

Chicken and Rice Skillet

1/2 teaspoon olive oil
2 cups ground boneless skinless chicken breasts
1/2 cup chopped onion
1/4 cup chopped red bell pepper
1/4 cup chopped green bell pepper
1 cup frozen green peas, thawed
1 (10-ounce) can reduced-fat cream of mushroom soup
1 3/4 cups water
1 cup long grain white rice
2 teaspoons salt

Heat the olive oil in a saucepan over medium heat. Add the chicken, onion and bell peppers. Cook until the chicken is no longer pink and the vegetables are tender, stirring frequently. Stir in the peas, soup, water, rice and salt. Bring to a boil; reduce heat. Simmer, covered, until the rice is tender. YIELD: **6 SERVINGS**.

Gussie Evans
Mobile Council

Tammy's Chicken Wraps

1 pound boneless skinless chicken breasts, cut into strips
Dale's Steak Seasoning
Lettuce, torn into bite-size pieces
Salad tomatoes, cut into quarters
1/2 cup (about) ranch salad dressing
1/4 to 1/2 cup vegetable oil
3 pita pockets, split
Shredded Cheddar cheese
Salt and pepper to taste

Combine the chicken with enough Dale's Steak Seasoning to cover in a bowl and mix well. Marinate in the refrigerator for 15 to 20 minutes, stirring occasionally. Drain, discarding the marinade. Grill the chicken over hot coals until cooked through. Toss lettuce and tomatoes in a microwave-safe bowl. Add the salad dressing and toss to coat. Microwave on High for 45 seconds; stir. Heat the oil in a skillet until hot. Brown the pita halves in the hot oil until brown on both sides. Sprinkle 1 side with the cheese. Remove from skillet. Pat the bottom of each pita half with a paper towel to remove the excess oil. Layer the pita halves with the chicken and lettuce and tomato mixture. Drizzle lightly with additional salad dressing. Sprinkle with salt and pepper. Roll to enclose the filling and wrap in foil. Substitute leftover roast beef for the chicken, using A.1. steak sauce in place of the ranch salad dressing.

YIELD: 6 SERVINGS.

Tammy Donner
Birmingham South Cahaba Council

Spicy White Chili

2 pounds boneless skinless chicken breasts, cut into 1-inch pieces
Boneless pork, cut into strips, chopped (optional)
5 (15-ounce) cans chicken broth
1 tablespoon chili powder
2 teaspoons cumin
1 teaspoon black pepper
1 teaspoon oregano
1 teaspoon salt
1 teaspoon coriander
1/4 teaspoon cayenne pepper
1/8 teaspoon ground cloves
2 (4-ounce) cans chopped green chiles, drained
1 large onion, chopped
4 ribs celery, chopped
3 garlic cloves, minced
Vegetable oil
Cornstarch or mesa flour
5 (15-ounce) cans white Northern beans
Shredded Monterey Jack cheese to taste

Combine the chicken, pork and broth in a stockpot. Bring to a boil; reduce the heat. Simmer until the chicken and pork are cooked through, stirring occasionally. Remove the chicken and pork to a platter with a slotted spoon, reserving the broth. Combine the chili powder, cumin, black pepper, oregano, salt, coriander, cayenne pepper and cloves in a bowl and mix well. Sauté the chiles, onion, celery and garlic in oil in a skillet. Stir in the spice mixture. Return the chicken and pork to the broth. Add the chile mixture and mix well. Simmer for 2 to 3 hours or until of the desired consistency, stirring occasionally. Remove from the heat. If time allows, let stand until cool. Chill, covered, for 8 to 10 hours. Reheat over low heat, stirring occasionally. Add a mixture of cornstarch and cold water. Simmer until thickened, stirring frequently. Stir in the undrained beans. Cook just until heated through, stirring frequently. Ladle into chili bowls. Sprinkle with cheese.

YIELD: 8 TO 10 SERVINGS.

Don Roy
Riverchase Council

White Chili

3 boneless skinless chicken breasts, cooked, chopped
2 (16-ounce) cans white Shoe Peg corn, drained
2 (16-ounce) cans Northern beans or navy beans, drained
2 (10-ounce) cans cream of mushroom soup
1 (16-ounce) can chicken broth
1 (16-ounce) can diced tomatoes with green chiles
1 pound Mexican Velveeta cheese, chopped
1 large onion, chopped

Combine all of the ingredients in a stockpot and mix well. Cook over medium heat for 1½ hours, stirring occasionally. Ladle over corn chips in chili bowls. You may cook in a CROCK-POT® Slow Cooker on Low for 4 hours. YIELD: **8 SERVINGS**.

Eulene Miller
Birmingham South Cahaba Council

Brunswick Stew

1 pound ground beef
1 large onion, chopped
2 cans Castleberry barbecue pork
2 (16-ounce) cans stewed tomatoes
2 (16-ounce) cans cream-style corn
2 (5-ounce) cans chunk chicken, drained, flaked
2 tablespoons lemon juice
2 tablespoons Worcestershire sauce
1 small bottle hot ketchup

Brown the ground beef in a skillet, stirring until crumbly; drain. Combine the ground beef, onion, pork, undrained tomatoes, corn, chicken, lemon juice, Worcestershire sauce and ketchup in a CROCK-POT® Slow Cooker and mix well. Cook, covered, on Low for 3 hours. YIELD: **6 TO 8 SERVINGS**.

Bertha Capps
Birmingham Life

CROCK-POT® Brunswick Stew

2 cans Castleberry barbecue pork
1 (28-ounce) can stewed tomatoes
1 (16-ounce) can whole kernel corn, drained
1 onion, chopped
1 (16-ounce) can cream-style corn
1 (16-ounce) can lima beans, drained
2 (5-ounce) cans canned chicken, drained, flaked

Mix all of the ingredients in a CROCK-POT® Slow Cooker. Cook, covered, on High for 4 hours or on Low for 10 hours. YIELD: 6 TO 8 SERVINGS.

Eulene Miller
Birmingham South Cahaba Council

Dove Breast Shish Kabobs

1/2 cup Italian salad dressing
1/2 cup Dale's Steak Seasoning
1 teaspoon minced garlic
Salt and pepper to taste
Dove breasts (allow 2 to 3 per person)
Cherry tomatoes
Green bell pepper chunks
Onions, cut into quarters
Medium mushrooms
Bacon slices, cut into halves

Combine the salad dressing, Dale's Steak Seasoning, garlic, salt and pepper in a bowl and mix well. Pour over the dove breasts, cherry tomatoes, bell pepper chunks, onion quarters and mushrooms in a shallow glass dish, turning to coat. Marinate, covered, in the refrigerator for 1 1/2 to 3 hours, turning occasionally. Drain, reserving the marinade. Wrap each breast with 1/2 slice bacon. Thread the breasts and vegetables on skewers. Grill over medium-hot coals until the vegetables are tender and the dove and bacon are cooked through, basting with the reserved marinade occasionally. Serve over hot cooked rice. YIELD: VARIABLE.

Kim Chichester
Birmingham South Cahaba Council

Smothered Quail

16 quail
Salt and pepper to taste
Flour
2 cups (4 sticks) butter

2 cups chicken broth
2 cups water
1/4 cup white wine

Season the quail with salt and pepper. Coat with flour. Cook the quail in the butter in a cast-iron skillet until brown on all sides. Add the broth and water and mix well. Cook, covered, over low heat for 1 hour or until the quail are tender, basting occasionally. Add the wine just before the end of the cooking time and mix well. **Yield: 10 to 16 servings.**

Sue Small
Selma Life

Taco Pie

1 (8-count) can crescent rolls
1 pound ground turkey
2 tablespoons chopped bell pepper
1 tablespoon beef bouillon granules

2 tablespoons chopped onion
1 (6-ounce) can tomato paste
3/4 cup water
1 envelope taco seasoning mix
8 ounces mozzarella cheese, shredded

Unroll the crescent roll dough. Separate into rectangles. Press the rectangles over the bottom and up the side of a 9-inch pie plate, pressing the edges and perforations to seal. Brown the turkey in a skillet, stirring until crumbly; drain. Stir in the bell pepper, bouillon granules and onion. Simmer until the onion and bell pepper are tender, stirring frequently. Stir in the tomato paste, water and seasoning mix. Layer the turkey mixture and cheese 1/2 at a time in the prepared pie plate. Bake at 400 degrees for 15 to 20 minutes or until brown and bubbly. **Yield: 8 servings.**

Gail Hyatt
Anniston Council

Basil-Lemon Turkey Breast

½ boneless turkey breast
½ cup chopped fresh basil
2 garlic cloves, minced
1 tablespoon grated lemon zest
2 lemons, thinly sliced
1½ cups thinly sliced carrots
¾ cup thinly sliced celery
1 Vidalia onion, chopped
1 cup water
1 cup reduced-sodium chicken broth

Loosen the skin carefully on the turkey breast. Combine the basil, garlic and lemon zest in a bowl and mix well. Spread the basil mixture under the skin and arrange the lemon slices over the basil mixture. Combine the carrots, celery, onion and water in a roasting pan and mix well. Arrange a roasting rack over the vegetable mixture. Place the turkey on the roasting rack. Roast at 325 degrees for 1 hour or until a meat thermometer placed in the thickest portion of the turkey registers 170 degrees, basting frequently. Remove the turkey to a cutting board. Let stand for 20 minutes. Discard the skin and slice. Drain the vegetable mixture. Combine the vegetable mixture and broth in a blender. Process until puréed. Pour into a saucepan. Cook just until heated through, stirring constantly. Serve warm with the turkey with steamed wild rice. YIELD: **6 TO 8 SERVINGS.**

Gussie Evans
Mobile Council

Bob's Grilled Catfish Fillets

2 tablespoons marinade
Juice of 1 lemon
1 teaspoon white vinegar
2 large catfish fillets
Pepper to taste
Lemon pepper to taste

Combine your favorite marinade, lemon juice and vinegar in a small bowl and mix well. Pour over the fillets in a shallow dish. Season with the pepper and lemon pepper on both sides of the fillets. Marinate in the refrigerator for 3 to 4 hours, turning twice. Place the fillets in a wire fish basket that has been sprayed with nonstick cooking spray; reserve the marinade. Grill the fillets over high heat for 10 minutes on each side; basting with the reserved marinade occasionally. YIELD: 2 SERVINGS.

Faith Kirby Richardson
Gadsden Life

Baked Catfish Fillets

Catfish fillets, rinsed, patted dry
Lemon pepper to taste
Italian-seasoned bread crumbs

Line a baking sheet with aluminum foil and spray with nonstick cooking spray. Sprinkle both sides of the fillets with the lemon pepper and bread crumbs. Place on the prepared baking sheet. Bake at 350 degrees for 25 minutes. Increase the heat and broil for 5 minutes, being careful not to burn the fish. Serve with buttered rice and assorted steamed vegetables. YIELD: VARIABLE.

Barbara O. Horton
Mobile Council

Baked Fish

2 tablespoons instant minced onion
2 tablespoons water
1/2 tablespoon basil
1/2 tablespoon paprika
2 tablespoons canola oil
1/8 teaspoon garlic powder
1 1/2 tablespoons lemon juice
1 pound white fish fillets
1 teaspoon parsley

Combine the minced onion and water in a small bowl and let stand for 10 minutes. Add the basil, paprika, canola oil, garlic powder and lemon juice and mix well. Pour the herb mixture over the fillets in a greased 6×10-inch baking dish. Bake at 350 degrees for 10 to 15 minutes or until the fish flakes easily. Sprinkle with the parsley and serve immediately. You may use cod, halibut or any white fish in this recipe. YIELD: 4 SERVINGS.

Gussie Evans
Mobile Council

Oven-Fried Fish

1 pound fish fillets
1/2 cup milk
1/2 cup fine bread crumbs
Salt and pepper to taste
2 tablespoons (1/4 stick) butter, melted

Dip the fillets in the milk and coat with the bread crumbs. Place on a well-greased baking sheet. Season with the salt and pepper. Drizzle with the melted butter. Bake at 400 degrees until the fish flakes easily and is golden brown. YIELD: 4 SERVINGS.

Sue Small
Selma Life

Glazed Salmon

3/4 pound salmon, rinsed, patted dry
1/4 cup balsamic vinegar
1 tablespoon Dijon mustard
1 teaspoon salt
Pepper to taste

Cook the salmon in a skillet srpayed with nonstick cooking spray over high heat for 3 minutes on each side. Remove the salmon to a plate. Add the vinegar to the skillet and cook over high heat until reduced by 1/2. Reduce the heat and add the mustard; mix well. Cook until a smooth glaze forms. Season the salmon with the salt and pepper. Return to the skillet and cook for 1 minute. Turn the salmon to coat both sides with the glaze and cook for 3 minutes. Divide into 2 portions and drizzle with the glaze. **YIELD: 2 SERVINGS.**

Barbara Reed
Montgomery Council

Easy Salmon Cakes

1 (12-ounce) can pink salmon, skin removed
1/3 cup chopped onion
1 egg, lightly beaten
1/2 cup flour
1 1/2 teaspoons baking powder
1 1/2 cups vegetable oil

Drain the salmon, reserving 2 tablespoons of the juice. Combine the salmon, reserved juice, onion, egg, flour and baking powder in a large bowl and mix well. Shape into 6 balls and flatten into patties. Heat the oil in a large skillet. Cook the salmon patties in the oil on each side until golden brown. Remove to paper towels to drain. **YIELD: 4 TO 6 SERVINGS.**

Jane B. Weatherly
Mobile Council

Salmon Croquettes

1 (15-ounce) can pink salmon, drained, deboned, flaked
1/2 cup evaporated milk
1/2 cup crushed cornflakes
1/4 cup dill pickle relish
1/4 cup finely chopped celery
2 tablespoon finely chopped onion
1/2 cup evaporated milk
1 cup crushed cornflakes
Vegetable oil for deep-frying
Tartar Sauce (below)

Combine the salmon, 1/2 cup evaporated milk, 1/2 cup crushed cornflakes, pickle relish, celery and onion in a large bowl and mix well. Shape by 1/4 cupfuls into cone shapes. Dip in 1/2 cup evaporated milk and coat with 1 cup crushed cornflakes. Heat the oil in a deep fryer to 365 degrees. Deep-fry the croquettes a few at a time for 2 1/2 minutes or until golden brown. Remove to paper towels to drain. Keep warm until serving time. Serve the croquettes with the Tartar Sauce. YIELD: 4 TO 6 SERVINGS.

Tartar Sauce

2/3 cup evaporated milk
1/4 cup mayonnaise
2 tablespoons dill pickle relish
1 tablespoon finely chopped onion

Combine the evaporated milk, mayonnaise, pickle relish and onion in a medium saucepan. Cook over medium-low heat until slightly thickened and heated through. Serve warm. YIELD: 1 CUP.

Hester P. Thompson
Birmingham Life

Dolly Parton's Salmon Patties

1 (15-ounce) can salmon, drained, deboned, flaked
2 eggs, beaten
1 small onion, finely chopped
1/4 cup flour
Salt and pepper to taste
Vegetable oil for frying

Combine the salmon, eggs, onion, flour, salt and pepper in a large bowl and mix well. Heat the oil in a large skillet. Drop the salmon mixture by spoonfuls into the hot oil. Fry until golden brown on both sides. **Yield: 4 to 6 servings.**

Virginia Killian
Gadsden Life

Crab Burgers

1 cup flaked crab meat
1/4 cup chopped celery
2 tablespoons chopped onion
1/2 cup shredded Cheddar cheese
1/2 cup mayonnaise
4 hamburger buns
Butter or margarine

Combine the crab meat, celery, onion and cheese in a bowl. Add the mayonnaise and mix well. Spread each hamburger bun half with the butter. Spread the crab meat mixture on each prepared hamburger bun half. Place on a baking sheet. Broil until hot and bubbly and lightly browned. You may use canned, fresh or imitation crab meat. **Yield: 8 servings.**

Dudley D. Pendleton
Birmingham South Life

Tuna Mushroom Casserole

½ cup water
1 teaspoon chicken bouillon granules
1 (10-ounce) package frozen green beans
1 cup chopped onion
1 cup sliced fresh mushrooms
¼ cup chopped celery
1 garlic clove, minced
½ teaspoon dillweed
½ teaspoon salt
⅛ teaspoon pepper
4 teaspoons cornstarch
1½ cups milk
½ cup shredded Swiss cheese
¼ cup mayonnaise
2½ cups medium noodles, cooked
1 (12-ounce) can tuna, drained, flaked
⅓ cup dry bread crumbs
1 tablespoon butter or margarine

Combine the water and bouillon in a saucepan and bring to a boil. Add the green beans, onion, mushrooms, celery, garlic, dillweed, salt and pepper and bring to a boil. Reduce the heat and simmer, covered, for 5 minutes or until the vegetables are tender. Dissolve the cornstarch in the milk in a bowl. Add to the vegetable mixture. Bring to a boil, stirring constantly. Cook for 2 minutes or until thickened; remove from the heat. Add the cheese and mayonnaise, stirring until the cheese melts. Fold in the noodles and tuna. Pour into a greased 2½-quart casserole dish. Heat the butter in a small skillet on the stove. Sauté the bread crumbs in the butter in a small skillet until golden brown. Sprinkle on top of the casserole. Bake at 350 degrees for 25 to 30 minutes or until heated through.

YIELD: 4 TO 6 SERVINGS.

Hester P. Thompson
Birmingham Life

Frogmore Stew

1 (3-ounce) package crab boil
1 (5-pound) bag new potatoes
2 (16-ounce) packages Polish sausage
2 (6-count) packages frozen corn on the cob halves
4 pounds fresh unpeeled shrimp

Fill a stockpot 3/4 full with water. Bring the water to a boil and add the crab boil. Add the potatoes and cook for 20 minutes. Cut each sausage in half and add to the pot. Cook for 15 minutes. Add the corn. Cook for 10 minutes. Add the shrimp. Cook for 7 minutes. Drain and discard the crab boil. You may serve this over rice if desired. **YIELD: 6 SERVINGS.**

Pam Dyer
Riverchase Council

Shrimp Casserole

1/2 teaspoon minced garlic
1/2 cup finely chopped onion
1/2 cup chopped green bell pepper
2 tablespoons butter, melted
1 (10-ounce) can cream of shrimp soup
2 tablespoons lemon juice
2 teaspoons Worcestershire sauce
1 1/2 cups cooked rice
1 1/2 pounds fresh peeled shrimp
Paprika to taste

Sauté the garlic, onion and bell pepper in the butter in a saucepan. Add the soup, lemon juice and Worcestershire sauce. Stir in the rice and shrimp. Pour into an 8x8-inch baking dish. Sprinkle with the paprika. Bake at 350 degrees for 35 minutes or until bubbly. **YIELD: 4 TO 6 SERVINGS.**

Chris Elsen
Gadsden Life

Shrimp Creole

1 cup thinly sliced onions
1 cup thinly sliced celery
1 cup green bell pepper cut into 2-inch strips
¼ cup vegetable oil
3½ cups canned tomatoes
1 (8-ounce) can tomato sauce
2 bay leaves
1 tablespoon sugar
1 tablespoon salt
1 tablespoon chili powder
⅛ teaspoon Tabasco sauce
2 pounds fresh shrimp, peeled, deveined
2 tablespoons flour
⅓ cup water

Sauté the onion, celery and bell pepper in the oil in an electric skillet at 300 degrees until tender. Add the tomatoes, tomato sauce, bay leaves, sugar, salt, chili powder and Tabasco sauce and mix well. Add the shrimp. Cover and reduce the heat. Simmer for 30 minutes. Add the flour and water and cook for 5 minutes longer or until thickened. Remove the bay leaves. Serve over rice. **YIELD: 6 SERVINGS.**

Eloise Bennett
Decatur Council

HELPFUL HINT

Freeze seafood in a carton of water to preserve its fresh flavor.

French-Fried Shrimp

1 cup pancake mix
1 teaspoon salt
Dash of pepper
¾ cup cold water
Vegetable oil for deep-frying
2 pounds fresh peeled shrimp

Combine the pancake mix, salt, pepper and cold water in a mixing bowl and beat for 2 minutes. Heat oil in a deep fryer to 375 degrees. Dip the shrimp the batter and deep-fry for 2 to 3 minutes. Remove to paper towels to drain. You may substitute lobster or scallops for the shrimp. YIELD: **6 SERVINGS**.

Betty Holloway
Birmingham Life

Jambalaya Deep Dish

2 pounds fresh shrimp, peeled, deveined
1 pound smoked sausage
1 (10-ounce) can French onion soup
1 (10-ounce) can beef broth
½ cup chopped green onions
½ cup chopped parsley
2 bay leaves
1 teaspoon salt
¼ teaspoon cayenne pepper
½ cup (1 stick) butter
2 cups rice
½ cup water

Combine the shrimp, sausage, French onion soup, beef broth, green onions, parsley, bay leaves, salt, cayenne pepper, butter, rice and water in a large deep baking dish that has been sprayed with non-stick cooking spray. Cover tightly with aluminum foil. Bake at 350 degrees for 1½ hours. Remove the bay leaves before serving.
YIELD: **6 SERVINGS**.

Dianne Tillman
Birmingham South Life

Shrimp and Pasta Packages

16 ounces angel hair pasta, cooked, drained
48 cooked peeled shrimp
1 cup (2 sticks) butter
1 red bell pepper, finely chopped
8 ounces mushrooms, sliced
1/2 cup chopped green onions
1/2 cup chopped fresh parsley
3 tablespoons soy sauce
2 teaspoons Worcestershire sauce
2 teaspoons garlic salt
1/2 teaspoon ginger
Dash of Tabasco sauce
1 (10-ounce) can chicken broth
15 fresh snow peas, sliced lengthwise

Cut aluminum foil into eight 12×12-inch squares. Divide the pasta evenly into 8 portions and place in the center of each foil square. Place 6 shrimp on top of each portion of pasta. Melt the butter in a large skillet. Add the bell pepper, mushrooms, green onions and parsley. Sauté until tender. Add the soy sauce, Worcestershire sauce, garlic salt, ginger and Tabasco sauce and mix well. Cook for 2 minutes. Add the chicken broth. Cook for 3 minutes. Pour the mixture evenly over each portion of pasta and shrimp. Top with the snow peas. Bring the sides of the foil squares up and fold over. Seal the two open ends. Place foil packages on a baking sheet. Bake at 350 degrees for 20 minutes. Remove from oven, cut an X in the top of each foil package and pull edges away. **Yield: 8 servings.**

Rita Wilson
Birmingham Life

Shrimp Rice Pilaf

1 garlic clove, finely chopped
1 medium onion, chopped
1 bell pepper, chopped
1/4 cup (1/2 stick) butter, melted
1 (8-ounce) can tomato sauce
2 or 3 dashes of Tabasco sauce
Salt to taste
1 cup cooked peeled shrimp
2 cups cooked rice

Sauté the garlic, onion and bell pepper in the melted butter in a skillet until tender. Add the tomato sauce, Tabasco sauce, salt and shrimp. Simmer, covered, for 10 minutes. Add the rice and mix well. Spoon into a greased 2-quart baking dish. Bake at 350 degrees for 15 to 20 minutes. YIELD: 4 TO 6 SERVINGS.

Catherine R. Bruce (Nan)
Bon Secour Life

Shrimp Scampi

1 pound fresh deveined peeled shrimp, butterflied
1/4 cup (1/2 stick) butter
1/4 cup dry white wine
1/4 cup chopped green onions
1 garlic clove, minced
1 tablespoon chopped parsley
1 teaspoon salt
1/4 teaspoon pepper

Combine the shrimp, butter, wine, green onions, garlic, parsley, salt and pepper in a large skillet. Cook for 10 to 15 minutes or until the shrimp turns pink and is cooked through. YIELD: 4 SERVINGS.

Betty Holloway
Birmingham Life

Noodles with Shrimp Scampi Sauce

3¾ cups wide egg noodles
⅔ cup butter or margarine
2 garlic cloves, minced
1 teaspoon basil
¾ pound fresh shrimp, peeled, deveined
1 tablespoon fresh lemon juice
Salt and freshly ground pepper to taste
2 teaspoons fresh chopped
Italian parsley or parsley
Lemon wedges

Cook the noodles using the package directions; drain and set aside. Melt the butter in a large skillet. Add the garlic and basil and sauté over low heat. Add the shrimp and cook for 3 to 4 minutes or until the shrimp turn pink, stirring constantly. Add the lemon juice, salt, pepper and parsley. Add the noodles and toss to mix well. Serve immediately with the lemon wedges. YIELD: 4 SERVINGS.

Anatalie Watson Fogg
Decatur Council

Shrimp Drop

1½ pounds fresh peeled shrimp
1 onion, chopped
1 potato, chopped
¼ cup finely chopped green onions
1 tablespoon parsley
1 egg
Salt and pepper to taste
Vegetable oil for deep-frying

Combine the shrimp, onion and potato in a food processor container. Process until finely chopped. Stir in the green onions, parsley and egg. Season with the salt and pepper. Drop by spoonfuls into hot oil. Deep-fry until golden brown. You may also drop by teaspoonfuls for appetizer servings. YIELD: 6 SERVINGS.

Mauntez Mayer
Anniston Council

Batter for Shrimp and Oysters

1 cup flour
½ teaspoon sugar
½ teaspoon salt
1 egg, beaten
2 tablespoons vegetable oil
1 cup ice water

Combine the flour, sugar and salt in a bowl. Mix in the beaten egg, oil and water. It is important that the water be very cold. Use as a batter for shrimp or oysters and deep-fry in hot oil until golden brown. YIELD: 1 CUP.

Susan Ragland
Birmingham South Cahaba Council

RIVERCHASE COUNCIL

The Riverchase Chapter annually supports the Gene Stallings Golf Tournament, which raises funds for the physically and mentally impaired.

Breads

Anne's Biscuits

2 cups self-rising flour
1 teaspoon baking powder
1/4 teaspoon baking soda

1/4 cup shortening
3/4 cup buttermilk

Combine the self-rising flour, baking powder and baking soda in a mixing bowl and mix well. Add the shortening and cut in with a pastry blender until the mixture is crumbly. Add the buttermilk and stir with a spoon until well mixed; the dough will be moist. Turn onto a lightly floured surface and knead lightly several times, adding a small amount of flour as necessary. Roll the dough to the desired thickness. Cut into biscuits using a 2-inch biscuit cutter. Arrange the biscuits on a lightly greased baking sheet. Bake at 500 degrees until brown. **Yield: 8 to 12 biscuits.**

Imogene Davis
Birmingham Life

Buttermilk Biscuits

2 cups flour, sifted
2 teaspoons baking powder
1 teaspoon salt
1 tablespoon sugar (optional)

1/2 teaspoon baking soda
1/2 cup shortening
1/2 cup (or more) buttermilk

Sift the flour, baking powder, salt, sugar and baking soda into a mixing bowl. Add the shortening and cut in with a pastry blender until crumbly. Stir in enough buttermilk gradually to make a medium dough. Turn the dough onto a lightly floured surface and knead lightly. Shape the dough into desired size balls to make drop biscuits or roll to the desired thickness and cut with a biscuit cutter. Arrange the biscuits on a greased baking sheet. Bake at 450 degrees for 15 to 20 minutes or to the desired brownness. **Yield: 8 to 12 biscuits.**

Gussie Evans
Mobile Life

Biscuits

4 cups self-rising flour
1 tablespoon sugar
1 tablespoon baking powder
²/₃ cup shortening
2 cups buttermilk
¼ cup (½ stick) butter, melted

Combine the self-rising flour, sugar and baking powder in a mixing bowl and mix well. Add the shortening and cut in with a pastry blender until the mixture is crumbly. Add the buttermilk and stir with a spoon until the mixture pulls from the side of the bowl. Turn the dough onto a floured pastry cloth and roll out. Knead the dough for 30 seconds and roll again. Brush the melted butter over half the dough, fold the dough over and roll to ½-inch thickness. Cut into biscuits with a biscuit cutter. Arrange the biscuits on a lightly greased baking sheet. Brush the tops with additional buttermilk. Bake at 450 degrees for 15 to 20 minutes or to the desired brownness. For crisper biscuits, arrange on baking sheets with enough space between to prevent touching. **YIELD: 2 DOZEN.**

Virginia Greene
Birmingham South Life

HELPFUL HINT

When a plastic bread wrapper melts onto the toaster or the coffeepot, rub some petroleum jelly on the spot, reheat the appliance and use a paper towel to rub off the plastic and the printing.

Potato Cheese Biscuits

1/2 cup instant potato flakes
1 tablespoon grated Parmesan cheese
1 (8- to 10-count) can biscuits
3 tablespoons melted butter

Combine the potato flakes and Parmesan cheese in a shallow dish. Separate the biscuits. Dip each biscuit in the melted butter to cover completely and roll in the cheese mixture to coat. Arrange the biscuits on a lightly greased baking sheet. Bake at 400 degrees until brown. YIELD: 8 TO 10 BISCUITS.

Barbara S. Lagle
Birmingham Life

Broccoli Corn Bread

1 (8-ounce) package corn bread mix
4 eggs
1/2 cup (1 stick) butter, melted
1 onion, chopped
2 cups shredded Cheddar cheese
1 (10-ounce) package frozen chopped broccoli, thawed

Combine the corn bread mix, eggs and melted butter in a large mixing bowl and mix well. Add the onion, cheese and broccoli and mix well. Pour into a greased 9×13-inch baking pan. Bake at 350 degrees for 30 minutes or until golden brown. Store any leftover corn bread in the refrigerator. YIELD: 12 SERVINGS.

Billie Woodruff
Mobile Council

Broccoli Corn Bread

2 eggs
1 cup cottage cheese
1 (10-ounce) package frozen chopped broccoli, thawed
3/4 cup chopped onion
6 tablespoons butter, melted
2 (8-ounce) packages corn bread or corn muffin mix
2 tablespoons butter, melted

Beat the eggs lightly in a large mixing bowl. Add the cottage cheese, broccoli, onion and 6 tablespoons melted butter and mix well. Add the corn bread mix and mix well. Pour the remaining 2 tablespoons melted butter into a 10-inch ovenproof skillet. Add the broccoli mixture. Bake at 350 degrees for 40 to 45 minutes or until golden brown. Cut into wedges and serve warm. Store any leftover corn bread in the refrigerator. YIELD: 12 TO 16 SERVINGS.

Hester P. Thompson
Birmingham Life

Mother's Broccoli Corn Bread

4 eggs
1/2 cup (1 stick) butter, melted
1 medium onion, chopped
8 ounces cottage cheese
1 (10-ounce) package frozen chopped broccoli, thawed
1 (8-ounce) package corn bread mix

Beat the eggs in a mixing bowl. Add the butter, onion, cottage cheese and broccoli and mix well. Add the corn bread mix and mix well. Pour the batter into a greased 9×13-inch baking pan. Bake at 350 degrees for 40 minutes or until brown. Serve warm. Store any leftover corn bread in the refrigerator. YIELD: 12 SERVINGS.

Sheila P. Brothers
Anniston Council

Corn Bread for Bland Diets

1 cup uncooked cream of wheat cereal
1 cup self-rising flour
4 teaspoons baking powder
½ teaspoon salt
1 cup buttermilk
1 egg, beaten
¼ cup vegetable oil

Combine the cereal, self-rising flour, baking powder and salt in a mixing bowl and mix well. Add the buttermilk, egg and oil and mix well. Pour into a greased cast-iron skillet. Bake at 400 degrees until golden brown. For Crackling Corn Bread, prepare batter as above but omit the vegetable oil and substitute 2 tablespoons bacon drippings. Add ¾ cup crumbled, crisp-cooked bacon to the batter and bake as above. YIELD: 8 TO 10 SERVINGS.

Betty Foshee
Decatur Council

Papa's Corn Bread

2 eggs
1 (8-ounce) can cream-style corn
1 cup sour cream
1 small onion, chopped
½ cup milk
1 (8-ounce) package corn bread mix

Beat the eggs in a mixing bowl. Add the cream-style corn, sour cream, onion and milk and mix well. Add the corn bread mix and mix well. Pour into a greased 8-inch ovenproof skillet. Bake at 400 degrees for 20 to 25 minutes or until golden brown. This corn bread is wonderful with chili. YIELD: 6 SERVINGS.

Susan Robbins
Riverchase Council

Mexican Corn Bread

1 cup self-rising cornmeal
1 (8-ounce) can cream-style corn
2 eggs, slightly beaten
1/3 cup melted shortening
3/4 cup buttermilk
2 tablespoons (about) chopped pickled jalapeño peppers
3/4 cup shredded Cheddar cheese
2 tablespoons butter

Combine the cornmeal, cream-style corn, eggs, melted shortening and buttermilk in a mixing bowl and mix well. Add the jalapeño peppers to taste and half the shredded cheese and mix well. Melt the butter in a cast-iron skillet. Pour the batter into the skillet and sprinkle with the remaining cheese. Bake at 400 degrees for 40 minutes or until brown. YIELD: 8 SERVINGS.

Lisa Burke
Birmingham Metro Council

Okra Corn Bread

1/2 cup hush puppy mix
1/2 teaspoon Cajun seasoning
1 (8-ounce) can cream-style corn
1 egg, beaten
1/2 cup milk
3 tablespoons vegetable oil
2 cups thinly sliced okra

Combine the hush puppy mix and Cajun seasoning in a mixing bowl and mix well. Add the cream-style corn, egg, milk and oil and mix well. Stir in the okra. Pour into a greased 8-inch square baking pan. Bake at 350 degrees for 45 minutes. Cut into squares.
YIELD: 9 SERVINGS.

Hazel E. Campbell
Birmingham Life

Hush Puppies

3/4 cup cornmeal mix
1 egg, beaten
1/2 cup (about) buttermilk
1/2 cup finely chopped onion

1 green onion, finely chopped
Pepper to taste
Vegetable oil for deep frying

Combine the cornmeal mix and egg in a mixing bowl. Add enough buttermilk to make the batter of the desired consistency. Add the onion, green onion and pepper and mix well. Drop the batter by spoonfuls into the hot oil. Deep-fry until golden brown on all sides, turning as necessary. Remove the hush puppies with a slotted spoon and drain on paper towels. Serve warm. YIELD: 4 TO 6 SERVINGS.

Faith Kirby Richardson
Gadsden Life

Hush Puppies

1 cup yellow cornmeal
1/4 cup flour
1 1/2 teaspoons baking powder
1/2 teaspoon salt

3/4 cup milk
1 egg, beaten
1 small onion, finely chopped
Vegetable oil for deep frying

Combine the cornmeal, flour, baking powder and salt in a mixing bowl. Add the milk and egg and mix until smooth. Stir in the onion. Heat the oil in a deep-fryer or electric skillet to 365 degrees. Drop the batter by teaspoonfuls into the hot oil. Deep-fry for 2 to 2 1/2 minutes or until golden brown on all sides, turning as necessary. Remove the hush puppies with a slotted spoon and drain on paper towels. Serve warm. YIELD: 4 TO 6 SERVINGS.

Hester P. Thompson
Birmingham Life

Vegetable Fritters

6 ounces self-rising white cornmeal mix
(about 1 cup plus 2 tablespoons)
1/2 cup flour
1/2 teaspoon crushed red pepper
2/3 cup buttermilk
1 egg, beaten
1 (16-ounce) can whole kernel corn, drained
1 (2-ounce) jar chopped pimentos
1/2 large green bell pepper, diced
4 green onions, thinly sliced
1 large carrot, shredded
1/2 cup vegetable oil
Sour cream

Combine the cornmeal, flour and red pepper in a mixing bowl and mix well. Add the buttermilk and egg and mix well. Stir in the corn, pimentos, green pepper, green onions and carrot and mix well. Heat the oil in a large nonstick skillet. Drop the batter by 1/3 cupfuls into the hot oil. Cook for 3 to 4 minutes on each side until golden brown. Drain the fritters on paper towels. Serve hot with sour cream. YIELD: 10 SERVINGS.

Donna Campbell
Anniston Council

HELPFUL HINT

For flavorful crumbs for coating fish, chicken or veal, combine leftover bread with citrus peel.

Coffee Cake

3/4 cup (1 1/2 sticks) margarine, softened
1 cup sugar
2 eggs
1 cup sour cream
2 cups flour
1 teaspoon baking powder
1 teaspoon baking soda
1/2 teaspoon salt
1 teaspoon nutmeg
Topping (below)

Cream the margarine and sugar in a mixing bowl until light and fluffy. Add the eggs and sour cream and beat until smooth. Sift the flour, baking powder, baking soda, salt and nutmeg together. Add to the sour cream mixture and beat until well blended. Pour the batter into a greased and floured cake pan. Sprinkle the Topping evenly over the batter. Refrigerate, covered, overnight. Bake, uncovered, at 325 degrees for 40 to 45 minutes or until golden brown. Yield: 6 to 8 servings.

Topping

3/4 cup packed brown sugar
1 teaspoon cinnamon
3/4 cup chopped pecans

Mix the brown sugar and cinnamon in a small bowl. Add the pecans and stir until well mixed. Yield: 1 1/2 cups.

Mary Alice Neal
Birmingham Life

Bubble Bread

1 cup sugar
½ cup packed brown sugar
4 teaspoons cinnamon
3 (8-count) cans fluffy large buttermilk biscuits
½ cup (1 stick) butter, melted
1 cup confectioners' sugar
1 to 2 tablespoons milk

Combine the sugar, brown sugar and cinnamon in a medium bowl and mix well. Separate the biscuits and cut each into quarters. Roll the biscuit pieces in the cinnamon mixture to coat and arrange in layers in a lightly greased bundt pan. Drizzle the butter over the biscuit layers. Bake at 350 degrees for 30 minutes or until golden brown. Invert the coffee cake onto a serving plate. Remove the pan carefully. Blend the confectioners' sugar and enough milk to make a glaze of the desired consistency. Spread the glaze over the hot coffee cake. Serve warm or cold. **YIELD: 10 TO 12 SERVINGS.**

Jamima M. Edney
Birmingham Life

Date Coffee Cake

⅓ cup mashed banana
½ cup (1 stick) butter, softened
3 eggs
1 teaspoon vanilla extract
3 cups unbleached flour
2 teaspoons baking powder
1 teaspoon baking soda
1½ cups water
1½ cups chopped dates
Topping (below)

Combine the banana and butter in a mixing bowl and beat until smooth and creamy. Add the eggs 1 at a time, beating after each addition. Beat in the vanilla. Combine the flour, baking powder and baking soda and mix well. Reserve a small amount of the flour mixture to mix with the dates. Add the remaining flour mixture and water alternately to the banana mixture, mixing well after each addition. Toss the reserved flour mixture with the dates until coated. Stir the coated dates into the batter. Spread the batter evenly in a greased and floured 9×13-inch cake pan. Sprinkle with the Topping. Bake at 350 degrees for 20 to 25 minutes or until a knife inserted in the center comes out clean. Cool in the pan on a wire rack. YIELD: 8 TO 10 SERVINGS.

Topping

⅓ cup chopped dates
⅓ cup chopped walnuts
⅓ cup flaked coconut

Combine the dates, walnuts and coconut in a bowl and mix well. YIELD: 1 CUP.

Louise Morrison
Tuscaloosa Council

Nutty Orange Coffee Cake

1 cup sugar
3/4 cup finely chopped pecans
1 tablespoon grated orange zest
2 (11-ounce) cans buttermilk biscuits
4 ounces reduced-fat cream cheese, softened
1/2 cup (1 stick) butter, melted
Glaze (below)

Combine the sugar, pecans and orange zest in a medium bowl, mix well and set aside. Separate the biscuits. Place about 3/4 teaspoon cream cheese in the center of each, fold over to enclose the cream cheese and press the edges together to seal. Lightly grease a 12-cup bundt pan. Roll each filled biscuit in the melted butter and then in the pecan mixture to coat. Arrange the biscuits with the curved side down in the grooves of the bundt pan; do not stack. Arrange any remaining biscuits around the center of the pan, filling in the spaces. Drizzle any remaining butter over the biscuits and sprinkle with any remaining pecan mixture. Bake at 350 degrees for 35 to 40 minutes or until golden brown. Invert the coffee cake onto a serving plate. Drizzle the Glaze over the coffee cake and serve immediately. YIELD: 10 TO 12 SERVINGS.

Glaze

1 1/2 cups confectioners' sugar
2 tablespoons fresh orange juice

Sift the confectioners' sugar into a small bowl. Add the orange juice and blend well. YIELD: 1 1/2 CUPS.

Chris Elsen
Gadsden Life

Quick Coffee Cake

2 cups flour
1 cup sugar
1/2 cup packed brown sugar
1 teaspoon baking powder
1 teaspoon baking soda
1/2 teaspoon salt
1/2 teaspoon cinnamon
2/3 cup vegetable oil
2 eggs
1 cup buttermilk
1 cup raisins (optional)
1/2 cup chopped nuts (optional)
Topping (below)

Combine the flour, sugar, brown sugar, baking powder, baking soda, salt and cinnamon in a mixing bowl and mix well. Add the oil and mix until the mixture is crumbly. Add the eggs and buttermilk and beat until well blended. Stir in the raisins and nuts. Pour the batter into a greased 9x13-inch cake pan. Sprinkle the Topping evenly over the batter. Refrigerate, covered, overnight if desired. Bake, uncovered, at 350 degrees for 30 minutes or until golden brown. YIELD: 10 TO 12 SERVINGS.

Topping

1/2 cup packed brown sugar
1/2 teaspoon cinnamon
1/2 teaspoon nutmeg
1/2 cup chopped nuts

Combine the brown sugar, cinnamon, nutmeg and nuts in a small bowl and mix well. YIELD: 1 CUP.

Barbara Seegmiller
Decatur Council

Sour Cream Coffee Cake

1 1/2 cups cake flour
1/2 cup all-purpose flour
1 teaspoon baking soda
1 teaspoon baking powder
1/2 cup (1 stick) butter, softened

1 cup sugar
1 egg, beaten
1 teaspoon vanilla extract
1 cup sour cream
Topping (below)

Mix the cake flour, all-purpose flour, baking soda and baking powder together and set aside. Cream the butter and sugar in a mixing bowl until light and fluffy. Add the egg and vanilla and beat until blended. Add half the flour mixture and mix just until the floured is blended. Blend in the sour cream. Add the remaining flour mixture and beat until blended. Spread half the batter in a lightly greased 10-inch tube pan. Sprinkle with half the Topping. Add layers of the remaining batter and the remaining Topping. Bake at 350 degrees for 40 to 45 minutes or until golden brown and the coffee cake tests done. Cool in the pan for 5 to 10 minutes. Invert the coffee cake onto a serving plate. YIELD: 10 TO 12 SERVINGS.

Topping

1/4 cup flour
3/4 cup packed brown sugar
1/4 teaspoon salt

1 cup chopped walnuts
1/4 cup (1/2 stick) butter

Combine the flour, brown sugar, salt and walnuts in a bowl. Cut the butter into small pieces. Add to the walnut mixture and mix with fingers until crumbly; do not overmix. YIELD: 2 CUPS.

Debbie Speaks
Montgomery Council

Sour Cream Coffee Cake

2 eggs
1 cup sugar
1/2 cup shortening
1 1/4 cups sour cream
1 teaspoon vanilla extract
1 teaspoon baking powder
1 teaspoon baking soda
1/2 teaspoon salt

2 cups flour
1/2 cup sugar
1/2 cup packed brown sugar
3 tablespoons flour
2 teaspoons cinnamon
3 tablespoons butter, melted
1 cup confectioners' sugar
2 tablespoons milk

Beat the eggs in a mixing bowl. Add the 1 cup sugar and shortening and beat until light and fluffy. Add the sour cream and vanilla and blend well. Add the baking powder, baking soda and salt and blend well. Add 2 cups flour gradually, beating until well blended after each addition. Pour half the batter into greased tube pan. Combine the 1/2 cup sugar, brown sugar, 3 tablespoons flour and cinnamon in a small bowl. Add the melted butter and mix with a fork until crumbly. Sprinkle about 1/3 of the topping mixture over the top. Add layers of the remaining batter and the remaining topping. Bake at 350 degrees for 50 to 60 minutes or until golden brown. Cool in the pan for 10 minutes. Invert the coffee cake onto a plate and reinvert onto a serving plate. Let stand until cooled completely. Blend the confectioners' sugar and milk in a small bowl until smooth and creamy. Drizzle over the coffee cake. You may add one or more of the following optional ingredients to the batter before pouring into the tube pan: 1/2 cup chopped nuts; 1 large apple, peeled, finely chopped; 3/4 cup dried blueberries; 3/4 cup chopped dried apricots; 3/4 cup chopped dates. YIELD: 16 SERVINGS.

Gussie Evans
Mobile Council

Apricot Quick Bread

1 cup dried apricots
1 cup sugar
2 tablespoons butter, softened
1 egg
2 cups flour
2 teaspoons baking powder
1 teaspoon salt
1/4 teaspoon baking soda
1/2 cup orange juice
1/4 cup water
1/2 cup chopped walnuts (optional)

Soak the apricots in warm water to cover for 30 minutes. Drain the apricots, cut into quarters and set aside. Combine the sugar, butter and egg in a mixing bowl and beat until light and fluffy. Combine the flour, baking powder, salt and baking soda and mix well. Combine the orange juice and 1/4 cup water. Add the flour mixture and orange juice to the sugar mixture alternately, mixing well after each addition. Stir in the apricots and walnuts. Pour into a greased loaf pan. Let stand for 20 minutes. Bake at 350 degrees for 1 hour or until a knife inserted in the center comes out clean. Cool in the pan for several minutes. Turn onto a wire rack to cool completely.
YIELD: 1 LOAF.

Francis Tucker
Selma Life

Amish Friendship Bread

Cinnamon-sugar
1 cup Starter (page 253)
1 cup sugar
1 cup vegetable oil
1 teaspoon vanilla extract
3 eggs
1 (6-ounce) package vanilla instant pudding
2 cups flour
2 teaspoons cinnamon
1 1/2 teaspoons baking powder
1/2 teaspoon baking soda
1/2 teaspoon salt
1/2 cup milk

Grease 2 large loaf pans well, sprinkle generously with cinnamon-sugar and set aside. Combine the Starter, sugar, oil, vanilla, eggs and pudding mix in a large mixing bowl and mix until well blended. Combine the flour, cinnamon, baking powder, baking soda and salt. Add the flour mixture to the Starter mixture alternately with the milk, mixing well after each addition. Divide the batter evenly between the prepared the loaf pans. Sprinkle with additional cinnamon sugar if desired. Bake at 325 degrees for 1 hour or until the loaves test done. Turn the loaves onto wire racks to cool. **YIELD: 2 LOAVES.**

Starter

Rules for creating and maintaining healthy starter:

- Do not use metal spoons or bowl for mixing.
- Do not refrigerate.
- Release air in the bag as necessary and reseal.
- It is normal for batter to thicken, bubble and ferment.
- Day 1: Combine 1 cup sugar, 1 cup all-purpose flour and 1 cup milk in a large sealable heavy-duty plastic bag. Squeeze out the air, seal the bag and knead gently to mix. Let the bag stand at room temperature overnight.
- Days 2 thru 5: Knead the bag gently, open the bag slightly to allow air to escape whenever necessary and reseal the bag.
- Day 6: Add 1 cup sugar, 1 cup all-purpose flour and 1 cup milk. Knead gently, squeeze out air and reseal the bag.
- Days 7 thru 9: Knead the bag gently, open the bag slightly to allow air to escape whenever necessary and reseal the bag.
- Day 10: Pour the batter into a large bowl. Add 1 cup sugar, 1 cup all-purpose flour and 1 cup milk and mix well. Divide the Starter into four 1-cup portions. Place 3 of the portions in sealable plastic bags to give as gifts to friends along with the recipe for Amish Friendship Bread. The fourth portion is for you to keep and can be used immediately to prepare a recipe for Amish Friendship Bread.

Sara Cooley
Birmingham Life

Banana Nut Bread

½ cup shortening
1 cup sugar
2 eggs
1 cup mashed bananas
2 cups flour
1 teaspoon baking powder
½ teaspoon baking soda
½ cup chopped nuts

Cream the shortening and sugar in a mixing bowl until light and fluffy. Add the eggs and mashed bananas and beat until well blended. Combine the flour, baking powder and baking soda. Add to the banana mixture and beat until well blended. Stir in the nuts. Pour into a greased loaf pan. Bake at 350 degrees for 1 hour or until the loaf tests done. Cool the banana bread in the loaf pan. Bread freezes well. YIELD: 1 LOAF.

Linda Ander
Montgomery Council

Beer Bread

3 cups self-rising flour
3 tablespoons sugar
1 (12-ounce) can beer
Chopped nuts (optional)
Cinnamon (optional)
¼ cup (½ stick) margarine, melted

Mix the self-rising flour, sugar and beer in a mixing bowl. Stir in the nuts and cinnamon. Pour into a greased loaf pan. Bake at 350 degrees for 50 minutes. Drizzle the margarine over the top. Bake for 10 minutes longer. Turn the loaf onto a serving plate. Serve hot. YIELD: 1 LOAF.

Mary Ann Stanley
Mobile Council

Pear Bread

1½ cups sugar
1½ cups corn oil
3 eggs
1 teaspoon vanilla extract
3 cups sifted flour
1½ teaspoons baking soda
1 teaspoon salt
1 teaspoon cinnamon
1 teaspoon nutmeg
½ teaspoon ground cloves
3 cups finely chopped peeled fresh pears

Combine the sugar, corn oil, eggs and vanilla in a mixing bowl and beat until well blended. Mix the flour, baking soda, salt, cinnamon, nutmeg and cloves together. Add to the sugar mixture gradually, beating well after each addition. Add the pears and stir until well mixed. Pour the batter into 2 greased and floured loaf pans. Bake at 350 degrees for 45 to 55 minutes or until the loaves test done; do not overbake. Cool in the pans for several minutes. Turn onto wire racks to cool. You may substitute apples for pears. YIELD: **2 LOAVES**.

Barbara Odom Horton (Mrs. Edward K., Sr.)
Mobile Council

HELPFUL HINT

Most sweet breads freeze well. Be sure they are completely cool and well wrapped before freezing.

Date Loaf

1 cup sugar
4 eggs
1 cup flour
2 teaspoons baking powder
½ teaspoon salt
1 pound pitted dates, chopped
1 pound English walnuts, chopped

Beat the sugar and eggs in a mixing bowl until until blended. Reserve a small amount of the flour. Combine the remaining flour, baking powder and salt and mix well. Add to the egg mixture and beat until well blended. Mix the reserved flour with the dates and walnuts. Add to the batter and mix well. Pour the batter into a greased loaf pan. Bake at 300 degrees for 2 hours or until the loaf tests done. Cool in the pan for several minutes. Turn onto a wire rack to cool completely. YIELD: 1 LOAF.

Elizabeth Cornwell
Selma Life

Zucchini Bread

3 eggs
1 cup vegetable oil
2 cups sugar
2 teaspoons vanilla extract
2 cups grated zucchini
3 cups flour
1 teaspoon salt
1 teaspoon baking soda
¼ teaspoon baking powder
1 tablespoon cinnamon
½ cup chopped nuts (optional)
½ cup raisins (optional)

Beat the eggs in a large mixing bowl. Add the oil, sugar and vanilla and beat until well blended. Stir in the zucchini. Mix the flour, salt, baking soda, baking powder and cinnamon together. Add to the zucchini mixture and mix well. Stir in the nuts and raisins. Pour into 2 greased loaf pans. Bake at 325 degrees for 1 hour or until the loaves test done. Cool in the pans for several minutes. Turn onto wire racks to cool completely. Loaves freeze well. YIELD: 2 LOAVES.

Louise Morrison
Tuscaloosa Council

Blueberry Muffins with Streusel Topping

1 egg
½ cup olive oil
¾ cup milk
2 cups self-rising flour
¾ cup sugar
2 cups blueberries
¼ cup sugar
Streusel Topping (below)

Grease 12 muffin cups on the bottoms only. Beat the egg in a medium mixing bowl. Add the olive oil and milk and mix well. Mix the self-rising flour and ¾ cup sugar together. Add to the egg mixture all at once and mix just until moistened; the batter will be lumpy. Drain the blueberries on paper towels and place in a bowl. Sprinkle the blueberries with the ¼ cup sugar and mix gently. Fold the blueberries into the muffin batter. Fill the prepared muffin cups ¾ full. Sprinkle with the Streusel Topping. Bake at 400 degrees for 20 minutes or until golden brown. Remove the muffins from the muffin cups to a wire rack immediately. YIELD: 1 DOZEN.

Streusel Topping

¼ cup sugar
2½ tablespoons flour
½ teaspoon cinnamon
1½ tablespoons butter

Combine the sugar, flour and cinnamon in a small bowl. Cut the butter into small pieces. Add to the sugar mixture and mix until crumbly. YIELD: ½ CUP.

Virginia Greene
Birmingham South Life

Low-Fat Banana Muffins

1 cup plus 5 tablespoons unbleached flour
3 tablespoons brown sugar
1 tablespoon pumpkin pie spice
1½ teaspoons baking powder
1 cup mashed bananas
¼ cup skim milk
3 tablespoons nonfat sour cream
1 egg white, well beaten

Grease and flour 6 muffin cups and set aside. Combine the flour, brown sugar, pumpkin pie spice and baking powder in a medium mixing bowl. Combine the mashed bananas, skim milk, sour cream and egg white in a small bowl and blend well. Add the banana mixture to the flour mixture and mix just until moistened. Fill the prepared muffin cups ⅔ full. Bake at 350 degrees for 20 minutes or until light brown. YIELD: 6 MUFFINS.

Gussie Evans
Mobile Council

Bran Muffins

2 tablespoons shortening
½ cup any flavor jelly
1 egg, beaten
1 cup All-Bran cereal
¾ cup buttermilk
1 cup flour
1 teaspoon baking powder
½ teaspoon baking soda

Combine the shortening and jelly in a mixing bowl and blend well. Add the egg and mix well. Add the cereal and buttermilk and mix well. Mix the flour, baking powder and baking soda together. Add the flour mixture to the cereal mixture and mix well. Spoon the batter into greased muffin cups of the desired size. Bake at 325 degrees for 40 minutes or until the muffins test done. YIELD: 6 MUFFINS.

Sue Small
Selma Life

Minnie Pearl's Bran Muffins

1 cup All-Bran cereal
1 cup boiling water
½ cup vegetable oil
2½ cups sifted flour
2½ teaspoons baking soda
1 teaspoon salt
1½ cups sugar
2 eggs, beaten
2 cups buttermilk
2 cups All-Bran cereal

Combine the 1 cup cereal and boiling water in a medium mixing bowl. Let stand until cool. Add the oil and mix well. Sift the flour, baking soda, salt and sugar together into a large mixing bowl. Beat the eggs and buttermilk together. Mix the egg mixture into the flour mixture. Stir in the remaining 2 cups cereal. Add the moist cereal mixture and mix well. Spoon the desired amount of batter into the desired number of greased muffin cups; store any remaining muffin batter in a covered container in the refrigerator. Bake at 400 degrees for 20 minutes or until lightly browned. **Editor's Note:** For safety, if the batter is to be stored before baking, we recommend that the equivalent amount of egg substitute be substituted for the fresh eggs. YIELD: 2 DOZEN.

Phoebe Arthur
Gadsden Life

HELPFUL HINT

Muffins can be easily removed from the pan if it is first placed on a damp towel.

Refrigerator Bran Muffins

1 (15-ounce) package Raisin Bran cereal
3 cups sugar
5 cups flour
5 teaspoons baking soda
2 teaspoons salt
1 teaspoon cinnamon
1 teaspoon ground cloves
1 teaspoon nutmeg
4 eggs, beaten
1 cup vegetable oil
4 cups buttermilk
2 teaspoons vanilla extract

Combine the cereal, sugar, flour, baking soda, salt, cinnamon, cloves and nutmeg in a large mixing bowl and mix well. Add the eggs, oil, buttermilk and vanilla and mix well. Fill the desired number of greased muffin cups ⅔ full. Bake at 400 degrees for 15 minutes. Store any remaining muffin batter in a covered container in the refrigerator for up to 4 weeks. **Editor's Note:** For safety, if the batter is to be stored before baking, we recommend that the equivalent amount of egg substitute be substituted for the fresh eggs. YIELD: 3 TO 3½ DOZEN.

Dottie Drennon
Birmingham South Cahaba Council

Onion Cheese Muffins

3 cups biscuit mix
1 teaspoon salt
3/4 cup shredded Cheddar cheese
1 (3-ounce) can French-fried onions, crumbled
1 egg
1 cup milk

Combine the biscuit mix, salt, cheese and onions in a large mixing bowl and mix well. Add the egg and milk and beat for 1 minute. Fill greased muffin cups 2/3 full. Bake at 400 degrees for 15 minutes or until golden brown. YIELD: 1 TO 1 1/2 DOZEN.

Eunice Henry
Selma Life

Orange Muffins

1/2 cup (1 stick) butter, softened
3/4 cup sugar
2 eggs
1 teaspoon baking soda
1 cup buttermilk
2 cups flour
1/2 teaspoon salt
1 cup raisins
Zest of 1 orange

Cream the butter and sugar in a large mixing bowl until light and fluffy. Add the eggs and beat well. Dissolve the baking soda in the buttermilk. Sift the flour and salt together. Add the flour mixture to the creamed mixture alternately with the buttermilk mixture, mixing well after each addition. Process the raisins and orange zest in a food processor until finely chopped. Add to the muffin batter and mix well. Spoon the batter into 12 greased muffin cups. Bake at 400 degrees for 20 minutes or until golden brown. YIELD: 1 DOZEN.

Hazel E. Campbell
Birmingham Life

Orange Raisin Muffins

2 teaspoons baking soda
1 cup buttermilk
1 cup (2 sticks) butter, softened
2 cups packed brown sugar
2 eggs
3 cups flour
1/4 cup grated orange zest
1 teaspoon vanilla extract
1 cup chopped pecans
1 cup raisins
Orange Glaze (below)

Dissolve the baking soda in the buttermilk. Beat the butter in a large mixing bowl until creamy. Add the brown sugar gradually, beating until well blended. Stir in the buttermilk mixture and the eggs, blending well. Add the flour, orange zest and vanilla and mix well. Add the pecans and raisins and mix well. Fill greased muffin cups 2/3 full. Bake at 350 degrees for 20 to 23 minutes or until golden brown. Remove the muffins from the cups immediately. Place on wire racks to cool. Drizzle the Orange Glaze over the muffins. You may substitute 1 cup chopped dates for the raisins. The batter may be stored in a covered container in the refrigerator for up to 24 hours before baking. YIELD: 1 1/2 DOZEN.

Orange Glaze

1/3 cup confectioners' sugar
1 tablespoon butter, melted
2 teaspoons fresh orange juice

Combine the confectioners' sugar, butter and orange juice in a small bowl and mix until smooth. YIELD: 1/2 CUP.

Mary D. Palmer
Birmingham Metro Council

Pecan Pie Mini-Muffins

1 cup packed brown sugar
½ cup flour
1 cup chopped pecans
2 eggs, beaten
⅔ cup butter, melted

Combine the brown sugar, flour and pecans in a mixing bowl. Blend the eggs and butter in a small bowl. Add to the pecan mixture and mix well. Fill greased miniature muffin cups ⅔ full. Bake at 350 degrees for 20 to 25 minutes or until golden brown and the muffins test done. Remove from the muffin cups immediately. Cool on wire racks. YIELD: 2½ DOZEN.

Linda McAdams
Shoals Life

Pumpkin Muffins

8 ounces raisins
¾ cup water
1 (15-ounce) can pumpkin
1¾ cups sugar
¾ cup beaten eggs
2½ cups flour
2 teaspoons baking powder
1 teaspoon baking soda
½ teaspoon salt
¼ teaspoon cinnamon
¼ teaspoon ground cloves
¼ teaspoon nutmeg
½ cup vegetable oil

Soak the raisins in water to cover until plumped. Combine ¾ cup water, pumpkin, sugar and eggs in a large mixing bowl and mix well. Mix the flour, baking powder, baking soda, salt, cinnamon, cloves and nutmeg together. Add to the pumpkin mixture and mix well. Drain the raisins. Add the raisins and oil to the batter and stir just until mixed. Spoon the batter into greased muffin cups. Bake at 400 degrees for 15 to 20 minutes or until golden brown and the muffins test done. Remove from the muffin cups. YIELD: 1 DOZEN.

Sarah Wanda Cook
Montgomery Life

Whole Wheat Honey Muffins

3/4 cup Fiber One cereal
1/2 cup golden raisins
1/2 cup shredded carrots
1 egg
1/4 cup honey
1/4 cup canola oil

1 1/4 cups buttermilk
1 teaspoon vanilla extract
1 1/4 cups whole wheat flour
1 teaspoon baking soda
1 teaspoon cinnamon

Combine the cereal, raisins, carrots, egg, honey, canola oil, buttermilk and vanilla in a mixing bowl and mix well. Let stand for 10 minutes. Combine the whole wheat flour, baking soda and cinnamon in a large mixing bowl. Make a well in the center. Add the cereal mixture and stir just until moistened. Spoon the batter into greased muffin cups. Bake at 375 degrees for 15 to 17 minutes or until a toothpick inserted in the center comes out clean; do not overbake. YIELD: 1 DOZEN.

Kathleen Griffis
Birmingham South Life

Quick Rolls

2 cups self-rising flour
1 cup milk

1 teaspoon sugar
4 teaspoons mayonnaise

Grease and flour 12 muffin cups and set aside. Combine the self-rising flour, milk, sugar and mayonnaise in a mixing bowl and beat until blended. Fill the prepared muffin cups 2/3 full. Bake at 400 degrees for 15 minutes or until golden brown. For 12 small rolls, reduce each ingredients by half and bake in small muffin cups. YIELD: 12 LARGE ROLLS.

Kathryn Morgan
Gadsden Life

Orange Rolls

2 (8-count) packages crescent rolls
2 Granny Smith apples, peeled
½ cup (1 stick) butter
1 cup sugar
1 cup orange juice
1 teaspoon vanilla extract

Separate the roll dough into triangles. Core the apples and cut each apple into 8 slices. Wrap each of the apple slices in a dough triangle and place in a greased 9×13-inch baking pan. Melt the butter in a small saucepan and remove from the heat. Add the sugar and mix well. Stir in the orange juice and vanilla. Pour the orange juice mixture over the rolls. Bake at 350 degrees for 30 minutes. Serve warm. YIELD: 16 SERVINGS.

Gloria "Carol" Lindley
Birmingham South Cahaba Council

Sweet Rolls

1 (10-count) can fluffy large buttermilk biscuits
½ cup (1 stick) butter, melted
¾ cup sugar
1 teaspoon cinnamon
3 ounces cream cheese, softened

Separate the biscuits. Roll each biscuit in the melted butter; roll in a mixture of cinnamon and sugar to coat well. Arrange the biscuits in a baking dish. Make a small hole in the center of each biscuit and add a spoonful of cream cheese to each hole. Bake at 350 degrees for 20 minutes or until golden brown. YIELD: 10 SERVINGS.

Fay Clark
Riverchase Council

Something Different Sweet Rolls

1 (2-layer) package yellow cake mix
2 envelopes dry yeast
5 cups flour
2 1/2 cups hot water
Butter, softened
Cinnamon-sugar
Topping (below)

Combine the cake mix, yeast and flour in a large mixing bowl and mix well. Add the water and mix well. Let the dough rise, loosely covered, in a warm place until doubled in bulk. Turn the dough onto a lightly floured surface. Roll into a rectangle. Spread the dough with butter and sprinkle with cinnamon-sugar. Roll the rectangle as for a jelly roll. Cut into 1 1/2- to 2-inch slices and arrange in a greased baking pan. Let the dough rise, loosely covered, until almost doubled in bulk. Spoon the Topping over the rolls. Bake at 375 degrees for 25 minutes or until golden brown.
Yield: 2 1/2 dozen.

Topping

1/2 cup (1 stick) butter
1/4 cup light corn syrup
1/4 cup packed brown sugar
Chopped nuts

Melt the butter in a saucepan. Add the corn syrup and brown sugar and mix well. Stir in the desired amount of nuts.
Yield: about 1 cup.

Barbara Seegmiller
Decatur Council

Exa's Rolls

1 envelope dry yeast
2 teaspoons sugar
¼ cup warm water
2 tablespoons (heaping) shortening
½ cup sugar
1 cup lukewarm water
2 teaspoons salt
2 eggs
5 cups flour
Margarine

Dissolve the yeast and 2 teaspoons sugar in ¼ cup warm water and set aside. Combine the shortening, ½ cup sugar, 1 cup lukewarm water, salt, eggs and 2 cups flour in a large mixing bowl and beat until well mixed. Add the yeast mixture and beat until creamy. Add the remaining 3 cups flour gradually, mixing with a spoon or by hand until well mixed. Spread a generous coating of shortening over the top of the dough. Let rise, loosely covered, for 1 hour. Punch the dough down and turn onto a lightly floured surface. Roll the dough into a rectangle. Cut the dough as for biscuits. Mark each dough circle with a ridge across the center. Melt a generous amount of margarine in a baking pan. Roll each dough circle in the melted margarine, fold over and arrange in the baking pan. Let the rolls rise, loosely covered, for about 2 hours for best results or cover, refrigerate overnight and let rise at room temperature on the following day. Bake at 400 degrees for 5 to 8 minutes or until golden brown. This was the secret recipe of Mrs. Exa Warren, who made Walgreen's in Sheffield famous for her rolls. YIELD: 2½ DOZEN.

Virginia Bowen
Shoals Life

Freeze and Bake Rolls

2 envelopes dry yeast
1½ cups (110- to 115-degree) water
2 teaspoons sugar
1½ cups (110- to 115-degree) milk
¼ cup vegetable oil
4 teaspoons salt
½ cup sugar
7½ to 8½ cups flour

Dissolve the yeast in the warm water in a large mixing bowl. Add the 2 teaspoons sugar and mix well. Let stand for 5 minutes. Add the milk, oil, salt and remaining ½ cup sugar. Stir in enough flour to make a stiff dough. Turn the dough onto a lightly floured surface and knead for 6 to 8 minutes or until smooth and elastic. Shape the dough into a ball and place in a large greased bowl, turning to coat the surface. Let the dough rise, loosely covered, in a warm place for about 1½ hours or until doubled in bulk. Punch the dough down. Divide the dough into easy to handle portions. Roll one portion at a time into a rectangle on a lightly floured surface. Cut into rolls and arrange on greased baking sheets. Let rise, loosely covered, for 20 to 30 minutes or until doubled in bulk. Bake at 375 degrees for 15 to 18 minutes or until golden brown. You may partially bake the rolls at 325 degrees for 15 minutes, cool completely, wrap tightly and store in the freezer. Bake the frozen rolls at 375 degrees for 12 to 15 minutes or until golden brown. YIELD: 3 TO 4 DOZEN.

Elba Skinner
Selma Life

Basic Refrigerator Rolls

6 tablespoons shortening
1 teaspoon salt
1/4 cup sugar
1 cup hot water
1 envelope dry yeast

2 tablespoons lukewarm water
1 egg, well beaten
3 1/2 to 4 cups sifted flour
Melted butter

Mix the shortening, salt, sugar and hot water in a large mixing bowl. Let stand until cooled to lukewarm. Dissolve the yeast in the lukewarm water in a small bowl. Add the yeast, egg and half the flour to the shortening mixture. Add enough of the remaining flour to make the dough easy to handle. Grease the top of the dough. Store, covered, in the refrigerator for several hours to overnight. Roll the dough into a rectangle on a lightly floured surface and cut into rolls. Dip the rolls into butter. Arrange in a baking pan. Bake at 425 degrees for 12 minutes or until brown. YIELD: 1 1/2 TO 2 DOZEN.

Earline Weaver
Shoals Life

Thirty-Minute Rolls

3 cups (about) self-rising flour
1/2 cup sugar
1 envelope dry yeast

1 1/2 cups water
1/2 cup shortening
1 egg

Mix 3 cups self-rising flour, sugar and dry yeast in a large mixing bowl. Heat the water and shortening in a saucepan to 225 degrees or until the shortening melts. Stir into the flour mixture. Add the egg and mix well. Add enough remaining flour to make a stiff dough. Turn the dough onto a lightly floured surface, roll and cut into rolls. Arrange the rolls on a greased baking sheet. Let rise for 30 minutes. Bake at 400 degrees until brown. YIELD: 1 1/2 DOZEN.

Imogene Davis
Birmingham Life

Aunt Luna's Refrigerator Rolls

1 envelope dry yeast
1/2 cup lukewarm water
1/2 cup shortening
1/2 cup cool water
1/3 cup sugar
1 teaspoon salt
1 egg, well beaten
3 cups flour

Dissolve the yeast in 1/2 cup lukewarm water. Combine the shortening and 1/2 cup cool water in a saucepan and heat until the shortening melts. Remove from the heat and let stand until cooled to lukewarm. Place the yeast mixture in a large mixing bowl. Add the shortening mixture and mix well. Stir in the sugar and salt. Add the beaten egg and flour alternately, mixing well after each addition. Let rise, loosely covered, in the refrigerator overnight. Turn the dough onto a lightly floured surface. Roll into a 1/4 inch thick rectangle and cut into rolls. Arrange the rolls a on greased baking sheet. Let rise, loosely covered, for 2 hours or until almost doubled in bulk. Bake at 450 degrees for 10 to 15 minutes or until golden brown. YIELD: 1 1/2 DOZEN.

Lola Duffey
Shoals Life

HELPFUL HINT

Hot rolls or biscuits will stay hot longer if you place aluminum foil under the napkin in the basket.

Club Soda Pancakes

2 cups biscuit mix
½ cup vegetable oil
1 egg, beaten
1¼ cups club soda

Combine the biscuit mix, oil and egg in a mixing bowl. Add the club soda and mix well. Ladle the desired amount of batter onto a hot greased griddle. Bake until bubbly around the edge, turn the pancake over and bake until golden brown on both sides.
YIELD: 1 DOZEN.

Narice Sutton
Birmingham Life

Belgian Waffles

4 egg yolks
3 tablespoons butter, melted
½ teaspoon vanilla extract
1 cup flour
½ teaspoon salt
1 cup milk
4 egg whites, stiffly beaten
Whipped cream
Sliced fresh strawberries

Beat the egg yolks in a mixing bowl at medium speed until thickened and pale yellow. Add the butter and vanilla and beat until blended. Mix the flour and salt together. Add the flour mixture to the egg yolk mixture alternately with milk, mixing well after each addition. Fold in the stiffly beaten egg yolks gently. Bake in a hot oiled Belgian waffle iron until golden. Serve with whipped cream and strawberries. YIELD: 8 SERVINGS.

Betty Foshee
Decatur Council

BIRMINGHAM METRO COUNCIL

The Birmingham Metro Council has many different projects for the inner city schools. One of the most rewarding projects is the annual field trip to the McWane Center.

Vegetables

Oven-Baked Asparagus

1 pound fresh asparagus
2 tablespoons butter or margarine
Salt and pepper to taste

Arrange the asparagus on a large piece of heavy-duty foil. Dot with the butter. Wrap the foil around the asparagus, pressing the edges to seal. Place the foil packet on a baking sheet. Bake at 350 degrees for 25 to 30 minutes or until tender-crisp. Season with the salt and pepper. YIELD: 4 SERVINGS.

Hester P. Thompson
Birmingham Life

English Pea and Asparagus Casserole

1 (15-ounce) can English peas, drained
1 (10-ounce) can cream of mushroom soup
1 (11-ounce) can asparagus tips, drained
2 hard-cooked eggs, sliced
Butter
2 cups shredded Cheddar cheese
1 sleeve butter crackers, crushed

Layer the peas, soup, asparagus and eggs in a buttered 9×13-inch baking pan. Dot with the butter. Top with the Cheddar cheese. Sprinkle with the cracker crumbs. Bake at 350 degrees for 30 minutes or until bubbly. You may omit the asparagus. YIELD: 8 SERVINGS.

Dilla Samuel
Gadsden Life

Lemon-Kissed Asparagus with Midgie Carrots

1 pound baby carrots
½ pound fresh asparagus
1 tablespoon fresh lemon juice
1 teaspoon lemon pepper
½ teaspoon grated lemon zest

Combine the carrots with enough water to cover in a saucepan. Simmer until tender; drain and rinse. Bring ½ inch of water to a boil in a skillet. Add the asparagus. Boil for 1 to 3 minutes, or until tender-crisp; drain and rinse. Combine the carrots and asparagus in a serving dish. Drizzle with the lemon juice. Sprinkle with the lemon pepper. Garnish with the lemon zest. **YIELD: 2 SERVINGS.**

Gussie Evans
Mobile Council

Quick Casserole

1 (15-ounce) can asparagus, drained
1 (15-ounce) can English peas, drained
1 (15-ounce) can whole potatoes, drained
1 (10-ounce) can cream of celery soup
Buttered bread crumbs

Combine the asparagus, peas, potatoes and soup in a bowl and mix well. Spoon into a baking dish. Top with the bread crumbs. Bake at 350 degrees for 30 minutes or until bubbly. You may substitute homemade white sauce for the cream of celery soup or slivered almonds for the bread crumbs. You may top with shredded Cheddar cheese. **YIELD: 6 SERVINGS.**

Faith Kirby Richardson
Gadsden Life

Baked Beans

2 (21-ounce) cans pork and beans
1 (15-ounce) can pineapple chunks, drained
1/2 cup packed brown sugar
1/4 cup barbecue sauce
2 tablespoons prepared mustard
1 tablespoon chopped onion
1 tablespoon Worcestershire sauce
1/8 teaspoon cayenne pepper

Combine the pork and beans, pineapple, brown sugar, barbecue sauce, mustard, onion, Worcestershire sauce and cayenne pepper in a bowl and mix well. Spoon into a baking dish. Bake at 400 degrees for 30 to 40 minutes or until brown and bubbly. YIELD: 8 SERVINGS.

Joann Foul
Gadsden Life

The Best Baked Beans

1/2 cup ketchup
1/4 cup packed brown sugar
1 tablespoon prepared mustard
2 (16-ounce) cans pork and beans
1 medium onion, chopped
1/4 cup (1/2 stick) butter
1 pound ground chuck

Combine the ketchup, brown sugar and mustard in a bowl and mix well. Stir in the pork and beans. Sauté the onion in the butter in a skillet until transparent. Stir in the ground chuck. Cook until the ground chuck is brown and crumbly, stirring constantly; drain. Add the ground chuck mixture to the pork and bean mixture and mix well. Spoon into a baking dish. Bake, covered, at 250 degrees for 2 to 3 hours or until brown and bubbly. YIELD: 6 TO 8 SERVINGS.

Mary Haynes
Birmingham South Cahaba

Turnip Greens and White Bean Bake

4 slices bacon
1 large onion, chopped
3 garlic cloves, minced
¼ to ½ teaspoon crushed red pepper
1 (15-ounce) can Italian-seasoned tomatoes
1½ pounds fresh turnip greens, rinsed, drained
1 (15-ounce) can Great Northern beans, drained
1 cup crumbled corn bread
2 tablespoons butter or margarine, melted

Fry the bacon in a skillet until crisp. Drain, reserving 1½ tablespoons drippings. Crumble the bacon. Stir the onion, garlic and red pepper into the reserved pan drippings. Cook over medium heat for 3 minutes or until tender, stirring frequently. Stir in the tomatoes. Bring to a boil, stirring frequently. Tear the turnip greens into 1-inch strips. Add the turnip greens to the tomato mixture gradually, stirring until wilted. Cook, covered, over medium-low heat for 10 minutes or until tender, stirring occasionally. Stir in the beans. Spoon into a greased shallow 1½-quart baking dish. Combine the corn bread and the butter in a bowl and toss to mix. Sprinkle over the prepared layer. Bake at 350 degrees for 25 minutes. Sprinkle with the bacon. Bake for 3 minutes longer. **YIELD: 4 SERVINGS.**

Dianne Tillman
Birmingham South Life

HELPFUL HINT

Chop onions and green peppers during their plentiful season and freeze them for later use in casseroles and soups.

Harvest Beets

1 pound fresh beets
½ cup lemon juice or vinegar
½ cup sugar
¼ cup water
1 tablespoon cornstarch
½ teaspoon salt

Combine the beets with enough water to cover in a saucepan. Cook until tender; drain. Peel the beets and slice. Transfer the beets to a serving bowl. Combine the lemon juice, sugar, water, cornstarch and salt in a saucepan. Cook over medium heat for 5 minutes, stirring occasionally. Pour over the beets. Let stand for 5 minutes before serving. YIELD: 6 SERVINGS.

Louise Morrison
Tuscaloosa Council

Pensacola Boarding House Beets

2 (16-ounce) cans sliced beets
½ cup sugar
½ cup cider vinegar
1 large sweet onion, sliced, separated into rings

Drain the beets, reserving the liquid. Combine the reserved liquid, sugar and vinegar in a saucepan. Bring to a boil, stirring frequently. Place the beets in a serving dish. Arrange the onion rings over the beets. Pour the reserved liquid over the prepared dish. Let stand until cool. Chill, covered, until ready to serve. YIELD: 8 TO 10 SERVINGS.

Jack D. Phillips
Birmingham South Life

Sweet-and-Sour Broccoli

4 medium tomatoes, halved, seeded
2 pounds broccoli, cut into 3/4-inch pieces
1 cup olive oil
2 cups frozen corn, thawed
2 large red bell peppers, chopped
1/4 cup plus 2 tablespoons lemon juice
1/4 cup white wine vinegar
1/4 cup sugar
1/2 teaspoon cinnamon
1/2 teaspoon pepper
1/2 cup raisins
1/2 cup pine nuts

Drain the tomatoes on a paper towel. Chill, covered, until ready to serve. Cook the broccoli in the oil in a skillet over medium heat for 12 to 15 minutes or until tender. Stir in the corn, bell peppers, lemon juice, white wine vinegar, sugar, cinnamon and pepper. Simmer for 5 minutes, stirring occasionally. Stir in the raisins and pine nuts. Simmer for 2 to 3 minutes or until thickened, stirring frequently. Spoon the mixture into a bowl. Chill, covered, for 2 hours. Spoon the broccoli mixture into the tomato halves.
Yield: 8 servings.

Rita Wilson, daughter of Helen Shirley
Birmingham Life

HELPFUL HINT

Place a heel of bread on top of broccoli to absorb odor when cooking.

Broccoli Casserole

1 (16-ounce) package frozen chopped broccoli
1 (10-ounce) can cream of chicken soup
1 (10-ounce) can chicken and rice soup, drained
1/4 cup instant rice
2 cups shredded Cheddar cheese
1/4 cup chopped onions
1/4 cup milk (optional)
1 (3-ounce) can French-fried onions

Cook the broccoli using package directions; drain. Combine the broccoli and the next 5 ingredients in a bowl and mix well, adding the milk if needed for desired consistency. Spoon the mixture into a baking dish. Sprinkle with the French-fried onions. Bake at 350 degrees for 25 to 30 minutes or until brown. YIELD: **8 SERVINGS**.

Diane Riccio
Riverchase Council

Broccoli Casserole

2 (10-ounce) packages frozen chopped broccoli
2 (10-ounce) cans cream of mushroom soup
2 eggs
1 cup shredded sharp Cheddar cheese
1 onion, chopped
1 tablespoon mayonnaise
1 cup shredded sharp Cheddar cheese
1 sleeve butter crackers, crushed
1/2 cup (1 stick) butter, melted

Cook the broccoli using the package directions; drain. Combine the broccoli, soup, eggs, 1 cup Cheddar cheese, onion and mayonnaise in a bowl and mix gently. Spoon into a baking dish. Bake at 350 degrees for 45 minutes or until firm in the middle. Sprinkle 1 cup Cheddar cheese over the top. Sprinkle with the cracker crumbs. Drizzle with the butter. Bake until light brown. YIELD: **8 SERVINGS**.

Evelyn T. Veazey
Opelika Life

Broccoli and Rice Casserole

2 (10-ounce) packages frozen chopped broccoli
1 (12-ounce) jar Cheez Whiz
1 (10-ounce) can cream of celery soup
1 (5-ounce) package yellow rice, cooked
French-fried onions

Steam the broccoli in a steamer for 5 minutes; drain. Combine the broccoli, Cheez Whiz, soup and rice in a bowl and mix gently. Spoon into a baking dish. Sprinkle with the French-fried onions. Bake at 400 degrees for 30 minutes or until brown. YIELD: **6 SERVINGS**.

Betty C. Gray
Montgomery Life

Rice and Broccoli Casserole

1 (10-ounce) package frozen chopped broccoli, thawed
1 small onion, chopped
½ cup chopped celery
1 tablespoon butter or margarine
1 (10-ounce) can cream of mushroom soup
1 (8-ounce) jar Cheez Whiz
1 (5-ounce) can evaporated milk
3 cups cooked rice

Cook the broccoli, onion and celery in the butter in a skillet over medium heat for 10 to 15 minutes or until tender. Stir in the soup, Cheez Whiz and evaporated milk and mix gently. Spoon the rice into a baking dish. Spoon the broccoli mixture over the top. Bake at 325 degrees for 35 to 40 minutes or until bubbly. YIELD: **6 SERVINGS**.

Doris Yarber
Shoals Life

Pattie's Owens Broccoli

2 (10-ounce) packages frozen chopped broccoli
½ pound Velveeta cheese
1 sleeve butter crackers, crushed
¼ cup (½ stick) butter, melted

Cook the broccoli using the package directions; drain. Combine the broccoli with the Velveeta cheese in a bowl and mix gently until the cheese is melted. Spoon into a baking dish. Combine the cracker crumbs and butter in a bowl and mix well. Sprinkle over the top. Bake at 375 degrees for 20 to 30 minutes or until brown. YIELD: 8 SERVINGS.

Pattie Smith
Gadsden Life

Cabbage Casserole

⅔ cup noodles
1 head of cabbage, chopped
½ cup chopped onion (optional)
1 or 2 bouillon cubes (optional)
1½ cups shredded Cheddar cheese
Salt and pepper to taste

Cook the noodles using the package directions; drain. Combine the cabbage, onion and bouillon cube with enough water to cover in a saucepan. Simmer until tender; drain. Combine the noodles and cabbage in a bowl and toss to mix. Stir in the Cheddar cheese. Sprinkle with salt and pepper. Spoon into a baking dish. Bake at 350 degrees for 30 minutes. You may top with additional shredded Cheddar cheese before baking. YIELD: 6 TO 8 SERVINGS.

Donna Roper
Birmingham South Cahaba Council

Glazed Carrots

2 cups sliced carrots
1 cup orange juice
½ cup sugar
2 tablespoons cornstarch
Dash of nutmeg

Combine the carrots with enough water to cover in a saucepan. Simmer until tender-crisp; drain. Transfer the cooked carrots to a serving dish. Combine the orange juice, sugar, cornstarch and nutmeg in a saucepan. Cook over medium heat until thickened, stirring constantly. Pour over the carrots. Let stand for 3 minutes before serving. YIELD: 6 SERVINGS.

Betty Holloway
Birmingham Life

Piccadilly Carrot Soufflé

3 pounds baby carrots, steamed, drained
2 cups sugar
¼ cup flour
1 tablespoon baking powder
1 tablespoon vanilla extract
6 eggs
1 cup (2 sticks) margarine, melted
Confectioners' sugar

Process the carrots in a food processor container until finely chopped. Add the sugar, flour, baking powder and vanilla and process until smooth. Add the eggs and margarine and process until blended. Spoon into a 9×13-inch baking pan. Bake at 350 degrees for 1¼ hours. Dust the top with confectioners' sugar. YIELD: 12 SERVINGS.

Virginia Greene
Birmingham South Life

Cauliflower Casserole

Florets of 1 head cauliflower
1 cup sour cream
1 cup shredded Cheddar cheese
1/2 cup crushed corn flakes
1/4 cup chopped green bell pepper
1/4 cup chopped red bell pepper
1/4 cup grated Parmesan cheese
Paprika

Place the cauliflower in a small amount of water in a saucepan Cook, covered, for 5 minutes or until tender-crisp; drain. Combine the cauliflower, sour cream, Cheddar cheese, corn flakes and the bell peppers in a bowl and mix gently. Spoon into a greased 2-quart baking dish. Sprinkle with the Parmesan cheese. Sprinkle with the paprika. Bake at 325 degrees for 30 to 35 minutes or until heated through. YIELD: 6 TO 8 SERVINGS.

Hester P. Thompson
Birmingham Life Member

Corn Casserole

1 (17-ounce) can cream-style corn
1 (16-ounce) can whole kernel corn
1 (9-ounce) package corn muffin mix
1 cup sour cream
1/2 cup (1 stick) margarine, melted

Combine the cream-style corn, whole kernel corn, muffin mix, sour cream and margarine in a bowl and mix well. Pour into a baking dish. Bake at 250 degrees for 45 to 50 minutes or until light brown. YIELD: 9 SERVINGS.

Fay Clark
Riverchase Council

Corn Casserole

1 onion, chopped
Butter
2 eggs, beaten
2 (17-ounce) cans cream-style corn
1 (16-ounce) can whole kernel corn, drained
1 (9-ounce) package corn bread mix
2/3 cup vegetable oil

Sauté the onion in butter in a skillet until transparent. Combine the onion, eggs, cream-style corn, whole kernel corn, corn bread mix and vegetable oil in a bowl and mix well. Pour into a 2-quart baking dish. Bake at 350 degrees for 40 to 45 minutes or until set and light brown. **YIELD: 8 TO 10 SERVINGS.**

Sherry A. Liles
Huntsville Council

Corn and Rice Casserole

1 (5-ounce) package yellow rice
1 3/4 cups shredded Cheddar cheese
1/4 cup (1/2 stick) butter, melted
1 (16-ounce) can whole kernel corn, drained
1 (10-ounce) can cream of chicken soup
3/4 cup shredded Cheddar cheese

Cook the rice using the package directions, omitting the salt. Combine the rice, 1 3/4 cups Cheddar cheese, butter, whole kernel corn and cream of chicken soup in a bowl and mix well. Spoon into a baking dish sprayed with nonstick cooking spray. Bake at 350 degrees for 20 to 30 minutes until bubbly. Sprinkle 3/4 cup Cheddar cheese over the top. Bake for 10 minutes longer. **YIELD: 6 SERVINGS.**

Mary Ann Stanley
Mobile Council

Corn Pudding

4 eggs
1 cup milk
1 (17-ounce) can cream-style corn
½ cup sugar
5 slices bread, crusts trimmed, cubed
1 tablespoon butter or margarine, softened

Combine the eggs and milk in a bowl and beat until blended. Add the corn and sugar and mix well. Arrange the bread cubes in a greased 9-inch square baking dish. Pour the corn mixture over the bread cubes. Dot with the butter. Bake at 350 degrees for 50 to 60 minutes or until a knife inserted near the center comes out clean.
YIELD: 9 SERVINGS.

Mary M. Storey
Anniston Council

Big Mama's Green Beans

3 slices bacon
2 to 3 pounds fresh green beans, trimmed, snapped
Salt and pepper to taste

Cook the bacon in a skillet until crisp. Place the green beans in a saucepan. Add enough water to cover the green beans by 1 inch. Add the bacon, drippings, salt and pepper. Cook over medium heat for 2 to 3 hours or until ½ inch water is left in the saucepan.
YIELD: 8 TO 10 SERVINGS.

Margie Stetson
Riverchase Council

Baked String Beans

2 slices bacon
1 beef bouillon cube
1 cup hot water
¼ to ½ teaspoon garlic salt
Pinch of pepper
1 (16-ounce) package frozen French-style green beans, thawed

Cook the bacon in a skillet until crisp. Remove the bacon with a slotted spoon, reserving 1 tablespoon of drippings. Crumble the bacon and set aside. Dissolve the bouillon cube in the water in a small bowl. Stir in the garlic salt and pepper. Combine the green beans and reserved bacon drippings in a baking dish. Pour the bouillon over the green beans. Bake, covered, at 350 degrees for 1 hour. Sprinkle with the crumbled bacon. YIELD: **6 SERVINGS**.

Hester P. Thompson
Birmingham Life

Green Bean Casserole

2 (16-ounce) cans French-style green beans
1 (10-ounce) can cream of mushroom soup
1 (3-ounce) can French-fried onions
1 cup shredded Cheddar cheese
¾ cup milk
⅛ teaspoon pepper

Combine the green beans, cream of mushroom soup, ½ of the onions, Cheddar cheese, milk and pepper in a bowl and mix well. Spoon into a 1½-quart baking dish. Bake at 350 degrees for 30 minutes. Top with the remaining onions. Bake until the onions are golden brown. YIELD: **6 SERVINGS**.

Dorothy Yarber
Shoals Life

Creamed Hominy

¼ cup (½ stick) butter
1 (15-ounce) can hominy, drained
1 cup whipping cream
Salt and pepper to taste

Melt the butter in saucepan. Stir in the hominy and whipping cream. Cook over low heat for 30 minutes, stirring frequently. Stir in the salt and pepper. You may sprinkle with chopped parsley. YIELD: 4 SERVINGS.

Sheila P. Brothers
Anniston Council

Hominy Casserole

1 (10-ounce) can cream of mushroom soup
1 (8-ounce) jar Cheez Whiz with jalapeño peppers
1 medium onion, chopped
2 (15-ounce) cans hominy, drained
Butter crackers, crushed
¼ cup (½ stick) margarine, melted

Combine the soup, Cheez Whiz and onion in a saucepan over low heat. Cook until heated through, stirring constantly. Add the hominy and mix well. Spoon into a baking dish. Sprinkle with the cracker crumbs. Drizzle with the margarine. Bake at 350 degrees for 25 to 30 minutes or until hot and bubbly. YIELD: 6 TO 8 SERVINGS.

Marie Hartley
Birmingham South Life

Hominy Casserole

2 (15-ounce) cans hominy with red and
green peppers, drained
1 (10-ounce) can cream of mushroom soup
1 (8-ounce) jar Cheez Whiz with jalapeño peppers
1 medium onion, chopped
1 sleeve butter crackers, crushed
½ cup (1 stick) margarine, melted

Combine the hominy, soup, Cheez Whiz and onion in a bowl and mix well. Spoon into a greased baking dish. Sprinkle with the cracker crumbs. Drizzle with the margarine. Bake at 325 degrees for 25 minutes. YIELD: 6 TO 8 SERVINGS.

Mary M. Storey
Anniston Council

Onion Patties

¾ cup flour
1 tablespoon cornmeal
1 tablespoon sugar
2 teaspoons baking powder
½ teaspoon salt
½ cup milk
2 to 2½ cups chopped onions
Vegetable oil for frying

Combine the flour, cornmeal, sugar, baking powder and salt in a bowl and mix well. Stir in the milk. Add the onions and mix well. Heat the oil in a skillet until hot. Drop the onion mixture by tablespoonfuls into the hot oil. Fry the patties until golden brown on both sides, turning once; drain. Serve immediately. YIELD: 8 SERVINGS.

Frankie Vaughn
Selma Life

Ragout

1 (15-ounce) can small peas, drained
4 hard-cooked eggs, sliced
½ cup sliced mushrooms
2 cups shredded Cheddar cheese
1 cup thick white sauce
1 (10-ounce) can tomato soup
3 tablespoons shredded Cheddar cheese

Layer the peas, eggs, mushrooms and 2 cups Cheddar cheese in a baking dish. Combine the white sauce and soup in a bowl and stir until blended. Pour over the top of the prepared dish. Sprinkle with 3 tablespoons Cheddar cheese. Bake at 350 degrees for 30 minutes or until the cheese is brown. **Editor's Note:** For a thick white sauce, melt 3 tablespoons butter in a saucepan. Add 3 to 4 tablespoons flour, ¼ teaspoon salt and ⅛ teaspoon pepper. Stir in 1 cup milk. Cook until thickened, stirring constantly. YIELD: 4 SERVINGS.

Virginia Sherrer
Selma Life

Vidalia Onion Casserole

1 (10-ounce) can cream of chicken soup
1 cup sour cream
2 medium Vidalia onions, sliced
Grated Parmesan cheese
1 sleeve butter crackers, crushed
2 tablespoons (¼ stick) butter or margarine, melted

Combine the soup and sour cream in a bowl and mix well. Add the onions and toss to coat. Spoon into a baking dish. Sprinkle with Parmesan cheese. Combine the cracker crumbs and butter in a bowl and mix well. Sprinkle over the top of the prepared dish. Bake at 300 to 325 degrees for 35 minutes. YIELD: 4 TO 6 SERVINGS.

Mary Ruth Thompson
Shoals Life

Green Tomato Pie

1 unbaked (9-inch) pie shell
2 medium onions, sliced
1 to 2 garlic cloves, minced
3 tablespoons vegetable oil
4 large green tomatoes, sliced
3 tablespoons chopped parsley
2 tablespoons flour
2 teaspoons salt
1/4 teaspoon pepper
1 cup shredded Cheddar cheese

Bake the pie shell at 400 degrees for 5 minutes. Sauté the onions and garlic in the oil in a large skillet until tender. Add the tomatoes. Cook over medium-high heat for 15 minutes or until tender, stirring occasionally. Add the parsley, flour, salt and pepper and mix gently. Spoon into the pie shell. Sprinkle with the Cheddar cheese. Bake at 400 degrees for 15 minutes or until brown. Let stand for 10 minutes before serving. **YIELD: 6 SERVINGS.**

Mary Ann Stanley
Mobile Council

Fresh Tomato Pie

2 cups baking mix
3/4 cup milk
1 teaspoon basil
1 teaspoon chives
1 teaspoon parsley
4 medium tomatoes, sliced
1 green bell pepper, sliced (optional)
1 1/2 cups shredded sharp Cheddar cheese
1/2 cup mayonnaise

Combine the baking mix and milk in a bowl and stir until blended. Press over the bottom and side of a greased 9-inch pie plate. Combine the basil, chives and parsley in a small bowl and mix well. Alternate layers of tomato and bell pepper, sprinkling the herb mixture over each layer. Combine the Cheddar cheese and mayonnaise in a bowl and mix well. Spread over the top of the prepared dish. Bake at 400 degrees for 20 to 25 minutes or until the crust and top are golden brown. Let stand for 10 minutes before serving. You may use a frozen 9-inch pie shell. YIELD: 4 SERVINGS.

Frankie Vaughn
Selma Life

HELPFUL HINT

Store tomatoes at room temperature for best flavor.
Do not wash them until ready to use.

Sweet Banana Pepper Pie

3 sweet banana peppers, sliced
6 eggs, beaten
1 (17-ounce) can cream-style corn
8 ounces Velveeta cheese, shredded

Arrange the banana peppers in an 8×8-inch greased baking dish. Combine the eggs, corn and Velveeta cheese in a bowl and mix well. Pour over the banana peppers. Bake at 325 degrees for 35 minutes or until set. You may use hot banana peppers in place of the sweet banana peppers. YIELD: 8 SERVINGS.

Donna Jean Bowman
Birmingham South Cahaba

Bachelor Potatoes

2 (10-ounce) packages frozen hash brown potatoes, thawed
2 1/4 cups shredded sharp Cheddar cheese
2 cups sour cream
1/2 cup milk
4 green onions, chopped
Salt and pepper to taste
3/4 cup shredded sharp Cheddar cheese

Combine the potatoes, 2 1/4 cups Cheddar cheese, sour cream, milk, green onions, salt and pepper in a bowl and mix well. Spoon into a baking dish. Sprinkle with 3/4 cup Cheddar cheese. Bake at 375 for 45 minutes. YIELD: 8 SERVINGS.

Sue Bryars
Birmingham South Cahaba

Charcoal Potatoes

2/3 cup margarine, softened
3 envelopes instant onion soup mix
6 medium potatoes

Combine the margarine and onion soup mix in a bowl and mix well. Make three 1/2-inch-lengthwise slits into the top of each potato. Spread the onion soup mixture over the tops of the potatoes. Wrap each potato in heavy-duty foil. Grill over medium-hot coals for 50 to 60 minutes or until the potatoes are tender, turning once. YIELD: **6 SERVINGS**.

Jo Ann Thomas
Selma Life

Cheese Potato Casserole

6 medium baking potatoes, peeled
2 eggs, beaten
1 1/2 cups milk
1 cup shredded sharp Cheddar cheese
2 tablespoons minced onion (optional)
1 1/4 teaspoons salt
1 cup shredded sharp Cheddar cheese

Combine the potatoes with enough water to cover in a saucepan. Cook until tender; drain. Mash the potatoes. Add the eggs, milk, 1 cup Cheddar cheese, onion and salt and beat until blended. Spoon into a baking dish sprayed with nonstick cooking spray. Sprinkle with 1 cup Cheddar cheese. Bake at 350 degrees for 30 minutes or until brown. You may prepare ahead and chill, covered, until ready to bake. YIELD: **8 SERVINGS**.

Mary Clark Christopher, friend of Faith Kirby Richardson
Gadsden Life

Irene's Hash Brown Potato Casserole

1 (32-ounce) package frozen hash brown potatoes
10 ounces shredded Cheddar cheese
1 (10-ounce) can cream of chicken soup
1 cup sour cream
½ cup chopped onion
¼ cup (½ stick) margarine, melted
½ teaspoon each salt and pepper
3 slices bread, crumbled
¼ cup (½ stick) margarine, melted

Combine the potatoes, Cheddar cheese, soup, sour cream, onion, ¼ cup margarine, salt and pepper in a bowl and mix well. Spoon into a greased 9×13-inch baking dish. Mix the bread crumbs with ¼ cup margarine in a bowl. Sprinkle over the top of the prepared dish. Bake at 350 degrees for 70 minutes. YIELD: 12 SERVINGS.

Virginia Bowen
Shoals Life

Taylor's Favorite Hash Brown Casserole

1 (32-ounce) package frozen hash brown potatoes
1 (10-ounce) can cream of mushroom soup
1 cup sour cream
Salt and pepper to taste
Shredded Cheddar cheese
1 sleeve butter crackers, crushed

Arrange the potatoes in a baking dish sprayed with nonstick cooking spray. Combine the soup, sour cream, salt and pepper in a bowl and stir until blended. Spread over the potatoes. Sprinkle with the Cheddar cheese. Sprinkle with the cracker crumbs. Bake at 350 degrees for 1 hour. YIELD: 12 SERVINGS.

Christie Huff
Birmingham South Cahaba

Creamed Potato Casserole

10 medium potatoes, peeled, cubed
1 cup chopped onion
Salt to taste
8 ounces cream cheese, softened

1/2 cup shredded sharp Cheddar cheese
1/2 cup sour cream
1/4 cup (1/2 stick) margarine
1/4 cup shredded sharp Cheddar cheese

Combine the potatoes, onion and salt with enough water to cover in a saucepan. Cook until the potatoes are tender; drain. Add the cream cheese, 1/2 cup Cheddar cheese, sour cream and margarine. Mash until smooth. Spoon into a buttered baking dish. Sprinkle with 1/4 cup Cheddar cheese. Bake at 350 degrees for 20 minutes.
YIELD: 6 TO 8 SERVINGS.

Wayne Clements
Tuscaloosa Council

Luscious Potato Casserole

16 ounces cottage cheese
1 cup sour cream
1/3 cup sliced green onions
1 small garlic clove, minced
2 teaspoons salt
Pepper to taste

5 cups chopped, cooked potatoes
1/2 cup shredded Cheddar cheese
Paprika

Combine the cottage cheese, sour cream, green onions, garlic, salt and pepper in a bowl and mix well. Stir in the potatoes. Spoon into a greased 9x13-inch baking dish. Sprinkle with the Cheddar cheese. Sprinkle with paprika. Bake at 350 degrees for 35 minutes.
YIELD: 8 TO 10 SERVINGS.

Mrs. Vauline Terry
Tuscaloosa Council

Make-Ahead Mashed Potatoes

6 medium potatoes, cooked, mashed
3 ounces cream cheese, cubed
1/2 cup sour cream
1/4 to 1/2 cup milk
1 tablespoon butter
1 teaspoon onion salt
1/4 teaspoon pepper
1 tablespoon butter
Paprika (optional)

Combine the potatoes, cream cheese, sour cream, milk, 1 tablespoon butter, onion salt and pepper in a bowl and mash until smooth. Spoon into a greased 9×13-inch or 1 1/2-quart baking dish. Chill, covered, for 8 hours. Melt 1 tablespoon butter. Pour over the potatoes. Sprinkle with the paprika. Bake at 350 degrees for 45 minutes. YIELD: 8 SERVINGS.

Sue Walton
Birmingham Life

Potato Wedges

4 baking potatoes
2 cloves garlic, minced
1 tablespoon olive oil
1/4 teaspoon pepper
1/8 teaspoon salt

Cut each potato lengthwise into halves. Cut each potato half lengthwise into wedges. Combine the potatoes with enough cold water to cover in a bowl. Let stand for 15 minutes; drain. Pat dry with a paper towel. Combine the potato wedges, garlic, olive oil, pepper and salt in a bowl and toss to coat. Arrange in a single layer on a baking sheet sprayed with nonstick cooking spray. Bake at 425 degrees for 20 minutes, turning once. You may use sweet potatoes in place of the baking potatoes. YIELD: 6 SERVINGS.

Ilean Moore
Decatur Council

Spinach Artichoke Casserole

2 (10-ounce) packages frozen chopped spinach
6 tablespoons (3/4 stick) butter
1 tablespoon flour
1/2 cup milk
1 (4-ounce) can sliced mushrooms
1/2 teaspoon salt
Pepper to taste
1/2 cup mayonnaise
1/2 cup sour cream
2 tablespoons lemon juice
1 (14-ounce) can artichoke hearts, drained

Cook the spinach using the package directions; drain. Melt the butter in a saucepan. Add the flour. Cook until bubbly, stirring constantly. Stir in the milk. Cook until thickened, stirring constantly. Add the spinach, mushrooms, salt and pepper and mix well. Combine the mayonnaise, sour cream and lemon juice in a bowl and stir until blended. Place the artichoke hearts in a 1 1/2-quart baking dish. Top with the spinach mixture. Spread the sour cream mixture over the top. Bake at 350 degrees for 30 minutes.

YIELD: 8 SERVINGS.

Nancy Kallus
Birmingham South Cahaba

HELPFUL HINT

To preserve both nutrients and flavor, cook vegetables with the least amount of water possible.

Spinach-Filled Stuffed Eggs

1 (10-ounce) package frozen chopped spinach
12 hard-cooked eggs
1/2 cup mayonnaise
2 tablespoons grated Parmesan cheese
2 tablespoons olive oil
Salt and pepper to taste

Cook the spinach using the package directions; drain. Squeeze the excess water out of the spinach. Peel the eggs and cut into halves lengthwise. Mash the egg yolks in a bowl. Add the spinach, mayonnaise, Parmesan cheese, olive oil, salt and pepper and mix well. Spoon into the egg whites. Place on a serving plate. Chill, covered, until ready to serve. YIELD: 24 SERVINGS.

Mary Howle
Anniston Council

Squash and Pepper Sauté

2 medium yellow squash, sliced
2 medium zucchini, sliced
1 sweet red bell pepper, sliced
1/4 cup olive or vegetable oil
1 envelope Italian salad dressing mix
3 tablespoons red wine vinegar

Stir-fry the squash, zucchini and bell pepper in the olive oil in a skillet over medium-high heat for 3 to 4 minutes or until tender-crisp. Sprinkle with the salad dressing mix. Toss to coat. Stir in the vinegar. YIELD: 6 SERVINGS.

Hester P. Thompson
Birmingham Life

Summer Squash Shells

5 slices bacon
6 yellow squash, ends trimmed
3 tomatillos, husked, chopped
3/4 cup shredded Monterey Jack cheese
1/2 cup chopped green onions
3/4 cup bread crumbs
2 to 3 tablespoons butter, melted

Fry the bacon in a skillet until crisp; drain. Crumble the bacon. Combine the squash with enough water to cover in a saucepan. Cook just until tender; drain. Let stand until partially cool. Cut squash lengthwise into halves. Scoop the pulp into a bowl, reserving the squash shells. Add the crumbled bacon, tomatillos, Monterey Jack cheese and green onions to the bowl and mix well. Spoon the mixture into the squash shells. Arrange in a 9×13-inch baking dish. Sprinkle with the bread crumbs. Drizzle with the butter. Bake at 350 degrees for 25 to 30 minutes or until golden brown. You may prepare in advance and chill, covered, until ready to bake.
YIELD: **6 SERVINGS**.

Rita Wilson, daughter of Helen Shirley
Birmingham Life

HELPFUL HINT

Yellow squash is best when it is 4 to 6 inches in length and smooth skinned.

Squash Casserole

4 cups sliced yellow squash
1/2 cup grated onion
8 ounces Velveeta cheese, shredded
12 butter crackers, crushed
1 egg
1/2 cup mayonnaise
1/4 cup (1/2 stick) margarine, melted
1 tablespoon sugar

Combine the squash and onion with enough water to cover in a saucepan. Cook until tender; drain. Combine the squash, onion, Velveeta cheese, cracker crumbs, egg, mayonnaise, margarine and sugar in a bowl and mix well. Spoon into a baking dish. Bake at 350 degrees for 30 minutes. YIELD: 12 SERVINGS.

Elouise Freeman
Mobile Council

Squash Casserole

1 pound yellow squash, sliced
1 small onion, chopped
2 eggs, beaten
1 cup milk
1 cup cracker crumbs
1/2 cup shredded Cheddar cheese
3 tablespoons butter, softened
Salt and pepper to taste
1/2 cup shredded Cheddar cheese

Combine the squash and onion with enough water to cover in a saucepan. Cook until tender; drain. Combine the squash, onion, eggs, milk, cracker crumbs, 1/2 cup Cheddar cheese, butter, salt and pepper in a bowl and mix well. Spoon into a buttered baking dish. Sprinkle with 1/2 cup Cheddar cheese. Bake at 375 degrees for 30 minutes or until firm and brown. YIELD: 8 SERVINGS.

Sheila P. Brothers
Anniston Council

Squash Casserole

1 pound yellow squash, cooked
1 (8-ounce) can sliced water chestnuts, drained
2 cups shredded sharp Cheddar cheese
1/2 cup (1 stick) margarine, melted
1/2 cup mayonnaise
1 tablespoon sugar
1 egg
1/2 onion, chopped
1/2 green bell pepper, chopped
Salt and pepper to taste
Shredded sharp Cheddar cheese or bread crumbs

Combine the squash and the next 10 ingredients in a bowl and mix well. Spoon into a baking dish. Bake, covered, at 350 degrees for 30 minutes. Sprinkle with Cheddar cheese or bread crumbs. Bake for an additional 10 minutes. YIELD: 4 SERVINGS.

Anatalie Watson Fogg
Decatur Council

Squash Casserole

2 pounds yellow squash, sliced
4 eggs, beaten
1/2 cup milk
1/4 cup (1/2 stick) butter
Cheddar cheese, sliced

Combine the squash with enough water to cover in a saucepan. Cook until tender; drain. Mash the squash in a bowl. Add the eggs, milk and butter and mix well. Spoon into a buttered baking dish. Top with Cheddar cheese. Bake at 350 degrees for 50 to 60 minutes or until hot and bubbly. YIELD: 6 SERVINGS.

Dilla Samuel
Gadsden Life

Squash Casserole

3 cups cooked yellow squash
6 tablespoons (¾ stick) butter, melted
1 teaspoon salt
½ teaspoon pepper
2 eggs, beaten
2 cups cracker crumbs
1 cup evaporated milk
1 cup shredded Cheddar cheese
1 cup chopped onion

Combine the squash, butter, salt and pepper in a bowl and mix gently. Stir in the eggs, cracker crumbs, evaporated milk, Cheddar cheese and onion. Spoon into a greased baking dish. Bake at 375 degrees for 40 minutes. YIELD: 6 SERVINGS.

Margaret W. Wilborn
Gadsden Life

Squash Supreme

2 cups yellow squash, cooked
1 carrot, finely grated
1 cup cream of chicken soup
1 cup sour cream
¼ cup grated onion
Pepper to taste
1 (16-ounce) package dry stuffing
Butter

Combine the squash, carrot, soup, sour cream, onion and pepper in a bowl and mix well. Cover the bottom of a buttered baking dish with ½ of the stuffing. Spoon the squash mixture over the top of the stuffing. Top with the remaining stuffing. Dot with butter. Bake at 350 degrees for 30 to 40 minutes or until brown. YIELD: 4 TO 6 SERVINGS.

Eulene Miller
Birmingham South Cahaba Council

Orange Rings

6 oranges
1½ cups mashed cooked sweet potatoes
2 eggs, beaten
1 cup packed brown sugar
½ cup raisins
1 tablespoon cornstarch
1 teaspoon cinnamon
1 teaspoon nutmeg
12 marshmallows

Cut the oranges in half. Squeeze the juice from the oranges to measure 1 cup. Scoop out the pulp from the orange halves. Discard the pulp, reserving the orange shells. Combine the sweet potatoes, orange juice, eggs, brown sugar, raisins, cornstarch, cinnamon and nutmeg in a bowl and mix well. Spoon the mixture into the reserved orange shells. Arrange the filled orange shells in a baking dish. Top each with a marshmallow. Bake at 300 degrees for 30 minutes. YIELD: 12 SERVINGS.

Louise Morrison
Tuscaloosa Council

Sweet Potato Soufflé

3 cups mashed cooked sweet potatoes
1 cup sugar
½ cup milk
¼ cup (½ stick) butter, melted
2 eggs, beaten
1 teaspoon orange extract
1 teaspoon pineapple extract
1 cup packed brown sugar
½ cup flour
¼ cup (½ stick) butter, melted
1 cup chopped pecans

Combine the sweet potatoes, sugar, milk, ¼ cup butter and eggs in a bowl and mix well. Stir in the orange and pineapple extracts. Spoon into a baking dish. Mix the brown sugar and flour in a bowl. Sprinkle over the prepared dish. Drizzle with the butter. Sprinkle with the pecans. Bake at 350 degrees for 30 to 35 minutes or until bubbly. YIELD: 8 SERVINGS.

Carolyn Wheeler
Selma Life

HELPFUL HINT

Substitute crushed wheat germ for buttered crumbs for an easy and nutritious topping.

Scalloped Tomatoes Au Gratin

4 cups chopped tomatoes
2 small onions, chopped
2 tablespoons sugar
½ teaspoon salt
½ teaspoon pepper
3 slices bread, toasted, cubed
½ cup grated Parmesan cheese
2 tablespoons butter, melted

Combine the tomatoes, onions, sugar, salt and pepper in a bowl and mix well. Spoon into a baking dish. Sprinkle with the bread cubes. Top with the Parmesan cheese. Drizzle with the butter. Bake at 325 degrees for 20 minutes. YIELD: 4 SERVINGS.

*Virginia Murphy
Montgomery Council*

Zucchini Bake

5 zucchini, sliced
2 large onions, cut into large chunks
½ cup grated Parmesan cheese
2 large tomatoes, sliced
½ cup grated Parmesan cheese

Layer the zucchini, onions, ½ cup Parmesan cheese and tomatoes in a baking dish. Sprinkle with ½ cup Parmesan cheese. Bake, covered, at 350 degrees for 50 to 60 minutes or until hot and bubbly. YIELD: 8 SERVINGS.

*Candy Bird
Birmingham South Cahaba*

Zucchini Casserole

4 or 5 medium zucchini
2 eggs, beaten
1 medium onion, chopped
1 cup mayonnaise
1 cup grated Parmesan cheese
1/3 cup chopped green bell pepper
Buttered bread crumbs

Combine the zucchini with enough water to cover in a saucepan. Cook until tender; drain. Mash the zucchini in a bowl. Add the eggs, onion, mayonnaise, Parmesan cheese and bell pepper and mix well. Spoon into a greased baking dish. Sprinkle with the buttered bread crumbs. Bake at 350 degrees for 30 minutes. YIELD: 8 SERVINGS.

Anatalie Watson Fogg
Decatur Council

Hettie's Vegetable Casserole

1 (16-ounce) package frozen mixed vegetables
1 cup chopped celery
1 cup mayonnaise
1 cup shredded Velveeta cheese
1/2 cup chopped onion
1 sleeve butter crackers, crushed
1/2 cup (1 stick) margarine, melted

Cook the mixed vegetables using the package directions; drain. Combine the mixed vegetables, celery, mayonnaise, Velveeta cheese and onion in a bowl and mix well. Spoon into a baking dish. Mix the cracker crumbs with the margarine in a bowl. Sprinkle over the top of the prepared dish. Bake at 350 degrees for 30 minutes. YIELD: 4 SERVINGS.

Mrs. Raymond E. Davis
Decatur Council

Vegetable Casserole

1 (16-ounce) can French-style green beans, drained
1 (16-ounce) can Shoe Peg corn, drained
1 (10-ounce) can cream of celery soup
1 (8-ounce) can water chestnuts, drained
1/2 cup chopped celery
1/2 cup chopped onion
1/2 cup chopped green bell pepper
1/2 cup each shredded Cheddar cheese and sour cream
Salt and pepper to taste
2 sleeves butter crackers, crushed
1/2 cup (1 stick) margarine, melted
1/2 cup sliced almonds

Combine the first 11 ingredients in a bowl and mix well. Spoon into a baking dish. Mix the cracker crumbs, margarine and almonds in a bowl. Sprinkle over the top of the prepared dish. Bake at 350 degrees for 45 minutes. YIELD: 8 SERVINGS.

Sarah Spratt
Anniston Council

Vegetable Casserole

1 (15-ounce) can mixed vegetables
1 (11-ounce) can Mexicorn
1 cup chopped celery
1 cup chopped onion
1 cup mayonnaise
1 cup shredded Cheddar cheese
1 sleeve butter crackers, crushed
1/2 cup (1 stick) margarine, melted

Drain the mixed vegetables and Mexicorn, reserving half the liquid. Combine the mixed vegetables, Mexicorn, reserved liquid, celery, onion, mayonnaise and Cheddar cheese in a bowl and mix well. Spoon into a baking dish. Sprinkle with the cracker crumbs. Drizzle with the margarine. Bake at 300 degrees for 25 to 30 minutes or until hot and bubbly. YIELD: 6 SERVINGS.

Lola Duffey
Shoals Life

Vegetable Medley

1 (10-ounce) package frozen lima beans
1 (10-ounce) package frozen English peas
1 (16-ounce) can French-style green beans
4 hard-cooked eggs, chopped
1 medium onion, chopped
2 cups mayonnaise
¼ cup olive oil or vegetable oil
1 teaspoon prepared mustard
1 teaspoon Worcestershire sauce
Dash of Tabasco sauce
Paprika

Cook the lima beans and peas separately using the package directions; drain. Cook the green beans in a saucepan over low heat until warm; drain. Combine the lima beans, peas and green beans in a serving dish and mix gently. Combine the eggs, onion, mayonnaise, olive oil, mustard, Worcestershire sauce and Tabasco sauce in a bowl and mix well. Pour over the vegetables. Sprinkle with the paprika. This may be served hot or cold. You may prepare this 1 day in advance and chill, covered, until ready to serve.

YIELD: 10 TO 12 SERVINGS.

Faye King
Huntsville Council

HELPFUL HINT

To crisp limp celery, place it in a deep jar of cold water in the refrigerator.

MOBILE COUNCIL

The Mobile Council provides tricycles to children affected by cerebral palsy or spina bifida. These trikes, known as "HOT TRIKES," allow the physically impaired child to participate with siblings or friends in bicycle adventures. The trikes are propelled by hand pedals incorporated in the handlebars. This not only allows the child to ride but is also a source of physical therapy.

Side Dishes

Dressing

4 cups crumbled corn bread
2 cups crumbled biscuits
1 onion, chopped
3½ cups broth
3 eggs
1 cup milk
2 teaspoons salt
½ teaspoon pepper
1 tablespoon poultry seasoning

Combine the corn bread, biscuits and onion in a large bowl and mix well. Combine the broth, eggs and milk in a small bowl and mix well. Pour over the corn bread mixture and mix well. Add the salt, pepper and poultry seasoning and mix well. Spoon into a greased baking dish. Bake at 425 degrees for 40 minutes.
YIELD: 6 TO 8 SERVINGS.

Cheryl Crosson
Anniston Council

Dressing

3 large or 5 medium onions, chopped
1 rib celery, chopped
Butter
Pan juices from a turkey or hen
8 eggs
1 box plain crackers, crushed
1 cake of corn bread, crumbled
Sage to taste

Cook the onions and celery in a small amount of butter in a skillet until tender. Combine the onions and celery and the pan juices with eggs in a large bowl and mix well. Add the crackers, corn bread and sage and mix well. Spoon into a greased baking dish. Bake at 500 degrees until bubbly around the edges. Reduce the oven temperature to 350 degrees. Bake for 1 hour longer.
YIELD: 8 TO 10 SERVINGS.

Kathryn Morgan
Gadsden Life

Corn Bread Dressing

1 recipe corn bread, crumbled
4 slices white bread, crumbled
¼ teaspoon pepper
4 chicken bouillon cubes
1 cup water
4 eggs, lightly beaten
1 bunch green onions, chopped
4 ribs celery, finely chopped
1 cup (2 sticks) margarine
1 (14-ounce) can chicken broth

Mix the corn bread, white bread and pepper in a large bowl. Dissolve the bouillon cubes in the water. Pour over the bread crumb mixture and mix well. Stir in the eggs. Sauté the green onions and celery in the margarine in a skillet until tender. Add the bread crumb mixture and mix well. Stir in the chicken broth. Spoon into a 9×14-inch baking pan. Bake at 400 degrees until golden brown. You may freeze in sealable plastic bags. **YIELD: 8 TO 10 SERVINGS.**

Gussie Evans
Mobile Council

Johnson's Sausage Dressing

1 pound sausage
1 large onion, chopped
2 ribs celery, chopped
½ cup (1 stick) margarine
2½ cups crumbled corn bread
2½ cups crumbled biscuits
1 teaspoon salt
¼ teaspoon pepper
1 tablespoon poultry seasoning
2 (14-ounce) cans chicken broth

Brown the sausage in a skillet, stirring until crumbly; drain. Cook the onion and celery in the margarine in a separate skillet until tender. Combine the corn bread, biscuits, salt, pepper and poultry seasoning in a large bowl and mix well. Add the broth, onion mixture and cooked sausage and mix well. Spoon into a baking dish. Bake at 350 degrees for 30 to 35 minutes. **YIELD: 6 TO 8 SERVINGS.**

James B. Johnson, Jr.
Tuscaloosa Council

Miss Minnie's Corn Bread Sausage Dressing

1 (7-ounce) package brown and serve sausage links
4 tablespoons margarine
1/2 cup chopped walnuts
1 cup chopped celery
1/2 cup chopped onion
1 (16-ounce) package corn bread stuffing
1 1/2 cups chopped apples
1 1/2 cups apple juice
1 1/4 cups water

Cut the sausages into slices. Heat 1 tablespoon of the margarine in a skillet until melted. Add the walnuts. Cook until light brown, stirring constantly. Remove the walnuts and place in a large bowl. Add the remaining 3 tablespoons margarine to the skillet. Heat until melted. Add the celery and onion. Cook until tender. Add to the walnuts. Add the sausage, stuffing and apples to the walnuts and mix well. Pour in the juice and water and mix well. Spoon into a greased 3-quart baking dish. Bake, covered, at 350 degrees for 1 hour or until heated through and brown. YIELD: 10 SERVINGS.

D. Christine Kirkley
Birmingham Life

HELPFUL HINT

Bent or dented measuring utensils give inaccurate measures.

Squash Dressing

2 cups sliced squash
1 onion, chopped
1 cup water
2 cups corn bread crumbs
2 eggs
1 (10-ounce) can cream of chicken soup
1/4 cup (1/2 stick) margarine, softened
1/4 teaspoon pepper
Shredded Cheddar cheese

Combine the squash, onion and water in a saucepan. Cook, covered, until tender. Drain and place in a large bowl. Mash the squash. Add the corn bread, eggs, soup, margarine and pepper and mix well. Spoon into a greased baking dish. Sprinkle with the cheese. Bake at 350 degrees for 25 minutes. **YIELD: 6 TO 8 SERVINGS.**

Frances Andrew
Decatur Council

Squash Dressing

2 cups cooked squash, drained
2 cups crumbled corn bread
1 medium onion, chopped
½ cup (1 stick) margarine, melted
3 eggs, beaten
1 (10-ounce) can cream of chicken soup
2 teaspoons sage

Combine the squash, corn bread, onion, margarine, eggs, soup and sage in a large bowl and mix well. Spoon into a greased baking dish. Bake at 350 degrees until brown. YIELD: **6 TO 8 SERVINGS**.

Virginia Sherrer
Selma Life

Garlic Grits

½ cup grits, cooked
1 roll garlic cheese
½ cup (1 stick) margarine, softened
2 eggs
¾ cup milk

Combine the hot grits and cheese in a bowl and mix well. Add the margarine, eggs and milk and mix well. Spoon into a baking dish. Bake at 350 degrees for 30 to 40 minutes. YIELD: **2 TO 4 SERVINGS**.

Robert A. Riddee
Opelika Life

Gourmet Grits with Cheese

6 cups whole milk
¾ cup (1½ sticks) butter
1½ cups quick-cooking grits
2 eggs, beaten
1½ teaspoons salt
¾ teaspoon white pepper
½ cup (1 stick) butter
6 ounces Gruyère cheese
¾ cup freshly grated Parmesan cheese

Bring the milk to a boil in a saucepan over medium heat, stirring frequently. Add ¾ cup butter and grits. Cook for 5 minutes or until thickened, stirring constantly. Remove from the heat. Stir a small amount of the hot mixture into the beaten eggs. Stir the eggs into the hot mixture. Stir in the salt and white pepper. Add ½ cup butter and Gruyère cheese and mix well. Spoon into a greased 9×13-inch baking dish. Sprinkle the Parmesan cheese over the top. Bake at 350 degrees for 1 hour. **YIELD: 12 SERVINGS.**

Mrs. Virginia Greene
Birmingham South Life

HELPFUL HINT

For easier cleanup, fill cooking pans immediately with hot water to soak. Use cold water for cereal, egg and milk dishes.

Jalapeño Cheese Grits

1 cup grits
½ cup (1 stick) margarine, softened
2 rolls jalapeño cheese
1 garlic clove, minced
1 (4-ounce) can chopped green chiles
2 eggs, beaten

Cook the grits using the package directions. Combine with the margarine, cheese, garlic, green chiles and eggs in a large bowl and mix well. Spoon into a greased baking dish. Bake at 350 degrees for 40 minutes. You may substitute rolls of garlic cheese for the jalapeño cheese and add chopped jalapeño peppers. YIELD: 8 SERVINGS.

Mrs. James H. Erwin (Julia)
Decatur Council

CROCK-POT® Macaroni and Cheese

8 ounces elbow macaroni, cooked
1 (12-ounce) can evaporated milk
¾ cup whole milk
¼ cup (½ stick) butter, melted
2 eggs, beaten
4 cups shredded Cheddar cheese
Salt to taste
White pepper to taste
¼ cup grated Parmesan cheese

Combine the macaroni, evaporated milk, whole milk, butter, eggs, 3 cups of the Cheddar cheese, salt and white pepper in a large bowl and mix well. Spoon into a CROCK-POT® Slow Cooker. Sprinkle the remaining 1 cup Cheddar cheese and Parmesan cheese over the top. Cook on Low for 3 hours. YIELD: 8 SERVINGS.

Donna Campbell
Anniston Council

Macaroni and Cheese

8 ounces macaroni
1/3 cup milk
1 tablespoon margarine
2 heaping tablespoons Cheez Whiz
Salt and pepper to taste

Cook the macaroni using the package directions; drain. Combine the cooked macaroni with the milk, margarine, Cheez Whiz, salt and pepper in a large saucepan and mix well. Cook until the cheese melts, stirring constantly. You may spoon the macaroni mixture into a baking dish, sprinkle shredded Cheddar cheese over the top and bake at 350 degrees for 10 to 15 minutes. YIELD: 4 SERVINGS.

Marian White
Decatur Council

Macaroni and Cheese

14 ounces macaroni
1/2 cup (1 stick) margarine, melted
6 eggs, lightly beaten
4 cups milk
1 pound Cheddar cheese, shredded
1 teaspoon salt

Cook the macaroni using the package directions until al dente; drain. Combine the cooked macaroni, margarine, eggs, milk, cheese and salt in a large bowl and mix well. Spoon the macaroni mixture into a 9×13-inch baking dish sprayed with nonstick cooking spray. Bake at 325 degrees for 40 minutes. YIELD: 12 TO 15 SERVINGS.

Deanie Williams
Birmingham Life

Baked Pasta

16 ounces shell pasta
1 (10-ounce) can cream of celery soup
1¼ cups milk
1 envelope Italian salad dressing mix
1 (15-ounce) container ricotta cheese
½ cup grated Parmesan cheese
2 (16-ounce) packages frozen mixed vegetables, thawed
¼ cup grated Parmesan cheese

Cook the pasta using the package directions; drain. Combine the soup, milk and dressing mix in a large bowl and mix well. Add the ricotta cheese and ½ cup Parmesan cheese and mix well. Add the cooked pasta and vegetables and mix well. Spoon into a 9x13-inch baking dish sprayed with nonstick cooking spray. Sprinkle ¼ cup Parmesan cheese over the top. Bake at 350 degrees for 45 to 50 minutes or until heated through. **YIELD: 6 TO 8 SERVINGS.**

Eula Mae Watson
Gadsden Life

Vegetable Lasagna

1 medium zucchini, coarsely chopped
8 ounces fresh mushrooms, sliced
1 onion, coarsely chopped
1 large green bell pepper, coarsely chopped
1 (15-ounce) can Italian tomatoes
Italian seasoning to taste
2 garlic cloves, pressed
1 (10-ounce) package frozen chopped spinach, thawed
7 or 8 lasagna noodles, cooked
1 large jar spaghetti sauce
4 cups shredded mozzarella cheese
16 ounces cottage cheese

Combine the zucchini, mushrooms, onion, bell pepper, tomatoes, Italian seasoning and garlic in a large skillet. Cook until vegetables are tender and liquid has almost completely evaporated. Drain the spinach, pressing out the excess moisture. Layer ½ of the noodles, ½ of the spaghetti sauce, the vegetable mixture, ½ of the mozzarella cheese, remaining noodles, remaining spaghetti sauce, spinach, cottage cheese and remaining mozzarella cheese in a 9×13-inch baking dish sprayed with nonstick cooking spray. Bake at 375 degrees for 30 minutes. **YIELD: 10 TO 12 SERVINGS.**

Kelli Lee
Anniston Council

HELPFUL HINT

To produce steam when microwaving, cover pasta tightly with plastic wrap.

Baked Ziti

3 cups spaghetti sauce
16 ounces ricotta cheese
1½ cups shredded mozzarella cheese
½ cup ziti, cooked

1½ cups shredded mozzarella cheese
½ cup grated Parmesan cheese

Spread ½ of the spaghetti sauce over the bottom of a 9x13-inch baking pan. Combine the ricotta cheese and 1½ cups mozzarella cheese in a bowl and mix well. Add the ziti and mix well. Spoon over the spaghetti sauce. Spread the remaining spaghetti sauce over the cheese mixture. Sprinkle 1½ cups mozzarella cheese and Parmesan cheese over the top. Bake at 350 degrees for 15 to 20 minutes or until heated through. Let stand for 10 minutes.
YIELD: 8 SERVINGS.

Judy Evans
Decatur Council

Cashew Rice Pilaf

1½ cups long grain rice
1 cup chopped carrots
1 cup chopped onions
1 cup golden raisins
¼ cup (½ stick) margarine
3 cups chicken broth

1 teaspoon salt
2 cups small English peas
1½ cups cooked wild rice
1 cup cashews
¼ cup sliced green onions

Sauté the long grain rice, carrots, onions and raisins in the margarine in a skillet until tender. Pour in the broth. Stir in the salt. Bring to a boil. Reduce the heat. Simmer, covered, for 20 minutes or until the liquid is absorbed. Stir in the peas, wild rice and cashews. Cook until heated through. Sprinkle the green onions over the top. YIELD: 12 SERVINGS.

Mrs. Vauline Terry
Tuscaloosa Council

Baked Mushroom Rice

1/4 cup (1/2 stick) butter, melted
1 cup long grain rice
1 (14-ounce) can chicken broth
1 (10-ounce) can French onion soup
1 (3-ounce) jar sliced mushrooms, drained

Combine the butter, rice, broth, soup and mushrooms in a bowl and mix well. Spoon into a 2-quart baking dish. Bake, covered, at 350 degrees for 1 hour. YIELD: 4 TO 6 SERVINGS.

Catherine R. Bruce
Bon Secour Life

Mushroom Rice Casserole

3/4 cup (1 1/2 sticks) butter
2 cups rice
2 (10-ounce) cans French onion soup
2 (14-ounce) cans beef consommé
2 (3-ounce) jars sliced mushrooms, drained
Pepper to taste

Heat the butter in a 9x13-inch baking dish in the oven until melted. Add the rice, soup, consommé, mushrooms and pepper and mix well. Bake, covered, at 350 degrees for 45 to 60 minutes or until bubbly. YIELD: 10 TO 12 SERVINGS.

Mrs. Edward K. Horton, Sr.
Mobile Council

Rice Dish

1 medium onion, chopped
1/4 cup (1/2 stick) butter or margarine
1 (7-ounce) can sliced mushrooms
1 (10-ounce) can French onion soup
1 cup rice

Sauté the onion in the butter in a skillet until tender. Drain the mushrooms, reserving the liquid. Add enough water to the liquid to measure 1 1/4 cups. Add the soup and the liquid to the onion mixture and mix well. Bring to a boil. Stir in the mushrooms and rice. Cook for 15 minutes. Spoon into a 2-quart baking dish. Bake, covered, at 350 degrees for 30 minutes. YIELD: 8 SERVINGS.

Chris Elsen
Gadsden Life

Baked Apples

10 to 12 medium Gala apples
Sugar to taste
Margarine or butter

Peel and cut the apples into quarters. Arrange over the bottom of a buttered 9x12-inch glass baking dish. Sprinkle generously with sugar. Dot generously with margarine. Bake at 450 degrees for 45 to 60 minutes, stirring after 25 minutes. YIELD: 8 TO 10 SERVINGS.

Jack D. Phillips
Birmingham South Life

Apple Carrot Casserole

2 (21-ounce) cans apple pie filling
1 (10-ounce) package baby carrots, cooked
1 (20-ounce) can crushed pineapple, drained
½ cup sugar
1 teaspoon apple pie spice
½ cup (1 stick) margarine
Paprika

Combine the pie filling, carrots, pineapple, sugar and pie spice in a large bowl and mix well. Spoon into a baking dish. Cut the margarine into thin slices. Place over the filling. Sprinkle with the paprika. Bake at 350 degrees for 30 minutes or until bubbly.
YIELD: 10 TO 12 SERVINGS.

Lois Dobson
Mobile Council

Apple Cheese Casserole

½ cup (1 stick) margarine, softened
½ to 1 cup sugar
8 ounces Velveeta or sharp cheese, shredded
¾ cup flour
1 (20-ounce) can sliced apples

Cream the margarine and sugar in a mixing bowl until light and fluffy. Add the cheese and flour and mix well. Pour the apples evenly in a buttered baking dish. Spread the cheese mixture over the top. Bake at 350 degrees for 30 minutes. YIELD: 4 TO 6 SERVINGS.

Gussie Evans
Mobile Council

Hot Fruit Compote

1 (12-ounce) package pitted prunes
1 (6-ounce) package dried apricots
1 (20-ounce) can pineapple chunks
1 (11-ounce) can mandarin oranges
1 (21-ounce) can cherry pie filling
1/2 cup cooking sherry

Arrange the prunes and apricots over the bottom of an 8x12-inch baking dish. Combine the pineapple, mandarin oranges, pie filling and sherry in a bowl and mix well. Pour over the dried fruit. Bake at 350 degrees for 1 hour. YIELD: 12 SERVINGS.

Jack D. Phillips
Birmingham South Life

Baked Grapefruit

4 pink grapefruit
1 teaspoon cinnamon
1/2 cup sugar
1/2 cup (1 stick) butter
3 tablespoons honey

Cut the grapefruit into halves crosswise. Remove the core. Separate the sections from the peel with a grapefruit knife. Combine the cinnamon and sugar in a bowl and mix well. Sprinkle over the halves. Place a 1/2-inch cube of butter in the center of each half. Drizzle the honey over the butter. Arrange on a baking sheet. Bake at 350 degrees for 10 to 15 minutes or until hot and bubbly. YIELD: 8 SERVINGS.

Mrs. Virginia Greene
Birmingham South Life

Baked Oranges

6 oranges
6 apples, peeled, chopped
1 (20-ounce) can crushed pineapple
1½ cups sugar
½ cup chopped pecans
3 tablespoons butter, melted

Cut the oranges into halves. Remove the orange sections from the peel, leaving a thin layer next to the peel. Reserve the orange shells. Combine the orange sections, apples, pineapple and sugar in a saucepan. Cook until very thick, stirring frequently. Spoon into the orange shells. Sprinkle the pecans over the filling. Drizzle the butter over the pecans. Place in a foil-lined baking pan. Pour enough water into the pan to measure ½ inch deep. Bake at 325 degrees until hot and bubbly. YIELD: 12 SERVINGS.

Sue Small
Selma Life

Pattie's Pineapple Scallops

4 cups fresh bread crumbs
1 (20-ounce) can pineapple chunks, drained
3 eggs, beaten
2 cups sugar
1 cup (2 sticks) butter, melted

Combine the bread crumbs and pineapple chunks in a bowl and mix well. Spread over the bottom of a greased 2-quart baking dish. Combine the eggs, sugar and butter in a bowl and mix well. Pour over the pineapple mixture. Bake at 350 degrees for 30 minutes. YIELD: 6 TO 8 SERVINGS.

Pattie Smith
Gadsden Life

Pineapple Casserole

2 (20-ounce) cans pineapple chunks
1 cup sugar
5 tablespoons flour
1½ cups shredded Cheddar cheese
1½ cups butter cracker crumbs
½ cup (1 stick) margarine, melted

Drain the pineapple, reserving ½ of the juice. Arrange the pineapple over the bottom of a buttered baking dish. Pour the reserved juice over the pineapple. Combine the sugar, flour and cheese in a bowl and mix well. Sprinkle over the pineapple. Sprinkle the cracker crumbs over the layers. Pour the margarine over the top. Bake at 350 degrees for 30 minutes. YIELD: **6 SERVINGS**.

Wayne Clements
Tuscaloosa Council

Pineapple Casserole

2 (15-ounce) cans pineapple tidbits, drained
¾ cup sugar
1½ cups shredded cheese
5 tablespoons flour
¼ cup (½ stick) margarine, melted
⅓ cup margarine, melted
32 butter crackers, crushed

Arrange the pineapple over the bottom of a buttered baking dish. Combine the sugar, cheese, flour and ¼ cup margarine in a bowl and mix well. Spread evenly over the pineapple. Combine ⅓ cup margarine and crackers in a bowl and mix well. Sprinkle over the top. Bake at 350 degrees for 20 minutes. YIELD: **6 TO 8 SERVINGS**.

Patsy Frost
Decatur Council

Joan's Giblet Gravy

2 (14-ounce) cans chicken broth
1 (10-ounce) can cream of chicken soup
3 tablespoons cornstarch
1/2 cup water
5 ounces chicken, cooked, chopped, or
1 (5-ounce) can chicken, drained
2 hard-cooked eggs, chopped
Salt and pepper to taste

Combine the broth and soup in a saucepan and mix well. Bring to a boil. Combine the cornstarch and water in a small bowl and stir until smooth. Pour into the boiling mixture. Cook until the mixture thickens, stirring frequently. Stir in the chicken and eggs. Season with salt and pepper. YIELD: 5 1/2 CUPS.

Kathryn Morgan
Gadsden Life

Basting Sauce

1/2 cup vegetable oil
3/4 cup lemon juice
1/4 cup water
1 1/2 tablespoons salt
3 tablespoons sugar
1 1/2 teaspoons Tabasco sauce
1/4 cup (1/2 stick) butter

Combine the oil, lemon juice, water, salt, sugar, Tabasco sauce and butter in a saucepan and mix well. Bring to a boil, stirring occasionally. Keep warm. YIELD: 2 CUPS.

Brenda Nelson
Dixie Chapter

Barbecue Sauce

1 cup each chopped onions and celery
1 cup chopped bell peppers
1/4 cup (1/2 stick) butter
6 tablespoons lemon juice
3 tablespoons Worcestershire sauce
3/4 cup packed brown sugar
1 cup ketchup
1/2 cup water
Salt and pepper to taste
Dash of Tabasco sauce

Sauté the onions, celery and bell peppers in the butter in a skillet until tender. Add the lemon juice, Worcestershire sauce, brown sugar, ketchup, water, salt, pepper and Tabasco sauce and mix well. Bring to a simmer. Simmer until thickened. YIELD: 4 TO 5 CUPS.

Brenda Nelson
Dixie Chapter

White Barbecue Sauce for Chicken

1 1/2 cups mayonnaise
1/2 cup water
1/4 cup white wine vinegar
1/4 cup lemon juice
2 tablespoons each sugar and pepper
2 tablespoons Worcestershire sauce

Whisk the mayonnaise, water, vinegar, lemon juice, sugar, pepper and Worcestershire sauce together in a bowl. Refrigerate until ready to use. Use 1/2 of the sauce to baste chicken while grilling. Serve chicken with remaining sauce. YIELD: 2 1/2 CUPS.

Betty Foshee
Decatur Council

Fruit Sauce for Ham

1/2 cup fruit cocktail
1/2 cup confectioners' sugar
1 tablespoon cornstarch
2 tablespoons butter
1 cup fruit cocktail
1 tablespoon lemon juice

Drain 1/2 cup fruit cocktail, reserving the juice. Combine the confectioners' sugar and cornstarch in a saucepan and mix well. Stir in the reserved juice. Bring to a boil. Add the butter and fruit cocktail. Bring to a simmer. Simmer for 5 minutes. Remove from the heat. Stir in the lemon juice. YIELD: 1 1/2 CUPS.

Jamima M. Edney
Birmingham Life

Hot Diggity Dog Sauce

1 pound ground beef
1/2 cup chopped onion
1 garlic clove, minced
1 (15-ounce) can tomato sauce
1/2 cup water
1/4 to 1/2 teaspoon chili powder
1/4 teaspoon salt

Brown the ground beef in a skillet, stirring until crumbly; drain. Add the onion, garlic, tomato sauce, water, chili powder and salt and mix well. Bring to a boil. Reduce the heat. Simmer for 10 minutes, stirring occasionally. Serve over hot dogs.
YIELD: 8 TO 10 SERVINGS.

Lacey Sizemore
Decatur Council

Secret Sauce

2 (15-ounce) cans whole tomatoes
1 (15-ounce) can whole tomatoes, drained
1 large onion, chopped
Salt and pepper to taste
2 tablespoons garlic salt
1 (15-ounce) can tomatoes with garlic

Combine the tomatoes, onion, salt and pepper in a blender container and process briefly. Pour into a large container. Add the garlic salt and tomatoes with garlic and mix well. Store, covered, in the refrigerator. YIELD: ABOUT 3 CUPS.

Derek Harrison
Shoals Life

Garlic Pickles

2 garlic heads
1 (1-gallon) jar sour pickles
5 pounds sugar
2 tablespoons mustard seeds
½ small can black peppercorns
Cinnamon sticks

Cut the garlic into slivers. Drain the pickles. Cut into the desired thickness. Combine the garlic, sugar, mustard seeds and peppercorns in a bowl and mix well. Alternate layers of pickles and the sugar mixture in the jar. Place cinnamon sticks in the jar. Let stand, covered, at room temperature for 3 days or longer. Place pickles in smaller jars. Refrigerate if desired. YIELD: 1 GALLON PICKLES.

Phoebe Arthur
Gadsden Life

Mock Apple Pickles or Red Hot Cucumber Pickles

10 fully mature cucumbers
1 cup pickling lime
1 gallon water
1 (1-ounce) bottle red food coloring
1 cup vinegar
1 tablespoon alum
2 cups vinegar
2 cups water
8 cups (or less) sugar
8 cinnamon sticks
1/4 cup red hot cinnamon candies

Peel the cucumbers and cut into round slices. Remove the seeds. Place in a crock. Cover with a brine of pickling lime dissolved in 1 gallon water. Let stand for 24 hours. Drain and rinse the cucumbers with water. Place in a saucepan with enough water to cover. Combine the food coloring, 1 cup vinegar and alum in a bowl and mix well. Pour into the saucepan with the cucumbers. Bring to a simmer. Simmer for 2 hours. Combine 2 cups vinegar, 2 cups water, sugar, cinnamon sticks and cinnamon candies in a saucepan. Cook until heated through. Pour into the saucepan with the cucumbers. Let stand, covered, for 24 hours. Drain, reserving the syrup. Bring the reserved syrup to a boil. Pour over the cucumbers. Let stand for 24 hours. Repeat the draining, heating and soaking. Cook the cucumber mixture until heated through; do not boil. Remove the cinnamon sticks. Pack the cucumbers into hot sterilized jars. Add the hot syrup, leaving 1/2 inch headspace; seal with 2-piece lids.
YIELD: 5 1/2 OR 6 (1-PINT) JARS.

Mary Ann Stanley
Mobile Council

Icicle Pickles

*Enough cucumbers to fill a
  1-gallon container*
1 cup lime
1 tablespoon powder alum

6 cups sugar
4 cups vinegar
2 tablespoons salt
2 tablespoons pickling spices

Rinse and slice the cucumbers. Place in a 1-gallon container. Cover with a solution of lime, alum and water. Refrigerate, covered, for 24 hours. Drain and rinse with cold water. Place in the container. Cover with cold water. Refrigerate, covered, for 24 hours; drain. Place in the container. Combine the sugar, vinegar, salt and pickling spices in a bowl and mix well. Pour over the pickles. Refrigerate, covered, for 24 hours. Pour into a saucepan. Bring to a simmer. Simmer for 20 minutes. Pack the pickles into hot sterilized jars. Add the simmering syrup, leaving ½ inch headspace; seal with 2-piece lids. YIELD: 1 GALLON PICKLES.

Ann Moon
Decatur Council

Kitchen Floor Pickles

1 gallon whole cucumbers
2 tablespoons alum
2 tablespoons salt

1 box pickling spices
4 cups vinegar
4 cups sugar

Pack the cucumbers in a 1-gallon crock. Combine the alum, salt, pickling spices and vinegar in a bowl and mix well. Pour over the cucumbers. Add enough water to cover the cucumbers. Store, covered, in a cool place for 1 month. Drain and rinse thoroughly. Cut the cucumbers into slices. Place the slices in the crock. Add the sugar to the crock. Shake until sugar is dissolved. YIELD: 1 GALLON PICKLES.

Christine Richardson
Shoals Life

Raw Cranberry Relish

2 oranges
1 pound cranberries
2 apples, peeled
2 cups sugar
Pinch of salt

Peel the oranges, reserving the rind of one. Put the oranges, reserved orange rind, cranberries and apples through a food grinder. Place in a container with a lid. Stir in the sugar and salt. Refrigerate, covered, for up to 1 month. You may also store in the freezer. YIELD: 10 TO 12 SERVINGS.

Jo Anne Morris
Bon Secour Life

Key Lime Butter

1 cup unsalted butter, softened
3 tablespoons confectioners' sugar
3 tablespoons Key lime juice
3 tablespoons sweetened condensed milk
1/2 teaspoon grated lime zest

Beat the butter in a mixing bowl until smooth. Add the confectioners' sugar, lime juice and condensed milk and mix well. Stir in the zest. Spoon into a container. Chill, covered, until firm. YIELD: 1 1/2 CUPS.

Susan Robbins
Riverchase Council

Emeril's Essence

5 tablespoons paprika
¼ cup salt
¼ cup garlic powder
2 tablespoons coarsely ground black pepper
2 tablespoons onion powder
2 tablespoons cayenne pepper
2 tablespoons dried oregano
2 tablespoons dried thyme

Combine the paprika, salt, garlic powder, black pepper, onion powder, cayenne pepper, oregano and thyme and mix well. Store in a tightly covered container for up to 3 months. YIELD: 1¼ CUPS.

Alice Walski
Birmingham Life

Seasoning Salt

⅓ cup nutmeg
⅓ cup pepper
5⅓ cups salt
2⅓ cups garlic salt

Combine the nutmeg, pepper, salt and garlic salt in a bowl and mix well. Process 1 cup at a time in a blender. Store in a tightly covered container. YIELD: 8⅓ CUPS.

Hazel Campbell
Birmingham Life

I LIKE ME **BOOKS**

Alabama Pioneer Councils provide *I Like Me* books to kindergarten and first grade students every year. The *I Like Me* book is personally made for each child and includes the student's name in the book twenty-one times. It also includes the names of the teacher, friends, and city and state. These books foster a positive self-concept and encourage positive patterns of behavior in children.

Desserts

Apple Crisp

2 (21-ounce) cans apple pie filling
1 (2-layer) package yellow cake mix
½ cup (1 stick) butter
1 cup chopped pecans

Spray a 9x13-inch baking dish with nonstick cooking spray. Spread the pie filling evenly in the prepared baking dish. Sprinkle the cake mix evenly over the pie filling. Cut the butter into thin slices. Dot the cake mix with the butter slices. Bake at 350 degrees for 30 to 35 minutes or until lightly browned. Sprinkle the pecans over the top. Bake for about 15 minutes longer or until the pecans are toasted. Serve the crisp warm with ice cream. YIELD: 10 SERVINGS.

Betty C. Gray
Montgomery Life

Apple Dumplings

1 (8-count) package crescent rolls
2 Granny Smith apples
1 cup orange juice
1 cup sugar
½ cup (1 stick) margarine

Separate the crescent roll dough into triangles. Peel the apples, core and cut each into quarters. Wrap each apple quarter in 1 of the dough triangles and arrange in a lightly greased 6x10-inch baking dish. Combine the orange juice, sugar and margarine in a saucepan. Heat until the sugar is completely dissolved and the margarine is melted. Spoon the hot mixture over the wrapped apples. Bake at 350 degrees until the rolls are brown and the apples are tender. YIELD: 8 SERVINGS.

Hazel Campbell
Birmingham Life

Pattie's Apple Dumplings

1 Granny Smith apple
Cinnamon to taste
1 (8-count) can crescent rolls
1 cup sugar
1 cup orange juice
1/2 cup (1 stick) butter

Cut the apple into eighths, discarding the core. Sprinkle each apple slice with cinnamon. Separate the crescent roll dough into triangles. Wrap each apple slice in a dough triangle; do not allow cinnamon to get on the dough. Arrange the dumplings in a lightly greased deep baking dish. Combine the sugar, orange juice and butter in a saucepan. Bring the mixture to a boil, stirring until the sugar dissolves and the butter melts. Spoon the hot mixture over the dumplings. Bake at 350 degrees for 25 to 30 minutes or until brown. Serve the dumplings with the hot sauce. YIELD: **8 SERVINGS**.

Pattie Smith
Gadsden Life

Blueberry Crunch Cake

1 (20-ounce) can crushed pineapple
3 cups blueberries
1 (2-layer) package yellow cake mix
1/2 cup (1 stick) (or more) margarine, melted
1/2 cup sugar
1 cup chopped pecans

Spread the undrained pineapple evenly in the bottom of a lightly greased 9×13-inch baking pan. Sprinkle the blueberries over the pineapple. Sprinkle the cake mix evenly over the blueberries. Drizzle the melted margarine over the cake mix and spread evenly. Add a small of water if desired. Sprinkle with 1/2 cup sugar and the pecans. Bake at 350 degrees for 30 to 40 minutes or until golden brown. YIELD: **10 SERVINGS**.

Shirley Crocker
Birmingham Life

Blueberry Delight

8 ounces cream cheese, softened
2 eggs
1 teaspoon vanilla extract
½ cup sugar
Crust (below)
2 (21-ounce) cans blueberry pie filling

Combine the cream cheese, eggs, vanilla and sugar in a mixing bowl and beat until smooth and creamy. Spread the mixture evenly over the hot Crust. Bake at 350 degrees for 15 minutes. The filling will be slightly shaky. Spoon the pie filling over the cheesecake. Refrigerate for 2 hours or longer before serving. Cut into squares. YIELD: **6 TO 8 SERVINGS.**

Crust

20 graham crackers
¼ cup sugar
½ cup (1 stick) butter or margarine, melted

Crush the graham crackers into fine crumbs and place in a bowl. Add the sugar and melted butter and mix well. Press the mixture evenly over the bottom of an 8×11-inch baking pan. Bake at 350 degrees for 5 minutes. YIELD: **1 CRUST.**

Sue Bryars
Birmingham South Cahaba Council

Blueberry Dessert

1 (20-ounce) can crushed pineapple
3 cups blueberries
3/4 cup sugar
1 (2-layer) package yellow cake mix
1/4 cup sugar
1/2 cup (1 stick) margarine, melted
Chopped pecans

Spread the undrained pineapple evenly in a lightly greased 9×13-inch baking dish. Spread the blueberries evenly over the pineapple. Sprinkle 3/4 cup sugar over the blueberries. Sprinkle the cake mix evenly over the fruit layers. Sprinkle the remaining 1/4 cup sugar evenly over the cake mix. Drizzle the margarine over the top. Bake at 350 degrees for 35 minutes. Sprinkle the desired amount of pecans over the top. Bake for about 10 minutes longer or until lightly browned. **YIELD: 8 TO 10 SERVINGS.**

Marsha Harberger
Riverchase Council

Broken Glass Cake

Crust (below)
Flavored Gelatin Cubes (page 345)
2 envelopes unflavored gelatin
½ cup cold water
½ cup boiling water
1½ cups hot pineapple juice
Whipped Cream (page 345)

Prepare the Crust and set the prepared cake pan aside. Prepare the Flavored Gelatin Cubes. Soften the unflavored gelatin in ½ cup cold water in a large bowl. Add ½ cup boiling water and stir until the gelatin is completely dissolved. Add the hot pineapple juice and mix well. Let stand until cooled completely. Add the Flavored Gelatin Cubes and mix gently. Fold the Whipped Cream into the mixture gently. Spoon the mixture into the prepared cake pan. Chill in the refrigerator overnight. Invert the gelatin cake onto a serving plate. Refrigerate until serving time. **Yield: 8 to 10 servings.**

Crust

18 graham crackers
⅓ cup sugar
½ teaspoon cinnamon
⅓ cup melted butter

Crush the graham crackers into fine crumbs. Combine the crackers with the sugar, cinnamon and melted butter and mix until the mixture is crumbly. Grease an angel food cake pan. Press the crumb mixture over the bottom and side of the pan. **Yield: 1 crust.**

Flavored Gelatin Cubes

1 (3-ounce) package strawberry gelatin
1½ cups boiling water
1 (3-ounce) package lime gelatin
1½ cups boiling water
1 (3-ounce) package lemon gelatin
1½ cups boiling water

Dissolve the strawberry gelatin in 1½ cups boiling water in a bowl. Pour into a 9-inch round cake pan. Chill until firm. Dissolve the lime gelatin in 1½ cups boiling water in a bowl. Pour into a 9-inch round cake pan. Chill until firm. Dissolve the lemon gelatin in 1½ cups boiling water in a bowl. Pour into a 9-inch round cake pan. Chill until firm. Cut all the flavored gelatins into small cubes, loosen from the sides of the pans and separate into cubes.
Yield: 8 to 10 servings.

Whipped Cream

2 cups whipping cream
½ cup sugar
Dash of salt

Combine the whipping cream, sugar and salt in mixing bowl. Beat at medium speed until the sugar is completely dissolved. Beat at high speed until peaks form; do not overbeat. **Yield: 3 cups.**

Barbara Seegmiller
Decatur Council

Butterscotch Delight

16 ounces cream cheese, softened
2 cups confectioners' sugar
Crust (below)
2 (4-ounce) packages butterscotch instant pudding mix
2 cups milk
16 ounces whipped topping

Combine the cream cheese and confectioners' sugar in a mixing bowl and beat until smooth and creamy. Spread over the Crust. Combine the pudding mixes and milk in a mixing bowl and beat until thickened. Spread over the cream cheese layer. Spread the whipped topping over the top. Chill until serving time.
YIELD: 8 TO 10 SERVINGS.

Crust

2 cups flour
1 cup (2 sticks) margarine
1 cup chopped pecans

Place the flour in a bowl. Cut in the margarine until crumbly. Add the pecans and mix well. Press the mixture evenly over the bottom of a 9×13-inch baking pan. Bake at 350 degrees for 25 minutes. Let stand until completely cooled, or place in the freezer for faster cooling. YIELD: 1 CRUST.

Doris Yarber
Shoals Life

Cheese Squares

2 (8-count) packages crescent rolls
19 ounces cream cheese, softened
1¼ cups sugar
1 egg yolk, beaten
2 teaspoons lemon juice
1 teaspoon vanilla extract
1 egg white
1 teaspoon water

Separate 1 package of the crescent roll dough into rectangles. Line a lightly greased 9×13-inch baking pan with the roll dough, sealing the edges and perforations together. Combine the cream cheese, sugar, egg yolk, lemon juice and vanilla in a mixing bowl and beat until smooth and creamy. Spread the cream cheese mixture evenly over the roll dough. Separate the remaining package of the crescent roll dough into rectangles. Place on top of the cream cheese mixture. Whisk the egg white with the water in a small bowl. Brush over the roll dough. Bake at 350 degrees for 20 to 25 minutes or until lightly browned. Cool and cut into squares. Serve plain or top with strawberries or blueberries. **YIELD: 8 TO 10 SERVINGS.**

Marsha Harbarger
Riverchase Council

HELPFUL HINT

Flavor whipped cream with cocoa or tint with food coloring for garnishes.

Petite Cherry Cheesecakes

16 ounces cream cheese, softened
¾ cup sugar
2 eggs
1 tablespoon lemon juice
1 teaspoon vanilla extract
36 vanilla wafers
1 (21-ounce) can cherry pie filling

Combine the cream cheese, sugar, eggs, lemon juice and vanilla in a mixing bowl and beat until smooth and creamy. Line 36 muffin cups with paper cupcake liners. Place a vanilla wafer in each cup. Fill each cup ⅔ full with the cream cheese mixture. Bake at 375 degrees for 15 to 20 minutes or until firm; do not allow the filling to brown. Let stand until cool. Top each cheesecake with a teaspoon of the cherry pie filling. Cheesecakes may be frozen before adding the pie filling. YIELD: 3 DOZEN.

Barclay Dempster
Mobile Council

Chocolate Cheesecake

1½ cups semisweet chocolate chips
2 eggs
1 cup sugar
1 cup sour cream

16 ounces cream cheese, softened
2 tablespoons melted butter
Crust (below)

Melt the chocolate chips in the top of a double boiler over hot water, stirring until smooth. Set the melted chocolate aside. Combine the eggs, sugar and sour cream in a mixing bowl. Beat for 1 minute or until smooth and well blended. Add the melted chocolate gradually, beating constantly. Beat in the cream cheese and butter gradually, beating constantly until well blended. Pour the cream cheese mixture into the prepared Crust. Bake at 325 degrees for 45 minutes or until the cheesecake is set in the center. Let stand at room temperature for 1 hour or longer to cool. Chill in the refrigerator for 6 hours or longer. Loosen the cheesecake from the side of the pan. Remove the side of the pan. Serve with whipped cream if desired. May substitute 2 crust-lined pie plates for the springform pan and bake for 35 minutes or until the centers are set.
YIELD: 10 TO 12 SERVINGS.

Crust

1½ cups graham cracker crumbs
2 tablespoons sugar

¼ teaspoon cinnamon
¼ cup (½ stick) butter, melted

Combine the first 3 ingredients in a mixing bowl and mix well. Add the butter and mix until the mixture is crumbly. Press the crumb mixture over the bottom and slightly up the side of a springform pan. The crumb mixture may be pressed into 2 pie plates instead of a springform pan. YIELD: 1 OR 2 CRUSTS.

Betty Darnell
Gadsden Life

No-Guilt No-Fat Cheesecake

2 cups nonfat cottage cheese
1/4 cup nonfat plain yogurt
1 egg white
1/4 cup frozen orange juice concentrate, thawed
1/3 cup frozen apple juice concentrate, thawed
1 teaspoon vanilla extract
Grape-Nuts Crust (below)

Place the cottage cheese in a blender container. Process until the cottage cheese is smooth. Add the yogurt, egg white, orange juice and apple juice concentrates and vanilla and process until smooth and creamy. Pour the cottage cheese mixture into the Grape-Nuts Crust. Bake at 350 degrees for 20 minutes or until set. Chill in the refrigerator until serving time. Serve topped with fresh fruit such as strawberries, blueberries or cherries. Each serving has approximately 105 calories. YIELD: 8 SERVINGS.

Grape-Nuts Crust

1 to 2 cups Grape-Nuts cereal
1 to 2 tablespoons frozen apple juice concentrate, thawed

Combine the desired amounts of cereal and apple juice concentrate in a bowl and mix well. Pat the mixture evenly over the bottom of a 9-inch pie plate. Bake at 350 degrees for 10 minutes. Let the crust cool for 10 minutes before adding the cottage cheese mixture. YIELD: 1 CRUST.

Gussie Evans
Mobile Council

Cheesecake

1 pound graham crackers
½ cup (1 stick) melted butter or margarine
1 (3-ounce) package lemon gelatin
1 cup boiling water
3 tablespoons lemon juice
8 ounces cream cheese, softened
1 cup sugar
1 teaspoon vanilla extract
1 (12-ounce) can evaporated milk, chilled

Crush the graham crackers into fine crumbs. Combine ⅔ of the crumbs and the melted butter in a bowl and mix until crumbly. Press over the bottom and sides of a 9×13-inch pan. Dissolve the gelatin in 1 cup boiling water. Add 3 tablespoons lemon juice. Let stand until cool. Combine the cream cheese, sugar and vanilla in a mixing bowl and beat until smooth and creamy. Add the cooled gelatin and beat until well blended. Whip the evaporated milk in a small bowl until peaks form. Fold the whipped evaporated milk into the cream cheese mixture gently. Spoon the mixture evenly into the prepared pan. Sprinkle with the remaining graham cracker crumbs. Chill for several hours. Cut into squares. YIELD: 12 SERVINGS.

Susan Y. May
Shoals Life

HELPFUL HINT

Prepared whipped topping has 20 fewer calories per tablespoon than sweetened whipped cream.

Chocolate Cobbler

1 cup flour
¾ cup sugar
1½ tablespoons baking cocoa
½ cup milk
1 teaspoon vanilla extract
½ cup (1 stick) butter
1 cup sugar
¼ cup baking cocoa
1½ cups boiling water

Combine the flour, ¾ cup sugar, 1½ tablespoons baking cocoa, milk and vanilla in a mixing bowl and mix until well blended. Melt the butter in a 9x13-inch baking pan. Pour the batter into the melted butter; do not stir. Mix 1 cup sugar and ¼ cup cocoa in a small bowl and sprinkle over the batter; do not stir. Drizzle the boiling water over the top; do not stir. Bake at 350 degrees for 30 minutes. Serve warm. YIELD: 8 TO 10 SERVINGS.

Judy Evans
Decatur Council

Easy Fruit Cobbler

½ cup (1 stick) margarine
1 cup each self-rising flour and sugar
¾ cup milk
1 (21-ounce) can strawberry pie filling

Melt the margarine in a baking dish. Combine the self-rising flour, sugar and milk in a mixing bowl and beat until smooth. Drizzle the batter into the margarine; do not stir. Spoon the pie filling over the batter; do not stir. Bake at 350 degrees for 1 hour or until golden brown. YIELD: 4 TO 6 SERVINGS.

Faye King
Huntsville Council

Fruit Cobbler

2 cups favorite fruit
1 cup milk
1 cup sugar
¼ cup (½ stick) margarine, melted
Dash of salt
4 slices bread
Butter, softened
Sugar to taste

Combine the fruit, milk, sugar, margarine and salt in a saucepan. Add enough water to cover the fruit. Cook over medium heat until the fruit is tender, stirring occasionally. Spread the bread with butter and sprinkle with sugar. Toast the bread in the oven or a toaster oven until golden brown. Cut 2 of the slices into small pieces and add to the fruit. Let the mixture stand for several minutes to soak up the fruit juices. Place the fruit mixture in a lightly greased baking dish. Top with the remaining toast slices. Bake at 350 degrees for 15 minutes. YIELD: 4 TO 6 SERVINGS.

Lillian Weaver
Huntsville Council

Sweet Potato Cobbler

2 large sweet potatoes
2 cups water
2 cups sugar
Dash of salt
1/3 teaspoon nutmeg
1/4 to 1/2 cup (1/2 to 1 stick) margarine, softened
Pastry Strips (below)

Peel the sweet potatoes and cut into small pieces. Combine the sweet potatoes, 2 cups water, sugar, salt and nutmeg in a saucepan. Bring the mixture to a boil, stirring until the sugar dissolves. Reduce the heat and simmer, covered, for 15 to 20 minutes or until the sweet potatoes are tender. Spread the margarine in a 9- or 10-inch baking pan. Pour the sweet potato mixture into the prepared pan. Arrange the Pastry Strips over the mixture. Bake at 350 degrees for 35 minutes or until golden brown. **YIELD: 4 TO 6 SERVINGS.**

Pastry Strips

3/4 cup flour
3 tablespoons vegetable oil
3 tablespoons cold water

Place the flour in a bowl. Add the oil and mix until the mixture is crumbly. Add the cold water and mix until the mixture holds together. Roll very thinly on a lightly floured surface and cut into strips.

Narice Sutton
Birmingham Life

Sweet Potato Cobbler

6 cups chopped peeled sweet potatoes
5 cups water
2 teaspoons vanilla extract
1 cup (2 sticks) margarine, melted
2 cups sugar
3 cups flour
1 cup shortening
1 cup milk

Combine the sweet potatoes and water in a saucepan. Simmer, covered, until the sweet potatoes are tender. Stir in the vanilla. Divide the margarine between 2 baking pans. Drain the sweet potatoes, reserving the liquid. Dissolve the sugar in the reserved liquid and set aside. Place the flour in a bowl. Add the shortening and cut in until the mixture is crumbly. Add the milk and mix until a dough forms. Turn the dough onto a lightly floured surface and roll into a rectangle. Roll the dough as for a jelly roll. Cut into 1-inch slices. Divide the sweet potatoes between the baking pans. Arrange the dough slices over the sweet potatoes. Spoon the sugared liquid over the top. Bake at 350 degrees for 1 hour or until golden brown.
YIELD: 6 TO 8 SERVINGS.

Elizabeth S. Dempsey
Anniston Council

HELPFUL HINT
Chill the bowl and beaters to whip cream faster and stiffer.

Sweet Potato Cobbler

2 large sweet potatoes
2¼ cups water
2 cups sugar
Dash of salt
⅓ teaspoon nutmeg
¼ cup (½ stick) butter or margarine
Pastry Strips (below)

Peel the sweet potatoes and slice enough crosswise to measure about 3 cups. Combine the sweet potatoes and water in a saucepan and simmer, covered, until tender. Drain the sweet potatoes, reserving the liquid. Combine the reserved liquid, sugar, salt and nutmeg and mix until the sugar dissolves. Melt the butter in a 9×13-inch baking dish. Add the drained sweet potatoes. Add the sugar mixture and arrange the Pastry Strips over the top. Bake at 350 degrees for 35 minutes. **YIELD: 8 TO 10 SERVINGS.**

Pastry Strips

¾ cup self-rising flour
3 tablespoons vegetable oil
3 tablespoons cold water

Combine the self-rising flour and oil in a bowl and mix until crumbly. Add the water and mix until the mixture forms a dough. Turn the dough onto a lightly floured surface. Roll the dough thinly and cut into 3-inch strips.

Mary Ann Sparks Fulmer
Shoals Life

Cream Puffs

1 cup water
3/4 cup (1 1/2 sticks) butter
1 cup flour
1/2 teaspoon salt
4 eggs
Butter pecan ice cream

1/4 cup sugar
1/4 cup cornstarch
2 (12-ounce) cans apricot nectar
1/3 cup peach brandy
Fresh or canned peach slices

Combine the water and butter in a saucepan. Bring to a full rolling boil. Mix the flour and salt together. Add to the boiling mixture all at once and cook over low heat until the mixture forms a ball and becomes smooth and satiny, stirring vigorously. Remove from the heat and place the dough in a large mixing bowl. Add the eggs 1 at a time, beating until smooth and satiny after each addition. Drop the dough in 3-tablespoon portions 3 inches apart onto a buttered baking sheet. Bake at 425 degrees for 20 to 30 minutes or until golden brown. Turn off the oven. Cut a slit in the side of each puff to allow the centers to dry. Return the baking sheet to the oven for about 20 minutes. Remove the puffs to a wire rack to cool. Cut the tops from the puffs; remove the soft centers and discard. Fill the puffs with ice cream, place the puffs on dessert plates and replace the cream puff tops. Mix the sugar and cornstarch in a saucepan. Add the apricot nectar, blending well. Cook over medium heat until the mixture comes to a boil, stirring constantly. Boil for 2 minutes, stirring constantly. Remove from the heat and stir in the peach brandy. Arrange the peach slices around the puffs and spoon the warm sauce over the peach slices. You may substitute strawberries with whipped cream or a favorite flavor pudding for the ice cream and peaches. YIELD: 15 SERVINGS.

Betty Foshee
Decatur Council

St. Éclair Cake

1 (1-pound) package graham crackers
2 (4-ounce) or 1 (6-ounce) package French vanilla instant pudding mix
3½ cups milk
8 ounces whipped topping
Chocolate Frosting (below)

Line a buttered 9×13-inch dish with graham crackers. Prepare the pudding mix with milk according to the package directions. Blend in the whipped topping. Alternate layers of the pudding mixture and the remaining graham crackers in the prepared dish, ending with graham crackers. Refrigerate for 2 hours. Frost with the Chocolate Frosting. Refrigerate for 24 hours before serving.

Yield: 8 to 10 servings.

Chocolate Frosting

2 packages Choco Bake
½ teaspoon light corn syrup
3 tablespoons butter, softened
2 teaspoons vanilla extract
1½ cups confectioners' sugar
2 to 3 tablespoons milk

Combine the Choco Bake, corn syrup, butter and vanilla in a small mixing bowl and beat until well blended. Add the confectioners' sugar and beat well. Add enough of the milk to make the frosting of the desired consistency and beat until smooth and creamy.

Yield: 2 cups.

Virginia Bowen
Shoals Life

Chocolate Éclair

1 (1-pound) package graham crackers
2 (4-ounce) packages vanilla instant pudding mix
3 cups milk
8 ounces whipped topping
1 (16-ounce) can dark chocolate frosting

Arrange enough of the graham crackers to cover the bottom of a 9×13-inch pan. Prepare the pudding mixes with the milk according to the package directions. Fold in the whipped topping. Spoon half the pudding mixture over the graham crackers. Arrange another layer of the graham crackers over the pudding mixture. Add layers of the remaining pudding mixture and graham crackers. Heat the frosting in the microwave for 1 minute to soften. Spread the frosting over the top. Refrigerate until serving time.
YIELD: 8 TO 10 SERVINGS.

Faye Grizzell
Birmingham South Life

Seven-Layer Finger Gelatin

4 (3-ounce) packages gelatin (each a different flavor)
6 envelopes unflavored gelatin
6 cups boiling water
1 (14-ounce) can sweetened condensed milk

Layer 1—Combine 1 package of flavored gelatin and 1 envelope unflavored gelatin in a bowl and mix well. Add 1 cup of the boiling water and stir until completely dissolved. Pour into a 9×13-inch pan. Chill for 20 minutes or until partially set.

Layer 2—Combine the condensed milk, 2 envelopes of the unflavored gelatin and 2 cups boiling water in a bowl and mix until the gelatin dissolves completely. Pour 1/3 of the mixture over the partially set layer. Chill for 20 minutes.

Layer 3—Repeat Layer 1 using a second package of flavored gelatin and an envelope of unflavored gelatin and pour over the gelatin layers. Chill for 20 minutes.

Layer 4—Pour half the remaining condensed milk mixture over the gelatin layers. Chill for 20 minutes.

Layer 5—Repeat Layer 1 using a third package of flavored gelatin and envelope of unflavored gelatin and pour over the gelatin layers. Chill for 20 minutes.

Layer 6—Pour the remaining condensed milk mixture over the gelatin layers. Chill for 20 minutes.

Layer 7—Repeat Layer 1 with the remaining flavored gelatin and unflavored gelatin and pour over the gelatin layers. Chill for 20 minutes or until completely congealed.

Cut the gelatin into 1½-inch squares or the size you desire. Select different flavor and/or colors of flavored gelatin. YIELD: **8 TO 10 SERVINGS**.

Editor's Note: Unflavored gelatin may dissolve more completely if allowed to soften in a tablespoon or two of cool water before adding the boiling water. Be sure to reduce the amount of boiling water if this method is used so the combination of cool and boiling water does not exceed 1 cup for each flavored layer and 2 cups for the condensed milk mixture.

Shirley M. Helms
Montgomery Life

Lemon Junk

1 (12-ounce) can evaporated milk
1 cup sugar
½ cup lemon juice
Graham cracker crumbs

Pour the evaporated milk into a mixing bowl. Chill in the freezer until almost frozen. Beat the evaporated milk until peaks form. Combine the sugar and lemon juice in a bowl and stir until well mixed. Fold lemon juice mixture into the beaten evaporated milk. Sprinkle the desired amount of graham cracker crumbs over the bottom of a square dish. Spoon the lemon juice mixture over the crumbs. Freeze, covered, until firm. YIELD: **6 TO 8 SERVINGS**.

Faye Grizzell
Birmingham South Life

Lemon Torte

8 ounces cream cheese, softened
1 (14-ounce) can sweetened condensed milk
1/3 cup lemon juice
Pecan Crust (below)
1 (6-ounce) package lemon instant pudding mix
2 1/2 cups cold milk
8 ounces whipped topping

Combine the cream cheese, condensed milk and lemon juice in a mixing bowl and beat until light and fluffy. Pour over the cooled Pecan Crust. Prepare the pudding mix with milk according to the package directions. Spread over the cream cheese layer. Top with the whipped topping. Refrigerate until serving time.
YIELD: **6** TO **8** SERVINGS.

Pecan Crust

1/2 cup (1 stick) butter
1 cup flour
1 cup chopped pecans

Beat the butter in a mixing bowl until creamy. Add the flour and pecans and mix until crumbly. Pat into a 9×13-inch baking dish. Bake at 350 degrees for 20 to 25 minutes or until light brown. Let stand until completely cooled. YIELD: **1** OR **2** CRUSTS.

Betty C. Gray
Montgomery Life

Payday Candy Bar Cake

Miniature marshmallows
Crust (below)
2/3 cup light corn syrup
1/2 cup (1 stick) margarine
2 cups peanut butter chips
2 cups salted peanuts
2 cups crisp rice cereal

Sprinkle enough miniature marshmallows over the hot baked Crust to cover completely. Return to the oven until the marshmallows puff up. Combine the corn syrup, margarine and peanut butter chips in the top of a double boiler over hot water. Cook until the margarine and peanut butter chips melt and the mixture is well blended, stirring frequently. Add the peanuts and cereal and mix well. Cover the marshmallow layer with the peanut mixture. Let stand until cool. Cut into squares. **YIELD: 6 TO 8 SERVINGS.**

Crust

1 (2-layer) package yellow cake mix
1 egg
1/2 cup (1 stick) margarine

Combine the cake mix, egg and margarine in a mixing bowl and mix until the mixture is crumbly. Pat evenly in a 9×13-inch baking pan. Bake at 350 degrees for 10 minutes or until light brown. **YIELD: 1 OR 2 CRUSTS.**

Mary Howle
Anniston Council

Fluffy Mint Dessert

40 cream-filled chocolate sandwich cookies
½ cup (1 stick) butter or margarine, melted
24 ounces whipped topping
2 cups pastel miniature marshmallows
1⅓ cups small pastel mints

Crush the cookies into crumbs. Reserve ¼ cup of the crumbs for garnish. Combine the remaining crumbs and melted butter in a bowl and mix well. Press the mixture into a 9×13-inch dish. Place the whipped topping in a large bowl. Fold in the marshmallows and mints. Spread the mixture evenly over the cookie crumb layer. Sprinkle with the reserved crumbs. Refrigerate, covered, for 1 to 2 days before serving. This is a wonderful dessert for Easter.
YIELD: 18 TO 20 SERVINGS.

Virginia A. Holland
Birmingham South Life

Clester Pineapple Dessert

12 graham crackers, crushed
36 large marshmallows
1 cup milk
16 ounces whipped topping
1 (20-ounce) can crushed pineapple, drained

Reserve a small amount of the crumbs for topping. Sprinkle the remaining crumbs over the bottom of a 9×13-inch dish. Combine the marshmallows and milk in the top of a double boiler over hot water. Heat until the marshmallows melt and the mixture is smooth and well blended. Let stand until cool. Place the whipped topping in a large mixing bowl. Fold in the marshmallow mixture and the drained pineapple. Spoon the mixture into the prepared dish. Sprinkle with the reserved crumbs. Chill in the refrigerator until firm. YIELD: 8 TO 10 SERVINGS.

Barbara Seegmiller
Decatur Council

Pineapple Prune Whip

1 tablespoon unflavored gelatin
¼ cup canned pineapple juice
½ cup prune juice
¼ cup canned pineapple juice
1 cup whipping cream, whipped
1 teaspoon vanilla extract or lemon juice
2 cups cooked chopped prunes, drained
4 slices canned pineapple, drained, chopped
18 large marshmallows, chopped, or
36 miniature marshmallows

Soften the gelatin in ¼ cup pineapple juice in a mixing bowl. Heat the prune juice and ¼ cup pineapple juice in a saucepan. Add to the softened gelatin mixture and stir until the gelatin dissolves completely. Chill until the mixture has thickened to the consistency of honey. Beat the mixture until frothy. Fold in the whipped cream, vanilla, prunes, chopped pineapple and marshmallows. Rinse 1 large or several individual gelatin molds with cold water. Fill the molds with the mixture. Chill until firm. Unmold onto a serving plate. Serve with heavy cream or whipped cream.

Yield: 6 to 8 servings.

Francis Tucker
Selma Life

HELPFUL HINT

Save calories by topping desserts with lightly sweetened non-fat sour cream instead of whipped cream.

Pumpkin Dessert

1 (29-ounce) can pumpkin
3 eggs
1 cup sugar
½ teaspoon cinnamon
1 (12-ounce) evaporated milk
1 (2-layer) package yellow cake mix
1 cup chopped pecans
½ cup (1 stick) margarine, melted
Icing (below)

Combine the pumpkin, eggs, sugar, cinnamon and evaporated milk in a mixing bowl and beat until well blended. Pour the mixture into a lightly greased 9×13-inch baking dish. Sprinkle the dry cake mix over the top. Pat the pecans into the cake mix. Drizzle the melted margarine over the top. Bake at 350 degrees for 1 hour. Let stand until completely cooled. Spread the Icing over the top. Store in the refrigerator. YIELD: 15 SERVINGS.

Icing

8 ounces cream cheese, softened
8 ounces whipped topping
12 ounces confectioners' sugar

Beat the cream cheese in a mixing bowl. Add the whipped topping and beat until well blended. Add the confectioners' sugar gradually, beating until smooth and creamy. YIELD: 3 CUPS.

Patricia V. Allen
Selma Life

Mile-High Strawberry Delight

2 egg whites, at room temperature
1 (10-ounce) package frozen strawberries, thawed
1 cup sugar
1 tablespoon lemon juice
Dash of salt
8 ounces whipped topping
Pecan Crunch (below)
Fresh strawberries, sliced
Chocolate sauce

Combine the egg whites, strawberries, sugar, lemon juice and salt in a large mixing bowl. Beat with an electric mixer at high speed for 20 minutes or until the mixture forms high peaks similar to a meringue. Fold in the whipped topping gently. Spread evenly over the Pecan Crunch in the pan. Sprinkle the reserved Pecan Crunch over the top. Freeze for 6 hours or longer. Top with the fresh sliced strawberries and a drizzle of chocolate sauce. **YIELD: 12 TO 16 SERVINGS.**

Pecan Crunch

1 cup flour
1/4 cup packed brown sugar
1/2 cup (1 stick) margarine, melted
1 cup chopped pecans

Combine the flour and brown sugar in a bowl and mix well. Add the melted margarine and mix until the mixture is crumbly. Stir in the pecans. Spread the mixture in a 9×13-inch baking pan. Bake at 350 degrees for 20 minutes or until golden brown, stirring every 5 minutes. Let stand until cool. Reserve 1/3 of the mixture for topping. Stir the remaining mixture and spread evenly in the pan. **YIELD: ABOUT 2 CUPS.**

Virginia Greene
Birmingham South Life

Quick Dessert

1 angel food cake
1 (6-ounce) package vanilla pudding mix
3 cups milk
Fresh strawberries, sliced
4 cups strawberry glaze
16 ounces whipped topping

Tear the cake into pieces and place in a glass bowl. Cook the pudding mix with the milk in a saucepan or microwave according to the package directions. Pour the hot pudding over the cake pieces. Let stand until cool. Combine the desired amount of fresh sliced strawberries with the strawberry glaze in a bowl and mix well. Spoon the strawberry mixture evenly over the cake and pudding. Spread the whipped topping over the top. Chill in the refrigerator for 2 to 3 hours before serving. YIELD: **6 TO 8 SERVINGS**.

Jo Anne Norris Emery
Bon Secour Life

Fruit Pizza

1 (20-ounce) package refrigerator sugar
cookie dough
8 ounces cream cheese, softened
1/3 cup sugar
1/2 teaspoon vanilla extract
Fresh or canned pineapple slices, drained
Maraschino cherries, drained, sliced
Mandarin oranges, drained
Kiwifruit, peeled, sliced
1/4 cup orange marmalade
1 tablespoon water

Slice the cookie dough and arrange the slices in a 10x15-inch baking pan. Press the slices together to cover the pan evenly. Bake at 350 degrees for 12 to 15 minutes or until light golden brown. Let stand until completely cooled. Combine the cream cheese, sugar and vanilla in a small mixing bowl and beat until light and fluffy. Spread the mixture evenly over the cookie layer. Arrange the fruit decoratively over the cream cheese layer. Blend the marmalade and water in a small bowl and spread over the fruit. Chill in the refrigerator for 1 hour or longer before cutting into squares.
YIELD: 12 SERVINGS.

Elba Skinner
Selma Life

HELPFUL HINT

Whipped cream will be fluffier and less likely to separate if sweetened with confectioners' sugar instead of granulated sugar.

Strawberry Pizza

8 ounces cream cheese, softened
2 cups confectioners' sugar
16 ounces whipped topping
Crust (below)
1 (21-ounce) can strawberry pie filling, or
2 (10-ounce) packages frozen strawberries, thawed

Beat the cream cheese in a mixing bowl. Add the confectioners' sugar gradually, beating until light and fluffy. Fold in the whipped topping. Spread the mixture evenly over the cooled Crust. Top with the strawberry pie filling. Chill until serving time. Cut into squares. YIELD: 10 TO 12 SERVINGS.

Crust

1 1/2 cups flour
1/4 cup packed brown sugar
1 cup (2 sticks) margarine, melted
1 cup chopped pecans

Sift the flour into a bowl. Add the brown sugar and mix well. Add the melted margarine and mix well. Stir in the pecans. Press the mixture into a 9x13-inch baking pan. Bake at 400 degrees for 12 minutes. Let stand until completely cooled. YIELD: 1 OR 2 CRUSTS.

Eloise Bennett
Decatur Council

Chocolate Trifle

1 (2-layer) package chocolate fudge cake mix
1 (6-ounce) package chocolate instant pudding mix
3 cups milk
½ cup strong brewed coffee
12 ounces whipped topping
6 (1.4-ounce) Heath candy bars, crushed

Prepare and bake the cake mix according to the package directions. Let stand until completely cooled. Prepare the pudding mix with the milk according to the package directions. Crumble the cake into pieces. Reserve ½ cup of the crumbs for topping. Spread half the remaining cake in a 4½- to 5-quart trifle bowl. Sprinkle with half the coffee. Spoon half the pudding over the cake layer and spread with half the whipped topping. Sprinkle with half the crushed candy. Repeat the layers with the remaining cake, coffee, pudding and whipped topping. Mix the reserved cake crumbs with the remaining crushed candy. Sprinkle over the top. Refrigerate for 4 to 5 hours before serving. **YIELD: 8 TO 10 SERVINGS.**

Hester P. Thompson
Birmingham Life

HELPFUL HINT

Place a piece of plastic wrap directly on the surface of custards and puddings after removing from the heat to prevent a "skin" from forming.

Chocolate Trifle

1 small package sugar-free instant chocolate pudding mix
1 large package sugar-free instant chocolate pudding mix
5 cups milk
1 bakery pound cake
2 (21-ounce) cans lite cherry pie filling
Whipped topping

Combine the pudding mixes in a mixing bowl. Add the milk and mix according to the package directions. Cut the cake into slices. Alternate layers of pound cake, pudding, pie filling and whipped topping in a trifle bowl until all the ingredients are used, ending with the whipped topping. Chill in the refrigerator for several hours to overnight. The trifle will keep in the refrigerator for up to 5 days.
YIELD: **8 TO 10** SERVINGS.

Variations

Pineapple Trifle—Prepare as above but substitute vanilla instant pudding mix for chocolate. Omit the cherry pie filling and substitute a large can of crushed pineapple that has been mixed with 1 tablespoon cornstarch and cooked over medium heat until thickened, stirring constantly. Let the pineapple mixture cool completely before adding to the trifle.

Sherry Trifle—Prepare as above but substitute vanilla instant pudding mix for chocolate and add sherry to taste to the pudding. Substitute a 32-ounce jar of strawberry preserves for the pie filling.

Nell C. Bell
Birmingham Life

Quick Cranberry Sherbet

1 (3-ounce) package cranberry gelatin
1 cup boiling water
1 cup sugar
2 cups buttermilk
Dash of salt

Dissolve the gelatin in 1 cup boiling water in a mixing bowl. Add the sugar and stir until dissolved. Blend in the buttermilk and salt. Pour into an ice cream freezer container. Freeze according to the manufacturer's instructions. Alternatively, freeze the mixture in the refrigerator-freezer, process in a blender until slushy, return to the freezer, and freeze until firm. YIELD: 1½ QUARTS.

Marjorie Tucker
Selma Life

Fig Ice Cream

4 eggs
2 cups sugar
2 (12-ounce) cans evaporated milk
1½ quarts milk
1 tablespoon vanilla extract
4 cups chopped peeled ripe figs

Beat the eggs in a large mixing bowl until frothy. Add the sugar and beat until thick and lemon-colored. Add the evaporated milk, milk and vanilla and beat until well blended. Stir in the figs. Pour the mixture into a 1-gallon ice cream freezer container. Freeze according to the manufacturer's instructions. YIELD: 1 GALLON.

Mrs. Donald B. Terry
Tuscaloosa Council

Peach Ice Cream

4 to 6 ripe peaches
1 tablespoon lemon juice
3 quarts half-and-half
3 cups sugar
2 tablespoons vanilla extract
1/4 teaspoon salt

Peel the peaches, cut into pieces and place in a blender or food processor container. Add the lemon juice and process until puréed. Set the peaches aside. Combine the half-and-half, sugar, vanilla and salt in an ice cream freezer container and stir until the sugar is completely dissolved. Add the peaches and mix well. Freeze according to the manufacturer's instructions. **YIELD: 3 QUARTS.**

Mary C. Martin
Birmingham Life

Dessert Ice Cream Balls

1/2 cup raisins
Rum
1/2 gallon vanilla ice cream
2 cups toasted coconut
1/2 to 3/4 cup crushed pecans or almonds

Cover the raisins with rum in a small bowl. Let stand for about 15 minutes or until plumped. Drain the raisins and discard the rum. Place the ice cream in a large mixing bowl. Let stand until softened. Add the raisins, 1 cup of the toasted coconut and the pecans and mix well. Shape the ice cream into balls about the size of a golf ball and roll in the remaining toasted coconut to coat. Place the ice cream balls in paper-lined muffin cups. Freeze until serving time. **YIELD: ABOUT 2 TO 2 1/2 DOZEN BALLS.**

Susan Robbins
Riverchase Council

Oreo Ice Cream Dessert

24 Oreo cookies
1/2 cup (1 stick) butter, melted
1/2 gallon vanilla ice cream, softened
Chocolate Sauce (below)
8 ounces whipped topping
Chopped nuts

Crush the cookies into crumbs and sprinkle evenly over the bottom of a 9×13-inch dish. Drizzle the melted butter over the crumbs. Spread the softened ice cream evenly in the prepared dish. Freeze until firm. Drizzle the Chocolate Sauce over the ice cream layer. Spread the whipped topping over the top and sprinkle with the desired type and amount of nuts. YIELD: 16 SERVINGS.

Chocolate Sauce

1 (4-ounce) package German's sweet chocolate
1/2 cup (1 stick) butter
2/3 cup sugar
1 (5-ounce) can evaporated milk
1/8 teaspoon salt
1 teaspoon vanilla extract

Combine the chocolate, butter, sugar, evaporated milk, salt and vanilla in a saucepan. Heat over low heat until the chocolate and butter melt, stirring frequently. Continue to cook over medium heat until the mixture comes to a boil, stirring constantly. Boil for 4 minutes, stirring constantly. Remove from the heat and let stand until cool. YIELD: 2 CUPS.

Susan Robbins
Riverchase Council

Amy's Ice Cream Sandwich Dessert

16 ounces whipped topping
1/3 cup Kahlúa
3 Skor candy bars
3 milk chocolate candy bars
24 ice cream sandwiches

Blend the whipped topping and Kahlúa in a mixing bowl. Chop the candy bars and mix together. Arrange half the ice cream sandwiches in a 9×13-inch pan. Spread a layer of half the whipped topping mixture over the sandwiches and sprinkle with half the candy bar mixture. Repeat the layers of ice cream sandwiches, whipped topping mixture and candy bar mixture. Freeze for 6 hours or longer before serving. YIELD: 12 SERVINGS.

Virginia Greene
Birmingham South Life

Maxie Pearl's Ice Cream Sandwiches

2 egg yolks
3/4 cup sugar
2 tablespoons flour
1/2 cup milk
Pinch of salt
1 teaspoon vanilla extract
2 egg whites, stiffly beaten
2 cups whipping cream, whipped
Graham crackers

Beat the egg yolks in the top of a double boiler. Add the sugar and flour and mix until smooth. Stir in the milk and salt. Cook the mixture over hot water until slightly thickened, stirring frequently. Remove from the heat. Let stand until cool. Blend in the vanilla. Fold in the stiffly beaten egg whites and whipped cream gently. Arrange a layer of graham crackers in an 8×8-inch pan. Spread the egg mixture evenly over the graham crackers. Add another layer of graham crackers and press down gently. Freeze before serving. Cut into servings the size of half graham crackers. YIELD: 4 TO 6 SERVINGS.

Benny Hyatt
Gadsden Life

Mama's Homemade Banana Pudding

3/4 cup sugar
3 tablespoons flour
2 eggs, beaten
3 cups milk
5 1/3 tablespoons margarine, melted

1 teaspoon vanilla extract
1 package vanilla wafers
3 or 4 bananas, sliced
Whipped topping

Mix the sugar and flour in a saucepan. Add the eggs and mix well. Stir in the milk and margarine. Cook over low heat until thickened, stirring constantly. Remove from the heat and stir in the vanilla. Alternate layers of vanilla wafers, cooked mixture and bananas in a serving dish until all the ingredients are used. Refrigerate until serving time. Serve with whipped topping.
YIELD: 6 TO 8 SERVINGS.

D. Christine Kirkley
Birmingham Life

Banana Pudding

2 (4-ounce) packages banana instant pudding mix
2 cups milk
1 (14-ounce) can sweetened condensed milk

16 ounces whipped topping
1 cup milk
1 teaspoon vanilla extract
Vanilla wafers
Bananas, sliced

Prepare the banana pudding with 2 cups milk using package directions. Blend in the condensed milk. Fold in the whipped topping. Add the remaining cup of milk and beat until well blended. Beat in the vanilla. Crush several of the vanilla wafers for garnish if desired. Alternate layers of vanilla wafers, pudding mixture and bananas in a serving bowl until all the ingredients are use. Garnish with a sprinkle of vanilla wafer crumbs. YIELD: 8 TO 10 SERVINGS.

Mary Haynes
Birmingham South Cahaba Council

Best Banana Pudding

2 (4-ounce) packages French vanilla instant pudding mix
3 cups milk
8 ounces cream cheese, softened
1 (14-ounce) can sweetened condensed milk
1 cup confectioners' sugar
16 ounces whipped topping
2 packages vanilla wafers
6 to 8 bananas, sliced
16 ounces whipped topping
1 teaspoon cinnamon

Prepare the pudding mixes with the milk according to the package directions and set aside. Combine the cream cheese, sweetened condensed milk and confectioners' sugar in a large mixing bowl and beat until smooth and creamy. Fold 16 ounces of the whipped topping into the prepared pudding. Fold the pudding mixture into the cream cheese mixture. Alternate layers of vanilla wafers, bananas and pudding mixture in a large pan until all the ingredients are used. Blend the remaining 16 ounces of the whipped topping with the cinnamon and spread over the layers. Refrigerate until serving time. YIELD: 8 TO 10 SERVINGS.

Susan Neuhoff
Montgomery Council

HELPFUL HINT

Substitute low-fat yogurt for milk and cream in puddings and other desserts or for sour cream or butter in uncooked frostings.

Old-Fashioned Banana Pudding

1 cup sugar
2/3 cup flour
2 dashes of salt
8 egg yolks, beaten
4 cups milk
1 teaspoon vanilla extract
Vanilla wafers
7 or 8 large bananas, sliced
8 egg whites
1/2 cup sugar

Combine 1 cup sugar, flour and salt in the top of a double boiler and mix well. Add the egg yolks and milk and mix well. Cook over boiling water until the mixture thickens, stirring constantly. Reduce the heat. Cook for 5 minutes longer, stirring frequently. Remove from the heat and stir in the vanilla. Spread a small amount of the pudding over the bottom of a 3-quart baking dish. Add layers of vanilla wafers, banana slices and pudding 1/3 at a time. Beat the egg whites until stiff but not dry peaks form. Add the remaining 1/2 cup sugar gradually, beating constantly until very stiff peaks form. Spread over the pudding, sealing to the edge. Bake at 400 degrees for 5 minutes or until golden brown. YIELD: 12 SERVINGS.

Virginia Greene
Birmingham South Life

HELPFUL HINT

Sprinkle bananas lightly with sugar to keep them from darkening on the top of desserts.

Cold Biscuit Pudding

6 cold biscuits
1½ cups hot water
½ cup (1 stick) margarine, melted
1¼ cups sugar
5 eggs, well beaten
1 teaspoon vanilla extract
4 cups (about) milk

Split the biscuits and place in a baking dish. Pour the hot water over the biscuits and let stand for several minutes to soften. Add the margarine and sugar and stir to mix. Stir in the eggs, vanilla and milk. Bake at 450 degrees for 45 minutes or until set and brown. **Yield: 8 servings.**

Variations

Orange Biscuit Pudding—Prepare the pudding mixture as above and add 2 cans of mandarin oranges and a teaspoon of orange extract to the biscuit mixture. Sprinkle grated orange rind on top before baking.

Coconut Biscuit Pudding—Prepare the pudding mixture as above and stir 1 cup coconut into the biscuit mixture before baking.

Joann Ford
Gadsden Life

HELPFUL HINT

Dress up bread puddings by using sweet breads, raisin bread or French bread.

Bread Pudding

4 to 5 cups torn 100% whole wheat bread crumbs
1 (12-ounce) can evaporated milk
1½ cups skim milk
½ cup (1 stick) margarine, melted
1¼ cups sugar
4 eggs, slightly beaten
2 teaspoons vanilla extract
1 (3.5-ounce) can flaked coconut
Whole nutmeg to taste

Place the crumbs in a large mixing bowl. Combine the evaporated milk and skim milk in a microwave-safe bowl. Microwave on High to just to below the boiling point. Pour the hot milk over the crumbs. Add the margarine, sugar and eggs and mix with a wire whisk until well mixed. Add the vanilla and coconut. Pour the mixture into a buttered 8x8-inch baking dish. Grate the nutmeg over the top. Place the baking dish in a larger baking pan with 1½ to 2 inches water. Bake at 325 degrees for 55 minutes or until a light golden color and a knife inserted in the center comes out clean. Cut into squares. Serve warm or cold with whipped topping, vanilla ice cream or raspberry jam. **Yield: 4 to 6 servings.**

Barbara Odom Horton (Mrs. Edward K., Sr.)
Mobile Council

HELPFUL HINT

Make bread pudding out of unusual breads such as coffee cake, sweet rolls or croissants.

Bread Pudding

11 slices bread, crumbled
1/2 cup (1 stick) margarine, melted
1 1/2 cups sugar
2 1/2 cups evaporated milk
2 1/2 cups milk
5 egg yolks, well beaten
1 1/2 teaspoons vanilla extract
Cinnamon and nutmeg to taste
Meringue (below)
Sauce (page 383)

Combine the bread and margarine in a large mixing bowl and mix well. Add the sugar, evaporated milk, milk, egg yolks, vanilla, cinnamon and nutmeg and mix well. Pour into a greased baking pan. Bake at 450 degrees for 15 minutes. Spread the Meringue over the pudding, sealing to the edge. Bake for 10 minutes longer or until golden brown. Pour the warm Sauce over the pudding.

YIELD: 6 TO 8 SERVINGS.

Meringue

5 egg whites
1/2 cup sugar

Beat the egg whites in a mixing bowl until soft peaks form. Add the sugar 1 tablespoon at a time, beating constantly. Beat until stiff peaks form.

HELPFUL HINT

The amount of sugar added determines the type of meringue produced. Add 2 tablespoons sugar for a soft meringue and 4 to 5 tablespoons for a hard meringue.

Sauce

1 cup each evaporated milk and milk
1 cup sugar
1½ tablespoons cornstarch
3 tablespoons margarine
2 tablespoons vanilla or rum extract

Mix the evaporated milk, milk, sugar, cornstarch and margarine in a microwave-safe bowl. Microwave on High for 4 minutes. Stir the mixture well and rotate the bowl about a half turn. Microwave for 4 minutes longer. Stir in the vanilla. YIELD: 3 CUPS.

Faye Grizzell
Birmingham South Life

Hot Dog Bun Pudding

1 cup raisins
2½ cups milk
2 cups sugar
½ cup (1 stick) margarine
6 eggs, beaten
1 teaspoon vanilla extract
1 package hot dog buns

Soak the raisins in warm water to cover until plumped. Drain and set aside. Combine the milk, sugar and margarine in a saucepan. Heat until the margarine melts and the sugar is completely dissolved, stirring frequently. Stir a small amount of the hot mixture into the beaten eggs; stir the eggs and vanilla into the hot mixture. Split the buns and arrange split side up in a 10×15-inch baking pan. Pour the milk mixture over the buns. Sprinkle the raisins over the top. Bake at 350 degrees for 25 to 30 minutes or until golden brown and a knife inserted in the center comes out clean. YIELD: 6 SERVINGS.

Hazel Campbell
Birmingham Life

Cinnamon Pudding

1²/₃ cups flour
2 teaspoons baking powder
1 cup sugar
2 teaspoons cinnamon
2 tablespoons melted margarine
1 cup milk
1½ cups packed brown sugar
1½ cups cold water
2 tablespoons margarine

Combine the flour, baking powder, sugar and cinnamon in a mixing bowl. Add the melted margarine and milk and beat until smooth. Pour the batter into a greased loaf pan. Combine the brown sugar, water and margarine in a saucepan. Bring to a boil, stirring constantly. Pour the mixture over the batter. Bake at 350 degrees for 30 minutes. Serve warm with ice cream.
YIELD: 8 TO 10 SERVINGS.

Francis Tucker
Selma Life

Pudding with Chocolate Sauce

2 cups self-rising flour
1 cup sugar
1 egg, beaten
1 cup milk
Chocolate Sauce (below)

Combine the self-rising flour, sugar, egg and milk in a mixing bowl and beat until well blended. Pour into a greased baking dish. Bake at 350 degrees for 30 minutes or until set. Serve with the Chocolate Sauce. YIELD: **4 TO 6 SERVINGS.**

Chocolate Sauce

2 cups sugar
2 tablespoons baking cocoa
2 cups milk

Mix the sugar and baking cocoa in a saucepan. Stir in the milk. Cook over medium heat until smooth and thickened, stirring constantly. YIELD: **2½ CUPS.**

Martha Mitchell
Decatur Council

HELPFUL HINT

Chocolate sauce is similar to chocolate syrup but has a heavier density due to the addition of milk, cream and/or butter.

Stove-Top Rice Pudding

4 cups milk
1/2 cup rice
3 eggs
3/4 cup sugar
1 teaspoon vanilla extract

Bring the milk to a simmer in a large saucepan. Add the rice and stir for 1 minute. Reduce the heat to low and cover. Cook for about 45 minutes or until only a trace of the milk is covering the rice. Beat the eggs in a small bowl. Add the sugar and vanilla and mix well. Stir about 1/2 cup of the hot rice into the egg mixture; stir the egg mixture into the saucepan. Cook for 5 minutes longer, stirring frequently. YIELD: 4 SERVINGS.

Debbie Speaks
Montgomery Council

Sweet Potato Pudding

5 eggs
2 cups milk
1 1/2 cups sugar
1/2 cup (1 stick) butter, melted
1 teaspoon vanilla extract
1/2 teaspoon allspice
3 cups grated peeled sweet potatoes

Beat the eggs in large mixing bowl. Add the milk, sugar, butter, vanilla and allspice and mix well. Stir in the sweet potatoes. Pour into a greased baking dish. Bake at 350 degrees until light brown and crisp on top. YIELD: 6 TO 8 SERVINGS.

Althea Dunn
Bon Secour Life

Jessie Isbell's Sweet Potato Pudding

2 eggs
½ cup sugar
1½ cups grated peeled sweet potatoes
1 cup coconut
½ cup raisins (optional)
¼ teaspoon each nutmeg, mace, ginger,
cinnamon or ground cloves
1 cup milk
1 (5-ounce) can evaporated milk
¼ cup (½ stick) butter, melted
1 teaspoon vanilla extract

Beat the eggs in a large mixing bowl. Add the sugar and mix well. Add the sweet potatoes, coconut, raisins and your choice of spices and mix well. Add the milk, evaporated milk, butter and vanilla and mix well. Pour the mixture into a greased baking pan. Bake at 350 degrees for 1 hour or until set. Serve with whipped cream.

Yield: 4 to 6 servings.

Variation

Prepare and bake the pudding as above for 45 minutes. Sprinkle 1½ cups marshmallows over the top and bake for 15 minutes longer or until golden brown.

Imogene Davis
Birmingham Life

Chocolate Gravy

1 cup sugar
1/4 cup baking cocoa
1/4 cup flour
1 cup milk
Butter

Combine the sugar, baking cocoa and flour in a deep skillet and mix well. Stir in the milk. Cook until thickened, stirring constantly. Add the desired amount of butter and stir until melted and well blended. Serve with hot biscuits for breakfast. YIELD: 1 3/4 CUPS.

Fay Clark
Riverchase Council

Chocolate Sauce Supreme

1 cup semisweet chocolate chips
1/4 cup (1/2 stick) butter
1 cup sifted confectioners' sugar
1/2 cup light corn syrup
1/4 cup creme de cacao (optional)
1/4 cup water
1 teaspoon vanilla extract
Dash of salt

Heat the chocolate chips and butter in the top of a double boiler over boiling water until melted. Add the confectioners' sugar, corn syrup, creme de cacao and water and mix until well blended. Cook until the sauce is thickened and smooth, stirring frequently. Add the vanilla and salt and blend well. Serve hot or cold over ice cream or other desserts. YIELD: 1 3/4 CUPS.

Virginia Greene
Birmingham South Life

Lemon Sauce

1 cup sugar
2 tablespoons flour
3 tablespoons lemon juice
Grated rind of ½ lemon
1 egg
1 cup hot water
⅛ teaspoon salt
1 tablespoon butter

Mix the sugar and flour in the top of a double boiler. Add the lemon juice and rind, egg, water, salt and butter and mix well. Cook over boiling water until thickened, stirring constantly. Serve the warm sauce over apple cake or pound cake or other desserts. Refrigerate any unused sauce and reheat as necessary. YIELD: 1½ CUPS.

Doris B. Thrasher
Gadsden Life

Sweetened Condensed Milk

1 cup nonfat dry milk powder
⅔ cup sugar
2 tablespoons melted butter
½ cup warm water

Mix the dry milk powder and sugar in a bowl. Add the butter and water and mix until smooth. Refrigerate, covered, overnight. Use this mixture as a substitute for one 14-ounce can sweetened condensed milk. YIELD: 1½ CUPS.

Betty Foshee
Decatur Council

ENVIRONMENT

The Alabama Chapter has embarked on an environmental project that will provide a bluebird house to every school in the state of Alabama. This project will place more than 1,400 bluebird houses around the state and will nurture the environment to support increases in the state bluebird population. This is the largest single bluebird house project ever completed in the United States by any one organization.

Cakes

Almond Skillet Cake

3/4 cup (1 1/2 sticks) margarine
1 1/2 cups sugar
2 eggs
1 1/2 cups flour
1 teaspoon almond extract
Slivered almonds

Melt the margarine in a skillet. Stir in 1 1/2 cups sugar. Beat in the eggs. Add the flour and beat well. Stir in the almond extract. Pour into a foil-lined cast-iron skillet. Sprinkle with almonds and additional sugar. Bake at 350 degrees for 30 to 40 minutes or until the cake tests done. YIELD: **8 SERVINGS**.

Dee Ann H. Weaver
Birmingham Life

Apple Cake

3 cups flour
3 tablespoons baking cocoa
1 teaspoon baking soda
1/2 teaspoon salt
2 teaspoons cinnamon
1/2 teaspoon nutmeg
1 1/2 cups olive oil
1 1/2 cups sugar
1/2 cup packed brown sugar
3 eggs, beaten
3 1/2 Granny Smith apples, peeled, chopped
1 cup chopped pecans
2 teaspoons vanilla extract

Mix the flour, baking cocoa, baking soda, salt, cinnamon and nutmeg in a bowl. Combine the oil, sugar and brown sugar in a mixing bowl. Add the eggs and beat well. Stir in the flour mixture. Fold in the apples, pecans and vanilla. Pour into a greased and floured 10-inch tube pan. Bake at 325 degrees for 1 1/2 hours or until the cake tests done. Cool in the pan for 10 minutes. Remove to a wire rack to cool completely. YIELD: **16 SERVINGS**.

Mrs. Virginia Greene
Birmingham Life

Apple Dapple Cake

½ cup vegetable oil
2 cups sugar
3 eggs
2 teaspoons vanilla extract
3 cups self-rising flour
3 apples, peeled, chopped
½ cup chopped pecans
Sauce (below)

Combine the oil, sugar, eggs, vanilla and self-rising flour in a mixing bowl and mix well. Stir in the apples and pecans. Pour into a greased and floured bundt pan. Bake at 350 degrees for 1 hour or until the cake tests done. Pour the Sauce over the hot cake. Let stand for 2 hours before serving. YIELD: 16 SERVINGS.

Sauce

1 cup packed brown sugar
¼ cup milk
½ cup (1 stick) margarine

Combine the brown sugar, milk and margarine in a saucepan. Bring to a boil. Boil slowly for 3 minutes. YIELD: 1¼ CUPS.

Dorothy Kimbrough
Decatur Council

HELPFUL HINT

Use a thread or dental floss to cut a cake instead of a knife.

Apple Cake

3 cups flour
1¼ teaspoons baking soda
1 teaspoon salt
2½ teaspoons cinnamon
3 eggs
2 cups sugar
1½ cups vegetable oil
2 tablespoons vanilla extract
3 cups chopped apples
1 cup chopped dates
1 cup chopped pecans

Mix the flour, baking soda, salt and cinnamon together. Beat the eggs in a mixing bowl until light. Add the sugar gradually, beating until fluffy. Add the oil, vanilla and flour mixture and mix well. Fold in the apples, dates and pecans. Pour into a greased and floured bundt pan. Bake at 325 degrees for 1½ hours or until the cake tests done. Cool in the pan for 10 minutes. Remove to a wire rack to cool completely. YIELD: 16 SERVINGS.

Margaret W. Wilborn
Gadsden Life

Blue Ribbon Banana Cake

2 cups flour
2 teaspoons baking powder
1 teaspoon baking soda
¼ teaspoon salt
½ cup shortening
1½ cups sugar
2 eggs, beaten
½ cup sour milk
1 teaspoon vanilla extract
3 bananas, mashed
1 cup chopped nuts

Mix the first 4 ingredients together. Cream the shortening and sugar in a mixing bowl until light and fluffy. Add the eggs and beat well. Add the flour mixture alternately with the milk and vanilla, beating constantly. Stir in the bananas and nuts. Pour into a greased and floured cake pan. Bake at 350 degrees for 25 to 30 minutes or until the cake test done. Cool on a wire rack. YIELD: 12 SERVINGS.

Joann Thomas
Selma Life

Banana Nut Cake

1 cup (2 sticks) butter, softened
2½ cups sugar
5 eggs
2 cups flour
1½ teaspoons baking soda
1 teaspoon salt
½ teaspoon baking powder
1½ cups milk
1 cup sour cream
1 cup mashed bananas
2 teaspoons vanilla extract

Cream the butter and sugar in a mixing bowl until light and fluffy. Beat in the eggs. Add the flour, baking soda, salt and baking powder and mix well. Beat in the milk, sour cream, bananas and vanilla. Pour into a greased and floured cake pan. Bake at 325 degrees for 1 hour or until the cake tests done. Cool on a wire rack. **Yield: 12 servings.**

Jo Anne Norris (Emery)
Bon Secour Life

Blackberry Wine Cake

1 (2-layer) package white cake mix
1 (3-ounce) package blackberry gelatin
½ cup (1 stick) butter
1 cup confectioners' sugar
1 cup blackberry wine

Prepare the cake mix using the package directions, adding the blackberry gelatin. Bake in a bundt pan using the package directions. Melt the butter in a saucepan. Add the confectioners' sugar and wine and mix until smooth. Pierce the top of the hot cake with a knife. Pour the sauce over the top. **Yield: 16 servings.**

Dilla Samuel
Gadsden Life

Black Walnut Apple Cake

2½ cups sifted cake flour
1 teaspoon baking powder
½ teaspoon baking soda
½ teaspoon salt
½ teaspoon cinnamon
½ teaspoon ground cloves
½ teaspoon nutmeg
¾ cup (1½ sticks) butter or margarine, softened
1¾ cups packed brown sugar
3 egg yolks
¾ cup milk
½ cup black walnuts, chopped
4 apples, grated
½ teaspoon black walnut extract
3 egg whites
¼ teaspoon cream of tartar
Frosting for Black Walnut Apple Cake (page 397)
½ cup black walnuts, chopped

Mix the cake flour, baking powder, baking soda, salt, cinnamon, cloves and nutmeg together. Beat the butter in a mixing bowl. Add the brown sugar and beat until light and fluffy. Beat in the egg yolks. Add the flour mixture alternately with the milk, beginning and ending with the flour mixture and beating well after each addition. Stir in ½ cup walnuts, apples and walnut extract. Beat the egg whites at high speed in a mixing bowl until foamy. Add the cream of tartar. Beat until stiff peaks form. Fold into the batter. Pour evenly into 3 greased and floured cake pans. Bake at 350 degrees for 25 to 30 minutes or until the layers test done. Cool in the pan for 10 minutes. Remove to wire racks to cool completely. Spread the Frosting for Black Walnut Apple Cake between the layers and over the top and side of the cake. Sprinkle with ½ cup walnuts. YIELD: 12 SERVINGS.

Frosting for Black Walnut Apple Cake

5 cups confectioners' sugar
1 teaspoon allspice
1¼ cups (2½ sticks) margarine, softened
¼ cup milk
½ teaspoon maple flavoring

Mix the confectioners' sugar and allspice together. Beat the margarine in a large mixing bowl. Add the confectioners' sugar mixture alternately with the milk, beating constantly until of a spreading consistency. Beat in the maple flavoring. YIELD: 5½ CUPS.

Betty Foshee
Decatur Council

Butter Pecan Bundt Cake

Sugar
Chopped pecans
1 (2-layer) package butter pecan cake mix
1 cup water
1 cup vegetable oil
4 eggs
1 (16-ounce) can coconut pecan icing

Grease a bundt pan with nonstick cooking spray. Sprinkle with sugar and pecans. Combine the cake mix, water, oil, eggs and icing in a mixing bowl and beat well. Pour into the prepared pan. Bake at 350 degrees for 50 minutes or until the cake tests done. Cool in the pan for 10 minutes. Invert onto a wire rack to cool completely. YIELD: 16 SERVINGS.

Paula D. Smith
Birmingham Metro Council

Carrot Cake

2 cups flour
2 cups sugar
1 teaspoon salt
2 teaspoons baking soda
2 teaspoons cinnamon
1½ cups vegetable oil
4 eggs
3 cups grated carrots
Icing (below)

Sift the flour, sugar, salt, baking soda and cinnamon into a mixing bowl. Add the oil and mix well. Add the eggs 1 at a time, beating well after each addition. Add the carrots. Pour into a greased and floured cake pan. Bake at 350 degrees for 45 minutes. Cool on a wire rack. Spread the Icing over the cooled cake. YIELD: 15 SERVINGS.

Icing

8 ounces cream cheese, softened
½ cup (1 stick) butter, softened
1 teaspoon vanilla extract
1 (1-pound) package confectioners' sugar
Crushed nuts
Shredded coconut (optional)

Beat the cream cheese, butter and vanilla in a mixing bowl until light and fluffy. Add the confectioners' sugar and beat well. Stir in the nuts and coconut. YIELD: 5 TO 5½ CUPS.

Jo Anne Norris (Emery)
Bon Secour Life

Carrot Cake

3 cups grated carrots
2 cups flour
2 cups sugar
2 teaspoons baking soda
1 teaspoon baking powder
½ teaspoon salt
1 teaspoon cinnamon
1 (4-ounce) package broken English walnuts
4 eggs, beaten
1½ cups vegetable oil
1 teaspoon vanilla extract
Cream Cheese Frosting (below)

Combine the carrots, flour, sugar, baking soda, baking powder, salt, cinnamon and walnuts in a mixing bowl and mix well. Add the eggs, oil and vanilla and mix until the oil is absorbed. Spoon into 3 greased and floured 9-inch cake pans. Bake at 350 degrees for 30 to 40 minutes or until the layers test done. Cool in the pan for 10 minutes. Remove to wire racks to cool slightly. Spread Cream Cheese Frosting between the warm layers and over the top and side of cake. YIELD: 12 SERVINGS.

Cream Cheese Frosting

8 ounces cream cheese, softened
½ cup (1 stick) margarine, softened
1 (1-pound) package confectioners' sugar
1 teaspoon vanilla extract

Beat the cream cheese and margarine in a mixing bowl until light and fluffy. Add the confectioners' sugar and vanilla and beat until smooth. YIELD: 5 CUPS.

Sarah (Conwill) Spratt
Anniston Council

Orange Carrot Cake

2 cups flour
1 teaspoon baking powder
1 teaspoon baking soda
1 teaspoon salt
1 teaspoon cinnamon
1 1/4 cups vegetable oil
1 cup packed light brown sugar
1 cup sugar
4 eggs
3 cups shredded carrots
Grated zest of 1 orange
1 teaspoon orange extract
Creamy Orange Frosting (below)

Mix the flour, baking powder, baking soda, salt and cinnamon together. Beat the oil, brown sugar and sugar in a mixing bowl. Add the eggs 1 at a time, beating well after each addition. Add the flour mixture gradually, beating constantly. Stir in the carrots, orange zest and orange extract. Spoon into 3 greased and floured 9-inch cake pans. Bake at 325 degrees for 35 minutes or until a wooden pick inserted in the center comes out clean. Cool in the pans for 10 minutes. Remove to wire racks to cool completely. Spread Creamy Orange Frosting between the layers and over the top and side of cake. YIELD: 12 SERVINGS.

Creamy Orange Frosting

12 ounces cream cheese, softened
3/4 cup (1 1/2 sticks) butter or margarine, softened
Finely grated zest of 1 orange
6 cups confectioners' sugar
1 teaspoon orange extract

Beat the cream cheese, butter and orange zest in a mixing bowl until smooth and creamy. Add the confectioners' sugar gradually, beating until smooth. Beat in the orange extract. YIELD: 7 CUPS.

Betty Darnell
Gadsden Life

Double Delight Chocolate Cake

6 ounces cream cheese, softened
½ cup shortening
½ teaspoon vanilla extract
½ teaspoon mint extract
3 cups confectioners' sugar
¼ cup hot water
3 cups confectioners' sugar
4 ounces baking chocolate, melted
2¼ cups flour
1½ teaspoons baking soda
1 teaspoon salt
¼ cup shortening
3 eggs
¾ cup milk

Beat the cream cheese, ½ cup shortening, vanilla and mint extract in a mixing bowl until creamy. Add 3 cups confectioners' sugar and mix well. Add the hot water alternately with 3 cups confectioners' sugar, beating constantly. Blend in the melted chocolate. Mix the flour, baking soda and salt together. Combine 2 cups of the chocolate cream cheese mixture and ¼ cup shortening in a mixing bowl and mix well. Add the eggs 1 at a time, beating well after each addition. Beat for 1 minute. Add to the flour mixture alternately with the milk, mixing well after each addition. Spoon into 2 greased and floured 9-inch round cake pans. Bake at 350 degrees for 30 to 40 minutes or until the layers test done. Cool in the pans for 10 minutes. Remove to wire racks to cool completely. Spread the remaining chocolate cream cheese mixture between the layers and over the top and side of the cake. YIELD: 12 SERVINGS.

Barbara Seegmiller
Decatur Council

Vida's Chocolate Cake

1/2 cup baking cocoa
1/2 cup boiling water
1 1/2 cups sugar
3 eggs
1/2 cup vegetable oil
1 1/2 cups buttermilk
1/2 teaspoon cinnamon
2 cups flour
Icing (below)

Mix the baking cocoa and boiling water in a mixing bowl. Cool slightly. Add the sugar, eggs, oil, buttermilk, cinnamon and flour and beat until smooth. Pour into 3 greased and floured round cake pans or a 9×13-inch cake pan. Bake at 400 degrees for 30 minutes or until the layers test done. Punch holes in the hot cake. Pour Icing over the top. YIELD: 12 TO 15 SERVINGS.

Icing

1 1/2 cups sugar
3 tablespoons flour
1 cup boiling water
1/2 cup (1 stick) butter
1 teaspoon vanilla extract

Combine the sugar, flour, water, butter and vanilla in a double boiler and mix well. Cook over simmering water until thickened and clear, stirring constantly. YIELD: 2 TO 2 1/2 CUPS.

Ruth Golden
Anniston Council

Chocolate Ice Box Cake

1¾ cups sifted cake flour
1⅓ cups sugar
2 teaspoons baking powder
¼ teaspoon baking soda
¾ teaspoon salt
⅔ cup shortening
2 ounces chocolate, melted
1 cup evaporated milk
1 teaspoon vanilla extract
2 eggs
1 cup whipping cream
½ cup confectioners' sugar
¼ teaspoon vanilla extract
4 chocolate candy bars, shaved

Sift the cake flour, sugar, baking powder, baking soda and salt into a mixing bowl. Add the shortening, melted chocolate, evaporated milk and 1 teaspoon vanilla. Beat at low speed until blended. Add the eggs and beat well. Pour into two greased 8×8-inch cake pans. Bake at 350 degrees for 30 to 35 minutes or until the layers spring back when touched in the center. Chill in the refrigerator. Beat the whipping cream in a mixing bowl until stiff peaks form. Fold in the confectioners' sugar and ¼ teaspoon vanilla. Split each cake layer into halves. Spread the cream mixture and sprinkle shaved chocolate between the layers and over the top of the cake. Chill for 8 to 12 hours before serving. Store in the refrigerator. **YIELD: 12 SERVINGS.**

Mary Alice Neal
Birmingham Life

Elaine's Chocolate Dream Cake

1 (2-layer) package devil's food cake mix
1 (12-ounce) jar hot caramel topping
16 ounces whipped topping
6 Heath or Skor candy bars, broken

Prepare and bake the cake using the package directions for a 9x13-inch glass cake dish. Poke small holes in the cake. Pour the caramel topping over the warm cake. Let stand until cool. Combine the whipped topping and candy bars in a bowl and mix well. Spread over the cooled cake. Chill, covered, in the refrigerator until ready to serve. YIELD: 15 SERVINGS.

Eulene Miller
Birmingham South Cahaba Council

Fudge Cake

1 cup (2 sticks) butter, softened
2 cups sugar
2 eggs
2 teaspoons vanilla extract
2 cups flour
1 1/4 cups milk
1/2 cup baking cocoa
1/2 teaspoon baking powder

Cream the butter and sugar in a mixing bowl until light and fluffy. Add the eggs and vanilla and beat well. Add the flour, milk, baking cocoa and baking powder and mix well. The batter will be thin. Pour into a greased 9x13-inch cake pan. Bake at 350 degrees for 30 minutes or until the cake tests done. Cool on a wire rack. YIELD: 15 SERVINGS.

Susan Ragland
Birmingham South Cahaba Council

Hot Fudge Cake

1 (2-layer) package chocolate cake mix
½ gallon vanilla ice cream, softened
3 ounces semisweet chocolate
2 ounces unsweetened chocolate
½ cup (1 stick) margarine
3 cups unsifted confectioners' sugar
1 (12-ounce) can evaporated milk
⅓ cup milk
1½ teaspoons vanilla extract

Prepare and bake the cake using the package directions for a 9×13-inch cake. Cool on a wire rack. Freeze in the freezer. Cut the frozen cake horizontally into 2 layers. Spread the ice cream between the layers. Return to the freezer. Freeze until firm. Melt the semisweet chocolate, unsweetened chocolate and margarine in a saucepan. Add the confectioners' sugar, evaporated milk and milk. Bring to a boil, stirring constantly. Remove from heat. Stir in the vanilla. Serve over the frozen ice cream cake. YIELD: 15 SERVINGS.

Anatalie Watson Fogg
Decatur Council

Texas Fudge Cake

2 cups flour
2 cups sugar
1 teaspoon cinnamon
1 teaspoon baking soda
1/2 cup (1 stick) margarine
1/2 cup vegetable oil
1 cup water
1/4 cup baking cocoa
1/2 cup buttermilk
2 eggs
1 teaspoon vanilla extract
Icing (below)

Mix the flour, sugar, cinnamon and baking soda in a large bowl. Combine the margarine, oil, water and baking cocoa in a saucepan. Bring to a boil, stirring constantly. Pour into the flour mixture and mix well. Add the buttermilk, eggs and vanilla and mix well. Pour into a greased and floured sheet cake pan. Bake at 400 degrees for 20 minutes. Spread Icing over the hot cake. **YIELD: 16 SERVINGS.**

Icing

1/2 cup (1 stick) margarine
6 tablespoons evaporated milk, or 5 tablespoons whole milk
1/4 cup baking cocoa
1 (1-pound) package confectioners' sugar
1 teaspoon vanilla extract
1 cup chopped nuts

Combine the margarine, evaporated milk and baking cocoa in a saucepan. Bring to a boil. Cook until smooth, stirring constantly. Remove from heat. Add the confectioners' sugar, vanilla and nuts and mix well. **YIELD: 5 1/2 CUPS.**

Judy Evans
Decatur Council

Swiss Chocolate Cake

1 (2-layer) package Swiss chocolate cake mix
1 (4-ounce) package vanilla instant pudding mix
1½ cups milk
1 cup vegetable oil
Icing for Swiss Chocolate Cake (below)

Combine the cake mix, pudding mix, milk and oil in a mixing bowl and beat well. Pour into 3 greased and floured cake pans. Bake at 325 degrees for 20 to 25 minutes or until the layers test done. Cool in the pans for 10 minutes. Remove to wire racks to cool completely. Cut each layer horizontally into halves using dental floss. Spread Icing for Swiss Chocolate Cake between the layers and over the top and side of cake. YIELD: 12 SERVINGS.

Icing for Swiss Chocolate Cake

8 ounces cream cheese, softened
1 cup confectioners' sugar
½ cup sugar
12 ounces whipped topping
½ cup chopped pecans
½ cup chopped milk chocolate candy bars

Beat the cream cheese, confectioners' sugar and sugar in a mixing bowl until smooth. Add the whipped topping, pecans and candy and mix well. YIELD: 3½ CUPS.

Margaret W. Wilborn
Gadsden Life

Triple Fudge Cake

1 (4-ounce) package chocolate cook-and-serve pudding
1 (2-layer) package devil's food cake mix
½ cup semisweet chocolate chips
½ cup chopped nuts
Whipped cream

Prepare the pudding mix in a large saucepan using the package directions. Stir the cake mix into the hot pudding. Beat at medium speed for 2 minutes. Pour into a greased and floured 9×13-inch cake pan. Sprinkle with the chocolate chips and nuts. Bake at 350 degrees for 35 to 40 minutes or until the cake tests done. Cool on a wire rack. Serve with whipped cream. YIELD: 15 SERVINGS.

Eunice Henry
Selma Life

Coconut Macaroon Cake

4 eggs
2 cups sugar
2 cups self-rising flour
1 cup buttermilk
1 cup vegetable oil
1 (3-ounce) can coconut
1 tablespoon coconut flavoring
1 cup sugar
½ cup water
1 tablespoon coconut flavoring

Beat the eggs and 2 cups sugar in a mixing bowl until light. Add the self-rising flour, buttermilk, oil, coconut and 1 tablespoon coconut flavoring. Pour into a 9×13-inch cake pan. Bake at 350 degrees for 45 minutes or until the cake tests done. Bring 1 cup sugar, water and 1 tablespoon coconut flavoring to a boil in a saucepan. Boil until the sugar dissolves. Pour over the hot cake. YIELD: 15 SERVINGS.

Margaret W. Wilborn
Gadsden Life

Allie's Coconut Cake

1 (2-layer) package white cake mix
1 (14-ounce) can sweetened condensed milk
1 (14-ounce) can coconut milk
8 ounces whipped topping
1 (12-ounce) package frozen fresh coconut, thawed

Prepare and bake the cake mix using the package directions for a 9×13-inch cake pan. Punch holes in the top of the cake while still hot. Pour the condensed milk and coconut milk over the cake. Let cake stand until completely cool. Spread whipped topping over the top. Sprinkle with coconut. Cut into squares. **YIELD: 15 SERVINGS.**

Mary Ann Stanley
Mobile Council

Coconut Cake

1 (2-layer) package golden butter-recipe cake mix
2 cups sugar
2 cups sour cream
1 (12-ounce) package frozen fresh coconut, thawed
8 ounces whipped topping

Prepare the cake mix using the package directions for 2 greased and floured 9-inch cake pans. Bake at 325 degrees for 20 minutes. Cool on a wire rack. Combine the sugar, sour cream and coconut in a bowl and mix well. Reserve 1 cup of the coconut mixture and chill in the refrigerator. Cut the cooled cake layers horizontally into halves. Spread the remaining coconut mixture between the layers. Mix the chilled reserved coconut mixture and whipped topping in a bowl. Spread over the top and side of the cake. Seal tightly in a cake carrier. Chill in the refrigerator for 3 days before serving. **YIELD: 12 SERVINGS.**

Dorothy Yarber
Shoals Life

Coconut Cake

1 (2-layer) package yellow cake mix
3 eggs
½ cup vegetable oil
1 cup milk
1 teaspoon vanilla extract
1 teaspoon baking powder
2 (6-ounce) packages frozen fresh coconut, thawed
2 cups sugar
1 cup sour cream

Beat the first 6 ingredients in a mixing bowl until smooth. Pour into 3 greased and floured cake pans. Bake at 350 degrees for 15 to 20 minutes or until the layers test done. Cool slightly on a wire rack. Reserve a small amount of the coconut. Mix the remaining coconut, sugar and sour cream in a bowl. Spread between the layers and over the top and side of the cake. Sprinkle the reserved coconut on the top and side of the cake. YIELD: 12 SERVINGS.

Barbara S. Lagle
Birmingham Life

Cream Nut Cake

1 (2-layer) package butter-recipe cake mix
1 cup (2 sticks) butter
2 cups sugar
5 egg whites
1 tablespoon vanilla extract
1 cup chopped pecans
½ cup pecan halves

Prepare the cake mix using the package directions for two 9-inch cake pans. Bake at 350 degrees for 30 minutes. Cool on a wire rack. Melt the butter and sugar in a double boiler. Beat the egg whites in a mixing bowl until stiff peaks form. Fold into the butter mixture. Cook for 1 hour, stirring constantly. Stir in the vanilla. Remove from heat. Beat until of the desired spreading consistency. Stir in the chopped pecans. Spread between the cake layers and over top of cake. Arrange the pecan halves on top. YIELD: 12 SERVINGS.

Doris Yarber
Shoals Life

Custard Chiffon Cake

3/4 cup milk, scalded
7 egg yolks
2 cups flour
1 1/2 cups sugar
1 tablespoon baking powder
1 teaspoon salt
1/2 cup vegetable oil
2 teaspoons vanilla extract
1 teaspoon lemon extract
1 cup egg whites
1/2 teaspoon cream of tartar

Blend the hot milk and egg yolks in a bowl. Let stand until cool. Mix the flour, sugar, baking powder and salt in a large mixing bowl. Make a well in the center. Add the oil, vanilla, lemon extract and cooled egg yolk mixture in the order listed and beat until smooth. Beat the egg whites and cream of tartar in a mixing bowl until stiff peaks form. Do not underbeat. Fold into the cake batter gradually. Do not stir. Spoon into a greased and floured tube pan. Bake at 325 degrees for 55 minutes. Increase the oven temperature to 350 degrees. Bake for 10 to 15 minutes longer or until a cake tester inserted in the center comes out clean. Cool on a wire rack.
Yield: 16 servings.

Barbara Seegmiller
Decatur Council

HELPFUL HINT

Dust flour in greased cake pans with a new powder puff.

Golden Fig Cake

1/2 cup sliced almonds
2 1/3 cups flour
1 1/4 teaspoons baking soda
1/4 teaspoon salt
2/3 cup butter, softened
1 cup packed brown sugar
4 eggs
2/3 cup orange marmalade
1/3 cup sour cream
2/3 cup amaretto or orange juice
1 cup chopped dried figs (6 ounces)

Butter a 9-cup bundt pan generously. Sprinkle with the almonds, patting gently to cover the sides. Mix the flour, baking soda and salt in a small bowl. Cream the butter and brown sugar in a large mixing bowl until light and fluffy. Add the eggs 1 at a time, beating well after each addition. Stir in the orange marmalade and sour cream. The mixture will look curdled. Add the flour mixture alternately with the amaretto, blending well after each addition. Stir in the figs. Pour into the prepared pan, spreading evenly. Bake at 350 degrees for 60 to 70 minutes or until a wooden pick inserted in the center comes out clean. Cool in the pan for 10 minutes. Invert onto a wire rack to cool completely. YIELD: 16 SERVINGS.

Frankie Vaughn
Selma Life

Fruit Cocktail Cake

2 cups flour
1½ cups sugar
2 teaspoons baking soda
2 eggs
1 (No. 303) can fruit cocktail (16 to 17 ounces)
½ cup packed brown sugar
Frosting (below)

Combine the flour, sugar, baking soda, eggs and fruit cocktail in a mixing bowl. Beat for 2 minutes. Pour into a greased and floured 9×13-inch cake pan or tube pan. Sprinkle with brown sugar. Bake at 350 degrees for 40 minutes or until the cake tests done. Spread Frosting over the hot cake. Y**IELD**: 15 **SERVINGS**.

Frosting

½ cup evaporated milk
¾ cup sugar
½ cup (1 stick) margarine
1 teaspoon vanilla extract
½ cup shredded coconut
½ cup nuts

Bring the evaporated milk, sugar and margarine to a boil in a saucepan. Boil for 3 minutes. Remove from heat. Beat for 2 minutes. Add the vanilla, coconut and nuts and mix well. Y**IELD**: 2 **CUPS**.

Mary Ann Stanley
Mobile Council

Fruitcake

1 cup (2 sticks) butter, softened
2 cups sugar
3 eggs
1 cup buttermilk
2 cups flour
1 teaspoon baking soda
1 cup blackberry jam
1 cup nuts
1 cup raisins
1 1/3 cups shredded coconut
1 tablespoon allspice

Cream the butter and sugar in a mixing bowl until light and fluffy. Add the eggs and buttermilk and mix well. Beat in the flour and baking soda. Stir in the jam, nuts, raisins, coconut and allspice. Pour into a greased and floured tube pan. Bake at 350 degrees for 1 hour or until the cake tests done. Cool on a wire rack. This cake can be frozen. YIELD: 16 SERVINGS.

Ann Moon
Decatur Council

Fruitcake

1 pound pitted dates
1 pound red candied cherries
4 slices candied pineapple
4 cups pecan halves
8 ounces shredded coconut
2 (14-ounce) cans sweetened condensed milk

Chop the dates, cherries, pineapple and pecans. Combine with the coconut and condensed milk in a large bowl and mix well. Spoon into a tube pan lined with foil. Bake at 325 degrees for 1 1/2 hours or until the cake tests done. Cool on a wire rack. YIELD: 16 SERVINGS.

Kathryn Morgan
Gadsden Life

Fruitcake

1 large package miniature marshmallows
1 cup milk
1 (13-ounce) package graham cracker crumbs
2 cups English walnut halves
1 pound Brazil nuts
1 pound pecan halves
1 (15-ounce) package raisins
1 small jar candied cherries

Melt the marshmallows in the milk in a saucepan over low heat. Pour the graham cracker crumbs into a large bowl. Reserve the package. Add the marshmallow mixture to the cracker crumbs and mix well. Stir in the walnuts, Brazil nuts, pecans, raisins and cherries. Place in a food storage bag. Pack into the reserved graham cracker package. Chill in the refrigerator until ready to serve. Unwrap and cut into slices using an electric knife. **YIELD: 12 SERVINGS.**

Irene B. McManus
Anniston Council

Dark Fruitcakes

1 (15-ounce) can pitted sour red cherries
1½ pounds candied cherries, chopped
1 pound mixed citrus, chopped (lemon and orange peel)
1 pound candied pineapple, chopped
1 (16-ounce) package dates, chopped
1 pound raisins
1 (12-ounce) package figs, chopped
4 pounds unshelled pecans, shelled, chopped
5 cups (or more) flour
1 teaspoon baking powder
1 tablespoon cinnamon
1 tablespoon allspice
1 teaspoon ground cloves
1 teaspoon nutmeg
½ teaspoon baking soda
1 cup (2 sticks) margarine, softened
2 cups packed brown sugar
7 egg yolks
1 small jar jelly
¾ cup dark corn syrup
½ cup wine or grape juice
2 teaspoons vanilla extract
7 egg whites, stiffly beaten

Drain the pitted cherries, reserving ½ cup juice. Combine the pitted cherries, candied cherries, mixed citrus, pineapple, dates, raisins, figs and pecans in a large bowl. Add 2 cups of the flour and toss to coat. Sift the remaining flour, baking powder, cinnamon, allspice, cloves, nutmeg and baking powder together. Cream the margarine and brown sugar in a mixing bowl until light and fluffy. Beat in the egg yolks 1 at a time. Add the reserved cherry juice and jelly and mix well. Add the flour mixture alternately with the corn syrup, wine and vanilla, beating well after each addition. Fold in the beaten egg whites. Fold in the fruit mixture. Add additional flour if needed for the desired consistency. Pour into five 1-pound loaf pans lined with greased nonrecycled brown paper. Bake at 250 degrees for 2 to 4 hours or until the loaves are moist when a knife is inserted in the center. YIELD: 5 LOAVES.

Mary Alice Neal
Birmingham Life

German Fruitcake

3 cups flour
1/2 teaspoon allspice
1/2 teaspoon nutmeg
1/2 teaspoon cinnamon
3/4 teaspoon baking soda
1 cup buttermilk
3/4 cup (1 1/2 sticks) butter, softened
2 cups sugar
4 eggs
2/3 cup cherry preserves
2/3 cup apricot preserves
2/3 cup pineapple preserves
1 cup chopped pecans
1 teaspoon vanilla extract

Sift the flour, allspice, nutmeg and cinnamon together. Stir the baking soda into the buttermilk. Cream the butter and sugar in a mixing bowl until light and fluffy. Beat in the eggs. Add the flour mixture and buttermilk mixture alternately, beating well after each addition. Fold in the cherry preserves, apricot preserves, pineapple preserves, pecans and vanilla. Pour into a greased and floured 10-inch tube pan. Bake at 325 degrees for 1 1/2 hours. Cool in the pan for 15 minutes. Invert onto a wire rack to cool completely. You can make this cake several weeks ahead of time and freeze.
YIELD: 16 SERVINGS.

Shirley M. Helms
Montgomery Life

So Easy Fruitcakes

2½ cups unsifted flour
1 teaspoon baking soda
2 eggs, lightly beaten
1 (28- or 29-ounce) jar mincemeat
1 (14-ounce) can sweetened condensed milk
1 cup red candied cherries
1 cup green candied cherries
1 cup candied pineapple
1 cup coarsely chopped pecans
1 teaspoon vanilla extract

Mix the flour and baking soda together. Combine the eggs, mincemeat, condensed milk, cherries, pineapple, pecans and vanilla in a large mixing bowl and mix well. Add the flour mixture and mix well. Pour into 2 greased 5×9-inch loaf pans. Bake at 300 degrees for 80 to 85 minutes or until a wooden pick inserted near the center comes out clean. Cool in the pans for 15 minutes. Invert onto wire racks to cool completely. Wrap each loaf in foil. Store in the refrigerator or in an unheated room. YIELD: **2 LOAVES.**

Sara H. Waldrop
Birmingham Life

HELPFUL HINT

To evenly distribute raisins and nuts in cake batter as it bakes, coat them in flour.

Southern Gingerbread

2½ cups flour
2 teaspoons baking soda
½ teaspoon baking powder
1½ teaspoons cinnamon
1 teaspoon ginger
½ teaspoon ground cloves
½ teaspoon allspice
¾ cup packed brown sugar
¾ cup molasses
¾ cup melted shortening
2 eggs, beaten
1 cup boiling water

Sift the flour, baking soda, baking powder, cinnamon, ginger, cloves and allspice together. Combine the brown sugar, molasses and shortening in a bowl and mix well. Add the eggs and mix well. Stir in the flour mixture. Add the water and mix well. Pour into 2 greased and floured 8x8-inch cake pans. Bake at 350 degrees for 30 to 40 minutes or until the cake tests done. Serve with lemon sauce or applesauce. **YIELD: 2 CAKES.**

Althea Dunn
Bon Secour Life

HELPFUL HINT

Be sure that the layers, filling and frosting of a cake are completely cooled before assembling.

Lemon Cake

1 (2-layer) package lemon cake mix
1 (4-ounce) package lemon instant pudding mix
¾ cup vegetable oil
¾ cup water
4 eggs
Glaze (below)

Combine the cake mix, pudding mix, oil and water in a mixing bowl and mix well. Add the eggs 1 at a time, beating well after each addition. Pour into a 9×13-inch cake pan sprayed with nonstick cooking spray. Bake at 325 degrees for 40 minutes or until a wooden pick inserted in the center comes out clean. Pierce holes in the hot cake with a fork. Pour the Glaze over the top. Let stand until cool. YIELD: 15 SERVINGS.

Glaze

2 cups confectioners' sugar
⅓ cup orange juice
2 teaspoons vegetable oil
2 teaspoons water

Combine the confectioners' sugar, orange juice, oil and water in a bowl and blend until smooth. YIELD: 2¼ CUPS.

Mary C. Martin
Birmingham Life

Graham Cracker Cake

1 pound graham crackers, finely ground
2 teaspoons (heaping) baking powder
1 cup (2 sticks) butter, softened
1½ cups sugar
5 eggs
1½ cups milk
1 cup shredded coconut
Pineapple Butter Icing (below)

Sift the graham cracker crumbs and baking powder together. Cream the butter and sugar in a mixing bowl until light and fluffy. Add the eggs 1 at a time, beating well after each addition. Add the graham cracker mixture and milk alternately, beating well after each addition. Stir in the coconut. Pour into 3 greased and floured cake pans. Bake at 375 degrees for 45 minutes or until the layers test done. Cool on a wire rack. Spread Pineapple Butter Icing between the layers and over the top and side of cake. Let stand for 24 hours before serving. YIELD: 12 SERVINGS.

Pineapple Butter Icing

½ cup (1 stick) butter, softened
1 cup drained crushed pineapple
1½ (1-pound) packages confectioners' sugar
Pinch of salt

Combine the butter, pineapple, confectioners' sugar and salt in a mixing bowl and blend well. Add additional confectioners' sugar if needed for the desired consistency. YIELD: 7 CUPS.

Shirley Crocker
Birmingham Life

Mystery Cake

1 (2-layer) package butter-recipe cake mix
1 (17-ounce) can fruit cocktail, drained
1 (4-ounce) package instant lemon pudding mix
1 (3-ounce) can flaked coconut
4 eggs
1/4 cup vegetable oil
2/3 cup packed brown sugar
2/3 cup chopped pecans
1/2 cup (1 stick) margarine
1 cup sugar
1/4 cup milk

Combine the cake mix, fruit cocktail, pudding mix, 1/2 of the coconut, eggs and oil in a mixing bowl. Beat at medium speed for 4 minutes. Pour into a greased and floured 9x13-inch cake pan. Mix the brown sugar and pecans in a bowl. Sprinkle over the batter. Bake at 325 degrees for 50 minutes or until a cake tester inserted in the center tests done. Melt the margarine in a saucepan. Add the sugar and milk. Bring to a boil. Cook for 2 minutes, stirring frequently. Stir in the remaining coconut. Pour over the hot cake. YIELD: 15 SERVINGS.

Betty Foshee
Decatur Council

HELPFUL HINT

Add chopped dates, candied cherries and almonds to any white frosting to lend a holiday air to ordinary cakes.

No Name Cake

1 (2-layer) package yellow cake mix
1 (16-ounce) can pecan or German chocolate frosting

Prepare the cake mix using the package directions. Stir in the frosting. Pour into a greased and floured loaf or tube pan. Bake at 350 degrees for 35 to 45 minutes or until the top tests done. Cool on a wire rack. YIELD: **16 SERVINGS**.

Rubie McInnis
Birmingham Life

Nut Cake

1 1/4 pounds vanilla wafers
2 (14-ounce) cans sweetened condensed milk
2 pounds pecans, shelled
2 pounds unshelled English walnuts, shelled
1 1/2 to 1 3/4 (15-ounce) packages raisins
1 (12-ounce) package frozen coconut

Process the vanilla wafers in a food processor until ground. Combine with the condensed milk in a large bowl and mix well. Let stand for 5 minutes. Add the pecans, walnuts, raisins and coconut and mix well. Pack into a buttered bundt pan. Chill, covered, for 8 to 12 hours. To serve, loosen around the edge of the cake with a knife. Invert onto a cake plate. You may dip the bottom of the pan in hot water for a few seconds before inverting if the cake is hard to remove from the pan. YIELD: **16 SERVINGS**.

Gaynell Bevis
Shoals Life

Lazy Daisy Oatmeal Cake

1 1/4 cups boiling water
1 cup quick-cooking oats
1/2 cup (1 stick) margarine, softened
1 cup sugar
1 cup packed brown sugar
2 eggs
1 teaspoon vanilla extract
1 1/2 cups flour
1 teaspoon baking soda
3/4 teaspoon cinnamon
1/2 teaspoon salt
1/4 teaspoon nutmeg
Frosting (below)

Pour the boiling water over the oats in a bowl. Let stand, covered, for 20 minutes. Beat the margarine,sugar and brown sugar in a mixing bowl until light and fluffy. Add the eggs and beat well. Blend in the vanilla. Stir in the oat mixture. Add the flour, baking soda, cinnamon, salt and nutmeg and mix well. Pour into a greased and floured 9x9-inch cake pan. Bake at 350 degrees for 45 to 50 minutes or until the cake tests done. Spread the Frosting over the top of the warm cake. YIELD: 9 SERVINGS.

Frosting

1/4 cup (1/2 stick) margarine, melted
1/2 cup packed brown sugar
3 tablespoons light cream
3/4 cup shredded coconut
1/4 cup chopped pecans

Combine the margarine, brown sugar and cream in a mixing bowl and mix well. Stir in the coconut and pecans. YIELD: 1 3/4 CUPS.

David J. Elkins
Selma Life

Easy Orange Cake

1 (2-layer) package yellow cake mix
1 1/3 cups orange juice
1/3 cup vegetable oil
3 eggs
1/2 teaspoon orange extract
Zest of 2 oranges
Orange Frosting (below)

Combine the cake mix, orange juice, oil, eggs, orange extract and orange zest in a mixing bowl. Beat at low speed for 1 minute or until mixed. Beat for 2 minutes at medium speed. Pour into a greased and floured 9x13-inch cake pan. Bake at 350 degrees for 30 to 40 minutes or until the cake tests done. Cool on a wire rack. Spread Orange Frosting over the cooled cake. YIELD: 15 SERVINGS.

Orange Frosting

1/4 cup (1/2 stick) butter, softened
4 ounces cream cheese or reduced-fat cream cheese, softened
1 teaspoon orange extract
1 teaspoon vanilla extract
Zest of 1 orange
Dash of salt
1 1/3 (1-pound) packages confectioners' sugar
1 tablespoon orange juice

Cream the butter and cream cheese in a mixing bowl until light and fluffy. Beat in the orange extract, vanilla, orange zest and salt. Add the confectioners' sugar gradually, beating well after each addition. Beat in enough of the orange juice to make of the desired consistency. Beat at high speed until creamy. YIELD: 5 3/4 CUPS.

Judy Brantley
Gadsden Life

Double Orange Refrigerator Cake

1 (3-ounce) package orange gelatin
3/4 cup boiling water
1/2 cup cold water
1 (2-layer) package orange supreme deluxe cake mix
1 envelope whipped topping mix
1 (4-ounce) package vanilla instant pudding mix
1 1/2 cups cold milk
1 teaspoon orange extract

Dissolve the gelatin in the boiling water in a bowl. Add the cold water. Prepare and bake the cake using the package directions for a 9x13-inch cake pan. Cool in the pan for 25 to 30 minutes. Pierce deep holes in the cake about 1 inch apart with an ice pick. Pour the gelatin mixture slowly into the holes. Chill in the refrigerator. Beat the whipped topping mix, pudding mix, milk and orange extract in a mixing bowl until stiff. Spread over the chilled cake. Garnish with thin orange slices. Store, covered, in the refrigerator or freezer.
YIELD: 15 SERVINGS.

Variations

For *Apple Cinnamon Refrigerator Cake*, substitute apple cinnamon cake mix, unflavored gelatin, rum extract and vanilla instant pudding mix.

For *Strawberry Refrigerator Cake*, substitute yellow cake mix, strawberry gelatin, strawberry extract and vanilla instant pudding mix.

For *Lemon Refrigerator Cake*, substitute lemon supreme cake mix, lime gelatin, lemon extract and lemon instant pudding mix.

For *Deep Chocolate Refrigerator Cake*, substitute deep chocolate deluxe cake mix, cherry gelatin, vanilla extract and chocolate instant pudding mix.

Barbara Seegmiller
Decatur Council

Honey Orange Cake

2 cups flour
2 teaspoons baking powder
¼ teaspoon baking soda
¼ teaspoon salt
½ cup shortening
½ cup sugar
½ cup honey
1 egg, beaten
½ cup finely shredded orange peel
1 teaspoon grated lemon peel
¼ cup orange juice

Sift the flour, baking powder, baking soda and salt together. Beat the shortening in a mixing bowl. Add the sugar gradually, beating constantly until light and fluffy. Add the honey and beat well. Beat in the egg. Stir in the orange peel and lemon peel. Add the flour mixture and orange juice alternately, beating well after each addition. The batter will be thick. Spread in a greased 8×8-inch cake pan. Bake at 350 degrees for 45 minutes or until the cake tests done. Cool on a wire rack. **YIELD: 8 SERVINGS.**

Mary Alice Neal
Birmingham Life

HELPFUL HINT

For an easy orange frosting, use vanilla frosting mix, subsituting orange juice for the water and adding grated orange zest.

Orange Pineapple Cake

1 (11-ounce) can mandarin oranges
1 (2-layer) package yellow cake mix
1½ cups vegetable oil
4 eggs
Frosting (below)

Drain the oranges, reserving the liquid. Combine the cake mix, oil and eggs in a mixing bowl and mix well. Add the reserved liquid and blend well. Stir in the oranges. Pour into a greased and floured medium square cake pan. Bake at 350 degrees for 25 to 30 minutes or until the cake tests done. Cool in the pan on a wire rack. Spread the Frosting over the top of the cooled cake. Store, covered, in the refrigerator. YIELD: 15 SERVINGS.

Frosting

1 (20-ounce) can crushed pineapple
1 (4-ounce) package vanilla instant pudding mix
12 ounces whipped topping

Combine the undrained pineapple and pudding mix in a bowl and mix well. Fold in the whipped topping. YIELD: 3 CUPS.

Linda J. Stough
Birmingham South Cahaba Council

Tropical Orange Cake

1 (2-layer) package white cake mix
1 cup water
2 eggs
1 (14-ounce) can sweetened condensed milk
2 teaspoons grated orange peel
1 (3-ounce) can flaked coconut (1 1/3 cups)
1/4 cup thawed frozen orange juice concentrate

Combine the cake mix, water, eggs, 1/3 cup of the condensed milk and orange peel in a mixing bowl. Beat at low speed until moistened. Beat at high speed for 3 minutes. Stir in 1 cup of the coconut. Pour into a greased and floured 9×13-inch cake pan. Bake at 350 degrees for 30 minutes. Cool in the pan on a wire rack. Combine the remaining condensed milk, remaining coconut and orange juice concentrate in a bowl and mix well. Spread over the cool cake. Chill, covered, in the refrigerator. YIELD: 15 SERVINGS.

Donna Jean Bowman
Birmingham South Cahaba Council

Out-Of-This-World Cake

1 (13-ounce) package graham cracker crumbs
2 cups sugar
2 teaspoons baking powder
4 eggs
1 cup milk
1 cup (2 sticks) margarine, melted
1 cup chopped pecans
1 (3-ounce) can flaked coconut
1 (8-ounce) can crushed pineapple
Icing (below)

Combine the graham cracker crumbs, sugar, baking powder, eggs, milk and margarine in a mixing bowl and mix well. Stir in the pecans and coconut. Pour into a greased and floured 9×13-inch cake pan. Bake at 350 degrees for 35 to 40 minutes or until the cake tests done. Pour the pineapple over the top of the warm cake. Cool in the pan on a wire rack. Spread Icing over the cooled cake.
YIELD: 15 SERVINGS.

Icing

½ cup (1 stick) margarine, softened
8 ounces cream cheese, softened
1 teaspoon vanilla extract
1 (1-pound) package confectioners' sugar

Beat the margarine, cream cheese and vanilla in a mixing bowl until creamy. Add the confectioners' sugar and beat well.
YIELD: 4½ CUPS.

Margaret W. Wilborn
Gadsden Life

Peanut Butter Cake

2 cups sugar
1¾ cups self-rising flour
3 eggs
1 cup milk
1 cup vegetable oil, or 1 cup (2 sticks) margarine, melted
1 cup peanut butter
1 teaspoon vanilla extract
Frosting (below)

Mix the sugar and self-rising flour in a mixing bowl. Add the eggs, milk, oil, peanut butter and vanilla and beat well. Pour into 3 greased and floured cake pans. Bake at 350 degrees for 45 minutes or until the layers test done. Spread the hot Frosting over the layers. YIELD: 12 SERVINGS.

Frosting

1 cup peanut butter
¼ cup (½ stick) margarine
¼ cup milk
2 cups confectioners' sugar

Combine the peanut butter, margarine, milk and confectioners' sugar in a saucepan. Cook over medium heat until smooth. YIELD: 3 CUPS.

Fay Clark
Riverchase Council

Pineapple Yum-Yum Cake

1 (2-layer) package yellow cake mix
3 eggs
1½ cups cold water
1 (4-ounce) package vanilla instant pudding mix
⅓ cup vegetable oil
1 (20-ounce) can crushed pineapple
8 ounces cream cheese, softened
1 cup sour cream
¼ cup confectioners' sugar
12 ounces whipped topping
1 (4-ounce) package French vanilla instant pudding mix

Combine the cake mix, eggs, water, pudding mix and oil in a mixing bowl and mix well. Pour into 3 greased 9-inch cake pans. Bake at 350 degrees for 20 to 25 minutes or until the layers test done. Cool in the pans for 5 minutes. Remove to a paper towel- or waxed paper-lined surface to cool completely. Drain the pineapple, reserving the juice. Beat the cream cheese and sour cream in a mixing bowl until smooth and creamy. Beat in the confectioners' sugar, whipped topping and pudding mix. Fold in the drained pineapple. Drizzle each layer with ⅓ of the reserved pineapple juice. Spread the pineapple mixture between the layers and over the top and side of cake. Chill, covered, for 2 days before serving to enhance the flavor. You may store in the refrigerator for 2 weeks.
YIELD: 12 SERVINGS.

Mauntez Mayer
Anniston Council

Pineapple Upside-Down Cake

1¼ cups sifted flour
1¼ teaspoons baking powder
¼ cup (½ stick) butter, softened
¾ cup sugar
1 egg, beaten
½ cup milk
¼ cup (½ stick) butter
1 cup packed brown sugar
1 (20-ounce) can sliced pineapple, drained
Cherries

Sift the flour and baking powder together. Beat ¼ cup butter in a mixing bowl. Add the sugar gradually, beating until light and fluffy. Add the egg and beat well. Add the flour mixture alternately with the milk, beating constantly. Melt ¼ cup butter in a cast-iron skillet. Add the brown sugar. Cook until melted, stirring constantly. Arrange the pineapple slices in the skillet. Place a cherry in the center of each pineapple slice. Pour the batter over the top. Bake at 350 degrees for 30 minutes. Invert onto a cake plate. May substitute peaches or apricots for the pineapple. YIELD: **8 TO 10 SERVINGS.**

Mary Alice Neal
Birmingham Life

HELPFUL HINT

To keep the cake fresh for several days longer, place an apple cut in half in the cake container.

Pineapple Delight

1 (2-layer) package yellow cake mix
1 (20-ounce) can crushed pineapple
½ cup sugar
1 (6-ounce) package vanilla instant pudding mix
8 ounces cream cheese, softened
16 ounces whipped topping
1 cup confectioners' sugar
Chopped nuts
Shredded coconut

Prepare and bake the cake using the package directions for a 9×13-inch cake pan. Punch holes in the warm cake. Combine the pineapple and sugar in a bowl and mix well. Spread over the cake. Prepare the pudding mix using the package directions. Spread over the pineapple layer. Beat the cream cheese, whipped topping and confectioners' sugar in a mixing bowl until smooth. Spread over the top. Sprinkle with nuts and coconut. YIELD: 15 SERVINGS.

Brenda Elliott
Decatur Council

Pistachio Nut Swirl Cake

1 (2-layer) package yellow cake mix
1 (4-ounce) package pistachio instant pudding mix
4 eggs
1 cup sour cream
½ cup vegetable oil
½ teaspoon almond extract
½ cup sugar
1 teaspoon cinnamon
½ cup finely chopped nuts

Combine the cake mix, pudding mix, eggs, sour cream, oil and almond extract in a large mixing bowl and beat until moistened. Beat at medium speed for 2 minutes. Mix the sugar, cinnamon and nuts in a bowl. Pour ½ of the batter into a greased and floured 10-inch tube pan. Sprinkle with ½ of the nut mixture. Pour ½ of the remaining batter over the nut mixture. Sprinkle with the remaining nut mixture. Pour remaining batter over the top. Bake at 350 degrees for 50 minutes or until the center springs back when lightly touched. Cool in the pan for 15 minutes. Remove to a wire rack to cool completely. **YIELD: 16 SERVINGS.**

Mary Alice Neal
Birmingham Life

HELPFUL HINT

Garnish cakes with tinted coconut. To tint coconut, shake it in a jar with a few drops of food coloring.

Aunt Pauline's Poor Man's Cake

½ (15-ounce) package raisins
1 cup sugar
½ cup shortening
Pinch of salt
½ teaspoon nutmeg
½ teaspoon ground cloves
½ teaspoon cinnamon
½ teaspoon allspice
½ cup chopped pecans
2 cups flour
2 teaspoons baking powder

Combine the raisins with water to cover in a saucepan. Bring to a boil. Boil for 10 minutes. Stir in the sugar and shortening. Let stand until cool. Add the salt, nutmeg, cloves, cinnamon, allspice and pecans and mix well. Stir in the flour and baking powder. Pour into a greased and floured 9×13-inch cake pan. Bake at 300 degrees for 25 minutes or until the cake tests done. Cool on a wire rack.
YIELD: 15 SERVINGS.

Marion Thompson
Gadsden Life

Poppy Seed Cake

1 (2-layer) package yellow cake mix
1 (4-ounce) package vanilla instant pudding mix
4 eggs
½ cup sour cream
½ cup cream sherry
½ cup vegetable oil
¼ cup poppy seeds

Combine the cake mix, pudding mix, eggs, sour cream, cream sherry, oil and poppy seeds in a mixing bowl. Beat at medium speed for 2 minutes. Pour into a greased 10-inch bundt or tube pan. Bake at 350 degrees for 50 minutes or until the cake tests done. Cool on a wire rack. YIELD: 16 SERVINGS.

Patricia Allen
Selma Life

Dutch Apple Pound Cake

3 cups flour
1 teaspoon baking soda
1 teaspoon salt
1½ cups vegetable oil
2 cups sugar
3 eggs, lightly beaten
2 teaspoons vanilla extract
3 cups chopped peeled Red Delicious apples
1 cup chopped pecans
Topping (below)

Sift the flour, baking soda and salt together. Beat the oil, sugar, eggs and vanilla in a mixing bowl. Add the flour mixture and beat well. The batter will be stiff. Fold in the apples and pecans. Spoon into a greased tube pan. Bake at 325 degrees for 1¼ hours or until the cake tests done. Pour Topping over the hot cake. Cover with foil. Let stand for 2 hours. Loosen with a spatula and invert onto a cake plate. YIELD: 16 SERVINGS.

Topping

1 cup packed brown sugar
½ cup (1 stick) margarine
¼ cup milk

Combine the brown sugar, margarine and milk in a saucepan. Cook for 3 minutes. YIELD: 1½ CUPS.

Ila Skidmore
Shoals Life

Banana Pound Cake

3 cups flour
1/2 teaspoon baking powder
1/2 teaspoon salt
1 cup (2 sticks) butter or margarine, softened
1/2 cup shortening
2 cups packed light brown sugar
1 cup sugar
5 eggs
1/2 cup milk
1 ripe large banana, mashed
1 cup chopped pecans
2 teaspoons vanilla extract
Caramel Glaze (below)

Mix the flour, baking powder and salt together. Beat the butter and shortening at medium speed for 2 minutes or until creamy. Add the brown sugar and sugar gradually, beating constantly for 5 to 7 minutes. Add the eggs 1 at a time, beating well after each addition. Add the flour mixture alternately with the milk, beating at low speed after each addition until blended and beginning and ending with the flour mixture. Stir in the banana, pecans and vanilla. Pour into a greased and floured 10-inch tube pan. Bake at 325 degrees for 1 hour and 5 minutes or until a wooden pick inserted near the center comes out clean. Cool in the pan on a wire rack for 10 minutes. Invert onto a cake plate. Drizzle with Caramel Glaze. YIELD: 16 SERVINGS.

Caramel Glaze

1/4 cup (1/2 stick) butter, softened
1/4 cup packed light brown sugar
1/4 cup sugar
1/4 cup heavy cream
1 teaspoon vanilla extract

Combine the butter, brown sugar, sugar and cream in a heavy saucepan. Bring to a boil over high heat, stirring frequently. Boil for 1 minute. Do not stir. Remove from heat. Stir in the vanilla. Cool until slightly thickened. YIELD: 3/4 CUP.

Ila Skidmore
Shoals Life

Bourbon Pound Cake

3 cups flour
¼ teaspoon baking soda
1 cup (2 sticks) butter, softened
3 cups sugar
6 eggs
1 cup sour cream
1 teaspoon vanilla extract
3 tablespoons bourbon

Sift the flour and baking soda together. Cream the butter and sugar in a mixing bowl until light and fluffy. Add the eggs 1 at a time, beating well after each addition. Beat in the sour cream until blended. Add the flour mixture ⅓ at a time, beating well after each addition. Stir in the vanilla and bourbon. Pour into a greased and floured 10-inch tube pan. Bake at 325 degrees for 1¼ hours or until the cake tests done. Cool on a wire rack. **YIELD: 16 SERVINGS.**

Shirley M. Helms
Montgomery Life

Coconut Sour Cream Pound Cake

3 cups flour
1/4 teaspoon baking soda
1/4 teaspoon salt
1 cup (2 sticks) butter or margarine, softened
3 cups sugar
6 eggs
1 cup sour cream
2 teaspoons coconut extract
1 1/4 teaspoons almond extract
2 cups flaked coconut
Glaze (below)

Mix the flour, baking soda and salt together. Cream the butter and sugar in a mixing bowl until light and fluffy. Beat in the eggs 1 at a time. Beat in the sour cream. Add the flour mixture gradually, beating well after each addition. Beat in the coconut extract and almond extract. Fold in the coconut. Pour into a greased and floured tube pan. Bake at 350 degrees for 1 hour or until the cake tests done. Cool slightly. Pierce holes in the top of the warm cake with a knife. Pour Glaze over the cake a small amount at a time, allowing the cake to absorb the Glaze. YIELD: 16 SERVINGS.

Glaze

2 cups sugar
1 cup water
3 tablespoons butter
3 tablespoons light corn syrup
1 teaspoon coconut extract

Combine the sugar, water, butter and corn syrup in a saucepan. Bring to a boil. Boil for 5 minutes. Remove from heat. Stir in the coconut extract. YIELD: 2 1/2 CUPS.

Betty Foshee
Decatur Council

Rhonda's Kentucky Pound Cake

2½ cups self-rising flour
2 cups sugar
1½ cups vegetable oil
4 eggs
1 tablespoon cinnamon

1 teaspoon vanilla extract
1 (8-ounce) can crushed
   pineapple
1 cup chopped pecans

Combine the self-rising flour, sugar, oil, eggs, cinnamon and vanilla in a mixing bowl and mix well. Stir in the pineapple. Fold in the pecans. Pour into a greased and floured tube pan. Bake at 325 degrees for 1¼ hours or until the cake tests done. Cool on a wire rack. YIELD: 16 SERVINGS.

Marie Hartley
Birmingham South Life

Shelia's Old-Fashioned Pound Cake

3 cups flour
1 teaspoon baking powder
1 cup (2 sticks) butter,
   softened
½ cup shortening

3 cups sugar
5 eggs
1 cup milk or buttermilk
2 teaspoons lemon extract
1 teaspoon vanilla extract

Mix the flour and baking powder together. Beat the butter and shortening in a mixing bowl. Add the sugar gradually, beating constantly until light and fluffy. Add the eggs 1 at a time, beating well after each addition. Add the flour mixture alternately with the milk, beating well after each addition. Stir in the lemon extract and vanilla. Pour into a greased and floured 10-inch tube pan. Bake at 350 degrees for 1¼ hours or until the cake tests done. Cool in the pan for 10 to 15 minutes. Remove from the pan to a wire rack to cool completely. YIELD: 16 SERVINGS.

Phoebe Arthur
Gadsden Life

Butter Peach Pound Cake

3 cups self-rising flour
2¼ cups sugar
1½ cups (3 sticks) margarine, melted
¾ cup milk
6 eggs
1 teaspoon lemon extract
1 teaspoon vanilla extract
1 cup mashed fresh peaches

Combine the self-rising flour, sugar, margarine, milk, eggs, lemon extract and vanilla in a mixing bowl. Beat at medium speed for 20 minutes. Fold in the peaches. Pour into a greased and floured tube pan. Place on the rack in a cold oven. Bake at 300 degrees for 70 minutes or until the cake tests done. Cool on a wire rack.
YIELD: 16 SERVINGS.

Mary Alice Neal
Birmingham Life

Granny Taylor's Plain Pound Cake

3 cups flour
2½ cups sugar
1½ cups (3 sticks) butter, melted
7 eggs
1 tablespoon vanilla extract

Combine the flour, sugar and butter in a mixing bowl and mix well. Add the eggs 1 at a time, beating well after each addition. Stir in the vanilla. Pour into a greased and floured tube pan or two 5x9-inch loaf pans. Bake at 300 degrees for 1½ hours or until the cake tests done. Cool on a wire rack. YIELD: 16 SERVINGS.

Eloise Bennett
Decatur Council

Meme's Pound Cake

1 cup (2 sticks) butter, softened
½ cup shortening
3 cups sugar
8 ounces cream cheese, softened
3 cups sifted cake flour
6 eggs
1 tablespoon vanilla extract

Cream the butter, shortening and sugar in a mixing bowl until light and fluffy. Add the cream cheese a small amount at a time, beating well after each addition. Add 1 cup of the cake flour and beat until blended. Beat in 3 of the eggs until blended. Do not overbeat. Add 1 cup of the cake flour and beat until blended. Add the remaining 3 eggs and beat until blended. Do not overbeat. Add the remaining 1 cup cake flour and vanilla and beat until blended. Pour into a greased and floured bundt or tube pan. Bake at 325 degrees for 1 to 1¼ hours or until the cake tests done. Cool in the pan for 10 minutes. Invert onto a wire rack to cool completely. **Yield: 16 servings.**

Susan Robbins
Riverchase Council

HELPFUL HINT

To reduce fat, cholesterol and calories in your favorite cake mix, substitute an equal amount of applesauce for the oil.

Pound Cake

1½ cups shortening
6 eggs
3 cups sugar
2½ cups all-purpose flour
½ cup self-rising flour
1 cup milk
1 teaspoon vanilla extract
Glaze (below)

Beat the shortening in a mixing bowl. Add the eggs and sugar, beating until light and fluffy. Add the all-purpose flour, self-rising flour, milk and vanilla and beat until smooth. Pour into a greased and floured tube pan. Bake at 325 degrees for 1½ hours or until the cake tests done. Cool in the pan for 10 minutes. Invert onto a wire rack to cool completely. Spread Glaze on the cooled cake. YIELD: 16 SERVINGS.

Glaze

1 cup confectioners' sugar
¼ cup (½ stick) margarine, melted
Juice of 1 lemon

Combine the confectioners' sugar, margarine and lemon juice in a mixing bowl and beat until smooth. YIELD: ABOUT 1 CUP.

Bettie Nabors
Anniston Council

Pound Cake

3 cups flour
1¼ teaspoons baking powder
½ teaspoon salt
1 cup water
½ teaspoon lemon extract
½ teaspoon vanilla extract
1½ cups (3 sticks) butter, softened
2¼ cups sugar
6 eggs

Sift the flour, baking powder and salt together. Mix the water, lemon extract and vanilla together. Beat the butter in a mixing bowl until smooth. Add the sugar a small amount at a time, beating constantly until light and fluffy. Beat in the eggs 1 at a time. Add the water mixture and flour mixture alternately, beating well after each addition. Pour into a greased and floured tube pan. Bake at 350 degrees for 1½ hours or until the cake tests done. Cool on a wire rack. **Yield: 16 servings.**

Mary Alice Neal
Birmingham Life

Pound Cake

3 cups flour
1/2 teaspoon baking powder
1/2 cup (1 stick) butter, softened
1/3 cup shortening
3 cups sugar

5 egg yolks
1 cup milk
2 teaspoons almond extract
2 teaspoons vanilla extract
5 egg whites

Mix the flour and baking powder together. Cream the next 4 ingredients in a mixing bowl until smooth. Add the flour mixture alternately with the milk, beating well after each addition. Add the almond extract and vanilla and mix well. Beat the egg whites in a mixing bowl until stiff peaks form. Fold gently into the batter. Pour into a greased and floured tube pan. Place on the rack in a cold oven. Bake at 300 degrees for 1 1/2 hours or until the cake tests done. Cool in the pan for 10 minutes. Cool on a wire rack. Place the cake crust-side up on a cake plate before serving. **YIELD: 16 SERVINGS.**

Virginia Greene
Birmingham South Life

Whipping Cream Pound Cake

1 cup (2 sticks) margarine, softened
3 cups sugar
6 eggs

3 cups flour
1 cup whipping cream
1/2 teaspoon salt
1 tablespoon vanilla extract

Cream the margarine and sugar in a mixing bowl until light and fluffy. Add the eggs 1 at a time, beating well after each addition. Add the flour and whipping cream alternately, beating at low speed until mixed. Add the salt and vanilla. Beat at high speed until smooth. The secret of this cake is the beating. Pour the batter into a greased 9-inch tube pan. Place on a rack in a cold oven. Bake at 300 degrees for 1 1/2 hours. Cool on a wire rack. **YIELD: 16 SERVINGS.**

Brenda Stone
Birmingham South Cahaba Council

Pumpkin Cake

3 cups flour
1 cup nuts
1 cup raisins or dates
2 cups sugar
1½ cups vegetable oil
2 teaspoons baking powder
2 teaspoons baking soda
1 tablespoon cinnamon
1 teaspoon allspice
1 teaspoon salt
2 cups cooked pumpkin
4 eggs
2 teaspoons vanilla extract
Buttermilk Glaze (below)

Combine the flour, nuts and raisins in a bowl and mix to coat. Combine the sugar, oil, baking powder, baking soda, cinnamon, allspice, salt and pumpkin in a mixing bowl and mix well. Add the flour mixture 1 cup at a time alternately with the eggs, beating well after each addition. Stir in the vanilla. Pour into a greased and floured tube pan. Bake at 350 degrees for 1 hour or until the cake tests done. Cool in the pan on a wire rack for 20 minutes. Pour the Buttermilk Glaze over the cake. Remove the cake from the pan just before serving. YIELD: 16 SERVINGS.

Buttermilk Glaze

1 cup sugar
½ teaspoon baking soda
½ cup buttermilk
1 teaspoon light corn syrup
½ teaspoon vanilla extract

Combine the sugar, baking soda, buttermilk, corn syrup and vanilla in a heavy saucepan. Bring to a boil. Cook to 234 to 240 degrees on a candy thermometer, soft-ball stage, stirring constantly.
YIELD: ABOUT 1 CUP.

Joann Thomas
Selma Life

Pumpkin Roll

2/3 cup cooked pumpkin
3/4 cup flour
1 teaspoon salt
1 teaspoon baking soda
1/2 teaspoon cinnamon

3 eggs
1 cup sugar
Chopped nuts
Confectioners' sugar
Cream Cheese Filling (below)

Grease a 12×17-inch jelly roll pan. Line the pan with waxed paper. Grease the waxed paper. Mix the pumpkin, flour, salt, baking soda and cinnamon in a bowl. Beat the eggs and sugar in a mixing bowl until smooth. Add the pumpkin mixture and mix well. Spread in the prepared pan. Sprinkle with nuts. Bake at 375 degrees for 15 minutes or until the cake tests done. Invert the cake onto a clean towel sprinkled with confectioners' sugar. Remove the waxed paper. Roll the warm cake in the towel as for a jelly roll from the short side and place on a wire rack. Cool for 1 hour. Unroll the cooled cake carefully and remove the towel. Spread the Cream Cheese Filling to the edge and reroll. Wrap in plastic wrap. Chill or freeze until serving time. Unwrap and place seam side down on a cake plate before serving. YIELD: 8 SERVINGS.

Cream Cheese Filling

8 ounces cream cheese, softened
2 tablespoons butter, softened

1 teaspoon vanilla extract
1 cup confectioners' sugar

Beat the cream cheese and butter in a mixing bowl until light and fluffy. Add the vanilla. Beat in the confectioners' sugar until smooth and creamy. YIELD: 1 1/2 CUPS.

Mary Alice Neal
Birmingham Life

Pumpkin Roll

1 cup flour
1 teaspoon baking soda
1/2 teaspoon salt
1/2 teaspoon nutmeg
1/2 teaspoon ginger
3/4 cup canned pumpkin
2 tablespoons lemon juice

3 eggs, beaten
3/4 cup sugar
1 tablespoon cinnamon
1 cup chopped nuts
Confectioners' sugar
Cream Cheese Filling (below)

Mix the flour, baking soda, salt, nutmeg and ginger together. Combine the pumpkin, lemon juice, eggs, sugar and cinnamon in a mixing bowl and mix well. Add the flour mixture and mix well. Pour into a greased and floured jelly roll pan. Sprinkle with nuts and confectioners' sugar. Bake at 350 degrees for 15 minutes or until the cake tests done. Dust a clean kitchen towel generously with confectioners' sugar. Invert the cake onto the towel. Roll the warm cake in the towel as for a jelly roll from the short side. Chill in the refrigerator just until the cake is chilled through. Unroll the cooled cake carefully and remove the towel. Spread Cream Cheese Filling to the edge and reroll. Sprinkle with confectioners' sugar. Wrap in plastic wrap and freeze until firm. YIELD: **8 SERVINGS**.

Cream Cheese Filling

8 ounces cream cheese, softened
2 tablespoons margarine, softened

1 teaspoon vanilla extract
1 cup confectioners' sugar

Beat the cream cheese, margarine and vanilla in a mixing bowl until light and fluffy. Add the confectioners' sugar and beat until smooth. YIELD: **1 1/2 CUPS**.

Margaret W. Wilborn
Gadsden Life

Red Velvet Cake

2½ cups self-rising flour
1 teaspoon baking soda
1½ cups sugar
1½ cups vegetable oil
2 eggs, lightly beaten
1 teaspoon white vinegar
1 teaspoon vanilla extract
1 cup buttermilk
2½ tablespoons red food coloring
Frosting (page 451)

Spray three 9-inch round cake pans with nonstick cooking spray. Line each with waxed paper. Sift the self-rising flour and baking soda together. Combine the sugar, oil, eggs, vinegar and vanilla in a medium mixing bowl. Beat for 2 minutes or until light and fluffy. Add the flour mixture gradually, beating at low speed just until incorporated. Add the buttermilk and food coloring and beat until blended. Pour into the prepared cake pans filling each halfway. Tap the pans on the counter to remove any air bubbles. Bake at 350 degrees for 30 minutes or until a cake tester inserted in the center comes out clean. Cool in the pans on a wire rack for 5 minutes. Invert onto wire racks sprayed with oil to cool completely or chill in the freezer for 10 to 15 minutes. To assemble, place 1 cake layer top side down on a cake plate. Spread ¼ inch Frosting over the layer using an offset spatula. Repeat with the remaining cake layers stacking to form a 3-layer cake. Spread the remaining Frosting over the top and side of the cake. Store in an airtight container for up to 1 week. YIELD: 12 SERVINGS.

Frosting

8 ounces cream cheese, softened
½ cup (1 stick) margarine, softened
1 (1-pound) package confectioners' sugar, sifted
1 cup finely chopped pecans
1 teaspoon vanilla extract

Beat the cream cheese and margarine in a medium mixing bowl for 2 minutes or until light and fluffy. Add the confectioners' sugar, pecans and vanilla. Beat at low speed until well mixed. You may chill for about 10 minutes or until of the desired spreading consistency before using. YIELD: **6 CUPS**.

Mary M. Storey
Anniston Council

Refrigerator Cake

1 pound graham crackers
1 pound marshmallows
1 cup milk
1 pound raisins
1 pound chopped nuts

Line a 5x9-inch loaf pan with plastic wrap, leaving an overhang. Crush the graham crackers in a bowl. Combine the marshmallows and milk in a saucepan. Cook over low heat until the marshmallows are melted. Add to the crushed graham crackers and mix well. Stir in the raisins and nuts. Spoon into the prepared pan and press down to pack. Cover with the plastic wrap. Chill for 24 hours. Unwrap and invert onto a serving plate. Cut into slices to serve. YIELD: **12 SERVINGS**.

Margaret W. Wilborn
Gadsden Life

Sausage Cake

1 pound mild bulk pork sausage
1 1/2 cups sugar
1 1/2 cups packed brown sugar
1 egg
1 teaspoon allspice
1 teaspoon cinnamon
1 teaspoon ground cloves
1 teaspoon nutmeg
1 cup coffee
2 teaspoons baking soda
3 cups flour
1 cup buttermilk
1 cup chopped nuts
1/2 cup raisins

Combine the sausage, sugar, brown sugar, egg, allspice, cinnamon, cloves and nutmeg in a bowl and mix well. Add the coffee, baking soda, flour, buttermilk, nuts and raisins and mix well. Pour into a greased and floured 9x13-inch cake pan. Bake at 350 degrees for 45 to 60 minutes or until the cake tests done. Cool on a wire rack.
YIELD: 15 SERVINGS.

Barbara Seegmiller
Decatur Council

HELPFUL HINT

Substitute yogurt for milk, sour cream, butter or margarine in uncooked frosting.

Scripture Mayonnaise Cake

3¾ cups unsifted flour (1 Kings 4:22)
3 tablespoons baking powder (Amos 4:5)
1 teaspoon baking soda (Amos 4:5)
Pinch of salt (Leviticus 2:13)
¼ teaspoon allspice (1 Kings 10:2)
2½ teaspoons nutmeg
½ teaspoon ground cloves
1 cup (2 sticks) butter, softened (Judges 5:25)
1¾ cups sugar (Jeremiah 6:20)
1¼ cups honey (Proverbs 24:13)
6 eggs (Job 39:14)
1 cup cold buttermilk
1 cup water (Genesis 24:11)
2 cups dried figs (Revelations 6:13)
2 cups raisins (1 Samuel 30:12)
1 cup almonds (Numbers 17:8)
1 tablespoon mayonnaise

Mix the flour, baking powder, baking soda, salt, allspice, nutmeg and cloves together. Cream the butter, sugar and honey in a mixing bowl until light and fluffy. Add the eggs 1 at a time, beating well after each addition. Add the flour mixture, buttermilk and water and mix well. Stir in the figs, raisins and almonds. Add the mayonnaise and mix well. Pour into a greased tube pan. Bake at 350 degrees for 1½ hours or until the cake tests done. Cool in the pan for 30 minutes. Invert onto a wire rack to cool completely. Say Psalms 23 while mixing the ingredients together. YIELD: 16 SERVINGS.

D. Christine Kinkley
Birmingham Life

Sock-It-To-Me Cake

1 (2-layer) package butter-recipe cake mix
1 cup sour cream
½ cup vegetable oil
¼ cup sugar
¼ cup water
4 eggs
Filling (below)
Glaze (below)

Combine the cake mix, sour cream, oil, sugar, water and eggs in a mixing bowl and beat until moistened. Beat at high speed for 2 minutes. Pour ⅔ of the batter into a greased and floured bundt pan. Sprinkle with the filling. Spread the remaining batter over the filling. Bake at 375 degrees for 45 to 55 minutes or until the cake springs back when lightly touched. Cool in the pan for 25 minutes. Invert onto a serving plate. Drizzle the Glaze over the cake. YIELD: 16 SERVINGS.

Filling

1 cup chopped pecans
2 tablespoons brown sugar
2 teaspoons cinnamon

Combine the pecans, brown sugar and cinnamon in a bowl and mix well. YIELD: ABOUT 1 CUP.

Glaze

1 cup confectioners' sugar
2 tablespoons milk

Combine the confectioners' sugar and milk in a bowl and mix until smooth. YIELD: 1 CUP.

Mary Gillis
Mobile Council

Spice Chiffon Cake

2 cups sifted flour
1½ cups sugar
1 tablespoon baking powder
1 teaspoon salt
1 teaspoon cinnamon
½ teaspoon each nutmeg, allspice and ground cloves
½ cup vegetable oil
7 medium egg yolks
¾ cup cold water
1 cup egg whites (7 egg whites)
½ teaspoon cream of tartar
Creamy Nut Icing (below)

Sift the first 8 ingredients together in a large bowl. Make a well in the center. Add the oil, egg yolks and water in the order listed and mix with a spoon until smooth. Do not use a mixer. Beat the egg whites and cream of tartar in a large mixing bowl until stiff peaks form. Do not under beat. Fold in the egg yolk mixture gently. Do not stir. Pour into an ungreased tube pan. Bake at 325 degrees for 55 minutes. Increase the oven temperature to 350 degrees. Bake for 10 to 15 minutes or until the cake tests done. Invert on a funnel to cool completely. Loosen the cake from the side of the pan. Invert onto a cake plate. Spread with Creamy Nut Icing. YIELD: 10 SERVINGS.

Creamy Nut Icing

½ cup butter-flavor shortening
2½ tablespoons flour
¼ teaspoon salt
½ cup milk
½ cup packed brown sugar
2 cup sifted confectioners' sugar
½ teaspoon vanilla extract
½ cup chopped nuts

Melt the shortening in a saucepan. Remove from heat. Blend in the flour and salt. Add the milk gradually, stirring constantly. Bring to a boil, stirring constantly. Boil for 1 minute. Do not be alarmed if the mixture curdles. Stir in the brown sugar. Remove from heat. Stir in the confectioners' sugar, vanilla and nuts. YIELD: 3½ CUPS.

Eloise Bennett
Decatur Council

Spiced Rum Cake and Glaze

1 (2-layer) package yellow cake mix
1 (4-ounce) package vanilla instant pudding mix
4 eggs
½ cup cold water
½ cup vegetable oil
½ cup spiced rum
1 cup chopped pecans
Glaze (below)

Combine the cake mix, pudding mix, eggs, water, oil and rum in a mixing bowl and mix well. Stir in the pecans. Pour into a greased and floured 10-inch tube pan or 12-cup bundt pan. Bake at 325 degrees for 1 hour. Cool in the pan on a wire rack. Loosen the cake from the side of the pan. Invert onto a cake plate. Prick the top of the cake. Drizzle Glaze evenly over top and side, spreading to smooth. YIELD: 16 SERVINGS.

Glaze

½ cup (1 stick) butter, softened
¼ cup water
1 cup sugar
½ cup spiced rum

Melt the butter in a saucepan. Stir in the water and sugar. Bring to a boil. Boil for 5 minutes, stirring constantly. Remove from heat. Stir in the rum. YIELD: 2 CUPS.

Eloise Bennett
Decatur Council

Sponge Cake

5 egg whites, at room
  temperature
Pinch of salt
5 egg yolks

1 cup sugar
1 teaspoon lemon extract
1 cup sifted flour

Beat the egg whites in a mixing bowl until foamy. Add the salt, beating until stiff peaks form. Beat the egg yolks in a mixing bowl until pale yellow. Stir in the sugar and lemon extract. Fold into the egg whites. Fold in the flour. Pour into an ungreased tube pan. Bake at 350 degrees for 45 minutes. Invert on a funnel to cool completely. Loosen the cake from side of pan. Invert onto a cake plate. **Note:** Sift the flour 5 times before measuring. YIELD: **16 SERVINGS.**

Imogene Davis
Birmingham Life

Strawberry Shortcake

1 (2-layer) package moist
  yellow cake mix
1 1/4 cups water
1/4 cup nonfat vanilla yogurt

3/4 cup egg substitute
1 1/2 cups fat-free whipped
  topping
1 1/2 cups sliced strawberries

Combine the cake mix, water, yogurt and egg substitute in a mixing bowl. Beat at low speed until moistened. Beat for 2 minutes at high speed. Pour into a greased and floured 9×13-inch cake pan. Bake at 350 degrees for 30 to 35 minutes or until a wooden pick inserted in the center comes out clean. Cool completely in the pan on a wire rack. Cut into squares and place on serving plates. Top with whipped topping and strawberries. YIELD: **15 SERVINGS.**

Gussie Evans
Mobile Council

Strawberry Gelatin Cake

1 (2-layer) package white cake mix
1 tablespoon flour
1 (3-ounce) package strawberry gelatin
1 cup vegetable oil
1/4 cup strawberry juice
4 egg yolks
3/4 cup frozen sliced strawberries
4 egg whites
Frosting (below)

Combine the cake mix, flour and gelatin in a mixing bowl and mix well. Add the oil and strawberry juice and beat well. Add the egg yolks 1 at a time, beating well after each addition. Stir in the strawberries. Beat the egg whites in a mixing bowl until stiff peaks form. Fold gently into the batter. Pour into 3 greased and floured 9-inch cake pans. Bake at 350 degrees for 25 to 30 minutes or until the layers test done. Cool in the pans on a wire rack. Spread Frosting between the layers and over the top and side of cake. YIELD: 12 SERVINGS.

Frosting

1/2 cup (1 stick) margarine, softened
3 ounces cream cheese, softened
1 (1-pound) package confectioners' sugar
1/4 cup frozen sliced strawberries

Cream the margarine and cream cheese in a mixing bowl until light and fluffy. Beat in the confectioners' sugar until smooth. Stir in the strawberries. YIELD: 5 CUPS.

Gladys Slaughter
Bon Secour Life

Sugarless Cakes

2 cups milk
2 cups pitted dates, chopped
2 teaspoons baking soda
2 eggs
1 cup vegetable oil
2 tablespoons artificial sweetener
1 teaspoon cinnamon
1 teaspoon nutmeg
3 cups flour
1 cup raisins
1 cup chopped pecans

Combine the milk, dates and baking soda in a saucepan. Bring almost to the boiling point. Let stand until cool. Combine the date mixture, eggs, oil, artificial sweetener, cinnamon and nutmeg in a mixing bowl and mix well. Beat in the flour. Stir in the raisins and pecans. Pour into 2 greased and floured small loaf pans. Bake at 325 degrees for 1 hour or until the loaves test done. Cool in the pans for a few minutes. Invert onto wire racks to cool completely.
YIELD: 2 LOAVES.

Virginia Bowen
Shoals Life

HELPFUL HINT
Add mayonnaise to cake mix to increase moistness.

Willamsburg Cake

Juice from 1 large orange
3/4 cup sugar
Rind from 1 large orange
1/2 to 1 cup raisins
1 cup pecans
1/2 cup (1 stick) butter, softened

1 cup sugar
2 eggs
2/3 cup buttermilk or sour milk
1 teaspoon vanilla extract
2 cups flour
1 teaspoon baking soda

Combine the orange juice and 3/4 cup sugar in a bowl and mix well. Force the orange rind, raisins and pecans through a meat grinder. Cream the butter and 1 cup sugar in a mixing bowl until light and fluffy. Add the eggs 1 at a time, beating well after each addition. Add the buttermilk, vanilla, flour and baking soda and beat well. Beat in the ground mixture. Pour into a greased and floured tube pan. Bake at 375 degrees for 40 to 50 minutes or until the cake tests done. Remove from the pan and place on a wire rack over a plate. Pour the warm orange juice mixture over the hot cake. Cool before serving. YIELD: 16 SERVINGS.

Frankie Vaughn
Selma Life

Fudge Icing

2 cups sugar
2 tablespoons baking cocoa
1/2 cup (1 stick) butter or margarine

1/3 cup evaporated milk
1/3 cup light corn syrup
1 teaspoon vanilla extract

Combine the sugar, baking cocoa, butter, evaporated milk and corn syrup in a saucepan. Bring to a boil. Boil for 1 minute. Remove from heat. Stir in the vanilla. Beat until of the desired spreading consistency. YIELD: 3 CUPS.

Susan Ragland
Birmingham South Cahaba Council

Chocolate Pour Icing

½ cup (1 stick) butter or margarine
¼ cup baking cocoa
6 tablespoons milk
⅛ teaspoon salt
1 teaspoon vanilla extract
2 tablespoons lemon juice
1 (1-pound) package confectioners' sugar, sifted
1 cup chopped nuts

Combine the butter, baking cocoa, milk and salt in a medium saucepan. Heat over medium heat until the butter melts, stirring constantly. Bring to a boil and remove from heat. Add the vanilla, lemon juice and confectioners' sugar and beat until smooth. Stir in the nuts. Use to pour over a hot sheet cake. YIELD: **6 CUPS**.

Virginia Sherrer
Selma Life

Vanilla Frosting

¼ cup shortening
1 ounce white chocolate bark
¼ teaspoon salt
⅓ cup milk
1½ teaspoons vanilla extract
3½ cups confectioners' sugar

Melt the shortening in a saucepan. Add the white chocolate bark and salt and stir until smooth. Stir in the milk and vanilla. Add the confectioners' sugar gradually, beating constantly. You may tint the frosting as desired. YIELD: **4 CUPS**.

Margaret W. Wilborn
Gadsden Life

ALABAMA READING INITIATIVE

Alabama Pioneers provided community support for the Alabama Reading Initiative. More than 250 volunteers in Birmingham, Huntsville, Mobile, and Montgomery devoted one hour per week to read with second graders to support the state's goal of every child reading on grade level.

Candy and Cookies

Forever Amber Candy

1 pound orange candy slices, chopped
2 (3½-ounce) cans flaked coconut
1 teaspoon orange extract
2 (14-ounce) cans sweetened condensed milk
1 cup chopped pecans
1 teaspoon vanilla extract
Confectioners' sugar to taste

Combine the first 6 ingredients in a bowl and mix well. Spread the mixture in a lightly greased 10×15-inch baking pan. Bake at 275 degrees for 30 minutes. Spoon the baked mixture into a bowl. Add the confectioners' sugar and mix well. Shape into small balls. Cool on wire racks. YIELD: 3 POUNDS.

Frances Hyatt
Gadsden Life

Chocolate-Covered Cherries

2½ cups confectioners' sugar
¼ cup (½ stick) margarine
1 tablespoon milk
½ teaspoon almond extract
2 (8-ounce) jars maraschino cherries with stems, drained
2 cups semisweet chocolate chips
2 tablespoons shortening

Mix the first 4 ingredients in a mixing bowl. Knead the mixture into a large ball. Roll out on a lightly floured surface. Cut into 2-inch circles. Wrap each circle around a cherry and roll lightly in hands. Arrange cherries stem up on a waxed paper-lined pan. Chill, covered, in the refrigerator for 8 to 12 hours or overnight. Melt the chocolate chips and shortening in a double boiler over simmering water or microwave in a microwave-safe bowl. Dip the cherries into the chocolate mixture, holding cherry by the stem. Place on waxed paper-lined pan. Let stand until cool. Store in an airtight container in the refrigerator for 1 to 2 weeks before serving. YIELD: 1 TO 2 POUNDS.

Sarah Breland
Riverchase Council

English Toffee Candy

1 cup (2 sticks) butter
1 cup sugar
1 tablespoon corn syrup
3 tablespoons water
1½ cups chopped pecans
1 cup semisweet chocolate chips
2 ounces unsweetened chocolate

Melt the butter in a 2-quart saucepan. Stir in the sugar gradually. Add the corn syrup and water and mix well. Cook to 290 degrees on a candy thermometer, soft-crack stage, stirring constantly. Add 1 cup of the pecans and mix well. Cook for 3 minutes longer, stirring constantly. Pour the candy onto a greased baking sheet. Let stand until cool. Melt ½ of the chocolate chips and ½ of the unsweetened chocolate in a saucepan. Spread over the top of the candy. Sprinkle with ¼ cup of the pecans. Let stand until the chocolate is firm. Melt the remaining chocolate chips and unsweetened chocolate in a saucepan. Turn the candy over. Spread with the remaining chocolate. Sprinkle with the remaining pecans. Chill, covered, in the refrigerator. Break into pieces to serve. You may spread all of the melted chocolate on one side of the candy. Sprinkle all of the pecans over the chocolate for this variation.
YIELD: 2 POUNDS.

Virginia Greene
Birmingham South Life

HELPFUL HINT

Choose a cool dry day to make candy. Some candies are especially sensitive to humid conditions.

Easy Chocolate Candy

Graham crackers
1 cup (2 sticks) butter, or 1/2 cup (1 stick) butter
and 1/2 cup (1 stick) margarine
1/2 cup sugar
1 cup chopped pecans
5 milk chocolate bars

Line a baking sheet with graham crackers. Combine the butter and sugar in a saucepan and mix well. Bring to a boil. Cook for 4 minutes, stirring constantly. Remove from the heat. Stir in the pecans. Spread the mixture over the graham crackers. Bake at 325 degrees for 12 minutes. Place the chocolate bars over the top. The chocolate will begin to melt immediately. Spread the chocolate evenly over the top. Let stand until cool. Break into pieces to serve.

YIELD: 1 1/2 POUNDS.

Christie Huff
Birmingham South Cahaba Council

Cow Pies

2 cups milk chocolate chips
1 tablespoon shortening
1/2 cup raisins
1/2 cup almonds or pecans

Melt the chocolate chips and shortening in a double boiler over simmering water, stirring until smooth. Remove from the heat. Add the raisins and almonds and mix well. Drop by tablespoonfuls onto waxed paper. Chill, covered, in the refrigerator until serving time.

YIELD: 1 POUND.

Debbie Morris
Birmingham South Cahaba Council

Divinity

3 cups sugar
3/4 cup corn syrup
1/2 cup water

2 egg whites
1 teaspoon vanilla extract
1 cup chopped nuts

Combine the sugar, corn syrup and water in a heavy saucepan and mix well. Cook over medium heat to 254 degrees on a candy thermometer, hard-ball stage, stirring constantly. Remove from the heat. Let stand until the temperature of the mixture reaches 220 degrees, stirring constantly. Beat the egg whites in a mixing bowl for 1 minute or until soft peaks form. Add the sugar mixture gradually in a fine stream, beating for 2 1/2 minutes or until stiff peaks form. Add the vanilla. Beat for 20 to 25 minutes or until the mixture begins to lose its gloss. Stir in the nuts. Drop by teaspoonfuls onto waxed paper. YIELD: ABOUT 1 1/2 POUNDS.

Jean Martin
Anniston Council

CROCK-POT® Fudge

2 pounds white chocolate bars
1 (4-ounce) German's chocolate bar
2 cups semisweet chocolate chips

1 (24-ounce) jar unsalted dry-roasted peanuts, pecans or walnuts

Place the white chocolate, German's chocolate, and chocolate chips in the CROCK-POT® Slow Cooker. Sprinkle the peanuts over the top. Cook on Low until the chocolate is melted. Stir the mixture well. Cook for 1 1/2 hours longer. Stir the mixture well. Drop by tablespoonfuls onto waxed paper. Let stand until cool. Store in an airtight container. YIELD: 4 1/2 POUNDS.

Nancy Walker
Decatur Council

Microwave Fudge with Pecans

1 (1-pound) package confectioners' sugar
1 1/2 tablespoons baking cocoa
1/2 cup (1 stick) butter, melted
1/4 cup evaporated milk
1 teaspoon vanilla extract
Chopped pecans (optional)

Combine the confectioners' sugar and baking cocoa in a microwave-safe bowl and mix well. Add the butter and mix until creamy. Stir in the milk. Microwave on High for 2 minutes. Add the vanilla and pecans and mix well. Spoon the mixture into a greased pan. Cool in the pan for several minutes. Chill, covered, in the refrigerator until firm. Cut into squares. YIELD: 1 1/4 POUNDS.

Pam Dyer
Riverchase Council

Old-Fashioned Peanut Butter Fudge

2 cups sugar
2/3 cup milk
1/3 cup baking cocoa
2 tablespoons light corn syrup
1/4 teaspoon salt
1 teaspoon vanilla extract
1 1/2 cups peanut butter

Combine the sugar, milk, baking cocoa, corn syrup and salt in a large saucepan and mix well. Cook over high heat until the sugar dissolves and the mixture comes to a boil, stirring constantly. Reduce the heat to medium. Cook until a small amount of the mixture forms a ball when dropped into cold water, stirring constantly. Remove from the heat. Add the vanilla and peanut butter and mix until smooth. Pour into pans sprayed with nonstick cooking spray. Let stand until firm. Cut into squares. You may increase or decrease the amount of peanut butter to your taste. YIELD: 2 TO 3 POUNDS.

Shirley Crocker
Birmingham Life

Melissa's Peanut Butter Fudge

2 cups sugar
1/2 cup evaporated milk
2 tablespoons butter
1 teaspoon vanilla extract
3/4 cup creamy peanut butter

Combine the sugar, evaporated milk and butter in a saucepan and mix well. Bring to a boil, stirring constantly. Cook for 3 minutes, stirring constantly. Remove from the heat. Add the vanilla and peanut butter and mix well. Pour into a dish sprayed with nonstick cooking spray. Let stand until firm. Cut into squares. YIELD: 1 TO 2 POUNDS.

Faith Kirby Richardson
Gadsden Life

Easy Velveeta Fudge

1/4 cup baking cocoa
1 (1-pound) package confectioners' sugar
4 ounces Velveeta cheese
1/2 cup (1 stick) butter
1 teaspoon vanilla extract

Sift the baking cocoa and confectioners' sugar into a bowl. Melt the Velveeta cheese and butter in a saucepan, stirring constantly. Add to the confectioners' sugar mixture and mix well. Press into a buttered glass dish. Let stand until cool. Cut into squares. You may place pecans in the buttered dish before adding the fudge if desired. Do not substitute margarine for the butter in this recipe.
YIELD: 1 TO 1 1/2 POUNDS.

Dilla Samuel
Gadsden Life

Goof Balls

1 cup (2 sticks) margarine, melted
2½ cups graham cracker crumbs
1 (1-pound) package confectioners' sugar
½ cup peanut butter
1 cup flaked coconut
1 cup chopped pecans
2 cups semisweet chocolate chips
½ block paraffin

Combine the margarine, graham cracker crumbs, confectioners' sugar, peanut butter, coconut and pecans in a bowl and mix well. Shape into balls. Melt the chocolate chips and paraffin in a double boiler over simmering water. Coat the balls in the chocolate mixture. Place on waxed paper. Chill, covered, in the refrigerator. YIELD: 4 POUNDS.

Shirley Crocker
Birmingham Life

Heath Bar

1 cup (2 sticks) margarine
1⅓ cups sugar
3 tablespoons water
1 tablespoon light corn syrup
1 cup coarsely chopped toasted almonds
10 (1.5-ounce) milk chocolate candy bars

Melt the margarine in a saucepan. Stir in the sugar, water and corn syrup. Cook over medium heat to 300 degrees on a candy thermometer, hard-crack stage, stirring occasionally. Stir in the almonds. Spread over the bottom of a greased 9×13-inch baking pan. Let stand until completely cool. Invert onto waxed paper. Melt the chocolate bars in a saucepan. Spread half the melted chocolate over the candy layer; let set. Invert the candy layer and spread with the remaining chocolate. Chill, covered with waxed paper, in the refrigerator until firm. Break into pieces. YIELD: 2½ TO 3 POUNDS.

Nelda Goodwin
Birmingham Life

Mounds

1 cup sugar
1½ cups light corn syrup
½ cup water
½ teaspoon coconut extract
5 cups flaked coconut
2 cups semisweet chocolate chips
½ block paraffin

Combine the sugar, corn syrup and water in a saucepan. Bring to a boil over high heat. Reduce the heat to medium-high. Cook until a small amount of the mixture forms a ball when dropped in cold water, stirring constantly. Remove from the heat. Add the coconut flavoring and coconut and mix well. Place the mixture in a bowl. Chill, covered, in the refrigerator. Shape into flat round patties. Place on baking sheets sprayed with nonstick cooking spray. Cover with plastic wrap and freeze until firm. Melt the chocolate chips and paraffin in a double boiler over simmering water. Dip the frozen patties into the chocolate mixture using tongs. Place on baking sheets. Chill, covered, in the freezer until firm. Store in airtight containers in the freezer until ready to serve. YIELD: **4 TO 4½ POUNDS.**

Shirley Crocker
Birmingham Life

HELPFUL HINT
It is usually more successful to make two separate batches of a candy than to double the recipe.

No-Bake Babies

2 cups sugar
1/4 cup baking cocoa
1/2 cup milk
1/2 cup (1 stick) butter
1/2 cup rolled oats
1 cup creamy or chunky peanut butter
1/2 cup raisins (optional)
2 teaspoons vanilla extract

Combine the sugar, baking cocoa, milk and butter in a saucepan and mix well. Bring to a boil. Cook for 1 1/2 minutes. Remove from the heat. Add the oats, peanut butter, raisins and vanilla and mix well. The mixture will be stiff. Drop by spoonfuls onto buttered waxed paper. Let stand until cool. YIELD: 2 POUNDS.

Susan Robbins
Riverchase Council

Orange Balls

2 (14-ounce) cans sweetened condensed milk
2 2/3 cups flaked coconut
1 pound orange candy slices, chopped
1 cup chopped pecans
1 teaspoon vanilla extract
Confectioners' sugar to taste

Combine the condensed milk, coconut, orange slices, pecans and vanilla in a bowl and mix well. Spread evenly in a greased and floured 10x15-inch baking pan. Bake at 275 to 300 degrees for 30 minutes. Let stand until cool. Shape into teaspoon-size balls with hands dampened with water. Roll in confectioners' sugar. Store in an airtight container. YIELD: 3 1/2 POUNDS.

Kim Merritt
Decatur Council

Microwave Peanut Brittle

1 cup raw peanuts
1 cup sugar
½ cup light corn syrup
Pinch of salt
1 teaspoon butter or margarine
1 teaspoon vanilla extract
1 teaspoon baking soda

Combine the peanuts, sugar, corn syrup and salt in a microwave-safe 1½-quart dish and mix well. Microwave on High for 7 to 8 minutes, stirring after 4 minutes. Blend in the butter and vanilla. Microwave for 2 minutes. Stir in the baking soda gently until the mixture is light and foamy. Pour the mixture onto a greased baking sheet and spread thinly. Let stand for 30 minutes to 1 hour or until cool. Break into pieces. YIELD: 1 POUND.

Adeline Neal
Birmingham Life

Toasted Pecan Clusters

3 cups pecan pieces
3 tablespoons butter or margarine, melted
12 ounces chocolate candy coating

Combine the pecans and butter in a 10x15-inch baking pan. Bake at 300 degrees for 30 minutes, stirring every 10 minutes. Melt the chocolate in a heavy saucepan over low heat. Remove from the heat. Cool for 2 minutes. Stir in the toasted pecans. Drop by rounded teaspoonfuls onto waxed paper. Let stand until cool. YIELD: 1½ POUNDS.

Faith Kirby Richardson
Gadsden Life

Walnut Penuche

1½ cups walnuts, coarsely chopped
⅔ cup butter
1 cup packed light brown sugar
1 (14-ounce) can sweetened condensed milk
½ teaspoon vanilla extract

Line an 8-inch-square pan with foil, allowing the foil to extend over the sides of the pan. Grease the foil lightly. Spread the walnuts in a 9-inch microwave-safe dish. Microwave on High for 6 to 7 minutes or until lightly toasted, stirring 3 times. Microwave the butter on Medium in a 2½- or 3-quart microwave-safe mixing bowl until melted. Stir in the brown sugar and condensed milk until well blended. Microwave on High for 7 to 9 minutes or until the sugar has completely dissolved and the mixture has thickened and is a caramel color, stirring 4 times. Remove the bowl to a heatproof surface. Beat in the vanilla. Beat the mixture for 3 to 4 minutes or until smooth and shiny. Add the walnuts. Beat at low speed until the walnuts are well distributed. Spread over the bottom of the prepared pan. Chill, covered, in the refrigerator for 2 to 3 hours or until firm. Remove the penuche from the pan by carefully lifting the foil ends. Remove the foil. Cut the penuche into 1-inch squares. Store, tightly covered, in a cool place. YIELD: 1½ POUNDS.

Howard and Elizabeth Dempsey
Anniston Council

HELPFUL HINT

Make candy in a saucepan with 3 or 4 times the volume of the combined ingredients so the candy can boil freely without boiling over.

S'mores-Golden Grahams

1½ cups milk chocolate chips
5 tablespoons butter
¼ cup light corn syrup
1 (10-ounce) package miniature marshmallows
1 teaspoon vanilla extract
1 (13-ounce) package Golden Graham cereal

Combine the chocolate chips, butter and corn syrup in a 3-quart saucepan and mix well. Stir in the marshmallows, reserving 1 cup of the marshmallows. Heat over low heat until the mixture is melted, stirring occasionally. Remove from the heat. Stir in the vanilla. Pour the marshmallow mixture over the cereal in a large bowl. Stir until the cereal is evenly coated. Add the reserved marshmallows and mix well. Press the mixture into a buttered 9×13-inch pan. Let stand for 1 hour or until firm. Cut into 24 large bars or 48 small bars. Store, loosely covered, at room temperature. YIELD: 2½ POUNDS.

Virginia Greene
Birmingham South Life

Spider Candies

1 cup chocolate chips
½ cup crisp rice cereal
¼ cup flaked coconut
Purchased eyes from specialty candy store
1 (3-ounce) can chow mein noodles

Melt the chocolate chips in a saucepan. Remove from the heat. Add the cereal and coconut and mix well. Drop by spoonfuls onto waxed paper. Place eyes on each and make legs with chow mein noodles. Chill, covered, in the refrigerator. YIELD: 1 POUND.

Carolyn G. Wheeler
Selma Life

Gooey Turtles

1/2 cup (1 stick) melted butter
1 1/2 cups vanilla wafer crumbs
2 cups semisweet chocolate chips
1 cup chopped pecans
1 (12-ounce) jar caramel topping

Combine the butter and vanilla wafer crumbs in a 9x13-inch baking pan and mix well. Press the crumb mixture evenly over the bottom of the pan. Sprinkle with the chocolate chips and pecans. Remove the lid from the caramel topping. Microwave on High for 1 to 1 1/2 minutes or until hot, stirring after 30 seconds. Drizzle the topping over the pecans. Bake at 350 degrees for 12 to 15 minutes or until the chocolate chips are melted. Cool in the pan on a wire rack. Chill, covered, in the refrigerator for 30 minutes. Cut into bars. You may use reduced-fat vanilla wafers, chocolate chips and caramel topping. YIELD: 2 1/2 POUNDS.

Jo Ann Thomas
Selma Life

Reese Cups

1 cup (2 sticks) butter, melted
1 (12-ounce) jar crunchy peanut butter
1 (1-pound) package confectioners' sugar
1 cup graham cracker crumbs
1 (1-pound) chocolate candy bar, melted

Combine the butter, peanut butter and confectioners' sugar in a bowl and mix with a spoon until creamy. Stir in the graham cracker crumbs. Press into a large pan. Pour the melted chocolate over the top. Chill, covered, in the refrigerator until firm. Cut into squares to serve. YIELD: 3 TO 3 1/2 POUNDS.

Ann Moon
Decatur Council

Reese Candy

1½ cups (3 sticks) margarine
1½ cups peanut butter
1 (1-pound) package confectioners' sugar
1½ cups graham cracker crumbs
2 cups chocolate chips

Melt 1 cup of the margarine and peanut butter in a saucepan, stirring until well combined. Remove from the heat. Add the confectioners' sugar and graham cracker crumbs and mix well with hands. Press into a 9×12-inch glass dish. Melt the remaining margarine and chocolate chips in a saucepan, stirring occasionally. Pour the chocolate mixture over the top. Let stand until cool. Cut into squares. YIELD: 4 POUNDS.

Sarah Breland
Riverchase Council

Vanilla Nut Roll

1 (14-ounce) can sweetened condensed milk
1 cup flaked coconut
2 cups chopped pecans
½ package vanilla wafers, crushed
Confectioners' sugar to taste

Combine the condensed milk, coconut, pecans and vanilla wafer crumbs in a bowl and mix well. Divide the mixture into 2 or 3 equal portions. Roll each portion into a log and coat with confectioners' sugar. Chill, covered, in the refrigerator. Cut into slices. You may press the mixture into a square pan and sprinkle with confectioners' sugar if desired. YIELD: 2 TO 2½ POUNDS.

Oneida C. Allen
Tuscaloosa Council

Olga's Angel Crisp Cookies

1 cup sugar
½ cup (1 stick) margarine
½ cup shortening
1 egg
2½ cups flour

1 teaspoon salt
1 teaspoon cream of tartar
1 teaspoon baking soda
1 teaspoon vanilla extract

Cream the sugar, margarine and shortening in a mixing bowl until light and fluffy. Beat in the egg. Add the flour, salt, cream of tartar, baking soda and vanilla and mix well. Chill the dough, covered, in the refrigerator. Shape into small balls. Place on nonstick cookie sheets. Press each ball with the bottom of a glass dipped in sugar to flatten thinly. Bake at 350 degrees for 8 to 10 minutes or until light brown. Cool on wire racks. **YIELD: ABOUT 5 DOZEN.**

Mrs. Raymond E. Davis
Decatur Council

Polly Jones' Apple Bars

3 eggs, beaten
2 cups sugar
1 cup vegetable oil
2 cups flour
½ teaspoon salt

1 teaspoon cinnamon
2 cups chopped peeled apples
Chopped nuts to taste
Confectioners' sugar to taste

Beat the eggs, sugar and oil in a mixing bowl until well combined. Add the flour, salt and cinnamon and mix well. Fold in the apples and nuts. Pour into a greased and floured 9×13-inch baking pan. Bake at 350 degrees for 40 to 45 minutes or until brown. Sprinkle with confectioners' sugar while warm. Let stand until cool. Cut into bars. **YIELD: 2 DOZEN.**

Kitty Logan Brown
Gadsden Life Council

Brownies

½ cup (1 stick) margarine
1 cup sugar
4 eggs
1 (16-ounce) can chocolate syrup
1 cup flour
1 cup finely chopped nuts
Frosting (below)

Cream margarine and sugar in a mixing bowl until light and fluffy. Add the eggs 1 at a time, beating well after each addition. Add the chocolate syrup and beat until smooth. Add the flour and nuts and mix well. Pour the mixture into a greased 10x15-inch baking pan. Bake at 350 degrees for 35 minutes or until the brownies pull away from the sides of the pan. Let stand until cool. Spread Frosting over brownies. Cut into bars. YIELD: 3 DOZEN.

Frosting

1⅓ cups sugar
6 tablespoons (¾ stick) margarine
⅓ cup milk
½ cup chocolate chips

Combine the sugar, margarine and milk in a saucepan and mix well. Bring to a boil. Boil for 1 minute, stirring constantly. Remove from the heat. Add the chocolate chips and stir until of spreading consistency. YIELD: 2 CUPS.

Barbara Seegmiller
Decatur Council

Brownies

1 cup (2 sticks) unsalted butter
2 ounces unsweetened chocolate
2 cups sugar
3 eggs
1 teaspoon vanilla extract
1 cup sifted flour
3/4 cup (or more) chopped nuts
1/2 cup chocolate chips

Melt the butter and unsweetened chocolate in a saucepan over medium heat. Remove from the heat. Add the sugar and mix well with a wooden spoon. Add the eggs 1 at a time, mixing well after each addition. Stir in the vanilla. Add the flour and mix well. Fold in 1/2 cup of the nuts. Spread the mixture evenly into a greased 9×13-inch baking pan. Sprinkle the remaining nuts and chocolate chips over the top. Bake at 350 degrees for 35 to 40 minutes or until the brownies pull away from the sides of the pan. Let stand until cool. Cut into bars. YIELD: 2 DOZEN.

Sharon Etheridge
Birmingham South Cahaba Council

Best-Ever Brownies

1 cup plus 2 tablespoons vegetable oil
2¼ cups sugar
5 eggs
2 tablespoons vanilla extract
¾ cup baking cocoa
1¾ cups flour
1 tablespoon salt
1½ cups chopped nuts

Beat the oil and sugar in a mixing bowl until well combined. Add the eggs 1 at a time, beating well after each addition. Beat in the vanilla. Add the the baking cocoa, flour and salt and mix well. Fold in the nuts. Pour the mixture into a greased 10x15-inch baking pan. Bake at 350 degrees for 20 to 25 minutes or until the brownies pull away from the sides of the pan. Let stand until cool. Cut into bars. You may frost the brownies if desired. **YIELD: 3 DOZEN.**

Margaret W. Wilborn
Gadsden Life Council

Caramel Brownies

2 cups baking mix
1 (1-pound) package light brown sugar
4 eggs
1 cup nuts
1 teaspoon vanilla extract

Combine the baking mix and brown sugar in a mixing bowl and mix well. Beat in the eggs until well blended. Add the nuts and vanilla and mix well. Pour the mixture into a greased 9x13-inch baking pan. Bake at 325 degrees for 25 minutes or until firm in the center. Let stand until cool. Cut into bars. **YIELD: 2 DOZEN.**

Sue Small
Selma Life Council

Katharine Hepburn's Brownies

1/2 cup (1 stick) butter
1/2 cup baking cocoa
2 tablespoons vegetable oil
1 cup sugar
2 eggs
1/2 teaspoon vanilla extract
1/4 cup flour
1/4 teaspoon salt
1 cup chopped pecans
Judy's Frosting (below)

Melt the butter in a heavy saucepan. Remove from the heat. Stir in the baking cocoa, oil and sugar. Add the eggs and vanilla and mix well. Stir in the flour and salt. Fold in the pecans. Pour the mixture into a greased 8-inch-square baking pan. Bake at 325 degrees for 30 minutes. Let stand until cool. Spread Judy's Frosting over the brownies. Cut into bars. YIELD: 1 1/3 DOZEN.

Judy's Frosting

1/4 cup (1/2 stick) butter
1/2 cup baking cocoa
1 teaspoon vanilla extract
Dash of salt
2 cups confectioners' sugar
3 tablespoons milk

Beat the butter in a mixing bowl at low speed until creamy. Add the baking cocoa, vanilla and salt and mix well. Beat in the confectioners' sugar and milk until of spreading consistency. YIELD: 2 1/2 CUPS.

Judy Brantley, Friend of Marion and Warren Thompson
Gadsden Life Member Club

Hershey Brownies

1/2 cup vegetable oil
1 cup sugar
1 teaspoon vanilla extract
2 eggs
1/2 cup flour

1/3 cup baking cocoa
1/4 teaspoon baking powder
1/4 teaspoon salt
1/2 cup chopped nuts

Beat the oil and sugar in a mixing bowl until well combined. Add the vanilla and mix well. Beat in the eggs. Add the flour, baking cocoa, baking powder and salt and mix well. Fold in the nuts. Pour the mixture into a greased 9-inch-square baking pan. Bake at 350 degrees for 20 to 25 minutes or until the brownies pull away from the sides of the pan. Let stand until cool. Cut into bars. You may frost the brownies if desired. YIELD: 1 1/3 DOZEN.

Sue Walton
Birmingham Life

Marbled Brownie Bars

2 (8-ounce) packages cream cheese, softened
2 eggs
2 tablespoons sugar

1 (22-ounce) package brownie mix
1 teaspoon vanilla extract

Beat the cream cheese, eggs, sugar and vanilla in a mixing bowl until light and fluffy. Prepare the brownie mix using the package directions. Spread half the brownie batter in a greased 9×13-inch baking pan. Spoon the cream cheese mixture over the brownie batter. Spread the remaining batter over the top. Swirl with a knife. Bake at 350 degrees for 35 to 40 minutes or until a wooden pick inserted in the center comes out clean. Let stand until cool. Cut into bars. YIELD: 1 1/3 DOZEN.

Mary C. Martin
Birmingham Life

Peanut Butter Brownie Pizza

1 (22-ounce) package brownie mix
8 ounces cream cheese, softened
1 cup packed brown sugar
¼ cup creamy peanut butter
2 (2-pack) peanut butter cups
½ cup chopped peanuts
1 ounce semisweet chocolate, melted
2 teaspoons melted butter

Prepare the brownie mix using the package directions. Pour into a large pizza pan sprayed with nonstick cooking spray. Spread the mixture evenly. Bake at 350 degrees until the brownie layer tests done. Let stand until cool. Combine the cream cheese, brown sugar and peanut butter in a mixing bowl and beat until creamy. Spread the cream cheese mixture over the baked layer. Chop the peanut butter cups and peanuts. Sprinkle over the cream cheese mixture, reserving some for topping. Combine the chocolate and butter in a bowl and mix well. Drizzle over the top. Sprinkle with the reserved peanut mixture. Cut into wedges. **YIELD: 16 SERVINGS.**

Stacy Yarborough
Birmingham South Cahaba Council

HELPFUL HINT

Slice bar cookies with a pizza cutter.

Chocolate Cake Cookies

1 cup packed light brown sugar
½ cup (1 stick) margarine, softened
1 egg
½ teaspoon baking soda
½ cup buttermilk or sour cream
½ cup baking cocoa
1½ cups flour
1 teaspoon vanilla extract
½ cup nuts
Frosting (below)

Cream the brown sugar and margarine in a mixing bowl until light and fluffy. Beat in the egg. Combine the baking soda and buttermilk in a bowl. Add to the creamed mixture and mix well. Sift the baking cocoa and flour together. Add to the creamed mixture and mix well. Stir in the vanilla. Fold in the nuts. Drop by tablespoonfuls onto nonstick cookie sheets. Bake at 350 degrees for 15 minutes. Remove to waxed paper. Spread with Frosting while hot. **Yield: 2 dozen.**

Frosting

3 ounces unsweetened chocolate
¼ cup (½ stick) margarine, softened
2¼ cups confectioners' sugar
¼ teaspoon salt
½ cup milk, scalded
½ teaspoon vanilla extract

Melt the chocolate in a saucepan, stirring constantly. Stir in the margarine. Combine the confectioners' sugar, salt and milk in a bowl and mix well. Add to the chocolate mixture and mix well. Stir in the vanilla. **Yield: 3 cups.**

Mary Alice Neal
Birmingham Life

Chocolate Chip Cookies

1 cup (2 sticks) butter, softened
1 cup vegetable oil
1 cup sugar
1 cup packed brown sugar
1 egg
2 teaspoons vanilla extract
3½ cups flour
1 teaspoon salt
1 teaspoon cream of tartar
1 teaspoon baking soda
1 cup rolled oats
1 cup crisp rice cereal
2 cups semisweet chocolate chips
1 cup chopped pecans

Beat the butter and oil in a mixing bowl until well combined. Add the sugar, brown sugar, egg and vanilla and mix well. Mix the flour, salt, cream of tartar and baking soda together. Add the flour mixture to the sugar mixture gradually, beating well after each addition. Stir in the oats, cereal, chocolate chips and pecans. Drop by teaspoonfuls onto greased cookie sheets. Bake at 375 degrees for 10 minutes. Cool on wire racks. YIELD: 4 TO 5 DOZEN.

Bill Johnson
Birmingham South Life

Chocolate Chip Cookies

½ cup (1 stick) butter, softened
1½ cups packed brown sugar
2 eggs
1 teaspoon vanilla extract
2⅔ cups baking mix
2 cups chocolate chips
½ cup (or more) nuts

Cream the butter and brown sugar in a mixing bowl until light and fluffy. Beat in the eggs 1 at a time. Stir in the vanilla. Add the baking mix gradually, mixing with a wooden spoon. Fold in the chocolate chips and nuts. Drop by spoonfuls onto greased cookie sheets. Bake at 375 degrees for 8 to 10 minutes or until brown. Cool on wire racks. YIELD: 2½ TO 3 DOZEN.

Mabel Smartt
Decatur Council

Chocolate Chip Cookies

²/₃ cup shortening, softened
½ cup sugar
½ cup packed brown sugar
1 egg
1 teaspoon vanilla extract

1½ cups flour
½ teaspoon baking soda
½ teaspoon salt
½ cup chopped nuts
1 cup chocolate chips

Beat the shortening, sugar, brown sugar, egg and vanilla in a mixing bowl until well combined. Combine the flour, baking soda and salt in a bowl and mix well. Add the flour mixture to the sugar mixture and mix well. Fold in the nuts and chocolate chips. Drop by teaspoonfuls onto ungreased cookie sheets. Bake at 350 degrees for 8 to 10 minutes or until brown. Cool on wire racks. YIELD: 3 DOZEN.

Linda Ander
Montgomery Council

Death-by-Chocolate Cookie

16 ounces semisweet
   chocolate, coarsely chopped
¼ cup (½ stick) butter or
   margarine
¾ cup packed brown sugar

2 eggs
1 teaspoon vanilla extract
½ cup flour
¼ teaspoon baking powder
2 cups chopped pecans

Melt 8 ounces of the chocolate with the butter in a saucepan, stirring constantly until smooth. Stir in the brown sugar, eggs and vanilla. Add the flour and baking powder and mix well. Remove from the heat. Fold in the remaining chocolate and pecans. Drop by ¼ cupfuls onto ungreased cookie sheets. Bake at 350 degrees for 12 to 13 minutes or until the cookies are puffed and firm to the touch. Cool on the cookie sheets for 1 minute. Remove to wire racks to cool completely. YIELD: 1½ DOZEN.

Edith Dixon
Birmingham Life

Fudgy Coconut Squares

1 cup (2 sticks) butter or margarine, softened
1 1/2 cups sugar
3 eggs
1 teaspoon vanilla extract
1 cup flour
1/4 cup baking cocoa
1/2 cup chopped walnuts
1 (14-ounce) can sweetened condensed milk
1 cup shredded coconut
2 cups confectioners' sugar
1/4 cup baking soda
5 tablespoons evaporated milk
2 tablespoons butter or margarine, melted
1/2 teaspoon vanilla extract

Cream 1 cup butter and sugar in a mixing bowl until light and fluffy. Add the eggs 1 at a time, beating well after each addition. Beat in 1 teaspoon vanilla. Combine the flour, baking cocoa and walnuts and mix well. Add the flour mixture to the creamed mixture and mix well. Spread into a greased 9x13-inch baking pan. Bake at 350 degrees for 30 minutes or until a wooden pick inserted near the center comes out clean. Combine the condensed milk and coconut in a bowl and mix well. Spread the coconut mixture carefully over the hot chocolate layer. Bake for 20 minutes or until the coconut is light brown. Combine the confectioners' sugar, baking soda, evaporated milk, 2 tablespoons butter and 1/2 teaspoon vanilla in a bowl and mix until smooth. Spread over the warm layer. Chill, covered, in the refrigerator for 1 hour. Cut into squares.

Yield: about 4 dozen.

Hester P. Thompson
Birmingham Life

Gay's Cowboy Cookies

¾ cup (1½ sticks) margarine, softened
1 cup sugar
1 cup packed light brown sugar
2 eggs
1 teaspoon vanilla extract
2 cups sifted flour
½ teaspoon salt
¾ teaspoon baking soda
1 teaspoon cinnamon
½ teaspoon ground cloves
2 cups quick-cooking oats
1 cup chopped pecans
1 cup raisins
1 cup semisweet chocolate chips

Cream the margarine, sugar and brown sugar in a mixing bowl until light and fluffy. Add the eggs 1 at a time, beating well after each addition. Beat in the vanilla. Sift the flour, salt, baking soda, cinnamon and cloves together. Add the flour mixture, oats, pecans, raisins and chocolate chips to the creamed mixture all at once, mixing well by hand. Drop by teaspoonfuls onto greased cookie sheets. Bake at 375 degrees for 8 to 12 minutes or until light brown; do not overbake. Cool on wire racks. You may add chopped maraschino cherries or flaked coconut and substitute milk chocolate chips for the semisweet chocolate chips. **YIELD: 6 DOZEN.**

Carole Jones
Bon Secour Life

Dishpan Cookies

2 cups packed brown sugar
2 cups vegetable oil
2 teaspoons vanilla extract
2 cups sugar
4 eggs
1 teaspoon almond extract
   (optional)
4 cups flour
1 teaspoon salt
2 teaspoons baking soda
1 1/2 cups rolled oats
4 cups cornflakes, crushed
1 cup chopped nuts (optional)
1 cup raisins (optional)

Combine the brown sugar, oil, vanilla, sugar, eggs and almond extract in a mixing bowl and beat until smooth. Add the flour, salt, baking soda, oats, cornflakes, nuts and raisins and mix well. Drop by teaspoonfuls onto ungreased cookie sheets. Bake at 325 degrees for 8 minutes. Cool on wire racks. YIELD: 4 TO 5 DOZEN.

Barbara Seegmiller
Decatur Council

Dream Bars

1 (2-layer) package French
   vanilla cake mix
1/3 cup butter, softened
1 egg
1 (21-ounce) can cherry
   pie filling
8 ounces cream cheese,
   softened
1 egg
1/2 cup sugar
1/2 teaspoon vanilla extract

Combine the cake mix, butter and 1 egg in a mixing bowl and mix well. Spread over the bottom of a nonstick 9×13-inch baking pan. Bake at 350 degrees for 15 minutes; the layer will not be completely baked. Spread the pie filling over the baked layer. Combine the cream cheese, 1 egg, sugar and vanilla in a bowl and mix well. Spread over the pie filling. Bake for 20 minutes or until brown. Let stand until cool. Cut into bars. YIELD: 2 DOZEN.

Fay Clark
Riverchase Council

Duchess Cookies

½ cup sifted flour
½ cup rolled oats
½ cup (1 stick) butter or margarine
2 eggs
1½ cups firmly packed brown sugar
1 teaspoon vanilla
2 tablespoons flour
½ teaspoon baking powder
½ teaspoon salt
½ cup candied cherries, chopped
½ cup flaked coconut
½ cup chopped pecans

Combine ½ cup flour and oats in a bowl and mix well. Cut in the butter until the mixture is crumbly. Spoon into a nonstick 8×12-inch baking pan. Bake at 350 degrees for 2 minutes. Spread the mixture evenly over the bottom of the pan. Bake for 10 minutes longer. Beat the eggs in a bowl, gradually beating in the brown sugar and vanilla until creamy. Combine 2 tablespoons flour, baking powder and salt in a bowl and mix well. Add to the creamed mixture and mix well. Fold in the cherries, coconut and pecans. Spread over the baked layer. Bake for 25 minutes. Cut into bars while warm. Let stand until cool before removing from the pan.
YIELD: 1½ TO 2 DOZEN.

Frankie Vaughn
Selma Life

HELPFUL HINT

Always place cookie dough on a cool cookie sheet;
it will spread on a hot cookie sheet.

Everyday Cookies

1 cup (2 sticks) butter or margarine, softened
1 cup sugar
1 cup packed light brown sugar
1 cup vegetable oil
2 eggs
1 teaspoon vanilla extract
3½ cups flour
1 teaspoon cream of tartar
1 teaspoon baking soda
1 teaspoon salt
1 cup crisp rice cereal
1 cup quick-cooking oats
1 cup shredded coconut
½ cup chopped pecans

Cream the butter, sugar, brown sugar and oil in a mixing bowl until light and fluffy. Add the eggs and vanilla and mix well. Combine the flour, cream of tartar, baking soda and salt in a bowl and mix well. Add to the creamed mixture and mix well. Stir in the cereal, oats, coconut and pecans. Drop by teaspoonfuls onto ungreased cookie sheets; flatten slightly. Place the cookie sheets on the lower oven rack. Bake at 350 degrees for 5 to 6 minutes. Remove the cookie sheets to the middle oven rack and bake for 5 minutes longer or until the cookies are light brown; do not overbake. Cool on wire racks. YIELD: **8 DOZEN**.

Jeanette Norton
Shoals Life

HELPFUL HINT

Make cookies a uniform size to assure even baking.

Expensive Cookies

4 cups flour
1 cup blended rolled oats
1 teaspoon salt
1 teaspoon baking powder
2 teaspoons baking soda
2 cups (4 sticks) butter, softened
2 cups sugar
2 cups packed brown sugar
4 eggs
2 teaspoons vanilla extract
4 cups chocolate chips
1 (8-ounce) milk chocolate bar, grated
3 cups chopped nuts (optional)

Mix the flour, oats, salt, baking powder and baking soda in a bowl. Cream the butter, sugar and brown sugar in a mixing bowl until light and fluffy. Stir in the eggs and vanilla. Add the flour mixture, chocolate chips, chocolate bar and nuts and mix well. Roll into balls. Place 2 inches apart on nonstick cookie sheets. Bake at 375 degrees for 10 minutes. Cool on wire racks. YIELD: 9 1/3 DOZEN.

Jamima M. Edney
Birmingham Life

Gooey Butter Bars

1/2 cup (1 stick) margarine, melted
1 (2-layer) butter cake mix
1 egg
3 cups confectioners' sugar
1/2 cup (1 stick) margarine, softened
8 ounces cream cheese, softened
2 eggs

Combine 1/2 cup margarine, cake mix and 1 egg in a bowl and mix well. Spread over the bottom of a nonstick 9×13-inch baking pan. Combine the confectioners' sugar, 1/2 cup margarine, cream cheese and 2 eggs in a bowl and mix well. Spread over the crust. Bake at 350 degrees for 30 to 40 minutes or until brown. Let stand until cool. Cut into bars. YIELD: 2 DOZEN.

Debby Sims
Gadsden Life

Christmas Kiss Cookies

2/3 cup margarine, softened
1/3 cup sugar
1 teaspoon vanilla extract
2 egg yolks
1 ounce white chocolate bark,
1/2 ounce melted, 1/2 ounce chopped
1 1/2 cups flour
1/2 teaspoon salt
2 egg whites, slightly beaten
3/4 cup finely chopped pecans
Vanilla Frosting (below)

Combine the margarine, sugar, vanilla, egg yolks and chocolate in a mixing bowl and mix well. Add the flour and salt and mix well. Roll dough into small balls. Dip the balls in the egg whites and coat with the pecans. Place on greased cookie sheets. Make an indentation in each ball with thumb. Bake at 350 degrees for 15 minutes. Cool on cookie sheets for several minutes. Remove to wire racks to cool completely. Fill each indentation with Vanilla Frosting. You may tint the frosting with food coloring if desired. YIELD: 3 1/2 DOZEN.

Vanilla Frosting

3 ounces cream cheese, softened
1/4 cup (1/2 stick) butter or margarine, softened
1 teaspoon vanilla extract
2 cups confectioners' sugar
Milk

Beat the cream cheese, butter and vanilla in a mixing bowl until smooth. Add the confectioners' sugar and beat well. Add enough milk to make of the desired consistency. YIELD: 2 1/2 CUPS.

Margaret W. Wilborn
Gadsden Life

Forgotten Kisses

2 egg whites, at room
  temperature
1/8 teaspoon cream of tartar
1/8 teaspoon salt
1/2 cup sugar
1 teaspoon vanilla extract
1/2 cup chopped nuts
1/2 cup miniature semisweet
  chocolate chips (optional)

Preheat the oven to 350 degrees. Beat the egg whites in a mixing bowl at high speed until frothy. Add the cream of tartar and salt. Add the sugar gradually, beating until stiff peaks form. Beat in the vanilla. Fold in the nuts and chocolate chips 1/2 at a time. Drop slightly rounded teaspoonfuls 1 inch apart onto greased cookie sheets. Turn off the oven. Place cookie sheets in the oven. Allow cookies to remain in the oven for up to 2 hours or overnight. YIELD: 3 DOZEN.

Mary Ann Stanley
Mobile Council

Fruitcake Cookies

1 cup (2 sticks) butter
1 1/2 cups packed brown sugar
3 eggs, beaten
1/2 cup buttermilk
1/2 teaspoon baking soda
3 cups flour
1 teaspoon cinnamon
6 slices candied pineapple,
  chopped
2 cups candied cherries,
  chopped
3/4 cup raisins
2 cups dates, chopped
6 cups pecans, chopped

Cream the butter and brown sugar in a mixing bowl until light and fluffy. Beat in the eggs, buttermilk, baking soda, flour and cinnamon. Add the pineapple, cherries, raisins, dates and pecans and mix well. Drop by teaspoonfuls onto buttered cookie sheets. Bake at 300 degrees for 20 minutes. Cool on wire racks. YIELD: 6 DOZEN.

Mary M. Storey
Anniston Council

Fruitcake Cookies

1 cup packed brown sugar
1/2 cup (1 stick) butter or margarine, softened
1 cup flour
1 pound dates, chopped
4 cups pecans, chopped
2 cups black walnuts, chopped
1 1/2 cups golden raisins
1 pound candied cherries, chopped
1/2 pound candied green pineapple, chopped
1/2 pound candied red pineapple, chopped
2 tablespoons molasses or honey
3 tablespoons milk
1 tablespoon baking soda
Pinch of salt
4 egg yolks
2 cups flour
1 teaspoon cinnamon
1 teaspoon nutmeg
4 egg whites, stiffly beaten

Cream the brown sugar and butter in a mixing bowl until light and fluffy. Combine 1 cup flour with the dates, pecans, walnuts, raisins, cherries and pineapple in a large bowl and mix to coat. Add the molasses, milk, baking soda, salt, egg yolks, 2 cups flour, cinnamon and nutmeg to the creamed mixture and mix well. Stir in the fruit mixture. Fold in the egg whites. Drop by teaspoonfuls onto greased cookie sheets. Bake at 300 degrees for 20 minutes. Cool on wire racks. **Yield: 6 dozen.**

Margaret W. Wilborn
Gadsden Life

Grace's Fruitcake Cookies

1 cup (2 sticks) butter, softened
1 cup sugar
5 eggs
1 cup self-rising flour
1/4 teaspoon cinnamon
1/4 teaspoon nutmeg
1/4 teaspoon ground cloves
1/4 teaspoon ginger
1 teaspoon flavoring of choice
1 ounce fruit juice
1 1/2 cups all-purpose flour
1 pound candied pineapple, finely chopped
1 pound candied cherries, finely chopped
8 cups pecans, finely chopped

Cream the butter and sugar in a mixing bowl until light and fluffy. Add the eggs and mix well. Combine 1 cup flour, cinnamon, nutmeg, cloves and ginger in a bowl and mix well. Add to the creamed mixture and mix well. Stir in the flavoring and fruit juice. Combine 1 1/2 cups flour, pineapple, cherries and pecans in a bowl and mix well. Add to the creamed mixture and mix well. Drop by teaspoonfuls onto nonstick cookie sheets. Bake at 350 degrees for 15 minutes. Cool on wire racks. The cookies may be made in batches, freezing the unused portions of dough in an airtight container until ready to bake. YIELD: **6 DOZEN**.

Grace O. Miller
Mobile Council

Crunch Grape-Nut Cookies

1/2 cup (1 stick) margarine
1/2 cup milk
1/2 teaspoon cinnamon
1 cup quick-cooking oats
1 cup Grape-Nuts cereal
1/2 cup sugar
1 cup nuts

Combine the margarine and milk in a heavy saucepan. Bring to a boil. Remove from the heat. Stir in the cinnamon, oats, cereal, sugar and nuts. Roll into 1-inch balls. Place on nonstick cookie sheets. Chill, covered, in the refrigerator until ready to serve.
YIELD: 2 DOZEN.

Eunice Henry
Selma Life

Mud Cookies

2 cups sugar
1/4 cup (1/2 stick) margarine
1/4 cup baking cocoa
1/2 cup milk
3 cups quick-cooking oats
1/2 cup peanut butter
1 teaspoon vanilla extract

Combine the sugar, margarine, baking cocoa and milk in a saucepan. Bring to a boil. Boil for 1 minute, stirring constantly. Add the oats, peanut butter and vanilla and mix well. Drop by spoonfuls onto a nonstick cookie sheet. Chill, covered, in the refrigerator until firm. YIELD: 2 DOZEN.

Jeanette Norton
Shoals Life

Neiman Marcus Cookies

5 cups rolled oats
2 cups (4 sticks) butter, softened
2 cups sugar
2 cups packed brown sugar
4 eggs
2 teaspoons vanilla extract
4 cups flour
1 teaspoon salt
2 teaspoons baking powder
2 teaspoons baking soda
4 cups chocolate chips
1 (8-ounce) milk chocolate bar, grated
3 cups chopped nuts

Process the oats in a blender to a fine powder. Cream the butter, sugar and brown sugar in a mixing bowl until light and fluffy. Add the eggs and vanilla and mix well. Combine the flour, ground oats, salt, baking powder and baking soda in a bowl and mix well. Add to the creamed mixture and mix well. Stir in the chocolate chips, milk chocolate bar and nuts. Roll into balls. Place 2 inches apart on cookie sheets. Bake at 375 degrees for 10 minutes. Cool on wire racks. YIELD: 9 1/3 DOZEN.

Sara Cooley
Birmingham Life

HELPFUL HINT

Substitute unsweetened cereal such as puffed rice for nuts in cookies.

Chloe Scott's Creamy Oat Cookies

1 cup (2 sticks) butter or margarine, softened
1 cup sugar
1 cup packed brown sugar
1 egg
1 cup vegetable oil
1 teaspoon vanilla extract
3½ cups flour
1 teaspoon baking soda
½ teaspoon salt
1 cup rolled oats
1 cup crushed cornflakes
½ cup flaked coconut
½ cup chopped peanuts or walnuts

Cream the butter, sugar and brown sugar in a mixing bowl, beating at medium speed until light and fluffy. Add the egg and mix well. Beat in the oil and vanilla. Combine the flour, baking soda and salt in a bowl and mix well. Add to the creamed mixture and mix well. Stir in the oats, cornflakes, coconut and peanuts. Roll dough into 1-inch balls. Place on ungreased cookie sheets. Flatten each ball with a fork dipped in sugar. Bake at 325 degrees for 15 minutes. Cool on the cookie sheets for several minutes. Remove to wire racks to cool completely. YIELD: 10 DOZEN.

Imogene Davis
Birmingham Life

HELPFUL HINT

*Cool cookies completely in a single layer on
a wire rack before storing.*

Vanishing Oatmeal Raisin Cookies

1 cup (2 sticks) butter or margarine, softened
1 cup packed brown sugar
1/2 cup sugar
2 eggs
1 teaspoon vanilla extract
1 1/2 cups flour
1 teaspoon baking soda
1 teaspoon cinnamon
1/2 teaspoon salt
3 cups quick-cooking or rolled oats
1 cup raisins

Cream the butter, brown sugar and sugar in a mixing bowl until light and fluffy. Add the eggs and vanilla and mix well. Combine the flour, baking soda, cinnamon and salt in a bowl and mix well. Add to the creamed mixture and mix well. Stir in the oats and raisins. Drop by rounded tablespoonfuls onto ungreased cookie sheets. Bake at 350 degrees for 10 to 12 minutes or until light brown. Cool on the cookie sheets for 1 minute. Remove to wire racks to cool completely. Store in an airtight container.
YIELD: ABOUT 4 DOZEN.

Mary M. Niver
Montgomery Life

Orange Slice Cookies

1 (9-ounce) package Jiffy cake mix
1 egg
1/3 cup (scant) vegetable oil
11 orange candy slices, chopped
1 cup chopped nuts

Combine the cake mix, egg, oil, orange slices and nuts in a mixing bowl and mix well. Drop by teaspoonfuls onto ungreased cookie sheets. Bake at 350 degrees for 10 minutes. Cool on wire racks.
YIELD: 2 DOZEN.

Virginia Killian
Gadsden Life

P-Nutty Bars

1 (2-layer) yellow cake mix
½ cup (1 stick) butter, softened
1 egg
20 miniature peanut butter cups, chopped
2 tablespoons cornstarch
1 (12-ounce) jar caramel topping
½ cup peanut butter
½ cup roasted peanuts, finely chopped
1 (16-ounce) can milk chocolate frosting

Mix the cake mix, butter and egg in a bowl until moistened. Stir in the peanut butter cups. Press the mixture into a greased 9x13-inch baking pan. Bake at 350 degrees for 20 minutes or until light brown. Mix the next 3 ingredients in a saucepan until smooth. Bring to a boil, stirring constantly. Cook for 2 to 3 minutes, stirring constantly. Remove from the heat. Stir in the peanuts. Spread over the baked layer. Bake for 10 minutes. Cool. Spread the frosting over the top. Chill, covered, in the refrigerator for 2 hours. YIELD: 3 DOZEN.

Mamie Parmer
Mobile Council

Peanut Butter-Chocolate Chunk Cookies

½ cup (1 stick) butter
¾ cup creamy peanut butter
½ cup sugar
½ cup packed brown sugar
1 egg
½ teaspoon vanilla extract
1 cup flour
¾ teaspoon baking soda
1 cup semisweet chocolate chunks

Cream the first 4 ingredients in a mixing bowl until light and fluffy. Stir in the egg and vanilla. Sift the flour and baking soda together. Stir into the creamed mixture. Fold in the chocolate chunks. Drop by spoonfuls onto nonstick cookie sheets. Bake at 350 degrees for 18 to 20 minutes or until brown. Cool on wire racks. YIELD: 1½ DOZEN.

James B. Johnson Jr.
Tuscaloosa Council

Chloe Scott's Peanut Butter Cookies

1 cup shortening
1 cup sugar
1 cup packed brown sugar
2 eggs
1 cup creamy or chunky peanut butter

3 cups flour
1 teaspoon salt
1 teaspoon baking powder
1 teaspoon baking soda
1 teaspoon vanilla extract
1 tablespoon cold water

Cream the first 4 ingredients in a mixing bowl until light and fluffy. Blend in the peanut butter. Sift the next 4 ingredients together. Stir into the creamed mixture. Beat in the vanilla and water. Shape by teaspoonfuls into balls. Place on nonstick cookie sheets. Press balls in a crisscross pattern with a fork. Bake at 350 degrees until golden brown. Cool on wire racks. YIELD: 3 DOZEN.

Imogene Davis
Birmingham Life

Pineapple Bars

2 cups sugar
1/2 cup (1 stick) margarine, melted
4 eggs
1 1/2 cups flour
1/2 teaspoon baking soda

1/2 teaspoon salt
1 (20-ounce) can crushed pineapple, drained
1 cup chopped nuts (optional)
Confectioners' sugar to taste

Beat the sugar and margarine in a mixing bowl until well combined. Beat in the eggs 1 at a time. Sift the flour, baking soda and salt together. Add to the sugar mixture alternately with the pineapple, beating well after each addition. Fold in the nuts. Pour into a greased 10×14-inch baking pan. Bake at 350 degrees for 35 to 40 minutes or until brown. Sprinkle with confectioners' sugar. Let stand until cool. Cut into bars. YIELD: 3 DOZEN.

Edna Vines
Decatur Council

Lemon-White Chocolate-Pistachio Cookies

2 1/4 cups flour
1 teaspoon baking soda
3/4 teaspoon salt
1 cup (2 sticks) butter, softened
1 1/2 cups packed brown sugar
2 eggs
1 teaspoon vanilla extract
1 tablespoon grated lemon zest
1 cup white chocolate chips
1 cup chopped unsalted pistachios

Mix the flour, baking soda and salt in a large bowl. Cream the butter and brown sugar in a mixing bowl until light and fluffy. Add the eggs, vanilla and lemon zest and mix well. Add the flour mixture, beating at low speed until well blended. Stir in the chocolate chips and pistachios. Drop by spoonfuls 2 inches apart onto ungreased cookie sheets. Bake at 350 degrees for 10 to 15 minutes or until brown. Cool on wire racks. YIELD: 4 TO 5 DOZEN.

Frankie Vaughn
Selma Life

Potato Chip Cookies

1 cup (2 sticks) margarine, softened
3/4 cup sugar
2 cups flour
1 teaspoon vanilla extract
3/4 cup chopped pecans
1 cup crushed potato chips

Cream the margarine and sugar in a mixing bowl until light and fluffy. Add the flour, vanilla and pecans and mix well. Fold in the potato chips. Drop by teaspoonfuls onto ungreased cookie sheets. Bake at 325 degrees for 12 to 15 minutes or until light brown. Cool on wire racks. YIELD: ABOUT 4 DOZEN.

Cheryl Crosson
Anniston Council

Potato Chip Cookies

1 cup sugar
2 cups (4 sticks) butter, softened
2 teaspoons vanilla extract
3 cups flour
1 cup chopped pecans
1½ cups crushed potato chips

Cream the sugar and butter in a mixing bowl until light and fluffy. Add the vanilla and flour gradually, beating well after each addition. Stir in the pecans. Fold in the potato chips. Drop by teaspoonfuls onto ungreased cookie sheets. Bake at 350 degrees for 10 to 12 minutes or until light brown. Cool on wire racks.
YIELD: 4 TO 4½ DOZEN.

Virginia Greene
Birmingham South Life

Powder Puff Cookies

1 cup sugar
1 egg
½ teaspoon baking soda
1 cup shortening
1 teaspoon vanilla extract
1 cup chopped pecans
2 cups sifted flour
1 teaspoon cream of tartar

Beat the sugar and egg in a mixing bowl until light. Add the baking soda, shortening, vanilla and pecans and mix well. Sift the flour and cream of tartar together. Add to the creamed mixture and mix well. Roll and knead the dough. Shape into 1-inch balls. Place on ungreased cookie sheets. Flatten each ball with a fork dipped in water. Bake at 350 degrees for 5 to 7 minutes or until brown. Cool on wire racks. YIELD: ABOUT 3 DOZEN.

Marie Hartley
Birmingham South Life

Pumpkin Cookies

1 cup shortening
1 cup sugar
1 egg
1 cup solid-pack pumpkin
2 cups flour
1 teaspoon cinnamon
1 teaspoon baking soda
1/2 teaspoon salt
1 cup raisins
Caramel Icing (below)

Cream the shortening and sugar in a mixing bowl until light and fluffy. Add the egg and pumpkin and mix well. Combine the flour, cinnamon, baking soda and salt in a bowl and mix well. Add to the creamed mixture and mix well. Stir in the raisins. Drop by teaspoonfuls onto nonstick cookie sheets. Bake at 315 degrees for 12 to 15 minutes or until brown. Cool on cookie sheets for several minutes. Remove to wire racks to cool completely. Frost with Caramel Icing. YIELD: 3 DOZEN.

Caramel Icing

3 tablespoons butter
1/4 cup milk
1/2 cup packed brown sugar
1 cup confectioners' sugar
1 teaspoon vanilla extract

Heat the butter, milk and brown sugar in a saucepan, stirring until the sugar is dissolved. Remove from the heat. Add the confectioners' sugar and vanilla and mix well. Let stand until cool. YIELD: 1 1/2 CUPS.

Ila M. Skidmore
Shoals Life

Crispy Ice Box Cookies

2 eggs, lightly beaten
1 cup (2 sticks) butter, melted
1 (1-pound) package dark brown sugar
4 cups sifted flour
1 teaspoon (scant) baking soda
1 teaspoon vanilla extract
1 cup pecan halves

Mix the eggs, butter and brown sugar in a mixing bowl. Add the flour gradually, beating well after each addition. Stir in the baking soda and vanilla. The mixture will be very firm. Add the pecans and mix well. Shape the dough into a roll. Chill, covered with foil or waxed paper, in the refrigerator. Cut the roll into thin slices using a sharp knife. Place on nonstick cookie sheets. Bake at 350 degrees for 20 minutes or until edges are brown. Cool on wire racks. Store in an airtight container. YIELD: 2 TO 2½ DOZEN.

Elsie Barton
Birmingham South Life

Refrigerator Cookies

½ cup shortening
½ cup packed brown sugar
¾ cup sugar
1 egg
1 teaspoon vanilla extract
½ cup chopped nuts
2 cups flour
½ teaspoon salt
2 teaspoons baking powder

Cream the shortening, brown sugar and sugar in a mixing bowl until light and fluffy. Beat in the egg. Stir in the vanilla and nuts. Add the flour, salt and baking powder and mix well. Divide the dough into 2 equal portions. Shape each portion into a 1½-inch diameter roll. Roll in waxed paper. Chill, covered, in the refrigerator for several hours or overnight. Cut each roll into thin slices. Place on nonstick cookie sheets. Bake at 350 degrees for 7 to 10 minutes or until brown. Cool on wire racks. YIELD: 2 DOZEN.

Sue Small
Selma Life

Lois' Snickerdoodles

1 cup shortening
1½ cups sugar
2 eggs
2¾ cups flour
2 teaspoons cream of tartar

1 teaspoon baking soda
½ teaspoon salt
2 tablespoons sugar
2 teaspoons cinnamon

Cream the shortening and 1½ cups sugar in a mixing bowl until light and fluffy. Beat in the eggs. Sift the next 4 ingredients together. Beat into the creamed mixture gradually. Chill the dough, covered, in the refrigerator for 2 hours or more. Shape into 1-inch balls. Roll each ball in a mixture of 2 tablespoons sugar and cinnamon. Place on nonstick cookie sheets. Bake at 400 degrees for 10 minutes or until light brown. Cool on wire racks. **YIELD: 4 DOZEN.**

Cheryl Crosson
Anniston Council

Chloe Scott's Old-Fashioned Sugar Cookies

3½ cups flour
2½ teaspoons baking powder
½ teaspoon salt
1½ cups sugar

1 cup (2 sticks) butter or
   margarine, softened
2 eggs
1 tablespoon vanilla extract

Sift the flour, baking powder and salt together. Cream the sugar, butter, eggs and vanilla in a mixing bowl until light and fluffy. Add the flour mixture to the creamed mixture gradually, beating well after each addition. Roll the dough into 1-inch balls. Place the balls 2 inches apart on lightly greased cookie sheets. Press carefully with the bottom of a glass greased with butter and dipped in sugar to ⅛-inch thickness. Bake at 400 degrees for 10 to 12 minutes or until edges are light brown. Cool on wire racks. **YIELD: ABOUT 4 DOZEN.**

Imogene Davis
Birmingham Life

Gladys P.'s Old-Fashioned Sugar Cookies

1/2 cup (1 stick) margarine
1/2 cup vegetable oil
1/2 cup sugar
1/2 cup confectioners' sugar
1 teaspoon vanilla extract
1 egg
2 cups flour
1/2 teaspoon cream of tartar
1/2 teaspoon baking soda
1/2 teaspoon salt

Cream the first 5 ingredients in a mixing bowl until light and fluffy. Beat in the egg. Combine the flour, cream of tartar, baking soda and salt in a bowl and mix well. Add to the creamed mixture gradually, beating well after each addition. Chill, covered, in the refrigerator overnight. Shape the dough into small balls. Roll in sugar. Place on ungreased cookie sheets. Flatten with a fork dipped in sugar. Bake at 350 degrees for 10 to 12 minutes or until light brown. Cool on wire racks. YIELD: 2 DOZEN.

Imogene Davis
Birmingham Life

Tea Cakes

1 cup sugar
1 cup shortening
2 eggs, beaten
2 teaspoons lemon or orange extract
1/4 cup milk
3 cups flour
1 cup cornmeal
2/3 teaspoon salt
1/2 teaspoon baking soda

Cream the sugar and shortening in a mixing bowl until light and fluffy. Add the eggs, flavoring and milk and mix well. Sift the flour, cornmeal, salt and baking soda together. Add gradually to the creamed mixture, beating well after each addition. Roll the dough 1/8 inch thick on a lightly floured surface. Cut with a cookie cutter. Place on greased cookie sheets. Bake at 375 degrees for 11 minutes. Cool on wire racks. YIELD: 4 DOZEN.

Dorothy Kimbrough
Decatur Council

Aunt Cora's Tea Cakes

2 eggs
1 cup sugar
1/4 cup milk
3 cups self-rising flour

1/2 cup (1 stick) butter, softened
1 teaspoon vanilla extract

Beat the eggs in a mixing bowl. Add the sugar and milk and mix well. Add the flour, butter and vanilla and mix well. Shape into balls. Place on nonstick cookie sheets. Press each ball with a fork dipped in sugar. Bake at 350 degrees for 15 minutes. Cool on wire racks. YIELD: 3 DOZEN.

Sheila P. Brothers
Anniston Council

MeMe's Teacakes

1 cup (2 sticks) butter, softened
1 1/2 cups sugar
2 eggs
3 tablespoons buttermilk

1 teaspoon vanilla extract
3 cups flour
1/2 teaspoon salt
1 teaspoon baking soda

Cream the butter and sugar in a mixing bowl until light and fluffy. Beat in the eggs. Stir in the buttermilk and vanilla. Combine the flour, salt and baking soda in a bowl and mix well. Add to the creamed mixture gradually, beating well after each addition. Divide the dough into 3 equal portions. Chill each portion, covered, in the refrigerator for 1 hour. Roll each portion 1/8 inch thick on a floured surface. Cut with a cookie cutter. Place on ungreased cookie sheets. Bake at 350 degrees for 8 minutes or until light brown. Cool on the cookie sheets for several minutes. Remove to wire racks to cool completely. YIELD: 4 DOZEN.

Virginia Greene
Birmingham South Life

Old-Fashioned Tea Cakes

1 cup shortening
1 cup sugar
1 egg, beaten
2 tablespoons buttermilk

2½ cups (or more) flour
¼ teaspoon salt
2 teaspoons baking powder
1 teaspoon vanilla extract

Beat the shortening in a mixing bowl at low speed. Add the sugar, egg and buttermilk and mix well. Sift the flour, salt and baking powder together. Add to the sugar mixture and mix well. Add the vanilla and mix well. Roll dough ¼ inch thick on a floured surface. Cut with a cookie cutter. Place on nonstick cookie sheets. Bake at 350 degrees for 8 minutes. Cool on wire racks. YIELD: 3 DOZEN.

Hazel E. Campbell
Birmingham Life

Pattie's Tea Cakes

2¼ cups sifted flour
¼ teaspoon salt
2 teaspoons baking powder
½ cup shortening

1 cup sugar
2 eggs, beaten
½ teaspoon vanilla extract
1 tablespoon milk

Sift the flour, salt and baking powder together. Cream the shortening and sugar in a mixing bowl until light and fluffy. Add the eggs and vanilla and mix well. Add the flour mixture and milk and mix well. Chill the dough, covered, in the refrigerator for 2 to 3 hours. Roll dough on a floured surface. Cut with a cookie cutter. Place on nonstick cookie sheets. Sprinkle with sugar. Bake at 375 degrees for 12 minutes. YIELD: 2 DOZEN.

Pattie Smith
Gadsden Life

PHYSICALLY AND MENTALLY CHALLENGED

Our chapter gives support to four main charities. They are Alabama Institute for Deaf and Blind (AIDB), Alabama's Special Camp for Children and Adults (Camp ASCCA), Camp Smile-A-Mile, and Camp Blue Bird. The Pioneers are always there to help answer the call of need to physically and mentally challenged people over the state of Alabama.

Pies

Apple Pie

2 York apples, sliced
1/2 cup sugar
1/4 teaspoon allspice
1/4 teaspoon nutmeg
1/2 cup (1 stick) butter, softened
1 cup packed brown sugar
1 cup flour

Arrange the apple slices in a buttered pie plate. Sprinkle with the sugar, allspice and nutmeg. Cream the butter in a mixer bowl until light and fluffy. Add the brown sugar and flour and mix well. Spread over the apple slices. Bake at 350 degrees for 30 minutes.
YIELD: 6 TO 8 SERVINGS.

Elba Skinner, Selma Life

Sugarless Apple Pie

1 (2-crust) pie pastry
6 apples, peeled, sliced
Lemon juice
1 (6-ounce) can frozen apple juice concentrate, thawed
2 tablespoons cornstarch
1 tablespoon margarine
1 teaspoon cinnamon, or 1/2 teaspoon cinnamon and 1/2 teaspoon nutmeg

Fit 1 pie pastry into a 10-inch pie plate. Sprinkle the apple slices with a small amount of lemon juice to prevent discoloration. Combine the apple juice concentrate and cornstarch in a saucepan. Bring to a boil, stirring constantly. Add the margarine and cinnamon and mix well. Stir in the apple slices. Pour into the pastry-lined pie plate. Cover with the remaining pastry, sealing the edge and cutting vents. Bake at 425 degrees for 30 minutes. Reduce the oven temperature to 375 degrees. Bake for 30 minutes longer.
YIELD: 6 TO 8 SERVINGS.

Eloise Bennett
Decatur Council

Dried Apple Custard

1 1/2 cups dried apples
Sugar to taste
4 eggs, lightly beaten
1/2 cup sorghum
1/2 cup milk
1/4 teaspoon vanilla extract
1/2 teaspoon apple pie spice
1 unbaked (9-inch) pie shell

Combine the dried apples and sugar in a saucepan and mix well. Cook until the mixture is heated through, stirring occasionally. Add the eggs, sorghum, milk, vanilla and apple pie spice and mix well. Pour into the pie shell. Bake at 300 degrees for 25 to 30 minutes or until the apples are tender. YIELD: **6 TO 8 SERVINGS**.

Louise Morrison
Tuscaloosa Council

Blueberry Pies

8 ounces cream cheese, softened
1/2 cup sugar
1 tablespoon lemon juice
16 ounces whipped topping
1 (2-crust) pie pastry
Bananas
1 (21-ounce) can blueberry pie filling, chilled

Combine the cream cheese, sugar, lemon juice and whipped topping in a bowl and mix well. Chill thoroughly in the refrigerator. Fit 1 pie pastry into each of 2 pie plates. Bake at 350 degrees until light brown. Let stand until cool. Arrange banana slices in each of the pastry-lined pie plates. Top each with half the cream cheese mixture. Chill until serving time. Spoon half the pie filling over each pie before serving. YIELD: **12 TO 16 SERVINGS**.

Marsha Harbarger
Riverchase Council

Blueberry Peach Pie

1 (2-crust) pie pastry
3 cups sliced fresh peaches
2 cups fresh blueberries
1 cup sugar
3 tablespoons cornstarch
1 teaspoon lemon juice
1/2 teaspoon cinnamon
2 to 3 tablespoons butter

Fit 1 pastry into a pie plate. Combine the peach slices, blueberries, sugar, cornstarch, lemon juice and cinnamon in a bowl and mix well. Pour into the pastry-lined pie plate. Dot with butter. Top with the remaining pie pastry, sealing the edge and cutting vents. Bake at 425 degrees for 15 minutes. Reduce the oven temperature to 350 degrees. Bake for 40 minutes. **YIELD: 8 SERVINGS.**

Gloria "Carol" Lindley
Birmingham South Cahaba Council

Jessie Isbell's Cantaloupe Cream Pie

1 cup sugar
2 tablespoons flour
3 eggs, beaten
1 cup puréed cantaloupe
1 teaspoon vanilla extract
2 tablespoons butter
1 baked (8-inch) pie shell
1 cup whipped cream or
  whipped topping

Combine the sugar and flour in a saucepan. Beat in the eggs 1 at a time. Stir in the cantaloupe purée. Cook over medium heat for 8 to 10 minutes or until the mixture boils and thickens, stirring constantly. Remove from the heat. Stir in the vanilla. Add the butter. Let stand until cool. Pour into the pie shell. Spread evenly with whipped cream. Chill until serving time. **YIELD: 6 TO 8 SERVINGS.**

Imogene Davis
Birmingham Life

Cream Cheese Brownie Pie

1 refrigerator pie pastry
8 ounces cream cheese, softened
3 tablespoons sugar
1 teaspoon vanilla extract
1 egg, lightly beaten
1 (15-ounce) package Thick 'n' Fudgy Hot Fudge Swirl Deluxe Brownie Mix
1/4 cup vegetable oil
1 tablespoon water
2 eggs, lightly beaten
1/2 cup chopped pecans
1 tablespoon water

Unfold the pastry into a pie plate. Remove the plastic wrap. Fit the pastry into the pie plate and trim the edge. Combine the cream cheese, sugar, vanilla and 1 egg in a mixing bowl and beat until smooth; set aside. Set aside the hot fudge packet from the brownie mix. Combine the brownie mix, vegetable oil, 1 tablespoon water and 2 eggs in a large bowl. Beat 50 strokes with a spoon. Spread 1/2 cup of the mixture in the pastry-lined pie plate. Top with the cream cheese mixture, spreading gently. Spread the remaining brownie mixture over the top. Sprinkle with the pecans. Bake at 350 degrees for 40 to 50 minutes or until the center is puffed and the crust is golden brown. Place the hot fudge from the packet in a small microwave-safe bowl. Microwave on High for 30 seconds. Stir in 1 tablespoon water. Drizzle the fudge over the pie. Let stand for 3 hours or until cooled completely. Chill until serving time.

YIELD: 6 TO 8 SERVINGS.

Narice Sutton
Birmingham Life

Caramel Pie

2 cups packed brown sugar
1 cup water
2 drops of maple extract
2 eggs, beaten
1/4 teaspoon salt
1/2 teaspoon baking soda
1 unbaked (9-inch) pie shell
Whipped cream
1/2 cup nut halves

Combine the brown sugar and water in a saucepan. Boil for 5 minutes. Let stand until cool. Add the maple extract, eggs, salt and baking soda and mix well. Pour into the pie shell. Bake at 350 degrees until a knife inserted near the center comes out clean. Top with unsweetened whipped cream and nut halves. YIELD: 6 TO 8 SERVINGS.

Francis M. Tucker
Selma Life

Coconut Caramel Pies

1 (7-ounce) package flaked coconut
1 cup chopped pecans
6 tablespoons (3/4 stick) margarine
8 ounces cream cheese, softened
1 (14-ounce) can sweetened condensed milk
16 ounces whipped topping
2 deep-dish graham cracker pie shells
1 (12-ounce) jar caramel ice cream topping

Cook the coconut and pecans in the margarine in a skillet until light brown, stirring constantly; drain well. Beat the cream cheese and condensed milk in a mixing bowl until blended and smooth. Fold in the whipped topping. Pour 1/4 of the cream cheese mixture into each pie shell. Top each with 1/4 of the coconut mixture. Drizzle each with 1/4 of the caramel topping. Repeat the layers. Freeze until firm. Serve frozen. YIELD: 12 TO 16 SERVINGS.

Patsy Frost
Decatur Council

Classic Chess Pie

1 (1-crust) pie pastry
2 cups sugar
2 tablespoons cornmeal
2 tablespoons flour
1/4 teaspoon salt
1/2 cup (1 stick) butter, melted
1/4 cup milk
1 tablespoon white vinegar
1/2 teaspoon vanilla extract
4 eggs, lightly beaten

Fit the pie pastry into a pie plate. Line with foil and fill with pie weights. Bake at 425 degrees for 4 to 5 minutes or until very light brown. Remove the pie weights and foil. Bake for 2 minutes longer. Combine the remaining ingredients in a bowl and mix well. Pour into the pie shell. Bake at 350 degrees for 50 to 55 minutes or until a knife inserted near the center comes out clean. **YIELD: 6 TO 8 SERVINGS.**

Faith Kirby Richardson
Gadsden Life

Black Skillet Chocolate Pies

3 cups sugar
6 tablespoons baking cocoa
6 tablespoons flour
1/8 teaspoon salt
3 cups milk
6 egg yolks, lightly beaten
3/4 cup (1 1/2 sticks) margarine
3 tablespoons vanilla extract
2 baked (9-inch) pie shells
6 egg whites
3/4 cup sugar

Combine 3 cups sugar, baking cocoa, flour and salt in a cast-iron skillet. Add the milk, egg yolks, margarine and vanilla and mix well. Cook until thickened, stirring constantly. Pour half the filling into each pie shell. Beat the egg whites in a mixing bowl until soft peaks form. Add 3/4 cup sugar gradually, beating constantly until stiff peaks form. Spoon half the egg whites onto each pie, sealing to the edge. Bake at 350 degrees for 12 to 15 minutes or until the meringue is brown. **YIELD: 12 TO 16 SERVINGS.**

Dorothy Kimbrough
Decatur Council

Chocolate Pie

1 cup sugar
1/8 teaspoon salt
1/4 cup cornstarch
5 tablespoons baking cocoa
4 egg yolks, lightly beaten
2 cups milk
1/4 cup (1/2 stick) margarine
1 baked (9-inch) pie shell
4 egg whites
1/4 teaspoon cream of tartar
1/3 cup sugar

Combine 1 cup sugar, salt, cornstarch, baking cocoa, egg yolks, milk and margarine in a double boiler. Cook until thickened, stirring constantly. Pour into the pie shell. Beat the egg whites with the cream of tartar in a mixing bowl until soft peaks form. Add 1/3 cup sugar gradually, beating constantly until stiff peaks form. Spoon over the pie filling, sealing to the edge. Bake at 350 degrees or broil until the meringue is light golden brown. **YIELD: 6 TO 8 SERVINGS.**

Kathryn Morgan
Gadsden Life

HELPFUL HINT

Use sugar cookie or gingersnap crumbs for crumb pie shells.

Chocolate Pies

2 cups sugar
3 tablespoons self-rising flour
3 tablespoons (heaping) baking cocoa
4 egg yolks, lightly beaten
2²/₃ cups milk
1 teaspoon vanilla extract
3 tablespoons butter
2 baked (9-inch) pie shells
4 egg whites
⅛ teaspoon cream of tartar
1 tablespoon sugar

Combine 2 cups sugar, flour and baking cocoa in a saucepan. Add the egg yolks, milk and vanilla and mix well. Cook over medium heat until heated through, stirring frequently. Add the butter. Cook until thickened, stirring constantly. Fill each pie shell. Beat the egg whites with the cream of tartar in a mixing bowl until soft peaks form. Add 1 tablespoon sugar, beating constantly until stiff peaks form. Spoon half the meringue onto each pie, sealing to the edge. Broil until the meringue is light brown. YIELD: **12 TO 16 SERVINGS**.

Mary Haynes
Birmingham South Cahaba Council

HELPFUL HINT

Pies with cream or custard fillings should be cooled to room temperature and then stored in the refrigerator.

Chocolate Pies

1/4 cup baking cocoa
1/2 cup flour
2 cups sugar
1 (12-ounce) can evaporated milk
6 egg yolks, lightly beaten
2 tablespoons butter
2 teaspoons vanilla extract
2 baked (9-inch) pie shells
6 egg whites, stiffly beaten

Mix the baking cocoa, flour and sugar in a saucepan. Stir in the evaporated milk. Fill the milk can with water. Stir into the cocoa mixture gradually. Add the egg yolks. Cook over medium heat until thickened, stirring constantly. Add the butter and vanilla, stirring until the butter melts. Pour half the filling into each pie shell. Spoon half the egg whites onto each pie, sealing to the edge. Bake at 350 degrees until the meringue is light golden brown.
YIELD: 12 TO 16 SERVINGS.

Sandra Sprinkle
Anniston Council

German Chocolate Pie

1 bar German's sweet chocolate
1/4 cup (1/2 stick) margarine
4 eggs, lightly beaten
1 (12-ounce) can evaporated milk
1 cup sugar
1 teaspoon vanilla extract
1 cup finely chopped coconut
1/2 cup chopped nuts
1 unbaked (10-inch) pie shell

Combine the chocolate and margarine in a large microwave-safe bowl. Microwave on Low for 3 minutes or until melted. Add the eggs, evaporated milk, sugar and vanilla and mix well. Stir in the coconut and nuts. Pour into the pie shell. Bake at 350 degrees for 1 hour or until set. YIELD: 6 TO 8 SERVINGS.

Kathryn Morgan
Gadsden Life

Hershey Bar Pie

1 (7-ounce) Hershey's chocolate bar with almonds
12 ounces whipped topping
1 baked (9-inch) pie shell

Grate the candy bar, grating around the almonds and leaving the almonds intact. Reserve 1 tablespoon of the grated chocolate. Combine the remaining grated chocolate, 3/4 of the whipped topping and the almonds in a bowl and mix well. Pour into the pie shell. Spread the remaining whipped topping over the top. Sprinkle with the reserved grated chocolate. Chill until serving time.
YIELD: 6 TO 8 SERVINGS.

Mary Alice Neal
Birmingham Life

Microwave Chocolate Pie

2 cups quick-cooking oats
1/3 cup packed brown sugar
1/3 cup butter, softened
1 cup sugar
3 tablespoons baking cocoa
3 tablespoons flour
1 (12-ounce) can evaporated milk
3 egg yolks, lightly beaten
3 tablespoons butter
1 teaspoon vanilla extract

Combine the oats, brown sugar and 1/3 cup butter in a bowl and mix well. Press onto the bottom and up the side of a 9-inch pie plate. Place an 8-inch pie plate directly on top of the crumb mixture and press down. Microwave on High for 2 to 3 minutes. Let cool. Combine the sugar, baking cocoa, flour and evaporated milk in a microwave-safe bowl and mix well. Microwave on High for 1 1/2 minutes. Stir in the egg yolks. Microwave on High for 3 to 6 minutes or until thickened. Stir in 3 tablespoons butter and vanilla. Pour into the cooled crust. Chill until serving time. Serve with whipped cream. YIELD: 6 TO 8 SERVINGS.

Frankie Vaughn
Selma Life

Chocolate Mousse Pie

1 tablespoon instant coffee granules
1/4 cup boiling water
8 ounces semisweet chocolate, cut into pieces
8 egg yolks
2/3 cup sugar
1 teaspoon vanilla extract
8 egg whites
1/2 teaspoon salt
1 1/2 cups whipping cream
1 1/2 teaspoons vanilla extract
1/2 cup confectioners' sugar

Generously butter a 9-inch pie plate; sprinkle with fine dry unseasoned bread crumbs. Dissolve the coffee granules in the boiling water in a cup. Combine the chocolate with the coffee mixture in a double boiler. Cook over low heat until the chocolate is melted, stirring occasionally. Beat the egg yolks in a bowl until thick. Add the sugar gradually, beating until the mixture is thick and pale yellow. Beat in the chocolate mixture gradually. Add 1 teaspoon vanilla. Beat the egg whites with the salt in a mixing bowl until stiff but not dry. Stir 1/4 of the egg whites into the chocolate mixture. Fold the chocolate mixture into the remaining egg whites. Fill the pie plate with enough of the chocolate mixture to be level with the edge of the pie plate. Place the remaining chocolate mixture in the refrigerator. Bake the pie at 350 degrees for 25 minutes. Turn off the oven. Let the pie stand in the closed oven for 5 minutes. Remove the pie from the oven and let stand for 2 hours. The cooked mousse will sink as the pie cools. When completely cool, press the mousse into the shape of a pie shell. Fill with the remaining mousse, mounding it like a pie filling. Chill for 2 to 3 hours. Beat the whipping cream, 1 1/2 teaspoons vanilla and confectioners' sugar in a mixing bowl until stiff peaks form. Spread over the pie or spoon into a pastry tube fitted with a star tip. Pipe onto the pie in a lattice pattern. Chill until serving time. YIELD: 6 TO 8 SERVINGS.

Judy Brantley
Gadsden Life

Old-Fashioned Chocolate Pie

¼ cup self-rising flour
1 cup sugar
½ cup baking cocoa, sifted
3 egg yolks, lightly beaten
2 cups milk
2 tablespoons butter
1 teaspoon vanilla extract
⅛ teaspoon salt

1 baked (9-inch) pie shell
¼ cup sugar
1 tablespoon cornstarch
3 egg whites, at room temperature
⅛ teaspoon salt
½ teaspoon cream of tartar

Sift the self-rising flour, 1 cup sugar and baking cocoa into a bowl and mix well. Stir in the egg yolks and milk. Pour into a double boiler. Cook until thickened, stirring frequently. Add the butter, vanilla and ⅛ teaspoon salt. Pour into the baked pie shell. Mix ¼ cup sugar with the cornstarch in a small bowl. Beat the egg whites, ⅛ teaspoon salt and cream of tartar in a mixing bowl until foamy. Add the cornstarch mixture gradually, beating constantly until stiff peaks form. Spread over the pie filling, sealing to the edge. Bake at 350 degrees for 15 minutes. YIELD: 8 SERVINGS.

Mrs. Virginia Greene
Birmingham South Life

Coconut Pie

4 eggs, beaten
½ cup self-rising flour
1⅓ cups sugar
¼ cup (½ stick) butter, melted

2 cups milk
1 teaspoon vanilla extract
1⅓ cups flaked coconut

Combine the eggs, self-rising flour, sugar, butter, milk, vanilla and coconut in a bowl and mix well. Pour into a pie plate. Bake at 325 degrees for 30 minutes or until golden brown. YIELD: 8 SERVINGS.

Jane B. Weatherly
Mobile Council

West Gadsden Cafe Coconut Pie

2/3 cup sugar
1/4 cup cornstarch
4 egg yolks, beaten
2 1/4 cups milk
1/4 cup (1/2 stick) butter
1 teaspoon vanilla extract
1 cup flaked coconut
1 baked (10-inch) pie shell

Combine the sugar and cornstarch in a large bowl and mix well. Add the egg yolks, milk, butter and vanilla and mix well. Pour into a double boiler. Cook until thickened, stirring frequently. Stir in the coconut. Pour into the pie shell. YIELD: 6 TO 8 SERVINGS.

Kathryn Morgan
Gadsden Life

Darn Good Pies

1 can flaked coconut
1 1/2 cups chopped pecans
1/2 cup (1 stick) margarine, melted
8 ounces cream cheese, softened
1 1/2 cups confectioners' sugar
12 ounces whipped topping
2 graham cracker pie shells
1 jar caramel ice cream topping

Mix the coconut and pecans together in a bowl. Spread in a shallow baking pan. Pour the melted margarine over the mixture. Bake at 350 degrees until toasted, stirring occasionally. Let cool. Beat the cream cheese and confectioners' sugar in a mixing bowl until blended and smooth. Fold in the whipped topping. Pour half the filling into each pie shell. Sprinkle each pie with half the toasted coconut mixture. Microwave the caramel topping until warm. Pour half the topping over each pie. Chill or freeze until serving time. YIELD: 6 TO 8 SERVINGS.

Shirley H. Crocker
Birmingham Life

Dreamsicle Pie

8 ounces cream cheese, softened
1 cup orange juice
1 (4-ounce) package vanilla instant pudding mix
1 (4-ounce) package orange gelatin
12 ounces whipped topping
1 (9-inch) graham cracker pie shell

Beat the cream cheese at high speed in a mixing bowl until smooth. Beat in the orange juice, pudding mix and gelatin. Fold in half the whipped topping. Pour into the pie shell. Top with the remaining whipped topping. Garnish with fresh orange slices. Chill for 3 hours. **YIELD: 6 TO 8 SERVINGS.**

Chris Elsen
Gadsden Life

Delight Pies

1 cup (2 sticks) margarine, softened
2 cups sugar
4 egg yolks
1 cup each flaked coconut, raisins and chopped nuts
1 teaspoon vanilla extract
1/8 teaspoon salt
4 egg whites, stiffly beaten
2 unbaked (9-inch) pie shells

Cream the margarine and sugar in a mixing bowl until light and fluffy. Beat in the egg yolks 1 at a time. Stir in the coconut, raisins, nuts, vanilla and salt. Fold in the egg whites. Pour half the filling into each pie shell. Bake at 325 degrees for 50 minutes. These pies freeze well. **YIELD: 12 TO 16 SERVINGS.**

Sandy Hudgins
Anniston Council

West Gadsden Cafe Egg Pie

5 eggs
2/3 cup sugar
1/8 teaspoon salt
1 teaspoon vanilla extract
7 tablespoons melted butter
2 cups milk
1 unbaked (9-inch) pie shell

Combine the eggs, sugar, salt and vanilla in a mixing bowl and beat well. Stir in the butter. Add the milk and mix well. Pour into the pie shell. Bake at 400 degrees for 30 minutes. **YIELD: 6 TO 8 SERVINGS.**

Kathryn Morgan
Gadsden Life

Egg Custard

1/4 cup (1/2 stick) butter or margarine, softened
2/3 cup sugar
2 eggs
3 tablespoons flour
3/4 cup evaporated milk
1/4 cup water
1 teaspoon vanilla extract
1 unbaked (9-inch) pie shell

Beat the butter in a mixing bowl until smooth and creamy. Add the sugar gradually, beating constantly until light and fluffy. Beat in the eggs 1 at a time. Add the flour and mix well. Stir in the evaporated milk, water and vanilla. Pour into the pie shell. Bake at 400 degrees for 20 minutes. Reduce the oven temperature to 300 degrees. Bake for 15 minutes. Let stand until cool. Chill thoroughly before serving. **YIELD: 6 TO 8 SERVINGS.**

Patricia V. Allen
Selma Life

Egg Custard

2 tablespoons cornstarch
¾ cup plus 2 tablespoons (about) sugar
2 cups milk
2 tablespoons butter
4 eggs
1 teaspoon vanilla extract
¼ teaspoon nutmeg
1 unbaked (9-inch) pie shell

Place the cornstarch in a 1-cup measure. Add enough sugar to measure 1 cup. Heat the milk and butter in a saucepan until the butter is melted; do not boil. Beat the eggs in a mixing bowl. Add the sugar mixture and mix well. Add the vanilla and nutmeg. Stir in the warm milk. Pour into the pie shell. Bake at 325 degrees for 35 minutes. Turn off the oven. Let the pie stand in the closed oven until the filling is set. YIELD: **6 TO 8 SERVINGS**.

Sandy Hudgins
Anniston Council

Mama's Egg Custard

3 eggs
2 cups milk
1 cup sugar
1 unbaked (9-inch) pie shell

Beat the eggs in a mixing bowl. Add the milk and sugar and beat well. Pour into the pie shell. Bake at 300 degrees until set. You may top with a meringue. YIELD: **6 TO 8 SERVINGS**.

Judy Burrow
Decatur Council

Old-Fashioned Egg Custard

6 eggs
1 cup plus 2 tablespoons sugar
1/8 teaspoon salt
3 cups milk
3 tablespoons margarine
2 1/4 teaspoons vanilla extract
2 unbaked (9-inch) pie shells
Nutmeg to taste

Combine the eggs, sugar and salt in a mixing bowl and beat well. Combine the milk and margarine in a saucepan. Cook over medium heat until the butter is melted, stirring frequently. Stir the vanilla into the egg mixture. Add the milk mixture and blend well. Pour into the pie shells. Sprinkle with nutmeg. Bake at 400 degrees for 10 minutes. Reduce the oven temperature to 300 degrees. Bake for 25 minutes or until the crust is brown. YIELD: 12 TO 16 SERVINGS.

Margaret W. Wilborn
Gadsden Life

Old-Fashioned Egg Custard Pie

3 eggs, beaten
3/4 cup sugar
1/4 teaspoon salt
1 teaspoon vanilla extract
1 tablespoon flour
1/2 teaspoon nutmeg
1 1/2 cups scalded milk
1 unbaked (9-inch) pie shell
Nutmeg to taste

Combine the eggs and sugar in a mixing bowl and beat well. Add the salt, vanilla, flour and 1/2 teaspoon nutmeg and mix well. Add the milk gradually, stirring constantly. Pour into the pie shell. Sprinkle with nutmeg. Bake at 400 degrees for 10 minutes. Reduce the oven temperature to 325 degrees. Bake for 25 minutes or until a knife inserted near the center comes out clean. Cool completely before serving. YIELD: 6 TO 8 SERVINGS.

Leon Howell
Mobile Council

Pattie's Egg Custard

1 unbaked (9-inch) pie shell
3 eggs, lightly beaten
¾ cup sugar
⅛ teaspoon salt
1 teaspoon lemon extract or vanilla extract
2 cups milk
¼ cup (½ stick) butter

Bake the pie shell at 400 degrees for 2 to 3 minutes or until very light brown. Combine the eggs, sugar, salt and lemon extract in a bowl and mix well. Bring the milk and butter to a boil in a saucepan. Add the egg mixture and mix well. Pour into the pie shell. Bake at 400 degrees until a knife inserted near the center comes out clean. YIELD: 6 TO 8 SERVINGS.

Pattie Smith
Gadsden Life

French Silk Pie

3 egg whites
1 cup sugar
12 saltine crackers, crushed
½ cup chopped pecans
1 teaspoon vanilla extract
½ cup (1 stick) margarine
¾ cup sugar
2 squares unsweetened chocolate, melted
2 eggs, lightly beaten
2 cups whipped topping
½ cup chopped pecans

Beat the egg whites in a mixing bowl until soft peaks form. Add 1 cup sugar gradually, beating constantly until very stiff peaks form. Fold in the cracker crumbs, ½ cup pecans and vanilla. Spread in a greased pie plate. Bake at 325 degrees for 30 minutes. Cool completely. Cream the margarine and ¾ cup sugar in a mixing bowl until light and fluffy. Stir in the chocolate. Add the eggs 1 at a time, beating at high speed for 5 minutes after each addition. Fold in the whipped topping and ½ cup pecans. Pour into the cooled crust. Chill for 2 hours or freeze until firm. YIELD: 8 SERVINGS.

Sue Small
Selma Life

Japanese Fruit Pies

2 cups sugar
1 cup (2 sticks) margarine, melted
4 eggs, lightly beaten
1 teaspoon white vinegar
1 teaspoon vanilla extract
1 cup chopped nuts
1 cup raisins
1 can flaked coconut
2 unbaked (9-inch) pie shells

Combine the sugar and margarine in a bowl and mix well with a spoon. Add the eggs and mix well. Add the vinegar, vanilla, nuts, raisins and coconut and mix well. Pour half the filling into each pie shell. Bake at 350 degrees for 50 minutes. YIELD: 12 TO 16 SERVINGS.

Kathryn Morgan
Gadsden Life

Fudge Pie

1/2 cup (1 stick) butter or margarine
2 squares unsweetened chocolate
1 cup sugar
2 eggs, lightly beaten
1/2 cup flour
1/4 teaspoon salt
1 tablespoon vanilla extract
1/2 cup chopped pecans

Combine the butter and chocolate in a saucepan Heat over low heat until melted. Add the sugar and eggs and mix well. Add the flour, salt and vanilla and mix well. Stir in the pecans. Pour into a greased pie plate. Bake at 325 degrees for 25 minutes. You may substitute 6 tablespoons baking cocoa plus 2 tablespoons vegetable oil for the unsweetened chocolate. YIELD: 6 TO 8 SERVINGS.

D. Christine Kirkley
Birmingham Life

Pecan Fudge Pie

1 (4-ounce) package German's sweet chocolate
1/4 cup (1/2 stick) margarine
1 (14-ounce) can sweetened condensed milk
1/2 cup hot water
2 eggs, beaten
1 teaspoon vanilla extract
1/2 teaspoon salt
1 1/4 cups chopped pecans
1 unbaked (9-inch) pie shell

Combine the chocolate and margarine in a medium saucepan. Heat over low heat until melted. Stir in the condensed milk, hot water and eggs; mix well. Remove from the heat. Stir in the salt and pecans. Pour into the pie shell. Bake at 350 degrees for 40 to 45 minutes or until a knife inserted near the center comes out clean. Chill for 3 hours. YIELD: 6 TO 8 SERVINGS.

Anne Hancock
Gadsden Life

Ice Cream Pie with Meringue Pecan Crust

1 egg white
1/4 cup sugar
1 1/2 cups chopped pecans
1 quart vanilla ice cream, softened
1/4 cup crushed pecans

Beat the egg white at high speed in a mixing bowl. Add the sugar 1 tablespoon at a time, beating constantly until stiff peaks form. Fold in the chopped pecans. Spread over the bottom and side of a buttered 9-inch pie plate. Bake at 400 degrees for 12 minutes or until light brown. Cool completely. Spread the ice cream over the crust. Cover and freeze until the ice cream is firm. Sprinkle with crushed pecans. YIELD: 6 TO 8 SERVINGS.

Jo Ann Thomas
Selma Life

Lazy Man Pie

1/2 cup (1 stick) margarine
1 cup flour
1 cup sugar
1 cup buttermilk
1 teaspoon vanilla extract
1 large can fruit

Melt the margarine in a 2-quart pie plate. Combine the flour, sugar, buttermilk and vanilla in a bowl and mix well. Pour into the pie plate. Spread the fruit over the flour mixture. Bake at 350 degrees for 40 to 55 minutes or until golden brown. **YIELD: 6 TO 8 SERVINGS.**

Louise Morrison
Tuscaloosa Council

Lemonade Pies

2 (4-ounce) packages vanilla instant pudding mix
2 cups milk
1 tub Crystal Light lemonade mix
16 ounces whipped topping
2 graham cracker pie shells

Combine the pudding mix, milk, lemonade mix and whipped topping in a bowl and mix well. Pour half the filling into each pie shell. **YIELD: 12 TO 16 SERVINGS.**

Shirley Cummings
Decatur Council

Lemon Meringue Pie

1 cup flour
1/4 teaspoon salt
2/3 cup vegetable oil
1/3 cup boiling water
1/2 cup flour
1 1/4 cups sugar
1/8 teaspoon salt
3 egg yolks, lightly beaten
1 1/2 cups water
1/2 cup lemon juice
Grated zest of 1 lemon
3 egg whites
2 tablespoons sugar
1/4 teaspoon cream of tartar

Combine 1 cup flour and 1/4 teaspoon salt in a bowl. Stir in the vegetable oil until crumbly. Add the boiling water 1 tablespoon at a time, stirring with a fork until the mixture forms a ball. Chill, wrapped in plastic wrap, for 30 minutes or longer. Roll into a circle on a lightly floured surface. Fit into a pie plate. Bake at 350 degrees until the crust is light brown. Combine 1/2 cup flour, 1 1/4 cups sugar and 1/8 teaspoon salt in a double boiler. Mix the egg yolks with 1 1/2 cups water in a bowl. Add the egg yolks to the mixture in the double boiler. Cook over boiling water for 10 minutes or until thickened, stirring frequently. Stir in the lemon juice and zest. Pour into the prepared pie crust. Beat the egg whites with 2 tablespoons sugar and cream of tartar in a mixing bowl until stiff peaks form. Spread over the top of the pie, sealing to the edge. Bake until the meringue is golden brown. **YIELD: 6 SERVINGS.**

Lucille C. Wright
Birmingham Life

West Gadsden Cafe Lemon Pie

4 egg yolks, beaten
1½ (14-ounce) cans sweetened condensed milk
½ cup frozen or fresh lemon juice
1 graham cracker or vanilla wafer pie shell

Combine the egg yolks, condensed milk and lemon juice in a bowl and mix gently. Pour into the pie shell. Chill until serving time. Do not use bottled lemon juice in this recipe. **YIELD: 6 TO 8 SERVINGS.**

Kathryn Morgan
Gadsden Life

Diabetic Lemon Pies

2 small packages sugar-free nonfat
vanilla instant pudding mix
1 (2-quart) package Crystal Light lemonade mix
3½ cups skim milk
2 (8-inch) graham cracker
pie shells
Light whipped topping

Combine the pudding mix and lemonade mix in a mixing bowl. Add the skim milk. Beat until very thick. Pour half the filling into each pie shell. Top with whipped topping. **YIELD: 12 TO 16 SERVINGS.**

Kathryn Morgan
Gadsden Life

Lemon Icebox Pie

½ cup fresh lemon juice, or 1 (6-ounce) can frozen lemonade concentrate, thawed
1 (14-ounce) can sweetened condensed milk
3 eggs, beaten
8 ounces whipped topping

Combine the lemon juice, condensed milk, eggs and whipped topping in a bowl and mix well. Pour into a 9-inch pie plate. Chill until serving time. Garnish with vanilla wafer crumbs. **YIELD: 8 SERVINGS.**

Dilla Samuel
Gadsden Life

Moonshine Pie

1½ cups sugar
5 tablespoons flour
1 cup milk
3½ tablespoons butter
1 teaspoon vanilla extract
3 egg whites, stiffly beaten
1 baked (9-inch) pie shell
Flaked coconut

Combine the sugar, flour, milk and butter in a saucepan. Cook until very thick, stirring frequently. Stir in the vanilla. Let stand until slightly cooled. Fold in the egg whites. Pour into the pie shell. Sprinkle with coconut. Bake at 400 degrees until brown.
YIELD: 6 TO 8 SERVINGS.

Rubie McInnis
Birmingham Life

Oh-So-Good Pie

6 tablespoons (3/4 stick) margarine, melted
3 eggs, lightly beaten
3 tablespoons flour
1 1/2 cups sugar
1 cup drained crushed pineapple
1 cup flaked coconut
1 unbaked (9-inch) pie shell

Combine the margarine, eggs, flour, sugar, pineapple and coconut in a bowl and mix well. Pour into the pie shell. Bake at 350 degrees for 1 hour or until set and brown. YIELD: 6 TO 8 SERVINGS.

Jamima M. Edney
Birmingham Life

Peach Cream Pie

6 fresh peach halves
1 unbaked (9-inch) pie shell
1 cup sugar
1 cup heavy cream
1/4 cup flour
1 teaspoon vanilla extract
Nutmeg to taste

Arrange the peach halves in the pie shell. Combine the sugar, heavy cream, flour and vanilla in a bowl and mix well. Pour over the peach halves. Sprinkle with nutmeg. Bake at 325 degrees until the filling is thick. YIELD: 6 TO 8 SERVINGS.

Sally Bates
Birmingham South

Peanut Butter Pie

1 cup confectioners' sugar
½ cup chunky peanut butter
1 baked (9-inch) pie shell
¼ cup cornstarch
⅔ cup sugar
¼ teaspoon salt

2 cups scalded milk
3 egg yolks, beaten
2 tablespoons butter
¼ teaspoon vanilla extract
3 egg whites, stiffly beaten

Combine the confectioners' sugar and peanut butter in a bowl, stirring until crumbly. Spread half the mixture in the pie shell. Combine the cornstarch, sugar and salt in a double boiler and mix well. Stir in the scalded milk. Pour a small amount of the mixture over the egg yolks in a bowl and mix well. Stir the egg yolks into the milk mixture. Cook until thickened, stirring frequently. Add the butter and vanilla and mix well. Pour into the pie shell. Spread the egg whites over the filling, sealing to the edge. Sprinkle with the remaining peanut butter mixture. Bake at 325 degrees until the meringue is brown. **Yield: 6 to 8 servings.**

Mary Alice Neal
Birmingham Life

Pecan Pie

⅓ cup shortening
½ cup packed brown sugar
½ cup milk
1 cup chopped pecans
3 eggs, lightly beaten

½ teaspoon salt
½ teaspoon vanilla extract
1 cup dark corn syrup
1 unbaked (9-inch) pie shell

Cream the shortening and brown sugar in a mixing bowl until light and fluffy. Add the next 6 ingredients and mix well. Pour into the pie shell. Bake at 425 degrees for 10 minutes. Reduce the oven temperature to 350 degrees. Bake for 25 minutes. **Yield: 6 to 8 servings.**

Elizabeth Cornwell
Selma Life

Pecan Cheese Pie

1/3 cup sugar
8 ounces cream cheese, softened
1 egg, beaten
1 teaspoon vanilla extract
1/4 teaspoon salt

1 unbaked (9-inch) pie shell
1 1/2 cups chopped pecans
1 cup light corn syrup
1/4 cup sugar
3 eggs, beaten
1 teaspoon vanilla extract

Cream 1/3 cup sugar and cream cheese in a mixing bowl until light and fluffy. Add 1 egg, 1 teaspoon vanilla and salt and mix well. Pour into the pie shell. Sprinkle with the pecans. Combine the corn syrup, 1/4 cup sugar, 3 eggs and 1 teaspoon vanilla in a bowl and mix well. Pour over the cream cheese mixture. Bake at 375 degrees for 35 to 40 minutes or until set. Cool completely. Chill until serving time. YIELD: 6 TO 8 SERVINGS.

Narice Sutton
Birmingham Life

West Gadsden Cafe Pecan Pie

1/4 cup (1/2 stick) (about) butter
1 cup pecan halves
5 eggs
2/3 cup sugar

1 cup Golden Eagle syrup
1 teaspoon vanilla extract
1 tablespoon vinegar
1 unbaked (9-inch) pie shell

Melt the butter in a saucepan. Stir in the pecans. Beat the eggs in a mixing bowl. Add the sugar, syrup and vanilla and mix well. Stir in the vinegar. Add the pecan mixture and mix well. Pour into the pie shell. Bake at 350 degrees for 1 hour or until set. YIELD: 6 TO 8 SERVINGS.

Kathryn Morgan
Gadsden Life

Mother's Pecan Pie

½ cup sugar
2 tablespoons flour
3 eggs
¼ cup (½ stick) butter, softened
1 cup light corn syrup
½ cup chopped pecans
1 unbaked (9-inch) pie shell

Mix the sugar and flour together. Beat the eggs in a mixing bowl. Add the butter, sugar mixture, corn syrup and pecans and mix well. Pour into the pie shell. Bake at 350 degrees for 50 minutes. **YIELD: 6 TO 8 SERVINGS.**

Sheila P. Brothers
Anniston Council

Caramel Pecan Pies

½ cup (1 stick) margarine, melted
7 ounces flaked coconut
1½ cups chopped pecans
1 (14-ounce) can sweetened condensed milk
8 ounces cream cheese, softened
16 ounces whipped topping
2 baked (9-inch) deep-dish pie shells
1 jar caramel ice cream topping

Combine the margarine, coconut and pecans in a bowl and mix well. Cream the condensed milk and cream cheese in a mixing bowl until light and fluffy. Fold in the whipped topping. Layer ¼ of the cream cheese mixture and ¼ of the pecan mixture in each pie shell. Drizzle each with half the ice cream topping. Repeat the layers. Freeze overnight. **YIELD: 12 TO 16 SERVINGS.**

Mary C. Martin
Birmingham Life

Pecan Meringue Pie

Butter
1 cup pecan pieces
1/8 teaspoon salt
1 cup sugar
1/4 cup sifted flour
1 cup half-and-half
3 egg yolks, lightly beaten
1 to 2 teaspoons vanilla extract
1 baked (9-inch) pie shell
3 egg whites
1/4 teaspoon cream of tartar
1 teaspoon vanilla extract
3 to 4 tablespoons sugar

Melt a small amount of butter in a nonstick skillet. Add the pecans and salt. Cook until the pecans are toasted, stirring frequently. Combine 1 cup sugar, flour, half-and-half and egg yolks in a double boiler. Cook for 35 to 45 minutes or until thickened, stirring frequently. Add 1 to 2 teaspoons vanilla and the toasted pecans and stir to mix. Pour into the pie shell. Beat the egg whites with the cream of tartar in a mixing bowl until soft peaks form. Add 1 teaspoon vanilla. Add 3 to 4 tablespoons sugar gradually, beating constantly until stiff peaks form. Spread over the pie filling, sealing to the edge. Bake at 350 degrees for 15 minutes or until brown.
YIELD: 6 TO 8 SERVINGS.

Catherine May
Mobile Council

Lottie's Pecan Chip Pies

1¼ cups sugar
¼ cup cornstarch
½ cup (1 stick) butter or
  margarine, softened
3 eggs, beaten

1 teaspoon vanilla extract
1 cup chopped pecans or
  walnuts
1 cup chocolate chips
2 unbaked (9-inch) pie shells

Combine the sugar and cornstarch in a bowl and mix well. Add the butter and eggs and mix well. Stir in the vanilla. Add the pecans and chocolate chips and mix well. Pour into the pie shells. Bake at 350 degrees for 35 to 45 minutes or until brown. YIELD: **12 TO 16 SERVINGS**.

Lottie Smith
Birmingham Metro Council

New Orleans Pecan Pie

3 egg yolks, lightly beaten
1 cup sugar
¼ cup sifted flour
⅛ teaspoon salt
1 cup sour cream
½ teaspoon lemon
  extract

1 baked (9- or 10-inch)
  pie shell
3 egg whites
¼ teaspoon cream of tartar
1 cup packed brown sugar
1 cup pecan pieces
½ teaspoon lemon extract

Combine the egg yolks, sugar, flour, salt and sour cream in a double boiler. Cook for 35 to 45 minutes or until thickened, stirring frequently. Stir in ½ teaspoon lemon extract. Pour into the pie shell. Beat the egg whites with the cream of tartar in a mixing bowl until soft peaks form. Add the brown sugar gradually, beating constantly until stiff peaks form. Fold in the pecans and ½ teaspoon lemon extract. Top the pie filling with the meringue, sealing to the edge. Bake at 325 degrees for 15 minutes or until brown. YIELD: **6 TO 8 SERVINGS**.

Catherine May
Mobile Council

Old-Fashioned Pecan Pie

1 cup sugar
1/4 cup (1/2 stick) butter, softened
2/3 cup corn syrup
1 tablespoon flour
1/4 teaspoon salt
3 eggs, lightly beaten
1 teaspoon vanilla extract
1 cup chopped pecans
1 unbaked deep-dish pie shell

Combine the sugar, butter and corn syrup in a bowl and blend well. Add the flour, salt and eggs and mix well. Stir in the vanilla and pecans. Pour into the pie shell. Bake at 350 degrees for 1 hour. The filling recipe can be doubled to make 3 shallower pies.
YIELD: **6 TO 8** SERVINGS.

Doris B. Thrasher
Gadsden Life

Pineapple Cream Cheese Pie

1 cup confectioners' sugar
8 ounces cream cheese, softened
8 ounces whipped topping
3/4 cup drained crushed pineapple
1 graham cracker pie shell

Cream the confectioners' sugar, cream cheese and whipped topping in a mixing bowl until light and fluffy. Stir in the pineapple. Pour into the pie shell. Garnish with graham cracker crumbs. Chill for 2 hours. YIELD: **8** SERVINGS.

Jackie Black
Montgomery Council

Pumpkin Custard Pie

1 (16-ounce) can pumpkin
3 egg yolks, lightly
  beaten
1 cup sugar
3/4 cup evaporated milk
1/4 teaspoon cinnamon
1/4 teaspoon nutmeg
3 egg whites, stiffly beaten
1 unbaked (9-inch) pie shell

Beat the pumpkin and egg yolks in a mixing bowl until blended and smooth. Add the sugar and evaporated milk and mix well. Stir in the cinnamon and nutmeg. Fold in the egg whites. Pour into the pie shell. Bake at 350 degrees for 1 hour. YIELD: 6 SERVINGS.

Jo Ann Thomas
Selma Life

Double-Layer Pumpkin Pie

4 ounces cream cheese,
  softened
1 tablespoon milk
1 tablespoon sugar
1 1/2 cups whipped topping
1 large graham cracker pie
  shell
1 cup cold milk
2 (4-ounce) packages vanilla
  instant pudding mix
1 (16-ounce) can pumpkin
1 teaspoon cinnamon
1/2 teaspoon ginger
1/2 teaspoon ground cloves

Combine the cream cheese, milk and sugar in a bowl and whisk until blended and smooth. Fold in the whipped topping. Spread over the bottom of the pie shell. Pour the milk into a large bowl. Add the pudding mix. Beat with a whisk for 1 minute; the mixture will be thick. Stir in the pumpkin, cinnamon, ginger and cloves. Spread over the cream cheese layer. Chill for 4 hours or until set. Garnish with additional whipped topping. YIELD: 6 TO 8 SERVINGS.

Ruth Dunlap
Shoals Life

Raisin Pie

1 cup raisins
1 cup (2 sticks) butter, melted
1 cup sugar
2 eggs, lightly beaten
1 teaspoon vanilla extract
1 teaspoon vinegar
1 unbaked (9-inch) pie shell

Combine the raisins, butter, sugar, eggs, vanilla and vinegar in a bowl and mix well. Pour into the pie shell. Bake at 350 degrees for 45 minutes. YIELD: 6 SERVINGS.

Eunice Henry
Selma Life

Strawberry Custard

2 tablespoons flour
1 unbaked deep-dish pie shell
2 cups sliced strawberries
1 cup sugar
2 tablespoons flour
1 or 2 eggs, beaten
1 teaspoon vanilla extract
1 cup milk
½ cup sugar
1 cup sour cream
1 teaspoon vanilla extract

Sprinkle 2 tablespoons flour over the bottom of the pie shell. Arrange the strawberry slices in the pie shell. Mix 1 cup sugar with 2 tablespoons flour in a bowl. Add the eggs, vanilla and milk and beat well. Pour over the strawberries. Bake at 350 degrees for 30 minutes or until set. Remove from the oven. Combine ½ cup sugar, sour cream and 1 teaspoon vanilla in a bowl and mix well. Spread over the top of the pie. Bake for 10 minutes longer or until the topping is set. You may top with meringue instead of sour cream mixture. YIELD: 6 TO 8 SERVINGS.

Frankie Vaughn
Selma Life

Diabetic Strawberry Pie

2 tablespoons cornstarch
1½ cups cold water
1 small package strawberry sugar-free gelatin
6 envelopes artificial sweetener
3 cups sliced strawberries
1 graham cracker pie shell
Light whipped topping

Combine the cornstarch with the cold water in a double boiler. Cook over medium heat until thickened and clear, stirring occasionally. Remove from the heat. Add the gelatin and artificial sweetener and mix well. Let stand until cool. Stir in the strawberries. Pour into the pie shell. Top with whipped topping.
YIELD: 6 TO 8 SERVINGS.

Kathryn Morgan
Gadsden Life

Melva's Strawberry Pies

1 (21-ounce) can strawberry pie filling
1 (14-ounce) can sweetened condensed milk
1 small can crushed pineapple, drained
1 cup miniature marshmallows
1 cup flaked coconut
1 cup chopped pecans
8 ounces whipped topping
2 graham cracker pie shells

Combine the pie filling, condensed milk, pineapple, marshmallows, coconut, pecans and whipped topping in a bowl and mix well. Pour into the pie shells. Chill until serving time. Freezes well.
YIELD: 12 TO 16 SERVINGS.

Susan Y. May
Shoals Life

West Gadsden Cafe Strawberry Pie

1 (14-ounce) can sweetened condensed milk
8 ounces cream cheese, softened
½ cup lemon juice
1 unbaked deep-dish pie shell
⅓ cup sugar
¼ cup cornstarch
1 large package frozen strawberries

Cream the condensed milk and cream cheese in a mixing bowl until light and fluffy. Stir in the lemon juice. Pour into the pie shell. Combine the sugar, cornstarch and strawberries in a saucepan. Cook until thickened, stirring frequently. Let stand until cool. Pour over the pie. Chill until serving time. YIELD: 6 TO 8 SERVINGS.

Kathryn Morgan
Gadsden Life

Strawberry Pie

1 cup sugar
4 tablespoons strawberry gelatin
3½ tablespoons cornstarch
1 cup warm water
Red food coloring
1 pint fresh strawberries, sliced
1 baked (9-inch) pie shell
Whipped topping

Combine the sugar, gelatin, cornstarch and warm water in a saucepan. Bring to a boil, stirring until the sugar and gelatin are dissolved. Stir in the food coloring. Cook over low heat until thickened. Let stand until cool. Fold in the strawberries. Pour into the pie shell. Chill until set. Top each serving with whipped topping. YIELD: 6 TO 8 SERVINGS.

Faith Kirby Richardson
Gadsden Life

Swedish Pie

1 egg, lightly beaten
1/2 cup packed brown sugar
1/2 cup sugar
1/2 cup flour
1 teaspoon baking powder
1/8 teaspoon salt
1 teaspoon vanilla extract
1 cup chopped apples
1 cup chopped pecans

Combine the egg, brown sugar, sugar, flour, baking powder, salt and vanilla in a large bowl and mix well. Fold in the apples and pecans. Pour into a greased 9-inch pie plate. Bake at 325 degrees for 30 to 35 minutes or until the apples are tender. You may serve with ice cream or whipped cream. **YIELD: 8 SERVINGS.**

Sue Small
Selma Life

Sweet Potato Pie

2 cups mashed cooked sweet potatoes
3 eggs, lightly beaten
1 cup sugar
1/2 cup (1 stick) margarine, softened
1 teaspoon vanilla extract
1 teaspoon cinnamon
1/2 to 1 teaspoon nutmeg
Evaporated milk
1 unbaked (9-inch) pie shell

Combine the sweet potatoes, eggs, sugar, margarine, vanilla, cinnamon and nutmeg in a bowl and mix well. Add enough evaporated milk to make the filling of the desired consistency. Pour into the pie shell. Bake at 350 degrees for 1 hour or until set. **YIELD: 6 TO 8 SERVINGS.**

Kathryn Morgan
Gadsden Life

Clara's Sweet Potato Pie

1 unbaked (9-inch) pie shell
1 cup sugar
2 egg yolks, lightly beaten
1/4 cup (1/2 stick) butter, softened
2 1/2 cups mashed cooked sweet potatoes
1/2 teaspoon lemon extract
1/2 teaspoon cinnamon
2 egg whites, stiffly beaten

Bake the pie shell at 350 degrees until almost done. Combine the sugar, egg yolks, butter, sweet potatoes, lemon extract and cinnamon in a bowl and mix well. Fold in the egg whites. Pour into the pie shell. Bake for 20 minutes. YIELD: **6 TO 8 SERVINGS.**

Pattie Smith
Gadsden Life

Oralee's Sweet Potato Custard Pie

1 1/2 cups mashed cooked sweet potatoes
1 (14-ounce) can sweetened condensed milk
1 egg, lightly beaten
1/2 cup (1 stick) margarine, softened
Vanilla extract to taste
1 unbaked (9-inch) pie shell

Combine the sweet potatoes, condensed milk, egg, margarine and vanilla in a bowl and mix well. Pour into the pie shell. Bake at 350 degrees for 35 to 40 minutes or until a knife inserted near the center comes out clean. YIELD: **6 TO 8 SERVINGS.**

Eloise Bennett
Decatur Council

Mary Lynn's Tang Pie

3 tablespoons (heaping) Tang
1 (14-ounce) can sweetened
  condensed milk
1 cup sour cream

8 ounces whipped topping
1 graham cracker pie shell
Whipped topping

Combine the Tang, condensed milk, sour cream and 8 ounces whipped topping in a bowl and mix well. Pour into the pie shell. Chill thoroughly. Top each serving with whipped topping. Chill 1 day before serving. YIELD: **6 TO 8 SERVINGS**.

Susan Y. May
Shoals Life

Tropical Pie

3/4 cup sugar
1/3 cup flour
1/4 teaspoon salt
1 1/4 cups milk
3 egg yolks, lightly beaten
1/2 cup orange juice
2 tablespoons lemon
  juice

1 tablespoon grated orange
  zest
1 teaspoon grated lemon zest
1 baked (9-inch) pie shell
3 egg whites
1/4 cup sugar
Maraschino cherries (optional)
Shredded coconut (optional)

Combine 3/4 cup sugar, flour, salt and milk in a double boiler. Cook over hot water for 20 minutes or until thick, stirring frequently. Stir a small amount of the hot mixture into the egg yolks; stir the egg yolks into the hot mixture. Cook for 5 minutes or until thick, stirring constantly. Remove from the heat. Add the next 4 ingredients. Pour into the pie shell. Beat the egg whites in a mixing bowl until soft peaks form. Add 1/4 cup sugar gradually, beating constantly until stiff peaks form. Spread over the pie filling, sealing to the edge. Decorate with maraschino cherries and coconut. YIELD: **6 TO 8 SERVINGS**.

Francis Tucker
Selma Life

Jessie Isbell's Walnut Pie

1½ cups chopped walnuts
3 eggs, lightly beaten
¾ cup sugar
¾ cup light corn syrup

2 tablespoons butter, melted
⅛ teaspoon salt
1 teaspoon vanilla extract
1 unbaked (9-inch) pie shell

Bring enough water to cover the walnuts to a boil in a saucepan. Drop in the walnuts. Boil for 3 minutes; drain well. Spread the walnuts in a single layer in a shallow baking pan. Bake at 350 degrees for 15 minutes, turning occasionally. Let cool. Combine the eggs, sugar, corn syrup, butter, salt and vanilla in a bowl and mix well. Stir in the walnuts. Pour into the pie shell. Bake at 350 degrees for 45 minutes or until a wooden pick inserted near the center comes out clean. YIELD: 6 TO 8 SERVINGS.

Imogene Davis
Birmingham Life

Wonderful Pie

1 (14-ounce) can sweetened condensed milk
8 ounces whipped topping
¼ cup lemon juice

2 (11-ounce) cans mandarin oranges, drained
1 cup chopped pecans
2 graham cracker pie shells

Combine the condensed milk, whipped topping, lemon juice, oranges and pecans in a bowl and mix well. Pour half the filling into each pie shell. Chill for 4 hours or longer. YIELD: 12 TO 16 SERVINGS.

Sue Walton
Birmingham Life

Aunt Polly's Tarts

2 cups graham cracker crumbs
16 ounces cream cheese, softened
3 egg yolks, lightly beaten
¾ cup sugar
3 egg whites, stiffly beaten
¾ cup sour cream
1 tablespoon sugar
½ teaspoon vanilla extract
1 (21-ounce) can cherry pie filling

Sprinkle the graham cracker crumbs into buttered miniature muffin cups. Shake out any excess. Beat the cream cheese, egg yolks and sugar in a mixing bowl until light and fluffy. Fold in the egg whites. Pour into the muffin cups. Bake at 350 degrees for 15 to 20 minutes or until set. While still warm, make an indentation in each tart. Combine the sour cream, 1 tablespoon sugar and vanilla in a bowl and mix well. Pour into a small baking dish. Bake at 400 degrees for 5 minutes. Spoon ½ teaspoon of the sour cream mixture into each indentation. Top each with 1 cherry. These tarts can be prepared ahead and frozen. Add the cherries after thawing.
YIELD: **60** TARTS.

Mary Ann Sparks Fulmer
Shoals Life

HELPFUL HINT

Fruit, mince and chiffon pies freeze well. Custard and meringue pies do not freeze well.

Lynda's Canadian Tarts

1 cup sugar
2 eggs, lightly beaten
½ cup (1 stick) margarine, melted
1 cup raisins
1 cup chopped pecans
1 cup flaked coconut
1 teaspoon vanilla extract
12 unbaked tart shells

Combine the sugar, eggs, margarine, raisins, pecans, coconut and vanilla in a bowl and mix well. Pour into the tart shells. Bake at 350 degrees for 25 to 30 minutes or until set. **YIELD: 12 SERVINGS.**

Brenda Self
Riverchase Council

Hattie's Coconut Tarts

½ cup (1 stick) margarine, melted
5 eggs, beaten
2 cups sugar
¾ cup buttermilk
1 to 1½ cups flaked coconut
2 teaspoons vanilla extract
16 unbaked tart shells, or 2 unbaked (10-inch) pie shells

Combine the margarine, eggs, sugar, buttermilk, coconut and vanilla in a bowl and mix well. Pour into the tart shells. Bake at 350 degrees for 40 minutes for tarts or 40 to 45 minutes for pies. **YIELD: 16 SERVINGS.**

Brenda Self
Riverchase Council

Cream Cheese Tarts

2 cups flour
1/2 cup confectioners' sugar
1 cup (2 sticks) butter, softened
8 ounces cream cheese, softened
3 to 4 teaspoons confectioners' sugar
Strawberry preserves

Combine the flour, 1/2 cup confectioners' sugar and butter in a mixing bowl and mix well. Shape into small balls. Press into greased miniature muffin cups. Make an indentation in the center of each tart. Bake at 350 degrees for 12 to 14 minutes or until set. Let cool. Combine the cream cheese and 3 to 4 teaspoons confectioners' sugar in a bowl and mix well. Spoon into the indentations. Top with preserves. YIELD: 24 SERVINGS.

Linda Ander
Montgomery Council

Bren's Pecan Tarts

1 (1-pound) package light brown sugar
3 tablespoons flour
3 eggs, lightly beaten
1/2 cup (1 stick) margarine, melted
3/4 cup milk
1 teaspoon vanilla extract
1 to 1 1/2 cups chopped pecans
16 unbaked tart shells, or 2 unbaked (10-inch) pie shells

Combine the brown sugar and flour in a large bowl and mix well. Add the eggs, margarine, milk and vanilla and mix well. Stir in the pecans. Pour into the tart shells. Bake at 350 degrees for 40 minutes for tarts or 40 to 45 minutes for pies. YIELD: 16 SERVINGS.

Brenda Self
Riverchase Council

Basic Substitutions

If the recipe calls for: | **You can substitute:**

Flour
1 cup sifted all-purpose flour . . . . 1 cup minus 2 tablespoons unsifted all-purpose flour
1 cup sifted cake flour . . . . 1 cup minus 2 tablespoons sifted all-purpose flour
1 cup sifted self-rising flour . . . . 1 cup sifted all-purpose flour plus 1½ teaspoons baking powder and a pinch of salt

Milk/Cream
1 cup buttermilk . . . . 1 cup plain yogurt, or 1 tablespoon lemon juice or vinegar plus enough milk to measure 1 cup—let stand for 5 minutes
1 cup whipping cream or half-and-half . . . . . ⅞ cup whole milk plus 1½ tablespoons butter
1 cup light cream . . . . ⅞ cup whole milk plus 3 tablespoons butter
1 cup sour cream . . . . 1 cup plain yogurt
1 cup sour milk . . . . 1 cup plain yogurt
1 cup whole milk . . . . 1 cup skim or nonfat milk plus 2 tablespoons butter or margarine

Seasonings
1 teaspoon allspice . . . . ½ teaspoon cinnamon plus ⅛ teaspoon cloves
1 cup ketchup . . . . 1 cup tomato sauce plus ½ cup sugar plus 2 tablespoons vinegar
1 teaspoon Italian spice . . . . ¼ teaspoon each oregano, basil, thyme, and rosemary plus dash of cayenne pepper
1 teaspoon lemon juice . . . . ½ teaspoon vinegar

Sugar
1 cup confectioners' sugar . . . . ½ cup plus 1 tablespoon granulated sugar
1 cup granulated sugar . . . . 1¾ cups confectioners' sugar, 1 cup packed light brown sugar or ¾ cup honey

Other
1 package active dry yeast . . . . ½ cake compressed yeast
1 teaspoon baking powder . . . . ¼ teaspoon cream of tartar plus ¼ teaspoon baking soda
1 cup dry bread crumbs . . . . ¾ cup cracker crumbs or 1 cup cornflake crumbs
1 cup (2 sticks) butter . . . . ⅞ cup vegetable oil or 1 cup margarine
1 tablespoon cornstarch . . . . 2 tablespoons all-purpose flour
1 cup dark corn syrup . . . . ¾ cup light corn syrup plus ¼ cup light molasses
1 cup light corn syrup . . . . 1 cup maple syrup
1⅔ ounces semisweet chocolate . . . . 1 ounce unsweetened chocolate plus 4 teaspoons granulated sugar
1 ounce unsweetened chocolate . . . . 3 tablespoons unsweetened baking cocoa plus 1 tablespoon butter or margarine
1 (1-ounce) square chocolate . . . . ¼ cup baking cocoa plus 1 teaspoon shortening
1 egg . . . . ¼ cup mayonnaise

Refrigeration Chart

Food	Refrigerate	Freeze
Beef steaks	1 to 2 days	6 to 12 months
Beef roasts	1 to 2 days	6 to 12 months
Corned beef	7 days	2 weeks
Pork chops	1 to 2 days	3 to 4 months
Pork roasts	1 to 2 days	4 to 8 months
Fresh sausage	1 to 2 days	1 to 2 months
Smoked sausage	7 days	Not recommended
Cured ham	5 to 7 days	1 to 2 months
Canned ham	1 year	Not recommended
Ham slice	3 days	1 to 2 months
Bacon	7 days	2 to 4 months
Veal cutlets	1 to 2 days	6 to 9 months
Stew meat	1 to 2 days	3 to 4 months
Ground meat	1 to 2 days	3 to 4 months
Luncheon meats	3 to 5 days	Not recommended
Frankfurters	7 days	1 month
Whole chicken	1 to 2 days	12 months
Chicken pieces	1 to 2 days	9 months

Freezing Tips

- List the date on all items before placing them in the freezer.

- Freezing canned hams or processed meats is not recommended. Frozen canned hams become watery and soft when thawed. Processed meats have a high salt content, which speeds rancidity when thawed.

- Do not freeze stuffed chickens or turkeys. The stuffing may incur bacterial contamination during the lengthy thawing process.

- Partially thawed food that still has ice crystals in the package can be safely refrozen. A safer test is to determine if the surface temperature is 40 degrees Fahrenheit or lower.

INDEX

Accompaniments. *See also* Pickles
  Key Lime Butter, 336

Appetizers. *See also* Cheese Balls;
    Dips; Snacks; Spreads
  Appetillas, 36
  Bacon Appetizer Crescents, 25
  Cheddar Crisps, 27
  Cheese Wafers, 28
  Cheesy Sausage Balls, 30
  Cocktail Meatballs, 33
  Cornelia's Party "Snausages", 32
  Easy-as-Pie Sausage Balls, 31
  Hidden Valley Ranch Buffalo
    Wings, 35
  Little Pizzas, 38
  McAllister Garlic Buffalo Wings, 34
  Olive Balls, 30
  Pinwheel Chicken Roll-Ups, 37
  Priatzo by Regina, 26
  Sausage Balls, 31, 32
  Sausage-Stuffed Mushrooms, 29
  Stuffed Mushrooms, 28
  Texas Tortillas, 38
  Vegetable Pizza, 39

Apples
  Apple Cake, 392, 394
  Apple Carrot Casserole, 326
  Apple Cheese Casserole, 326
  Apple Cinnamon Refrigerator
    Cake, 426
  Apple Crisp, 340
  Apple Dapple Cake, 393
  Apple Dumplings, 340
  Apple Pie, 514
  Apple Punch, 43
  Apple Salad, 75
  Baked Apples, 325
  Black Walnut Apple Cake, 396
  Brandon's Fruit Salad, 81
  Caramel Apple Dip, 17
  Chicken Salad Supreme, 120
  Dried Apple Custard, 515
  Dutch Apple Pound Cake, 437
  Miss Minnie's Corn Bread Sausage
    Dressing, 315
  Mock Apple Pickles or Red Hot
    Cucumber Pickles, 334
  Old-Fashioned Fruit Salad, 82
  Pattie's Apple Dumplings, 341
  Polly Jones' Apple Bars, 478
  Raw Cranberry Relish, 336
  Sauce, 33

  Sugarless Apple Pie, 514
  Swedish Pie, 549
  Tappy Apple Salad, 74

Apricots
  Apricot Quick Bread, 251
  Apricot Salad, 75, 76
  German Fruitcake, 417
  Grilled Ham Steak, 160
  Hot Fruit Compote, 327

Artichokes
  Capital Chicken Casserole, 180
  Spinach Artichoke Casserole, 298
  Spinach Dip, 23

Asparagus
  Asparagus Mold, 90
  Congealed Asparagus Salad, 89
  English Pea and Asparagus
    Casserole, 274
  Lemon-Kissed Asparagus with Midgie
    Carrots, 275
  Oven-Baked Asparagus, 274
  Quick Casserole, 275

Avocados
  Chunky Guacamole, 19
  Nine-Layer Taco Dip, 24
  Peach Mango Guacamole, 20
  Veggie Guacamole, 20

Bananas
  Banana Nut Bread, 254
  Banana Nut Cake, 395
  Banana Pound Cake, 438
  Banana Pudding, 377
  Berry 'n' Banana Salad, 76
  Best Banana Pudding, 378
  Blue Ribbon Banana Cake, 394
  Blueberry Pies, 515
  Brandon's Fruit Salad, 81
  Date Coffee Cake, 246
  Fresh Fruit with Lemon Yogurt
    Dressing, 80
  Fruit Salad, 81
  Fruity Smoothie, 42
  Low-Fat Banana Muffins, 258
  Mama's Homemade Banana
    Pudding, 377
  Old-Fashioned Banana Pudding, 379
  Old-Fashioned Fruit Salad, 82
  Peanut Butter and Banana
    Sandwich, 40

INDEX

Tropical Berry Blast Smoothie, 43

Beans
Baked Beans, 276
Barb's Minestrone Soup, 57
Bean Dip, 18
Beef and Bean Supper Dish, 137
Chauvinist Chili, 136
Chili, 135
Chloe Scott's Baked Beans, 134
Corn Bread Salad, 98
Easy Red Beans and Rice, 175
Frito Salad, 100
Mexican Bean Dip, 18
Mexican Bean Soup, 54
Nine-Layer Taco Dip, 24
Santa Fe Soup, 63, 64, 65
Spicy Cabbage Beef Soup, 54
Spicy White Chili, 216
Taco Soup, 67, 68
The Best Baked Beans, 276
Turnip Greens and White Bean Bake, 277
Tuscan White Bean Salad, 90
White Chili, 217

Beef. *See also* Ground Beef
Best-Ever Pot Roast, 124
Corned Beef and Cabbage Casserole, 133
Easy Baked Beef Stew, 132
Easy Roast Beef, 128
Eye-of-Round Roast, 126
Hungarian Goulash, 130
Italian Roast Beef Sandwich, 129
Margaret's Special Roast Beef, 127
New England Boiled Dinner, 125
One-Two-Three Stew, 132
Roast Beef, 125
Rump Roast, 129
Slow and Easy Roast, 128
Swiss Steak, 131

Beverages
Apple Punch, 43
Fruity Smoothie, 42
Punch, 44
Simple Punch, 44
Sparkling Summer Tea, 45
Spiced Tea Mix, 45
Tropical Berry Blast Smoothie, 43
Tropical Smoothie, 42

Biscuits
Anne's Biscuits, 236
Biscuits, 237
Buttermilk Biscuits, 236
Potato Cheese Biscuits, 238

Black Beans
Black Bean Hummus, 17
Cuban Pork Chops, 166
Layered Taco Salad, 114
Mexican Bean Soup, 54
Santa Fe Soup, 63, 64, 65
Taco Soup, 68
Tex-Mex Corn Chowder, 48
Veggie Guacamole, 20

Blackberries
Blackberry Wine Cake, 395
Fruitcake, 414

Blueberries
Berry 'n' Banana Salad, 76
Blueberry Crunch Cake, 341
Blueberry Delight, 342
Blueberry Dessert, 343
Blueberry Muffins with Streusel Topping, 257
Blueberry Peach Pie, 516
Blueberry Pies, 515

Breads. *See also* Biscuits; Coffee Cakes; Corn Bread; Muffins; Rolls
Amish Friendship Bread, 252
Apricot Quick Bread, 251
Banana Nut Bread, 254
Beer Bread, 254
Belgian Waffles, 271
Club Soda Pancakes, 271
Date Loaf, 256
Hush Puppies, 242
Pear Bread, 255
Starter, 253
Vegetable Fritters, 243
Zucchini Bread, 256

Broccoli
Broccoli and Rice Casserole, 281
Broccoli Casserole, 280
Broccoli Corn Bread, 238, 239
Broccoli Mushroom Chowder, 48
Broccoli Salad, 91, 92
Broccoli Slaw, 106
Dot Salad and Dressing, 93
Garden Broccoli Cauliflower Salad, 94

INDEX

Mother's Broccoli Corn Bread, 239
Pattie's Owens Broccoli, 282
Rice and Broccoli Casserole, 281
Sweet-and-Sour Broccoli, 279
Vegetable Pizza, 39
Zippy Chicken Stir-Fry, 213

Brownies
Best-Ever Brownies, 481
Brownies, 479, 480
Caramel Brownies, 481
Hershey Brownies, 483
Katharine Hepburn's Brownies, 482
Marbled Brownie Bars, 483
Peanut Butter Brownie Pizza, 484

Cakes. *See also* Fruitcakes; Pound Cakes
Allie's Coconut Cake, 409
Almond Skillet Cake, 392
Apple Cake, 392, 394
Apple Cinnamon Refrigerator Cake, 426
Apple Dapple Cake, 393
Aunt Pauline's Poor Man's Cake, 436
Banana Nut Cake, 395
Black Walnut Apple Cake, 396
Blackberry Wine Cake, 395
Blue Ribbon Banana Cake, 394
Butter Pecan Bundt Cake, 397
Carrot Cake, 398, 399
Chocolate Ice Box Cake, 403
Coconut Cake, 409, 410
Coconut Macaroon Cake, 408
Cream Nut Cake, 410
Custard Chiffon Cake, 411
Deep Chocolate Refrigerator Cake, 426
Double Delight Chocolate Cake, 401
Double Orange Refrigerator Cake, 426
Easy Orange Cake, 425
Elaine's Chocolate Dream Cake, 404
Fruit Cocktail Cake, 413
Fudge Cake, 404
Golden Fig Cake, 412
Graham Cracker Cake, 421
Honey Orange Cake, 427
Hot Fudge Cake, 405
Lazy Daisy Oatmeal Cake, 424
Lemon Cake, 420
Lemon Refrigerator Cake, 426
Mystery Cake, 422
No Name Cake, 423
Nut Cake, 423
Orange Carrot Cake, 400
Orange Pineapple Cake, 428

Out-Of-This-World Cake, 430
Peanut Butter Cake, 431
Pineapple Delight, 434
Pineapple Upside-Down Cake, 433
Pineapple Yum-Yum Cake, 432
Pistachio Nut Swirl Cake, 435
Poppy Seed Cake, 436
Pumpkin Cake, 447
Pumpkin Roll, 448, 449
Red Velvet Cake, 450
Refrigerator Cake, 451
Sausage Cake, 452
Scripture Mayonnaise Cake, 453
Sock-It-To-Me Cake, 454
Southern Gingerbread, 419
Spice Chiffon Cake, 455
Spiced Rum Cake and Glaze, 456
Sponge Cake, 457
Strawberry Gelatin Cake, 458
Strawberry Refrigerator Cake, 426
Strawberry Shortcake, 457
Sugarless Cakes, 459
Swiss Chocolate Cake, 407
Texas Fudge Cake, 406
Triple Fudge Cake, 408
Tropical Orange Cake, 429
Vida's Chocolate Cake, 402
Williamsburg Cake, 460

Candy. *See also* Fudge
Chocolate-Covered Cherries, 464
Cow Pies, 466
Divinity, 467
Easy Chocolate Candy, 466
English Toffee Candy, 465
Forever Amber Candy, 464
Gooey Turtles, 476
Goof Balls, 470
Heath Bar, 470
Microwave Peanut Brittle, 473
Mounds, 471
No-Bake Babies, 472
Orange Balls, 472
Reese Candy, 477
Reese Cups, 476
S'mores-Golden Grahams, 475
Spider Candies, 475
Toasted Pecan Clusters, 473
Vanilla Nut Roll, 477
Walnut Penuche, 474

Carrots
Apple Carrot Casserole, 326
Barb's Minestrone Soup, 57

INDEX 561

Basil-Lemon Turkey Breast, 220
Best-Ever Pot Roast, 124
Broccoli Salad, 92
Carrot and Zucchini-Stuffed Chicken
    Breasts, 190
Carrot Cake, 398, 399
Cashew Rice Pilaf, 323
Cheddar Chowder, 49
Chicken Cannelloni, 192
Chicken Potpie, 209
Corn Salad, 95
Dreamland's Marinated Coleslaw, 110
German Cabbage and Sausage, 175
Glazed Carrots, 283
Green Bean Salad, 101
Ham Chowder, 50
Healthy Chicken Soup, 55
Hearty Potato Soup, 58
Ho-Bo Potatoes, 155
Kraut Salad, 102
Lemon-Kissed Asparagus with Midgie
    Carrots, 275
New England Boiled Dinner, 125
Orange Carrot Cake, 400
Piccadilly Carrot Soufflé, 283
Pork Chops and Vegetables, 169
Potato Soup, 61, 62
Spaghetti Sauce, 155
Squash Supreme, 303
Sunshine Salad, 83
Sweet and Sour Pork Chops, 168
Vegetable Chicken Soup, 71
Vegetable Fritters, 243
Vegetable Pizza, 39
Whole Wheat Honey Muffins, 264
Zippy Chicken Stir-Fry, 213

Catfish
Baked Catfish Fillets, 221
Bob's Grilled Catfish Fillets, 221

Cauliflower
Broccoli Salad, 92
Cauliflower Casserole, 284
Garden Broccoli Cauliflower
    Salad, 94
Vegetable Chicken Soup, 71
Vegetable Pizza, 39

Cheese Balls. *See also* Spreads
Cheese Ball, 8, 9
Chicken Cheese Ball, 11
Ground Pepper Cheese Ball, 9
Pineapple Cheese Ball, 10

Salmon Ball, 12
Snowball Cheese Balls, 10
Tuna Ball, 12

Cheesecakes
Cheesecake, 351
Chocolate Cheesecake, 349
No-Guilt No-Fat Cheesecake, 350

Cherries
Aunt Polly's Tarts, 553
Cherry Salad, 77
Chocolate Trifle, 372
Chocolate-Covered Cherries, 464
Dark Fruitcakes, 416
Dream Bars, 490
Duchess Cookies, 491
Fruit Pizza, 369
Fruit Salad, 81
Fruitcake, 414, 415
Fruitcake Cookies, 495, 496
German Fruitcake, 417
Grace's Fruitcake Cookies, 497
Hot Fruit Compote, 327
Petite Cherry Cheesecakes, 348
7-Cup Salad, 82
So Easy Fruitcakes, 418
Tropical Pie, 551

Chicken
Alma's Baked Chicken, 184
Angel Chicken Pasta, 187
Baked Chicken, 184
Baked Chicken Breasts, 185
Brunswick Stew, 217
Capital Chicken Casserole, 180
Carrot and Zucchini-Stuffed
    Chicken Breasts, 190
Cashew Chicken, 191
Chicken and Dumpling Casserole, 203
Chicken and Dumplings, 202
Chicken and Rice Skillet, 214
Chicken and Shrimp Casserole, 197
Chicken Cannelloni, 192
Chicken Casserole, 188, 193
Chicken Cheese Ball, 11
Chicken Cordon Bleu Casserole, 194
Chicken Crunch, 195
Chicken Dressing, 199
Chicken Enchiladas, 204, 205
Chicken Fantastic, 206
Chicken Jun Jun, 207
Chicken Pie, 207
Chicken Potpie, 208, 209

562 INDEX

Chicken-Rice Casserole, 189
Chicken Salad, 118, 119
Chicken Salad Supreme, 120
Chicken Salad Tacos, 214
Chicken Supreme, 212
Chicken with a Spanish Flair, 212
Copycat Kentucky Fried Chicken, 182
Creamy Chicken Bake, 185
Creole Chicken Salad, 120
CROCK-POT® Brunswick Stew, 218
CROCK-POT® Chicken
  Dressing, 198
Deborah's Chicken Delight, 186
Drunk Chicken, 181
Easy Chicken and Dumplings, 202
Easy Chicken Potpie, 210
Great Chicken, 195
Healthy Chicken Soup, 55
Hidden Valley Ranch Buffalo Wings, 35
Hot Chicken Salad, 121
Joan's Giblet Gravy, 330
Joyce's Barbecued Chicken, 181
Light and Sticky Chicken, 189
Lipton Chicken, 186
Liz's Chicken and Dressing, 200
McAllister Garlic Buffalo Wings, 34
Mother's Chicken Dressing, 201
Nana Stetson's Chopped Liver, 16
Oriental Chicken Casserole, 196
Pan-Fried Chicken, 187
Pinwheel Chicken Roll-Ups, 37
Poppy Seed Chicken Casserole, 196
Provençal Chicken, 211
Shirley's Chicken and Rice, 188
Spicy White Chili, 216
Sticky Chicken, 190
Tammy's Chicken Wraps, 215
Terri's Chicken String Bean
  Casserole, 183
Vegetable Chicken Soup, 71
Very Quick-and-Easy Chicken
  Gumbo Soup, 51
White Chili, 217
Zippy Chicken Stir-Fry, 213

Chili
  Chauvinist Chili, 136
  Chili, 135
  Spicy White Chili, 216
  White Chili, 217

Chocolate
  Amy's Ice Cream Sandwich
    Dessert, 376

Best-Ever Brownies, 481
Black Skillet Chocolate Pies, 519
Brownies, 479, 480
Chocolate Cake Cookies, 485
Chocolate Cheesecake, 349
Chocolate Chip Cookies, 486, 487
Chocolate Cobbler, 352
Chocolate Éclair, 359
Chocolate Frosting, 358
Chocolate Gravy, 388
Chocolate Ice Box Cake, 403
Chocolate Mousse Pie, 524
Chocolate Pie, 520
Chocolate Pies, 521, 522
Chocolate Pour Icing, 461
Chocolate Sauce, 375, 385
Chocolate Sauce Supreme, 388
Chocolate Trifle, 371, 372
Chocolate-Covered Cherries, 464
Cow Pies, 466
Cream Cheese Brownie Pie, 517
CROCK-POT® Fudge, 467
Death-by-Chocolate Cookie, 487
Deep Chocolate Refrigerator Cake, 426
Double Delight Chocolate Cake, 401
Easy Chocolate Candy, 466
Elaine's Chocolate Dream Cake, 404
English Toffee Candy, 465
Expensive Cookies, 493
Fluffy Mint Dessert, 364
Forgotten Kisses, 495
French Silk Pie, 531
Frosting, 479, 485
Fudge Cake, 404
Fudge Icing, 460
Fudge Pie, 532
Fudgy Coconut Squares, 488
Gay's Cowboy Cookies, 489
German Chocolate Pie, 522
Gooey Turtles, 476
Goof Balls, 470
Heath Bar, 470
Hershey Bar Pie, 523
Hershey Brownies, 483
Hot Fudge Cake, 405
Judy's Frosting, 482
Katharine Hepburn's Brownies, 482
Lemon-White Chocolate-Pistachio
  Cookies, 504
Lottie's Pecan Chip Pies, 543
Microwave Chocolate Pie, 523
Microwave Fudge with Pecans, 468
Mile-High Strawberry Delight, 367
Mounds, 471

INDEX 563

Neiman Marcus Cookies, 499
No Name Cake, 423
No-Bake Babies, 472
Old-Fashioned Chocolate Pie, 525
Old-Fashioned Peanut Butter
  Fudge, 468
P-Nutty Bars, 502
Peanut Butter Brownie Pizza, 484
Peanut Butter-Chocolate Chunk
  Cookies, 502
Pecan Fudge Pie, 533
Pudding with Chocolate Sauce, 385
Reese Candy, 477
Reese Cups, 476
S'mores-Golden Grahams, 475
Spider Candies, 475
Swiss Chocolate Cake, 407
Texas Fudge Cake, 406
Toasted Pecan Clusters, 473
Triple Fudge Cake, 408
Vida's Chocolate Cake, 402

Chowders
  Broccoli Mushroom Chowder, 48
  Cheddar Chowder, 49
  Ham Chowder, 50
  Tex-Mex Corn Chowder, 48

Cobblers
  Chocolate Cobbler, 352
  Easy Fruit Cobbler, 352
  Fruit Cobbler, 353
  Sweet Potato Cobbler, 354, 355, 356

Coconut
  Allie's Coconut Cake, 409
  Berry 'n' Banana Salad, 76
  Bread Pudding, 381
  Butter Pecan Bundt Cake, 397
  Caramel Pecan Pie, 541
  Chloe Scott's Creamy Oat
    Cookies, 500
  Coconut Biscuit Pudding, 380
  Coconut Cake, 409, 410
  Coconut Caramel Pies, 518
  Coconut Macaroon Cake, 408
  Coconut Pie, 525
  Coconut Sour Cream Pound
    Cake, 440
  Darn Good Pies, 526
  Delight Pies, 527
  Dessert Ice Cream Balls, 374
  Duchess Cookies, 491
  Everyday Cookies, 492

  Forever Amber Candy, 464
  Frosting, 413, 424
  Fruitcake, 414
  Fudgy Coconut Squares, 488
  German Chocolate Pie, 522
  Goof Balls, 470
  Graham Cracker Cake, 421
  Hattie's Coconut Tarts, 554
  Icing, 398
  Japanese Fruit Pies, 532
  Jessie Isbell's Sweet Potato
    Pudding, 387
  Lynda's Canadian Tarts, 554
  Melva's Strawberry Pies, 547
  Moonshine Pie, 537
  Mounds, 471
  Mystery Cake, 422
  Nut Cake, 423
  Oh-So-Good Pie, 538
  Orange Balls, 472
  Out-Of-This-World Cake, 430
  Pineapple Delight, 434
  7-Cup Salad, 82
  Snowball Cheese Balls, 10
  Spider Candies, 475
  Topping, 246
  Tropical Orange Cake, 429
  Tropical Pie, 551
  Vanilla Nut Roll, 477
  West Gadsden Cafe Coconut
    Pie, 526

Coffee Cakes
  Bubble Bread, 245
  Coffee Cake, 244
  Date Coffee Cake, 246
  Nutty Orange Coffee Cake, 247
  Quick Coffee Cake, 248
  Sour Cream Coffee Cake, 249, 250

Cookies. *See also* Brownies; Tea Cakes
  Chloe Scott's Creamy Oat
    Cookies, 500
  Chloe Scott's Old-Fashioned Sugar
    Cookies, 508
  Chloe Scott's Peanut Butter
    Cookies, 503
  Chocolate Cake Cookies, 485
  Chocolate Chip Cookies, 486, 487
  Christmas Kiss Cookies, 494
  Crispy Ice Box Cookies, 507
  Crunch Grape-Nut Cookies, 498
  Death-by-Chocolate Cookie, 487
  Dishpan Cookies, 490

Dream Bars, 490
Duchess Cookies, 491
Everyday Cookies, 492
Expensive Cookies, 493
Forgotten Kisses, 495
Fruitcake Cookies, 495, 496
Fudgy Coconut Squares, 488
Gay's Cowboy Cookies, 489
Gladys P.'s Old-Fashioned Sugar
   Cookies, 509
Gooey Butter Bars, 493
Grace's Fruitcake Cookies, 497
Lemon-White Chocolate-Pistachio
   Cookies, 504
Lois' Snickerdoodles, 508
Mud Cookies, 498
Neiman Marcus Cookies, 499
Olga's Angel Crisp Cookies, 478
Orange Slice Cookies, 501
Peanut Butter-Chocolate Chunk
   Cookies, 502
Pineapple Bars, 503
P-Nutty Bars, 502
Polly Jones' Apple Bars, 478
Potato Chip Cookies, 504, 505
Powder Puff Cookies, 505
Pumpkin Cookies, 506
Refrigerator Cookies, 507
Vanishing Oatmeal Raisin
   Cookies, 501

Corn Bread
   Broccoli Corn Bread, 238, 239
   Chicken Dressing, 199
   Corn Bread Dressing, 313
   Corn Bread for Bland Diets, 240
   Corn Bread Salad, 97, 98
   Crackling Corn Bread, 240
   CROCK-POT® Chicken
      Dressing, 198
   Dressing, 312
   Johnson's Sausage Dressing, 314
   Liz's Chicken and Dressing, 200
   Mexican Corn Bread, 241
   Miss Minnie's Corn Bread Sausage
      Dressing, 315
   Mother's Broccoli Corn
      Bread, 239
   Mother's Chicken Dressing, 201
   Okra Corn Bread, 241
   Papa's Corn Bread, 240
   Squash Dressing, 316, 317
   Turnip Greens and White Bean
      Bake, 277

Corn. *See also* Hominy
   Brunswick Stew, 217
   Cheddar Chowder, 49
   Corn and Rice Casserole, 285
   Corn Casserole, 284, 285
   Corn Dip, 19
   Corn Pudding, 286
   Corn Salad, 95
   CROCK-POT® Brunswick
      Stew, 218
   Five-Can Soup, 66
   Frito Salad, 100
   Frogmore Stew, 227
   Green Bean Salad, 101
   Marinated Vegetable Salad, 115
   Mexican Bean Soup, 54
   Mexican Corn Bread, 241
   New England Boiled Dinner, 125
   Okra Corn Bread, 241
   Quick-and-Easy Ground Beef
      Vegetable Soup, 70
   Santa Fe Soup, 63, 64, 65
   Seven-Can Soup, 66
   Sweet-and-Sour Broccoli, 279
   Sweet Banana Pepper Pie, 293
   Taco Soup, 67, 68, 69
   Tex-Mex Corn Chowder, 48
   The Hog Pit Corn Salad with
      Hominy, 96
   Vegetable Casserole, 308
   Vegetable Fritters, 243
   Vegetable Salad, 116
   Vegetable Soup, 70
   Vegetable Soup for Canning, 71
   Vegetable Soup with Beef, 69
   Veggie Guacamole, 20
   White Chili, 217

Crab Meat
   Crab Burgers, 225
   Hot Crab Dip, 24
   Seafood Gumbo, 52
   Tabasco Seafood Gumbo, 53

Cranberries
   Apple Punch, 43
   Cranberry Salad, 78, 79
   Quick Cranberry Sherbet, 373
   Raspberry Congealed Salad, 88
   Raw Cranberry Relish, 336

Crusts
   Crust, 342, 344, 346, 349, 363, 370
   Grape-Nuts Crust, 350

Pastry Strips, 354, 356
Pecan Crust, 362

Cucumbers
Broccoli Salad, 92
Cucumber Salad, 99
Cukes and Cream, 100
Marinated Potato Salad, 104
Salad Lover's Delight, 118

Desserts. *See also* Cakes; Candy; Cheesecakes; Cobblers; Cookies; Ice Cream; Pies; Puddings
Apple Crisp, 340
Apple Dumplings, 340
Blueberry Crunch Cake, 341
Blueberry Delight, 342
Blueberry Dessert, 343
Broken Glass Cake, 344
Butterscotch Delight, 346
Cheese Squares, 347
Chocolate Éclair, 359
Chocolate Trifle, 371, 372
Clester Pineapple Dessert, 364
Cream Puffs, 357
Flavored Gelatin Cubes, 345
Fluffy Mint Dessert, 364
Fruit Pizza, 369
Lemon Junk, 361
Lemon Torte, 362
Mile-High Strawberry Delight, 367
Pattie's Apple Dumplings, 341
Payday Candy Bar Cake, 363
Pineapple Prune Whip, 365
Pineapple Trifle, 372
Pumpkin Dessert, 366
Quick Dessert, 368
Seven-Layer Finger Gelatin, 360
Sherry Trifle, 372
St. Éclair Cake, 358
Strawberry Pizza, 370

Desserts, Sauces
Chocolate Gravy, 388
Chocolate Sauce, 385
Chocolate Sauce Surprise, 388
Lemon Sauce, 389
Sauce, 383, 393

Desserts, Toppings
Pecan Crunch, 367
Topping, 437
Whipped Cream, 345

Dips. *See also* Guacamole
Bean Dip, 18
Black Bean Hummus, 17
Caramel Apple Dip, 17
Corn Dip, 19
Hot Crab Dip, 24
Mexican Bean Dip, 18
Michelle's Black-Eyed Pea Dip, 21
Nine-Layer Taco Dip, 24
Outback-Style Dip, 21
Ro-Tel Dip, 22
Shrimp Dip, 25
Spinach Dip, 23
Taco Dip, 23

Dove
Dove Breast Shish Kabobs, 218

Egg Dishes
Brunch Casserole, 170
Brunch Puff, 170
Garlic Grits, 317
Gourmet Grits with Cheese, 318
Grits and Sausage Casserole, 171
Ham and Cheese Quiche, 163
Ham and Egg Pizza, 162
Jalapeño Cheese Grits, 319
Karmen's Breakfast Pizza, 174
Make-Ahead Breakfast Bake, 172
Sausage Casserole, 173
Sausage, Egg and Cheese Quiche, 173
Spinach-Filled Stuffed Eggs, 299
Tramp Eggs, 176
Weekend Breakfast Casserole, 161

Emeril's Essence, 337

Fillings
Cream Cheese Filling, 448, 449
Filling, 454

Fish. *See also* Catfish; Salmon; Tuna
Baked Fish, 222
Oven-Fried Fish, 222

Frostings/Icings. *See also* Glazes
Caramel Icing, 506
Chocolate Frosting, 358
Chocolate Pour Icing, 461
Cream Cheese Frosting, 399
Creamy Nut Icing, 455
Creamy Orange Frosting, 400
Frosting, 413, 424, 428, 431, 451, 458, 479, 485

INDEX

Frosting for Black Walnut Apple
    Cake, 397
Fudge Icing, 460
Icing, 366, 398, 402, 406, 430
Icing for Swiss Chocolate Cake, 407
Judy's Frosting, 482
Orange Frosting, 425
Pineapple Butter Icing, 421
Vanilla Frosting, 461, 494

Fruitcakes
Dark Fruitcakes, 416
Fruitcake, 414, 415
German Fruitcake, 417
So Easy Fruitcakes, 418

Fudge
CROCK-POT® Fudge, 467
Easy Velveeta Fudge, 469
Melissa's Peanut Butter Fudge, 469
Microwave Fudge with Pecans, 468
Old-Fashioned Peanut Butter
    Fudge, 468

Glazes
Buttermilk Glaze, 447
Caramel Glaze, 438
Glaze, 247, 420, 440, 444, 454, 456
Orange Glaze, 262

Grapefruit
Baked Grapefruit, 327
Fresh Fruit with Lemon Yogurt
    Dressing, 80

Grapes
Apple Salad, 75
Chicken Salad, 118
Exotic Turkey Salad, 121
Old-Fashioned Fruit Salad, 82
Stained Glass Salad, 84

Green Beans
Baked String Beans, 287
Big Mama's Green Beans, 286
Chicken Casserole, 193
Chicken Fantastic, 206
Five-Can Soup, 66
Green Bean Casserole, 287
Green Bean Salad, 101
Marinated Vegetable Salad, 115
Meal-in-One Casserole, 145
Tuna Mushroom Casserole, 226
Vegetable Casserole, 308

Vegetable Salad, 116
Vegetables Medley, 309

Green Peas
Cashew Rice Pilaf, 323
Chicken and Dumpling Casserole, 203
Chicken and Rice Skillet, 214
Chicken Potpie, 209
Corn Bread Salad, 98
English Pea and Asparagus
    Casserole, 274
English Pea Salad, 104
Marinated Vegetable Salad, 115
Quick Casserole, 275
Ragout, 290
Swiss Steak, 131
Vegetable Medley, 309
Vegetable Salad, 116

Grits
Garlic Grits, 317
Gourmet Grits with Cheese, 318
Grits and Sausage Casserole, 171
Jalapeño Cheese Grits, 319

Ground Beef
Asian Beef and Noodles, 134
Barbecued Meatballs, 146
Beef and Bean Supper Dish, 137
Beef Stroganoff, 156
Brunswick Stew, 217
Chauvinist Chili, 136
Chili, 135
Chloe Scott's Baked Beans, 134
Cocktail Meatballs, 33
Cottage Meat Loaf, 149
CROCK-POT® Lasagna, 143
Elloise's Teenagers Delight, 158
Enchilada Pie, 138
Farmhouse Muffins, 159
Five-Can Soup, 66
Forgotten Minestrone, 56
Goulash, 141
Green Enchiladas, 137
Ground Beef Casserole, 140
Hamburger Pepper Casserole, 141
Hash, 142
Ho-Bo Potatoes, 155
Hot Diggity Dog Sauce, 332
Macaroni and Cheese Casserole, 142
Meal-in-One Casserole, 144, 145
Meat Loaf, 148
Meatballs, 147
Mexican Bean Soup, 54

INDEX

Mexican Casserole, 153
Mexican Meat Loaf, 150
Micro Meat Loaf, 151
Oriental Casserole, 154
Priatzo by Regina, 26
Quick-and-Easy Ground Beef
　Vegetable Soup, 70
Quick Mushroom Supper, 153
Rotel Spicy Meat Loaf, 151
Santa Fe Soup, 63, 64, 65
Seven-Can Soup, 66
Spaghetti Sauce, 155
Spicy Cabbage Beef Soup, 54
Spoonburgers, 157
Stuffed Green Peppers, 139
Stuffed Meat Loaf, 152
Taco Dip, 23
Taco Soup, 67, 68, 69
Tater Tot Casserole, 157
The Best Baked Beans, 276
Vegetable Soup with Beef, 69

Guacamole
Chunky Guacamole, 19
Peach Mango Guacamole, 20
Veggie Guacamole, 20

Gumbos
Seafood Gumbo, 52
Tabasco Seafood Gumbo, 53
Very Quick-and-Easy Chicken
　Gumbo Soup, 51

Ham
Appetillas, 36
Bourbon-Glazed Ham, 159
Chicken Cordon Bleu Casserole, 194
Grilled Ham Steak, 160
Ham and Cheese Quiche, 163
Ham and Egg Pizza, 162
Ham Chowder, 50
My Mother's Great Ham, 160
Pitty Pat's Sweet Potato Salad, 113
Salad Lover's Delight, 118
Weekend Breakfast Casserole, 161

Hominy
Creamed Hominy, 288
Hominy Casserole, 288, 289
The Hog Pit Corn Salad with
　Hominy, 96

Ice Cream
Amy's Ice Cream Sandwich Dessert, 376

Dessert Ice Cream Balls, 374
Fig Ice Cream, 373
Maxie Pearl's Ice Cream
　Sandwiches, 376
Oreo Ice Cream Dessert, 375
Peach Ice Cream, 374
Quick Cranberry Sherbet, 373

Lemon
Diabetic Lemon Pies, 536
Glaze, 444
Lemon Cake, 420
Lemon Icebox Pie, 537
Lemon Junk, 361
Lemon Meringue Pie, 535
Lemon Refrigerator Cake, 426
Lemon Sauce, 389
Lemon Torte, 362
Lemon Yogurt Dressing, 80
Lemon-White Chocolate-Pistachio
　Cookies, 504
Lemonade Pies, 534
Punch, 44
Spiced Tea Mix, 45
Tropical Pie, 551
West Gadsden Cafe Lemon Pie, 536
Wonderful Pie, 552

Lima Beans
CROCK-POT® Brunswick
　Stew, 218
Vegetable Medley, 309
Vegetable Soup, 70
Vegetable Soup for Canning, 71

Meat Loaf
Cottage Meat Loaf, 149
Meat Loaf, 148
Mexican Meat Loaf, 150
Micro Meat Loaf, 151
Rotel Spicy Meat Loaf, 151
Stuffed Meat Loaf, 152

Meatballs
Barbecued Meatballs, 146
Meatballs, 147

Meringues, 382

Muffins
Blueberry Muffins with Streusel
　Topping, 257
Bran Muffins, 258
Low-Fat Banana Muffins, 258

568 INDEX

Minnie Pearl's Bran Muffins, 259
Onion Cheese Muffins, 261
Orange Muffins, 261
Orange Raisin Muffins, 262
Pecan Pie Mini-Muffins, 263
Pumpkin Muffins, 263
Refrigerator Bran Muffins, 260
Whole Wheat Honey
    Muffins, 264

Mushrooms
Baked Mushroom Rice, 324
Beef Stroganoff, 156
Broccoli Mushroom Chowder, 48
Capital Chicken Casserole, 180
Chicken Crunch, 195
Dove Breast Shish Kabobs, 218
Hamburger Pepper Casserole, 141
Meal-in-One Casserole, 144, 145
Mushroom Rice Casserole, 324
Oriental Chicken Casserole, 196
Ragout, 290
Rice Dish, 325
Sausage-Stuffed Mushrooms, 29
Shrimp and Pasta Packages, 230
Spinach Artichoke Casserole, 298
Stuffed Meat Loaf, 152
Stuffed Mushrooms, 28
Tammy's Chicken Wraps, 215
Tuna Mushroom Casserole, 226
Vegetable Lasagna, 322
Weekend Breakfast Casserole, 161

Okra
Okra Corn Bread, 241
Seafood Gumbo, 52
Tabasco Seafood Gumbo, 53
Vegetable Soup, 70
Vegetable Soup for Canning, 71

Oranges
Baked Oranges, 328
Brandon's Fruit Salad, 81
Cranberry Salad, 78, 79
Dark Fruitcakes, 416
Double Orange Refrigerator
    Cake, 426
Dreamsicle Pie, 527
Easy Orange Cake, 425
Forever Amber Candy, 464
Fresh Fruit with Lemon Yogurt
    Dressing, 80
Fruit Pizza, 369
Glaze, 247, 420

Golden Fig Cake, 412
Honey Orange Cake, 427
Hot Fruit Compote, 327
Mandarin Pork Chops, 167
Mary Lynn's Tang Pie, 551
Nutty Orange Coffee Cake, 247
Old-Fashioned Fruit Salad, 82
Orange Balls, 472
Orange Biscuit Pudding, 380
Orange Carrot Cake, 400
Orange Frosting, 425
Orange Glaze, 262
Orange Jello Salad, 85, 86
Orange Muffins, 261
Orange Pineapple Cake, 428
Orange Raisin Muffins, 262
Orange Rings, 304
Orange Rolls, 265
Orange Slice Cookies, 501
Raw Cranberry Relish, 336
Romaine and Orange Salad, 86
Spiced Tea Mix, 45
Stained Glass Salad, 84
Tropical Orange Cake, 429
Tropical Pie, 551
Williamsburg Cake, 460
Wonderful Pie, 552

Oysters
Batter for Shrimp and Oysters, 233
Oyster Spread, 16
Seafood Gumbo, 52
Tabasco Seafood Gumbo, 53

Pasta
Angel Chicken Pasta, 187
Baked Pasta, 321
Baked Ziti, 323
Barb's Minestrone Soup, 57
Cabbage Casserole, 282
Chicken Cannelloni, 192
CROCK-POT® Lasagna, 143
CROCK-POT® Macaroni and
    Cheese, 319
Forgotten Minestrone, 56
Goulash, 141
Ground Beef Casserole, 140
Healthy Chicken Soup, 55
Hungarian Goulash, 130
Macaroni and Cheese, 320
Macaroni and Cheese Casserole, 142
Meal-in-One Casserole, 144
Noodles with Shrimp Scampi
    Sauce, 232

Provençal Chicken, 211
Shrimp and Pasta Packages, 230
Spaghetti Sauce, 155
Tuna Mushroom Casserole, 226
Vegetable Lasagna, 322
Very Quick-and-Easy Chicken Gumbo Soup, 51

Peaches
Blueberry Peach Pie, 516
Brandon's Fruit Salad, 81
Butter Peach Pound Cake, 442
Cream Puffs, 357
Peach Cream Pie, 538
Peach Ice Cream, 374
Peach Mango Guacamole, 20
Peach Salad, 87

Pears
Pear Bread, 255
Raspberry Congealed Salad, 88

Pickles
Garlic Pickles, 333
Icicle Pickles, 335
Kitchen Floor Pickles, 335
Mock Apple Pickles or Red Hot Cucumber Pickles, 334

Pies. *See also* Tarts
Apple Pie, 514
Black Skillet Chocolate Pies, 519
Blueberry Peach Pie, 516
Blueberry Pies, 515
Caramel Pecan Pies, 541
Caramel Pie, 518
Chocolate Mousse Pie, 524
Chocolate Pie, 520
Chocolate Pies, 521, 522
Clara's Sweet Potato Pie, 550
Classic Chess Pie, 519
Coconut Caramel Pies, 518
Coconut Pie, 525
Cream Cheese Brownie Pie, 517
Darn Good Pies, 526
Delight Pies, 527
Diabetic Lemon Pies, 536
Diabetic Strawberry Pie, 547
Double-Layer Pumpkin Pie, 545
Dreamsicle Pie, 527
Dried Apple Custard, 515
Egg Custard, 528, 529
French Silk Pie, 531
Fudge Pie, 532

German Chocolate Pie, 522
Hershey Bar Pie, 523
Ice Cream Pie with Meringue Pecan Crust, 533
Japanese Fruit Pies, 532
Jessie Isbell's Cantaloupe Cream Pie, 516
Jessie Isbell's Walnut Pie, 552
Lazy Man Pie, 534
Lemon Icebox Pie, 537
Lemon Meringue Pie, 535
Lemonade Pies, 534
Lottie's Pecan Chip Pies, 543
Mama's Egg Custard, 529
Mary Lynn's Tang Pie, 551
Melva's Strawberry Pies, 547
Microwave Chocolate Pie, 523
Moonshine Pie, 537
Mother's Pecan Pie, 541
New Orleans Pecan Pie, 543
Oh-So-Good Pie, 538
Old-Fashioned Chocolate Pie, 525
Old-Fashioned Egg Custard, 530
Old-Fashioned Egg Custard Pie, 530
Old-Fashioned Pecan Pie, 544
Oralee's Sweet Potato Custard Pie, 550
Pattie's Egg Custard, 531
Peach Cream Pie, 538
Peanut Butter Pie, 539
Pecan Cheese Pie, 540
Pecan Fudge Pie, 533
Pecan Meringue Pie, 542
Pecan Pie, 539
Pineapple Cream Cheese Pie, 544
Pumpkin Custard Pie, 545
Raisin Pie, 546
Strawberry Custard, 546
Strawberry Pie, 548
Sugarless Apple Pie, 514
Swedish Pie, 549
Sweet Potato Pie, 549
Tropical Pie, 551
West Gadsden Cafe Coconut Pie, 526
West Gadsden Cafe Egg Pie, 528
West Gadsden Cafe Lemon Pie, 536
West Gadsden Cafe Pecan Pie, 540
West Gadsden Cafe Strawberry Pie, 548
Wonderful Pie, 552

Pineapple
Apple Carrot Casserole, 326
Apricot Salad, 75, 76
Baked Beans, 276
Baked Oranges, 328

INDEX

Blueberry Dessert, 343
Cheese Ball, 8
Cherry Salad, 77
Clester Pineapple Dessert, 364
Cranberry Salad, 78
Dark Fruitcakes, 416
Exotic Turkey Salad, 121
For Goodness Sakes Salad, 79
Fruit Pizza, 369
Fruit Salad, 81
Fruitcake, 414
Fruitcake Cookies, 495, 496
German Fruitcake, 417
Grace's Fruitcake Cookies, 497
Hot Fruit Compote, 327
Lime Jello Salad, 84
Melva's Strawberry Pies, 547
Molded Lime Salad, 85
Oh-So-Good Pie, 538
Old-Fashioned Fruit Salad, 82
Orange Jello Salad, 85, 86
Orange Pineapple Cake, 428
Out-Of-This-World Cake, 430
Pattie's Pineapple Scallops, 328
Peach Mango Guacamole, 20
Peach Salad, 87
Pineapple Almond Cream Cheese Spread, 14
Pineapple Bars, 503
Pineapple Butter Icing, 421
Pineapple Casserole, 329
Pineapple Cheese Ball, 10
Pineapple Cream Cheese Pie, 544
Pineapple Delight, 434
Pineapple Prune Whip, 365
Pineapple Trifle, 372
Pineapple Upside-Down Cake, 433
Pineapple Yum-Yum Cake, 432
Punch, 44
Rhonda's Kentucky Pound Cake, 441
7-Cup Salad, 82
Simple Punch, 44
Snowball Cheese Balls, 10
So Easy Fruitcakes, 418
Stained Glass Salad, 84
Sunshine Salad, 83
Sweet and Sour Pork Chops, 168
Tappy Apple Salad, 74
Tropical Berry Blast Smoothie, 43

Pizzas
Fruit Pizza, 369
Ham and Egg Pizza, 162
Karmen's Breakfast Pizza, 174
Little Pizzas, 38
Marc's Pizza Dogs, 40
Peanut Butter Brownie Pizza, 484
Strawberry Pizza, 370
Vegetable Pizza, 39

Pork. *See also* Ham; Sausage
Barbecued Meatballs, 146
Brunswick Stew, 217
CROCK-POT® Brunswick Stew, 218
CROCK-POT® Pork Chops, 165
Cuban Pork Chops, 166
Mandarin Pork Chops, 167
Pork Chop Bake, 166
Pork Chops and Vegetables, 169
Rio Grande Pork Roast, 164
Spicy White Chili, 216
Stuffed Pork Chops, 169
Sweet and Sour Pork Chops, 168

Potatoes
Andrea's Hash Brown Casserole, 172
Bachelor Potatoes, 293
Best-Ever Pot Roast, 124
Charcoal Potatoes, 294
Cheddar Chowder, 49
Cheese Potato Casserole, 294
Corned Beef and Cabbage Casserole, 133
Creamed Potato Casserole, 296
Easy Baked Beef Stew, 132
Easy Potato Soup, 61
French Onion Potato Soup, 57
Frogmore Stew, 227
German Cabbage and Sausage, 175
Ham and Egg Pizza, 162
Ham Chowder, 50
Hamburger Pepper Casserole, 141
Hash, 142
Hearty Potato Soup, 58
Ho-Bo Potatoes, 155
Irene's Hash Brown Potato Casserole, 295
Karmen's Breakfast Pizza, 174
Low-Fat Potato Soup, 58
Luscious Potato Casserole, 296
Make-Ahead Mashed Potatoes, 297
Marinated Potato Salad, 104
Meal-in-One Casserole, 145
New England Boiled Dinner, 125
Perfect Potato Salad, 105
Pork Chops and Vegetables, 169
Potato Cheese Biscuits, 238
Potato Chip Cookies, 504, 505

Potato Soup, 59, 60, 61, 62
Potato Wedges, 297
Quick Casserole, 275
Shrimp Drop, 233
Tater Tot Casserole, 157
Taylor's Favorite Hash Brown Casserole, 295
Vegetable Soup, 70
Vegetable Soup for Canning, 71

Pound Cakes
Banana Pound Cake, 438
Bourbon Pound Cake, 439
Butter Peach Pound Cake, 442
Coconut Sour Cream Pound Cake, 440
Dutch Apple Pound Cake, 437
Granny Taylor's Plain Pound Cake, 442
Meme's Pound Cake, 443
Pound Cake, 444, 445, 446
Rhonda's Kentucky Pound Cake, 441
Shelia's Old-Fashioned Pound Cake, 441
Whipping Cream Pound Cake, 446

Puddings
Banana Pudding, 377
Best Banana Pudding, 378
Bread Pudding, 381, 382
Cinnamon Pudding, 384
Coconut Biscuit Pudding, 380
Cold Biscuit Pudding, 380
Hot Dog Bun Pudding, 383
Jessie Isbell's Sweet Potato Pudding, 387
Mama's Homemade Banana Pudding, 377
Old-Fashioned Banana Pudding, 379
Orange Biscuit Pudding, 380
Pudding with Chocolate Sauce, 385
Stove-Top Rice Pudding, 386
Sweet Potato Pudding, 386

Pumpkin
Double-Layer Pumpkin Pie, 545
Pumpkin Cake, 447
Pumpkin Cookies, 506
Pumpkin Custard Pie, 545
Pumpkin Dessert, 366
Pumpkin Muffins, 263
Pumpkin Roll, 448, 449

Quail
Smothered Quail, 219

Rabbit
Barbecue Rabbit in Barbecue Sauce, 177

Raspberries
Fruity Smoothie, 42
Raspberry Congealed Salad, 88

Rice
Baked Mushroom Rice, 324
Broccoli and Rice Casserole, 281
Broccoli Casserole, 280
Cashew Chicken, 191
Cashew Rice Pilaf, 323
Chicken and Rice Skillet, 214
Chicken and Shrimp Casserole, 197
Chicken Casserole, 188, 193
Chicken Fantastic, 206
Corn and Rice Casserole, 285
Easy Red Beans and Rice, 175
Jambalaya Deep Dish, 229
Lipton Chicken, 186
Mushroom Rice Casserole, 324
Pork Chop Bake, 166
Quick-and-Easy Ground Beef Vegetable Soup, 70
Quick Mushroom Supper, 153
Rice and Broccoli Casserole, 281
Rice Dish, 325
Sausage Casserole, 173
Shirley's Chicken and Rice, 188
Shrimp Casserole, 227
Shrimp Rice Pilaf, 231
Stove-Top Rice Pudding, 386
Stuffed Green Peppers, 139
Tabasco Seafood Gumbo, 53
Vegetable Soup with Beef, 69
Very Quick-and-Easy Chicken Gumbo Soup, 51
Zippy Chicken Stir-Fry, 213

Rolls
Aunt Luna's Refrigerator Rolls, 270
Basic Refrigerator Rolls, 269
Exa's Rolls, 267
Freeze and Bake Rolls, 268
Orange Rolls, 265
Quick Rolls, 264
Something Different Sweet Rolls, 266
Sweet Rolls, 265
Thirty-Minute Rolls, 269

Salads, Dressings
Buttermilk Dressing, 92

Creamy Topping, 87
Lemon Yogurt Dressing, 80
Mayonnaise Dressing, 91
Mexican Dressing, 114
Oil and Vinegar Dressing, 94, 101
Oil and Vinegar Salad Dressing, 86
Olive Oil and Vinegar Dressing, 106
Oriental Salad Dressing, 103
Slaw Dressing, 117
Sour Cream Dressing, 89
Sweet/Sour Dressing, 117
Vinegar Salad Dressing, 99
Wine Vinegar Dressing, 93

Salads, Fruit
Apple Salad, 75
Apricot Salad, 75, 76
Berry 'n' Banana Salad, 76
Brandon's Fruit Salad, 81
Cherry Salad, 77
Cranberry Salad, 78, 79
For Goodness Sakes Salad, 79
Fresh Fruit with Lemon Yogurt Dressing, 80
Fruit Salad, 81
Lime Jello Salad, 84
Molded Lime Salad, 85
Old-Fashioned Fruit Salad, 82
Orange Jello Salad, 85, 86
Peach Salad, 87
Raspberry Congealed Salad, 88
Romaine and Orange Salad, 86
7-Cup Salad, 82
Stained Glass Salad, 84
Strawberry Almond Salad, 88
Sunshine Salad, 83
Tappy Apple Salad, 74

Salads, Main Dish
Chicken Salad, 118, 119
Chicken Salad Supreme, 120
Creole Chicken Salad, 120
Exotic Turkey Salad, 121
Hot Chicken Salad, 121
Macaroni Salad, 102

Salads, Vegetable. *See also* Slaw
Asparagus Mold. 90
Broccoli Salad, 91, 92
Cabbage Salad, 107
Congealed Asparagus Salad, 89
Corn Bread Salad, 97, 98
Corn Salad, 95
Cucumber Salad, 99

Cukes and Cream, 100
Dot Salad and Dressing, 93
English Pea Salad, 104
Frito Salad, 100
Garden Broccoli Cauliflower Salad, 94
Green Bean Salad, 101
Kraut Salad, 102
Layered Taco Salad, 114
Marinated Potato Salad, 104
Marinated Vegetable Salad, 115
Perfect Potato Salad, 105
Pitty Pat's Sweet Potato Salad, 113
Polly's Oriental Salad, 103
Salad Lover's Delight, 118
The Hog Pit Corn Salad with Hominy, 96
Tuscan White Bean Salad, 90
Vegetable Salad, 116

Salmon
Dolly Parton's Salmon Patties, 225
Easy Salmon Cakes, 223
Glazed Salmon, 223
Salmon Ball, 12
Salmon Croquettes, 224

Sandwiches
Crab Burgers, 225
Italian Roast Beef Sandwich, 129
Peanut Butter and Banana Sandwich, 40
Spoonburgers, 157
Tammy's Chicken Wraps, 215

Sauces. *See also* Desserts, Sauces
Barbecue Sauce, 177, 331
Basting Sauce, 330
Hot Diggity Dog Sauce, 332
Sauce, 33, 34
Secret Sauce, 333
Spaghetti Sauce, 155
Tartar Sauce, 224
White Barbecue Sauce for Chicken, 331

Sausage
Andrea's Hash Brown Casserole, 172
Barb's Minestrone Soup, 57
Brunch Casserole, 170
Chauvinist Chili, 136
Cheesy Sausage Balls, 30
Chloe Scott's Baked Beans, 134
Cornelia's Party "Snausages", 32

Easy Red Beans and Rice, 175
Easy-as-Pie Sausage Balls, 31
Frogmore Stew, 227
German Cabbage and Sausage, 175
Grits and Sausage Casserole, 171
Jambalaya Deep Dish, 229
Johnson's Sausage Dressing, 314
Karmen's Breakfast Pizza, 174
Little Pizzas, 38
Make-Ahead Breakfast Bake, 172
Miss Minnie's Corn Bread Sausage
    Dressing, 315
Sausage Balls, 31, 32
Sausage Cake, 452
Sausage Casserole, 173
Sausage, Egg and Cheese
    Quiche, 173
Sausage Roll, 174
Sausage-Stuffed Mushrooms, 29

Seasoning Salt, 337

Shrimp
Batter for Shrimp and Oysters, 233
French-Fried Shrimp, 229
Frogmore Stew, 227
Jambalaya Deep Dish, 229
Noodles with Shrimp Scampi
    Sauce, 232
Raine's Shrimp Butter, 15
Seafood Gumbo, 52
Shrimp and Pasta Packages, 230
Shrimp Casserole, 227
Shrimp Creole, 228
Shrimp Dip, 25
Shrimp Drop, 233
Shrimp Rice Pilaf, 231
Shrimp Scampi, 231
Tabasco Seafood Gumbo, 53

Shellfish. See Crab Meat; Oysters; Shrimp

Side Dishes. See also Grits; Rice
Apple Carrot Casserole, 326
Apple Cheese Casserole, 326
Baked Apples, 325
Baked Grapefruit, 327
Baked Oranges, 328
Corn Bread Dressing, 313
CROCK-POT® Macaroni and
    Cheese, 319
Dressing, 312
Fruit Sauce for Ham, 332
Hot Fruit Compote, 327

Joan's Giblet Gravy, 330
Johnson's Sausage Dressing, 314
Macaroni and Cheese, 320
Miss Minnie's Corn Bread Sausage
    Dressing, 315
Pattie's Pineapple Scallops, 328
Pineapple Casserole, 329
Raw Cranberry Relish, 336
Squash Dressing, 316, 317

Slaw
Blanch's Delicious Slaw, 105
Broccoli Slaw, 106
Coleslaw, 107, 108
Crunchy Coleslaw, 109
Crunchy Slaw, 108
Dreamland's Marinated Coleslaw, 110
Marinated Slaw, 110
Race Track Slaw, 111
Spicy Coleslaw, 112

Snacks
Glazed Pecans, 41
Spiced Candied Pecans, 42
Toasted Party Mix, 41

Soups/Stews. See also Chili; Chowders;
    Gumbos
Barb's Minestrone Soup, 57
Brunswick Stew, 217
CROCK-POT® Brunswick Stew, 218
Easy Baked Beef Stew, 132
Easy Potato Soup, 61
Five-Can Soup, 66
Forgotten Minestrone, 56
French Onion Potato Soup, 57
Frogmore Stew, 227
Healthy Chicken Soup, 55
Hearty Potato Soup, 58
Low-Fat Potato Soup, 58
Mexican Bean Soup, 54
One-Two-Three Stew, 132
Potato Soup, 59, 60, 61, 62
Quick-and-Easy Ground Beef
    Vegetable Soup, 70
Santa Fe Soup, 63, 64, 65
Seven-Can Soup, 66
Spicy Cabbage Beef Soup, 54
Squash Soup, 67
Taco Soup, 67, 68, 69
Vegetable Chicken Soup, 71
Vegetable Soup, 70
Vegetable Soup for Canning, 71
Vegetable Soup with Beef, 69

INDEX

Spinach
Cheddar Chowder, 49
Salad Lover's Delight, 118
Spinach Artichoke Casserole, 298
Spinach Dip, 23
Spinach-Filled Stuffed Eggs, 299
Strawberry Almond Salad, 88
Vegetable Chicken Soup, 71
Vegetable Lasagna, 322

Spreads
Charleston Cheese, 13
Cheese Ring Spread, 13
Herbed Cheese Spread, 14
Nana Stetson's Chopped Liver, 16
Olive Pimento Cheese Spread, 15
Oyster Spread, 16
Pineapple Almond Cream Cheese Spread, 14
Raine's Shrimp Butter, 15

Squash
Squash and Pepper Sauté, 299
Squash Casserole, 301, 302, 303
Squash Dressing, 316, 317
Squash Soup, 67
Squash Supreme, 303
Summer Squash Shells, 300

Strawberries
Belgian Waffles, 271
Berry 'n' Banana Salad, 76
Cream Cheese Tarts, 555
Diabetic Strawberry Pie, 547
Easy Fruit Cobbler, 352
Fresh Fruit with Lemon Yogurt Dressing, 80
Frosting, 458
Fruity Smoothie, 42
Melva's Strawberry Pies, 547
Mile-High Strawberry Delight, 367
Quick Dessert, 368
Strawberry Almond Salad, 88
Strawberry Custard, 546
Strawberry Gelatin Cake, 458
Strawberry Pie, 548
Strawberry Pizza, 370
Strawberry Refrigerator Cake, 426
Strawberry Shortcake, 457
Tropical Berry Blast Smoothie, 43
West Gadsden Cafe Strawberry Pie, 548

Sweet Potatoes
Clara's Sweet Potato Pie, 550
Cuban Pork Chops, 166
Jessie Isbell's Sweet Potato Pudding, 387
Oralee's Sweet Potato Custard Pie, 550
Orange Rings, 304
Pitty Pat's Sweet Potato Salad, 113
Sweet Potato Cobbler, 354, 355, 356
Sweet Potato Pie, 549
Sweet Potato Pudding, 386
Sweet Potato Soufflé, 305
Wedges, 297

Sweetened Condensed Milk, 389

Tarts
Aunt Polly's Tarts, 553
Bren's Pecan Tarts, 555
Cream Cheese Tarts, 555
Hattie's Coconut Tarts, 554
Lynda's Canadian Tarts, 554

Tea Cakes
Aunt Cora's Tea Cakes, 510
MeMe's Tea Cakes, 510
Old-Fashioned Tea Cakes, 511
Pattie's Tea Cakes, 511
Tea Cakes, 509

Tomatoes
Barb's Minestrone Soup, 57
Bean Dip, 18
Black Bean Hummus, 17
Brunswick Stew, 217
Chauvinist Chili, 136
Chicken Cannelloni, 192
Chicken Salad Tacos, 214
Chili, 135
Chunky Guacamole, 19
Corn Bread Salad, 97, 98
CROCK-POT® Brunswick Stew, 218
Cucumber Salad, 99
Dove Breast Shish Kabobs, 218
Five-Can Soup, 66
Forgotten Minestrone, 56
Fresh Tomato Pie, 292
Frito Salad, 100
Goulash, 141
Green Tomato Pie, 291
Hungarian Goulash, 130
Meatballs, 147
Mexican Bean Dip, 18
Mexican Bean Soup, 54

Nine-Layer Taco Dip, 24
Pam's Homemade Salsa, 22
Provençal Chicken, 211
Quick-and-Easy Ground Beef
   Vegetable Soup, 70
Ro-Tel Dip, 22
Rotel Spicy Meat Loaf, 151
Salad Lover's Delight, 118
Santa Fe Soup, 63, 64, 65
Scalloped Tomatoes Au Gratin, 306
Seafood Gumbo, 52
Secret Sauce, 333
Seven-Can Soup, 66
Shrimp Creole, 228
Spaghetti Sauce, 155
Squash Soup, 67
Stuffed Green Peppers, 139
Sweet-and-Sour Broccoli, 279
Taco Soup, 67, 68, 69
Tammy's Chicken Wraps, 215
Tex-Mex Corn Chowder, 48
Turnip Greens and White Bean
   Bake, 277
Vegetable Chicken Soup, 71
Vegetable Lasagna, 322
Vegetable Pizza, 39
Vegetable Soup, 70
Vegetable Soup for Canning, 71
Vegetable Soup with Beef, 69
Veggie Guacamole, 20
Weekend Breakfast Casserole, 161
White Chili, 217
Zucchini Bake, 306

Toppings. *See also* Desserts, Toppings
Streusel Topping, 257
Topping, 244, 246, 248, 249, 266

Tuna
Tuna Ball, 12
Tuna Mushroom Casserole, 226

Turkey
Basil-Lemon Turkey Breast, 220
Exotic Turkey Salad, 121

Salad Lover's Delight, 118
Taco Pie, 219
Taco Soup, 68

Vegetables. *See also* Artichokes;
   Asparagus; Avocados; Beans;
   Black Beans; Broccoli;
   Carrots; Cauliflower; Corn;
   Cucumbers; Green Beans;
   Green Peas; Hominy; Lima Beans;
   Mushrooms; Okra; Potatoes;
   Salads, Vegetable; Spinach;
   Squash; Sweet Potatoes; Tomatoes;
   Zucchini
Baked Pasta, 321
Harvest Beets, 278
Hettie's Vegetable Casserole, 307
Michelle's Black-Eyed Pea Dip, 21
Onion Patties, 289
Pensacola Boarding House Beets, 278
Ragout, 290
Turnip Greens and White Bean
   Bake, 277
New England Boiled Dinner, 125
Sweet Banana Pepper Pie, 293
Vegetable Casserole, 308
Vegetable Medley, 309
Vidalia Onion Casserole, 290

Venison
Venison Roast, 176

Zucchini
Carrot and Zucchini-Stuffed
   Chicken Breasts, 190
Forgotten Minestrone, 56
Squash and Pepper Sauté, 299
Vegetable Lasagna, 322
Zucchini Bake, 306
Zucchini Bread, 256
Zucchini Casserole, 307

Calling All Cooks

These cookbooks are perfect gifts for holidays, weddings, anniversaries, and birthdays.

You may order as many of our cookbooks as you wish for the price of $10.00 each, plus $2.00 postage and handling per book. Mail this form to the address below or save postage and handling charges by picking up your books at the Chapter Pioneer Office:

Alabama Chapter #34
Cookbooks
3196 Highway 280 South, Room 301N
Birmingham, Alabama 35243

		Quantity	Total
Calling All Cooks	$10.00 ea.	_____	$ _____
Calling All Cooks two	$10.00 ea.	_____	_____
Calling All Cooks three	$10.00 ea.	_____	_____
Calling All Cooks four	$10.00 ea.	_____	_____
Celebrations	$10.00 ea.	_____	_____
Postage and Handling	$ 2.00 ea.	_____	_____
Total			$ _____ *

Name _____ (Please Print)

Address _____

City _____ State _____ Zip _____

(___) _____
Area Code/Telephone Number

*Please make check payable to Bell South Telephone Pioneers
At the present time we do not accept credit cards
Photocopies will be accepted